DATE DUE

DEMCO, INC. 38-2931

HARVARD SOCIOLOGICAL STUDIES
VOLUME IV

THE STUDIES IN THIS SERIES ARE PUBLISHED BY THE DEPARTMENT OF
SOCIAL RELATIONS OF HARVARD UNIVERSITY, WHICH, HOWEVER, ASSUMES
NO RESPONSIBILITY FOR THE VIEWS EXPRESSED

LAND USE

in

CENTRAL BOSTON

BY

WALTER FIREY

UNIVERSITY OF TEXAS

HD268
.B7
F52

90408

GREENWOOD PRESS, PUBLISHERS

NEW YORK   1968

Reprinted with permission of the

HARVARD UNIVERSITY PRESS

First Greenwood reprinting, 1968

LIBRARY OF CONGRESS catalogue card number: 68-23288

PRINTED IN THE UNITED STATES OF AMERICA

TO
MY PARENTS

PREFACE

THE LAST few years have seen an intensified interest in the problems and theory of urban land use. This new interest has been manifest in the most varied quarters. City planners, concerned with the outward drift of metropolitan residents, the continued decline in the municipal tax base, the aggravated problems of traffic congestion, and an accumulating housing deficit, have been looking for a broader and more adequate fund of factual knowledge in terms of which to formulate their planning blueprints. In another quarter antiquarians and historically minded citizens have been awakening to the fact that a real civic value attaches to historic shrines and that urban planning ought to reckon with such things. Realtors, investors, property owners, and home financing agencies have all been seeking for basic principles of land use in terms of which they might anticipate trends that affect their interests. Finally, land use theorists—social ecologists, economic geographers, *Standortstheoretikers,* and others—have been inquiring into the very foundations of urban land use structure. Established generalizations have succumbed before criticism and as yet no new ones have been formulated in their place.

This book was undertaken with the object of applying some of the newer viewpoints and principles of sociological theory to the field of land use. It was originally submitted as a doctoral dissertation to the Department of Sociology at Harvard University. In its present form it has been somewhat adapted to bring out more explicitly the practical planning implications of the systematic analysis that is presented. But its approach and treatment remain that of a strictly scientific study. Its central problem, in terms of which the empirical data have been gathered and arranged, is a frankly theoretical one. This problem concerns the scope of cultural values and community sentiments in conditioning land use patterns of central Boston. Boston was selected as being fairly representative of the older American cities whose time span embraces not only the commercialistic and rationalistic culture of the present but also the more "theocentric" and aristo-

vii

cratic culture of earlier periods when noncommercial land uses had relatively greater competitive strength. Its use as a test case should therefore bring out some hitherto neglected factors in land use analysis.

My own interest in the problems and theory of urban land use dates back to undergraduate years when, in courses on social ecology, urban sociology, migration, and population, I came to appreciate the need for a systematic conceptual framework in terms of which empirical data might have scientific meaning. The urgency of this need became even more evident to me during my graduate studies and it eventually prompted me to undertake the present research. My object in this study has been to show how systematic sociological theory has something to offer land use analysis, whether it be in terms of empirical research, scientific generalization, or practical planning.

In making this study I have incurred many obligations. Only the most outstanding of them can be acknowledged here, and they not at all adequately. To Professor Jesse F. Steiner I owe my first interest in social ecology; to him too I am grateful for stimulation and wise counsel in the course of my professional development. For guidance and encouragement at the beginning of this particular research I am indebted to the late Professor James Ford, who never saw the study through to completion but who, through his enthusiasm and confidence, enormously promoted its consummation.

My most evident and most profound debt is to the two teachers who introduced me to advanced sociological theory and thereby revealed the rich possibilities which theory offers for research, scientific understanding, and practical action. Whatever of methodological soundness and conceptual systematization this work may possess must be credited to them. To Professor Talcott Parsons I especially owe my application of the structural-functional approach to social action, particularly economic, and my recognition of the relativity of social "facts" to a conceptual framework. These two viewpoints permeate the whole land use analysis offered in this study. To Professor Pitirim A. Sorokin I am indebted for the invaluable concept of sociocultural integration and for the realization that subjective data are indeed accessible to verifiable, scientific knowledge—a viewpoint which is central to the methodology of this study. To both I am obliged for the essentially phenomenological approach of this study, a position which in my judgment must form the epistemology for a scientific sociology.

There are many other acknowledgments that I should like to make but to which I cannot do justice. One of these I should like to mention specifically. Professor Carle C. Zimmerman greatly encouraged me by his enthusiasm for the study and particularly helped me in the conceptual organization of certain chapters. Colleagues and friends both in sociology and in other fields have stimulated me in many intangible ways, through informal discussions, joint participation in seminars, etc. Dr. R. Freed Bales, Dr. George W. Mackey, Mr. George H. Grosser, Mr. Luke M. Smith, Mr. Richard F. Arens, and Mr. William J. Firey have been of particular help. I want to thank too the many informants who in one way or another made accessible the information on which this study was based. For financial assistance in the publication of this book I am indebted to a revolving fund placed at the disposal of the Harvard University Press by the Department of Sociology recently absorbed in the new Department of Social Relations.

WALTER FIREY

East Lansing, Michigan
February 22, 1946

CONTENTS

xi

TABLES

FIGURES

LAND USE IN CENTRAL BOSTON

CHAPTER 1

INTRODUCTION TO THE PROBLEM

Types of Ecological Theory. Social ecology is concerned with explaining the territorial arrangements that social activities assume. Its task is to discover and to explain the regularities which appear in man's adaptations to space. In this respect it is a generalizing science whose framework should be a system of theoretical propositions that are both empirically sound and logically integrated.

Since its emergence as a definite field of research ecology has developed a number of distinct theories, each of which has tried to bring a conceptual order out of man's relationships with physical space. When these theories are subjected to a careful analysis their differences turn out to be, in large part, variations upon a single conception of the society-space relationship. Briefly, this conception ascribes to space a determinate and invariant influence upon the distribution of human activities. The socially relevant qualities of space are thought to reside in the very nature of space itself, and the territorial patterns assumed by social activities are regarded as wholly determined by these qualities. There is no recognition, except in occasional fleeting insights, that social values may endow space with qualities that are quite extraneous to it as a physical phenomenon. Moreover there is no indication of what pre-conditions there may be to social activities' becoming in any way linked with physical space.[1]

This general conception of the society-space relationship may, for want of a better term, be called "ecological determinism." The determinism consists in the premise that social activities, in their territorial layouts, always constitute the dependent, "caused" variable, with physical space being the independent and "causing" factor. It is only in this sense that the expression "de-

[1] This whole range of problems constitutes the methodological *corpus* of the present study. See Pitirim A. Sorokin, *Sociocultural Causality Space Time* (Durham: 1943), pp. 113–122, 136–139 for a statement and analysis of our position.

3

terminism" is to be used in the present study. Any other connotations that the term may have are therefore to be excluded.[2]

Variations upon this theoretical position consist mainly in the different degrees of explicitness with which it is set forth by particular ecological theories. In this respect there is quite a range of variation among the theories, within which certain clearcut groupings seem to emerge.

In one grouping there fall those ecological theories which claim that social activities distribute themselves according to uniform geographical patterns. These patterns are thought to manifest certain natural forces which automatically sift and sort social activities over physical space. Any active role on the part of human beings, apart from that of compliance, is expressly or tacitly denied. Theories of this type have shown a pronounced empiricistic bias, with a marked disinclination to consider basic problems of theory. Consequently they reveal the least awareness of the determinism that is implied in their position. An appropriate title for this group of theories is that of "idealized descriptive schemes." Of these there are two main varieties, the concentric theory and the sector theory. The difference between the two concerns the kind of geographical configuration which social activities supposedly take on in their use of land.

A second grouping of ecological theories comprises those which acknowledge the active role played by human beings in adapting to space. However, they restrict this active role to one in which individuals and groups fully apprehend their spatial environs and then try to adapt to those environs with a minimum of cost. This restriction in effect vitiates the whole idea of active human volition. It implies that the properties of space, being inherently given in nature, can only be dealt with through passively learning and then complying. Physical space thus becomes the final "determinant" and the element of will or volition becomes an empty one.[3] Although this *reductio* is not always perceived by

[2] Cf. Milla Aïssa Alihan, *Social Ecology* (New York: 1938), pp. 127–130, 247, and *passim;* and Warner E. Gettys, "Human Ecology and Social Theory," *Social Forces*, 18: 469–476 (May, 1940) for an analysis of the determinism characteristic of ecology.

[3] For an analysis of this logical regression, characteristic of all utilitarian or "rationalistic" theories, see Talcott Parsons, *The Structure of Social Action* (New York: 1937), pp. 60–69.

the theories in question there is nevertheless a fairly clear recognition by them of the deterministic implications of their position. Because of the emphasis which these theories put upon the factors of full knowledge and least cost in actual spatial adaptation they may fittingly be called "empirically rationalistic theories." [4]

The principal difference that appears among such rationalistic theories is in regard to the inflexibleness with which the cognitive-adaptive process is thought to operate. There are two positions on this issue, which we may call "literal rationalism" and "empirically compromised rationalism." Only a few of the rationalistic ecologists are committed to the first position by insisting upon the literal applicability of their theories to land utilization. Most ecologists who fall into the empirically rationalistic category are realistic enough to see discrepancies between their theory and actual land use. But rather than abandon their theory they have supplemented it with a blanket category of "limiting factors" into which they put all factors that might account for the admitted discrepancies. In this way they reconcile the logical demands of their theory with demonstrable reality.

The third grouping of theories that may be made, in terms of the explicitness with which they set forth their deterministic premises, is that which we shall call the "methodological rationalists." Theories of this type are by far the most sophisticated of the ecological formulations. Their procedure is to sharply distinguish "real" patterns of spatially distributed activities from "virtual" or "pure" patterns. The "pure" patterns are nothing but constructs arrived at through deducing the kind of spatial order that would result if human beings had complete knowledge of their situation and so located as to minimize cost. Thus, the methodological rationalists deliberately isolate, for heuristic purposes only, the two elements of cognition and efficiency. Then they proceed to construct by means of rigorous deduction a complete system of propositions regarding the "pure" process of social adaptation to physical space. The existence of extraneous elements influencing the "real" process is fully admitted but these are deliberately excluded in the interests of a "pure" theory.

---

[4] A more rigorous definition of the term "rationalistic" will be presented later in this chapter.

We may classify these groupings of ecological theory in the
following form:

    I. Idealized descriptive schemes
        A. The concentric theory
        B. The sector theory
   II. Empirically rationalistic theories
        A. Literal rationalism
        B. Empirically compromised rationalism
  III. Methodologically rationalistic theories

Having established this classification and the *differentia* for it
we are now in a position to outline in a little more detail the
specific characteristics of each of the "schools" and to indicate
the logical consequences that follow from their common theoretical position. It is in terms of these characteristics and logical consequences that the problem of the present study has had its
origin. Therefore an outline of them is a necessary preliminary to
any positive formulation of the problem and hypothesis that have
guided this research.

Idealized Descriptive Schemes. Let us consider first the idealized descriptive schemes, beginning with the concentric theory.
This theory, formulated by Ernest W. Burgess and commonly
known as the Burgess zonal hypothesis, has limited itself to the
large American city and has carefully avoided forcing its generalizations onto other kinds of communities.[5] Within these limits
the theory posits a typical patterning of social and economic types
which appear as a series of concentric circles surrounding a central point. This central point is formed by the conjunction of two
or more communicative routes.

In the circular plane that surrounds this junction point there is
supposed to be a segregation of social and economic types into five
concentric zones. The first zone, lying athwart the intersection
of communicative routes, is occupied by the business district of
the city. Surrounding the business district there is a second zone,
known as the area of transition. In this circular band are sup-

---

    [5] Ernest W. Burgess, "The Growth of a City: an Introduction to a Re-
search Project," in Robert E. Park *et al.* (ed.), *The City* (Chicago: 1925),
pp. 47–62.

posedly located the main tenement and rooming-house districts of the city, as well as light manufacturing plants and scattered businesses that have ventured out of the retail center. This is the area of immigrants, transients, bohemians, and criminals. Beyond the zone of transition is placed the working-class district of single-family or two- and three-decker dwellings. The fourth concentric zone, lying at the edge of the city, consists of high-class apartment dwellings and exclusive restricted districts of single-family residences. Beyond this, in the suburban area, are the commuters' homes, comprising thus a fifth zone in the scheme.

The total configuration is envisioned as a self-regulating mechanism whereby "a process of distribution takes place which sifts and sorts and relocates individuals and groups by residence and occupation." [6] Each increment of population gravitates naturally to its predestined zone, so that the city's growth consists of an outward extension of each zone into the one lying just beyond it.

Nowhere in the theory is there a definite statement of the *modus operandi* by which people and groups are propelled to their appointed niches in space. Yet the whole emphasis upon the inevitability of the pattern implies a disavowal that they have any active part in the locational process. Indeed the very idea of a typical land use pattern, holding true for every American city, is predicated upon a deterministic premise, upon a denial that social values, ideals, or purposes can significantly influence the use of land. To be sure, Burgess acknowledges that some cities depart from the demands of his scheme. He points out that:

It hardly needs to be added that neither Chicago nor any other city fits perfectly into this ideal scheme. Complications are introduced by the lake front, the Chicago River, railroad lines, historical factors in the location of industry, the relative degree of the resistance of communities to invasion, etc.[7]

He adds, however, that these are only "interesting minor modifications." [8] At the very best he concedes that cultural factors may exert a "resistance," but the theoretical implications of this

[6] *Ibid.*, p. 54.
[7] *Ibid.*, pp. 51–52.
[8] *Ibid.*, p. 54.

point are not perceived and it receives no further consideration.

It is not our purpose at this point to give a logical critique of this theory or of those to follow. Our task at the moment is limited to presenting the theory and deducing from it the methodological premises upon which it rests. In a certain ·sense the very lack of explanatory analysis in the concentric theory protects it from logical criticism. The exposition that Burgess and his followers have given of the theory has been almost wholly on a descriptive level. A proper evaluation of it must therefore be in terms of empirical data. To this task we shall devote ourselves in Chapter II of the study.

Turning to the other of the idealized descriptive schemes, namely, the sector theory, we find once again a rather empiricistic and anti-theoretical point of view. The sector theory is a rather recent development in ecology and originated in response to demonstrable inadequacies that the concentric theory had revealed to research ecologists and real estate economists. As formulated by Homer Hoyt the sector theory envisions a circular expanse of space occupied by a city.[9] At the center of the city lies the business district. Then, extending outwards from this center, in the form of sectors or "slices," are the residential districts of the city. The preferred residential districts, i.e., those which command the highest rent, comprise one or perhaps several sectors. Low rent residential districts lie in another sector or sectors. Districts that are intermediate in terms of class position, desirability, and rent lie in still other sectors. Each type of residential district is thus embraced within one or more sectors extending from the very heart of the city to its periphery.

The explanation that Hoyt adduces for this idealized pattern is as follows:

High rent or high grade residential neighborhoods must almost necessarily move outward toward the periphery of the city. The wealthy seldom reverse their steps and move backward into the obsolete houses which they are giving up. On each side of them is usually an inter-

---

[9] Homer Hoyt, *The Structure and Growth of Residential Neighborhoods in American Cities* (Washington: 1939), pp. 74–78, 112–122; Arthur M. Weimer and Homer Hoyt, *Principles of Urban Real Estate* (New York: 1939), pp. 60–70.

mediate rental area, so they cannot move sideways. As they represent the highest income group, there are no houses above them abandoned by another group. They must build new houses on vacant land. Usually this vacant land lies available just ahead of the line of march of the area because, anticipating the trend of fashionable growth, land promoters have either restricted it to high grade use or speculators have placed a value on the land that is too high for the low rent or intermediate rental group. Hence the natural trend of the high rent area is outward, toward the periphery of the city in the very sector in which the high rent area started.[10]

Presumably the sectors comprising the intermediate and low rent residential uses are formed out of the residual slice not lying in the path of the expanding high rent sector, although Hoyt is not express upon this point.

In the sector theory there is found the same determinism that characterizes the concentric hypothesis. Expressions such as "natural trend" and "almost necessary outward movement" [11] indicate the negligible role that Hoyt would ascribe to social values, ideals, or purposes in land utilization. There is no definite place in the scheme for departures away from the sector pattern, except by means of references to "natural barriers" and "certain extraordinary factors" [12] which obstruct the free operation of natural forces.

Strictly speaking, of course, neither the concentric theory nor the sector theory is of recent origin. Both represent variations upon older "radial" and "ring" conceptions of city growth and they find their statements in standard real estate manuals, in agricultural economics, and even in classical political theory. The city plans proposed by Plato and Aristotle provided definite concentric circles for each of the major urban functions, namely, worship, legislation and adjudication, dwelling, and defense.[13] In Aristotle's scheme a radius or sector was formed by the link between a city and its port. Agricultural economists, beginning with

[10] *Ibid.*, p. 116.
[11] *Loc. cit.*
[12] Weimer and Hoyt, *Principles of Urban Real Estate,* pp. 66, 68.
[13] Plato, *Laws,* Bk. VI, tr. by B. Jowett, 2d ed. (Oxford: 1875); Aristotle, *Politics,* Bk. VII, chap. xii, tr. by William Ellis, Everyman's Library (New York: 1919).

Adam Müller in 1809, and extending through von Thünen and Schäffle, have formulated concentric patterns that correspond to the types of agricultural production surrounding a market place.[14] Urban geographers and real estate theorists have long pointed out the radial aspects of urban expansion from a nucleus of original settlement.[15] Essentially the Burgess-Hoyt theories are a restatement of these older principles, put into more strictly ecological terms.

The status of the idealized descriptive schemes must be determined on the basis of their empirical adequacy to generalizing the structure of urban settlement patterns. In Chapter II of the present study we shall try to establish this point through an examination of selected data pertinent to the problem.

Empirically Rationalistic Theories. The next group of theories to be considered comprises the empirically rationalistic theories. These, like the idealized descriptive schemes, begin by positing a central point at which communicative routes intersect. Here is the place of "highest accessibility" [16] and here "the largest number of individuals interact for the satisfaction of needs." [17] But rather than looking for typical geographical patterns around this point, the empirically rationalistic theories have sought some universal regulative principle that would explain the spatial orderliness of human activities. This regulative principle they claim to find in the automatic process of competition and selection. Every person and group is regarded as being engaged in a constant struggle for the point of highest accessibility. The result of this

[14] On Müller's theory, see: Gottfried Pfeifer, "Über raumwirtschaftliche Begriffe und Vorstellungen und ihre bisherige Anwendung in der Geographie und Wirtschaftswissenschaft," *Geographische Zeitschrift,* 34: 321–340, 411–425 (1928), pp. 414–415. Von Thünen's theory, set forth in his *Der Isolierte Staat* (1826), is summarized in Richard T. Ely and George S. Wehrwein, *Land Economics* (New York: 1940), p. 68. On Schäffle's theory, see Tord Palander, *Beiträge zur Standortstheorie* (Uppsala: 1935), p. 120.

[15] Jean Brunhes, *Human Geography* (New York: 1920), pp. 196–229; Richard M. Hurd, *Principles of City Land Values* (New York: 1905), chap. i; Frederick M. Babcock, *The Valuation of Real Estate* (New York: 1932), pp. 61–63.

[16] Calvin F. Schmid, "Land Values as an Ecological Index," *Research Studies of the State College of Washington,* 9: 16–36 (March: 1941), p. 23.

[17] A. B. Hollingshead, "Human Ecology," in Robert E. Park, (ed.), *An Outline of the Principles of Sociology* (New York: 1939), p. 104.

struggle is a selective process by which each person and group gravitates to the location that befits its competitive strength. From this there emerges a "natural" distribution over space of the component functions of a community, so arranged that the available space is being most efficiently utilized.

To support their reasoning the rationalists have assumed two major premises, which are set forth with varying degrees of explicitness by different writers. The first one is to the effect that the only consideration which guides a social system (whether it be a person or group) in its choice of location is the one of cost. Indeed, Angell has asserted that an ecological approach to social interaction is only possible because, in contemporary culture, all associations tend to be "fiscal enterprises." [18] Not only business establishments, but supposedly dwellings, churches, libraries, etc., locate solely in response to "fiscal" considerations of income and expenditure. All the interests of a social system thus become subsumed to the one of minimizing cost. In regard to dwellings, for instance, Haig asserts that:

In choosing a residence purely as a consumption proposition, one buys accessibility precisely as one buys clothes or food. He considers how much he wants the contacts furnished by the central location, weighing the "costs of friction" involved — the various possible combinations of site rent, time value, and transportation costs; he compares this want with his other desires and his resources and he fits it into his scale of consumption, and buys.[19]

And McKenzie writes that: "Underlying all forms of urban segregation are the factors of income and rent." [20] Social systems thus become strictly economic units. Whatever spatial position within a settlement conduces to the most economic functioning of a social system will be the object of that system's competitive bargaining. Thus cost, as the measure of frustration to the achieve-

[18] Robert C. Angell, "Discussion," *American Sociological Review*, 1: 189–192 (April: 1936).
[19] Robert Murray Haig, "Towards an Understanding of the Metropolis — the Assignment of Activities to Areas in Urban Regions," *Quarterly Journal of Economics*, 40: 402–434 (May, 1926), p. 423.
[20] R. D. McKenzie, *The Metropolitan Community* (New York: 1933), p. 247.

ment of ends, becomes the sole criterion by which social systems judge locations. Sentiments, values, and ideals presumably play no significant role in the process.

The second major premise is corollary to the first one, though logically distinct. According to this premise the only socially significant property of physical space lies in its impeding social interaction — i.e., in its cost-imposing quality. Thus Hurd, in an early work, asserted that:

> Since (land) value depends on economic rent, and rent on location, and location on convenience, and convenience on nearness, we may eliminate the intermediate steps and say that value depends on nearness.[21]

And Quinn has written in a recent article:

> Ecological units tend to be distributed within an area so that the ecological distance traversed in adjusting to limited environmental factors and to other men is reduced to the minimum.[22]

Various other terms for the premise are used by the rationalists, such as "time-cost distance,"[23] "median location,"[24] "shortest energy-distance,"[25] and similar expressions. But all of them consider spatiality as something which has to be paid for, in the sense that social systems, in dealing with it, must suffer a qualified attainment of their ends. Obviously the ideal location for any social system would be the point of highest accessibility, for there the impediment put by spatiality upon social interaction is at a minimum. It is easier for people to come together and deal with one another there than at any other point in a given territory. However the supply of such accessible locations is necessarily

---

[21] Richard M. Hurd, *Principles of City Land Values* (New York: 1905), p. 13.

[22] James A. Quinn, "The Hypothesis of Median Location," *American Sociological Review*, 8: 148–156 (April, 1943), p. 149.

[23] R. D. McKenzie, "The Scope of Human Ecology," in Ernest W. Burgess (ed.), *The Urban Community* (Chicago: 1926), pp. 170–171.

[24] Quinn, *op. cit.*

[25] George Kingsley Zipf, *National Unity and Disunity* (Bloomington: 1941), p. 161.

limited and must therefore be allocated among competing social systems.

In this way the rationalists are led to their view that the competitive process is the universal regulative principle of land use. Given on the one hand a multiplicity of social systems all seeking least costful locations [26] and, on the other hand, a limited supply of accessible locations (whose only relevance to these social systems is in minimizing time-cost-energy expenditure), there is bound to be a competition for advantageous location.

This competition for advantageous location is supposed to operate automatically, on a biotic, sub-cultural level.[27] In the words of Dawson and Gettys, "the distributive process through which all human units are located as to position and function is impersonal and almost completely unconscious."[28] And Quinn has written:

Ecological interaction occurs upon different levels from those of truly social interaction. Human social interaction involves consensus, exchange of meaning through symbol communication, and imaginative playing of the roles of others. Ecological interaction, in contrast, involves only an indirect, impersonal form of mutual modification by which each living man influences others by increasing or decreasing the supplies of environmental factors upon which the others depend. Ecological interaction cannot be conceived as social except in the sense that it influences social interaction.[29]

Volition and purpose thus become inconsequential, adventitious features of the competitive process. They have no causative

---

[26] "Least costful" in the sense of facilitating the greatest over-all surplus of income over expenditure for the individual social system. This is equivalent to the "highest profit combination" of location with other productive agents. The land that is least costful in this sense naturally becomes, by virtue of its desirability, the most costful on the real estate market. Care must be taken to avoid confusing these two very different referents of the term "costful."

[27] Alihan, *op. cit.*, p. 31 and *circ.*

[28] Carl A. Dawson and Warner E. Gettys, *An Introduction to Sociology* (New York: 1929), p. 220. The same idea may be found quite expressly in the works of Park, McKenzie, Davie, Hollingshead, Ratcliffe, Hurd, and Haig.

[29] Quinn, "Human Ecology and Interactional Ecology," *American Sociological Review*, 5: 713–722 (October, 1940), p. 722.

power of their own. The real dynamic force is thought to be the necessity for every social system to economize and in that way maintain itself within a dynamic equilibrium — the "web of life." [30] In order to economize there must be a "struggle for position — that is, for a sustenance niche and a spatial location in which the individual or institution may survive and function." [31]

The adaptive agents in the competitive struggle are viewed as independent, autonomous social systems each of which exists as a free agent in "the biotic community." [32] These agents are envisioned as bargaining freely with each other for the limited supply of accessible space. The outcome of this competitive bidding is a natural process of selection which distributes social activities over space according to their economic strength. Retail business, able to turn accessibility to the greatest profit, preempts the central locations. Other commercial functions, in proportion to their economizing ability, distribute themselves around the periphery and at other transportation junctions. Prosperous families pick those locations which are most convenient and pleasant in the area that remains. Finally, to the unwanted residue of land there gravitate the least economizing social systems — transients, single roomers, low-income families, morally reprehensible interests, and the like. All together these land uses constitute a self-regulating equilibrium of forces — a "biotic community." [33] And in Park's rather unequivocal words:

The ties that unite its individual units are those of a free and natural economy, based on a natural division of labor. Such a society is territorially organized and the ties which hold it together are physical and vital rather than customary and moral.[34]

---

[30] Hollingshead, op. cit., pp. 66–67.

[31] McKenzie, "Demography, Human Geography, and Human Ecology," in L. L. Bernard (ed.), The Fields and Methods of Sociology (New York: 1934), pp. 58–59. For an analysis of the Darwinistic implications of this position, with its recourse to concepts borrowed from biology, see Alihan, op. cit., chap. v.

[32] Cf. on this point Alihan, op. cit., p. 95.

[33] Hollingshead, op. cit., p. 67.

[34] Park, "Human Ecology," American Journal of Sociology, 42: 1–15 (July, 1936), p. 15. See also his "Succession, an Ecological Concept," American Sociological Review, 1: 171–179 (April, 1936), p. 178.

This line of reasoning, logically implied in the two initial premises of rationalism, constitutes what is known in economic theory as the "substitution principle." According to this principle any productive agent is technically capable of being applied to a number of different uses or ends. Which of these ends the productive agent will be applied to depends upon the relative economizing ability of these several uses in exploiting other productive agents. That one use or end which can so conjoin the particular productive agent with other productive agents as to achieve the greatest returns with the least cost (attending the exploitation of all the agents) will be the one to which the given productive agent is eventually applied.[35] The rationalistic ecologists have treated physical space entirely as a productive agent which can be variously combined with other agents so as to yield differing degrees of utility. That particular social system — say, a retail store — which can so combine accessible location with whatever other productive agents are necessary for its functioning as to extract the greatest economic returns from the land with the least cost (in the use of all these agents) will be the system that preëmpts the choice location.[36] Other social systems, less efficient in converting accessibility to profit, will mechanically arrange them-

[35] In technical economic terminology the "greatest returns with least cost" will be at the "highest profit combination" of inputs, a point which may be quite at variance from the "least cost combination" of inputs. To forestall any confusion arising out of terminological differences it will be well to emphasize that "cost" in our usage is not equivalent to "input" or to pecuniary valuation of input; rather "cost" refers to degree of departure from maximal end-attainment on the part of a system — i.e., the degree to which maintenance of identity is qualified. In this sense "profit" is a measure of "noncost." This usage does no violation to economic analysis and it affords a much more lucid translation of economic variables into a sociological frame of reference.

[36] The clearest incorporation of the substitution principle into ecological theory is that of Andreas Predöhl, a German theorist of industrial location. Predöhl has explicitly made of this principle the conceptual framework for his ecological theory. His work lies more directly in the methodologically rationalistic tradition, however, despite apparent lapses into a reification of his "pure" theory at a number of points. See his: "The Theory of Location in its Relation to General Economics," *Journal of Political Economy*, 36: 371–390 (June, 1928). Haig's formulation likewise states the substitution principle rather clearly, though without the technical economic terminology. *Op. cit.*, p. 420.

selves over space in accordance with their economizing ability. The result is a maximally efficient pattern of land use. In the words of Ratcliffe:

Thus, in the central business district of a large city the structural arrangement of land uses might be represented as constituting an economic machine whose parts have been arranged and rearranged until there is approached the maximum of efficiency in the performance of its commercial functions.[37]

And Haig writes:

It may be suggested as an hypothesis that the layout of a metropolis — the assignment of activities to areas — tends to be determined by a principle which may be termed the minimizing of the costs of friction.[38]

The efficiency and orderliness of this "biotic community" is thus regarded as an inevitable result of the free play of competitive forces. In McKenzie's words: "The underlying assumption is that the fact of a struggle is associated with the function of order." [39] And Hollingshead writes that: "It is competition in a market which gives society its more or less ordered ecological base." [40] At no point do the rationalists feel the need to invoke any cultural factors to explain spatial order: each social system is an independent being whose only relationship with other social systems is one of bargaining and contracting; the interests which prompt it to seek location are given in its very nature and involve only the idea of minimizing cost; and the resulting competition between it and the other social systems, all equally autonomous, is inherent in the biotic process. Out of this self-regulating process there emerges a spatial orderliness that comports with a "maximum of efficiency" in the functioning of the community.

At this point in the reasoning there arises a question of logical

[37] Richard U. Ratcliffe, *The Problem of Retail Site Selection,* Michigan Business Studies, vol. 9, no. 1, (Ann Arbor: 1939), p. 60.

[38] Haig, *op. cit.,* p. 422.

[39] McKenzie, "Demography, Human Geography, and Human Ecology," *op. cit.,* pp. 58–59.

[40] Hollingshead, *op. cit.,* p. 97.

inference. The rationalists have properly reasoned from their initial premises to the conclusion that every social system is forever struggling for a least costful location. This, they show, necessarily puts it into competition with other social systems, since the supply of "least costful" locations is limited and has to be allocated. In this way they establish their hypothesis regarding the inevitability and universality of competition. From this, however, they leap to the statement that the spatial layout resulting from this free play of competition has a spontaneous, natural stability and order. But this supposition in no way follows from the original premises. Only by recourse to a supplementary prop can any case be made for the hypothesis of a natural order emerging from competitive struggle. The rationalistic ecologists are not themselves aware of this necessity. However, anyone who is familiar with orthodox economics will recognize in the rationalists' reasoning a basic hypothesis of utility analysis.[41]

The substance of this hypothesis, to which the rationalists are unwittingly committed, is that the utility of the part coincides with the utility of the whole. According to this principle, each enterprise, in rationally seeking its own maximum utility, will inevitably contribute toward the maximum utility of the whole society, provided there are no artificial restrictions upon the natural laissez faire regime. In seeking its own selfish good it thereby furthers the good of all. The reasoning here is that, granting the substitution principle, the supply of a particular productive agent will be allocated among its possible uses in such a way that the last unit of the agent applied to a given use yields a surplus of returns over cost which is equal to that yielded by the last unit applied to each other use. At this point the utility accruing to the society is a maximum. Likewise at this point the utility accruing to each enterprise is a maximum. Things could not be otherwise if the substitution principle is accepted. For let us assume the contrary: suppose that a last unit of productive agent, x, is applied to a particular use in such a way that its surplus of returns over cost is less than that of the last unit of productive agent, y, applied to each other use in the society. This

---

[41] Our own evaluation of the adequacy of this hypothesis must wait upon our empirical analysis. At present we are concerned only with indicating the line of reasoning that is presupposed in rationalistic ecology.

could only mean that x would yield more utility if it were applied to a different use. In these circumstances, then, x is not being put to its most economic use. Hence whatever enterprise depends upon x for its functioning is not realizing a maximum of utility, and society too is not realizing as much utility as if x were put to a different use. Following the principle of substitution, x will eventually be put to that use which can most economically exploit it. In this way the utility of the part and the utility of the whole are both maximized, each varying positively with the other.

Nowhere in the ecological literature is this hypothesis expressly referred to. But without it there would be no way for the rationalists to explain how orderly land use could emerge from the competitive struggle of a multitude of independent social systems.[42] Only on the supposition that the interests of the whole are coördinate with the interests of the part could the rationalists account for any orderliness in land use. Without such a supposition all references to "least time-cost distance," "shortest energy-distance," "minimizing of the costs of friction," etc., would hardly have meaning; for the question would arise: shortest distance for whom, the enterprise or the community, the part or the whole? There might well be a complete dichotomy between the two, and the very core of rationalistic ecology would be vitiated.

Consider Ratcliffe's statement:

The process of adjustment in city structure to a most efficient land-use pattern is through the competition of uses for the various locations. The use which can extract the greatest profit from a given site will be the successful bidder. The outgrowth of this market process of competitive bidding for sites among the potential users of land is an orderly pattern of land use spatially organized to perform most efficiently the economic functions which characterize urban life.[43]

If this statement is dissociated from the hypothesis that the utility of the part coincides with the utility of the whole, it becomes ambiguous and untenable. Only on such a principle does

---

[42] For the definitive refutation of this hypothesis, from a sociological viewpoint, see Vilfredo Pareto, *Mind and Society* (New York: 1935), paragraphs 2128–2145. We shall return to this point in a later chapter.

[43] Ratcliffe, *op. cit.*, pp. 5–6.

it follow that "a most efficient land-use pattern" (utility of the whole) results from the successful bidding for choice sites by "the use which can extract the greatest profit" (utility of the part). To be sure, few if any of the rationalists perceive the problem here, but that in no way alters their theoretical position. Implicit in their concepts of "least time-cost distance" and the like is the assumption of an identity between the utility of the part and the utility of the whole. Apart from this proposition there could be no conception of a stable pattern of land use that maintained its orderliness through the automatic process of competition.

This unwitting commitment to a basic hypothesis of utility economics has profound implications for rationalistic ecology and goes far to account for certain empirical difficulties that confront it. The nature of these difficulties will become clear during our empirical analysis of pertinent data in succeeding chapters. Our present task is limited to an exposition of the theory and the logical grounds upon which it rests.

It should be evident from the foregoing analysis that the rationalists have made of spatial adaptation a strictly economic phenomenon. They have begun by regarding all social systems as purely economic units. They have then postulated that the only socially relevant quality of space is its costfulness as an economic good. From these two premises they have logically deduced that the city is a natural mechanism whose processes lead to a most efficient territorial layout of social activities.

If this is so there arises the question of how it is ever possible for man's use of land to deviate from a most economic arrangement. To account for the obvious irregularities that manifest themselves in land use the rationalistic ecologists have advanced two different kinds of explanation. It is in terms of these two types of explanation that the empirically rationalistic theories may be classified.

First there are a few ecologists, the literal rationalists, who view actual departures from their theory as in no way qualifying the adequacy of the theory. The departures, in other words, are not to be attributed to the influence of non-economic factors such as values or ideals. Rather they result from an inability of human beings to perfectly apprehend and comply with their spatial environs. This inability derives from unavoidable limitations upon the powers of human cognition. Thus "ignorance and error" become the sole cause of non-rational land use. Haig states this explanation in the following words:

There are many other special circumstances which also operate to distort the outlines of the ideal urban layout or to retard conformity to it. Ignorance, inertia, chance, and personal idiosyncrasies, all play a part. The physical characteristics of the terrain and the peculiarities of the transportation system are important factors influencing the pattern. Conditions of land tenure may retard or facilitate conformity to it. Similarly the absence of competitive pressures is responsible for much bad location.[44]

And Ratcliffe writes that:

Site bids are too often matters of trial and error. The complexity of the forces impinging upon each site precludes any accurate measurement of its future utility. The widespread use of leases tends to perpetuate errors in site selection and to delay the process of rearrangement.[45]

In this point of view the ultimately causative factors remain those of cognition and efficiency. At no point do the literal rationalists feel any need of incorporating new factors in their theoretical formulation. Such extraneous elements as meanings and values are to them ephemeral hindrances to the more basic economic factors.

Most of the empirical rationalists, however, deal with the manifest discrepancies between theory and reality in a different way. Being less puristic in matters of theory they have compromised the logical requirements of their scheme through the "residual category" device.[46] In other words, they readily acknowledge the reality and effectiveness of social values in spatial adaptation; but they make no attempt to incorporate this empirical concession into their theoretical system. Their procedure has been the com-

---

[44] Haig, *op. cit.*, pp. 429–430.
[45] Ratcliffe, *op. cit.*, p. 6.
[46] A good criticism on this point is that of Warner E. Gettys, *op. cit.*, p. 471. Cf. Alihan, *op. cit.*, p. 128, although hers is a rather polemical critique without any systematic framework of its own.

mon one of granting a causative efficacy to nonrationalistic factors without in any way altering the rationalistic scheme itself.[47] All factual departures from the kind of spatial order called for by the theory are lumped together into a loose category of "limiting" or "complicating" factors. This category embraces "customs," "moral attitudes and taboos," "political and administrative measures," "cultural biases," "traditional patterns," and the like. These are supposed to limit or complicate the natural competitive process, but they are not regarded as ultimate causative factors.

McKenzie, one of the more realistic ecologists, primarily concerned with descriptive research rather than with theory, typifies the empirically compromised position. He writes:

The human community, like the community of lower organisms, is fundamentally the product of biotic and environmental forces. . . . Man, however, is a cultural animal and is able, therefore, to modify his natural environment and to create, within limitations, his own habitat.[48]

And Park, one of the founders of ecology, expresses a compromised rationalism when he says that:

Human ecology has, however, to reckon with the fact that in human society competition is limited by custom and culture. The cultural superstructure imposes itself as an instrument of direction and control upon the biotic substructure.[49]

However, in Park's judgment the basic process remains that of natural competition:

The incidence of this more or less arbitrary control which custom and consensus imposes upon the natural social order complicates the

[47] Essentially this is but a particular case of "statistical positivism," characterized by its "admitting an empirical role to normative elements without disturbing the positivistic framework." The normative element remains extraneous and random so far as the theoretical system is concerned. See Parsons, *op. cit.*, p. 80.

[48] McKenzie, "Human Ecology," *Encyclopedia of the Social Sciences*, p. 314.

[49] Park, "Human Ecology," *op. cit.*, p. 15; see also his "Succession, an Ecological Concept," *op. cit.*, p. 175.

social process but does not fundamentally alter it — or, if it does, the effects of biotic competition will still be manifest in the succeeding social order and the subsequent course of events.[50]

Hollingshead considers the causative role of culture to be as follows:

Competition, in ecological relations, gives rise to a balance between competing forces in a situation; whereas custom, as a social process, tries to regulate and fix the equilibrium attained by competition, and gives rise to a stable condition.[51]

This empirically compromised rationalism is the prevailing theory of ecology today and it accordingly merits a particularly searching inquiry. In Part I of this work we shall undertake an empirical examination of its premises and generalizations as well as those of the literal rationalistic position. Only thus can the adequacy of ecological rationalism be properly appraised.

Methodologically Rationalistic Theories. All of the theories we have so far considered claim a high degree of descriptive accuracy for themselves. There is, however, a third grouping of ecological theories whose concern with realistic description of land use patterns is incidental to their preoccupation with methodological rigor. These we have called the methodologically rationalistic theories. On the surface there might appear to be little difference between these theories and the empirically rationalistic theories just discussed. Both treat social systems as strictly economizing agents and both consider space purely as an impediment to social interaction. Adequate cognition becomes in both of them the sole orienting link between social systems and physical space. But here the resemblance ends. The methodologically rationalistic theories, far from claiming any descriptive accuracy, deliberately "fictionalize" the process of spatial adaptation. The foremost representative of this kind of rationalism is Alfred Weber. Indeed his theory, and the minor revisions made of it by his disciples, comprise the whole of methodological rationalism.[52]

---

[50] Park, "Human Ecology," *op. cit.*, p. 13.

[51] Hollingshead, *op. cit.*, p. 127.

[52] Since the content of Weber's ecology is limited entirely to the locational processes of industrial production there might be some question as to the

Weber begins by sharply distinguishing "pure" theory from "realistic" theory.[53] In the pure theory Weber aims at a deductively constructed system of locational laws valid for all sociocultural regimes. His laws, in other words, are to be independent of any particular historical period. As he puts it:

To be specific, we shall exclude from the purview of the pure theory all locational factors of a purely social and cultural nature which our analysis of reality reveals. We shall not even investigate how far the natural and technical factors contain in their present form social and cultural elements which are due to the particular economic and social order, the particular civilization of today.[54]

Above all, the laws are to be logically deducible from specified initial premises and are to be logically compatible with each other. In this way they are to constitute a closed theoretical system. "Naturally, this system will apply only in terms of these premises and no further."[55] Being pure — i.e., predicated on no particular social values — the laws ostensibly describe the way in which social systems, unhampered by the vagaries of volition, would "virtually" adapt to physical space. They purport to get at the underlying processes that are ever at work beneath the surface appearance of real spatial adaptation.

In developing his conceptions of space and of social systems Weber resembles very closely the empirically rationalistic theorists. However, unlike them, he regards his postulates as heuris-

---

propriety of discussing a theory thus restricted in an analysis of ecological theories. However, in view of our own position that all spatial adaptation, viewed from a certain standpoint, is reducible to a common set of elements, there seemed no legitimate reason for excluding a theory from consideration merely because it confined itself to the locational processes of one kind of social system, namely, industry. Furthermore, the methodology of Weber's theory is so important that any failure to discuss it in a study of this character would seriously weaken the strength of our thesis.

[53] The pure theory appears in Alfred Weber, *Theory of the Location of Industries,* tr. with introduction and comments by Carl Joachim Friedrich (Chicago: 1929). The realistic theory is developed in his "Industrielle Standortslehre," in *Grundriss der Sozialökonomik,* vol. 6, chap. iii (Tübingen: 1914).

[54] Weber, *op. cit.,* pp. 22–23.

[55] *Ibid.,* p. 11.

tic constructs and nothing more. Regarding these two factors Weber writes:

By "locational factor" we mean an advantage which is gained when an economic activity takes place at a particular point or at several such points rather than elsewhere. An advantage is a saving of cost, i.e., a possibility for the industry to produce at this point a certain product at less cost than elsewhere, to accomplish the entire productive and distributive process of a certain industrial product cheaper at one place than at another.[56]

This definition clearly limits the significance of space to that of imposing unequal advantages upon various locations. Space is viewed only as a hindrance to the efforts of social systems to operate economically. Furthermore the statement considers social systems (specifically, industries) as being purely economizing agents so far as the process of selecting a location is concerned. Whatever other real properties they may have are deliberately excluded in the interests of a pure theory. In this definition Weber has thus stated the premises from which he logically deduces the remainder of his theory.

The locational factors are of three kinds, apart from those which are unique to particular industries: (a) places of consumption; (b) transportation costs, which in turn are reducible to: (b') weight of goods and raw materials, and (b'') distance to be traversed; and finally (c) labor costs at different places. The first of these, place of consumption, is assumed as constant throughout Weber's analysis. The other two factors constitute the variables with which Weber operates. Essentially his method consists of holding one locational factor constant and then deducing from his premises how industry would locate in terms of the other, the variable factor. This he calls the method of "isolation." In his own analysis Weber has chosen to confine himself to only two combinations of constant-variable factors, although he might have pursued additional such combinations.[57]

First Weber imagines that labor costs at different places are equal, and that the places of consumption are given. How then

---

[56] *Ibid.*, p. 18.
[57] Friedrich, "Editor's Introduction," *op. cit.*, p. xxv.

should an industry locate? Clearly it should locate at whatever point will minimize: (a) the aggregate weight of raw material and finished goods which must be moved if an industry is to operate; and (b) the aggregate distance over which an industry must move its materials. Obviously the determining factor here will be the ratio that prevails for a given industry between the weight of raw materials and the weight of finished goods. This ratio Weber calls the "material index." Those industries, for example, whose finished product is light in proportion to the weight of raw materials used will locate near the source of raw materials. Other industries will distribute themselves in a comparable manner, according to the relative make-up of their transportation costs — i.e., according to their respective material indexes.

Continuing with his "experimental isolation" of the locational factors Weber now asks: given the places of consumption and given the "proper" location for an industry in terms of the material index, what departure from such an optimum will be caused by unequal labor costs at different places? Under these specifications he deduces that an industry should comply with the pull of lower labor costs in direct ratio to the share borne by the labor coefficient in the total production costs. An industry whose labor costs are high in proportion to the total weight of materials that must be transported will deviate a great deal from the optimum as defined by the material index. But an industry with negligible labor costs relative to the weight of transported materials will not deviate significantly from the material index optimum.[58]

These are the only two "experimental isolations" which Weber himself makes although additional logical possibilities readily present themselves. But for present purposes it is sufficient for us to see what his method consists of and, more briefly, what he does with it.

As a result of the operation of the three locational factors there are set into motion two kinds of secondary locational forces, the agglomerative forces and the deglomerative forces. The former consist of the advantages which accrue to an industry, in the way of better market connections and lower overhead costs, through being close to other industries. The end-result of these forces is a spatial agglomeration of industries within certain areas. Con-

[58] Weber, *op. cit.*, chaps. iii–iv.

tinued spatial agglomeration reduces aggregate costs of an industry up to a certain point, but beyond this point the added rent which the desired area can command as a result of the agglomeration outweighs the gain attending convenient location. Thus a deglomerative force is created. When the deglomerative forces exceed the agglomerative forces there is a tendency for a given industry to move outward from the place of concentration.[59]

In this pure theory Weber has tried to eliminate whatever is culturally relative. The theory lays no claim to real descriptive accuracy but only to an *eo ipso* validity. Of course, Weber in no way regards his theory as a mere fantasy, but seeks to fit it to reality through further deductive reasoning. This he does through turning the causal relationship the other way around and viewing the three locational factors now as dependent variables rather than as independent ones. But here as before he excludes from his scheme all social or cultural ("historical") factors, saying:

> But it is obvious that this historical basis is something entirely different from what we are looking for at present. This historical basis is the material, so to speak, which is transformed; whereas we are looking for a basis or theory of this transformation itself.[60]

So, rather than explaining the origin of population aggregates (places of consumption) and the places of raw materials in terms of historical backgrounds Weber assumes a hypothetical original economy. He imagines an empty country that is being settled by an agricultural population. The problem of how this population acquires its skills and techniques embarrasses Weber, for such elements are purely cultural variables that cannot be admitted into a pure theory; yet they obviously will influence the settlement patterns formed by a new agricultural population.[61] Despite

---

[59] *Ibid.*, chap. v.

[60] *Ibid.*, p. 213.

[61] Weber's solution of this crucial point completely vitiates the "purity" of his theory, for he admits that the only way to understand the settlement pattern which an agricultural population will take on is in terms of an *empirical analysis* by which one can explain the techniques a population uses in developing the agricultural possibilities of land. Thus a cultural variable has forcibly intruded itself into Weber's supposedly pure scheme. Cf. *op. cit.*, p. 223.

this difficulty Weber proceeds with his deductive reasoning. With an agricultural population established, the places of consumption and the location of exploitable raw materials are automatically fixed.[62] On the basis of this land use pattern there arise primary industries, locating according to the principles formulated in the first part of Weber's theory. In turn primary industries, once located, establish the places of consumption and raw materials in terms of which derivative industries will distribute themselves.

There remains only one locational factor left unexplained. That is the one of unequal labor costs at various places. Here Weber admits that:

This is the great gap in our analysis so far. . . . This problem will have to be solved by the "realistic" theory. For at this point it becomes necessary to consider *particular economic systems*.[63]

In his later work on locational theory Weber undertakes to briefly develop this realistic theory.[64] Here he argues that the only way in which sociocultural factors can create an industrial locational pattern that deviates from the one described by pure theory is by influencing the layout of the labor supply. And even this has been true only since the advent of modern capitalism, under which transportation costs have become so low and places of consumption have become so settled that the location and accessibility of labor is a more important consideration than these in choosing a location. Industry thus has been able to emancipate itself from the pure theory formula and to locate in compliance with culturally varying locations of labor supply. The influence of culture upon the location of labor takes place through two main avenues: (a) localities made wealthy through some historical advantage or circumstance will create a population surplus which will attract labor-using industries;[65] (b) the laboring masses locate not only in response to economic advantage but

[62] *Ibid.*, p. 215.
[63] *Ibid.*, p. 225. The emphasis is ours.
[64] "Industrielle Standortslehre," *op. cit.*
[65] *Ibid.*, pp. 74–76.

also to nonrational feelings and localistic sentiments (*Heimatsge-fühl*).[66]

Oskar Engländer, following in the methodologically rationalistic tradition, has criticized Weber for limiting the significance of culture to that of influencing the location of labor supply. Engländer indicates that capitalism, as an embodiment of historically relative values, may exert an influence upon industrial location through such means as the system of exchange, the organization of production, and the layout of population, as well as the availability of labor.[67]

In developing his own theory, however, Engländer deliberately excludes these cultural factors, not by way of denying their real importance but rather in the interests of a "pure" theory. Thus in terms of methodology Engländer's theory closely resembles that of Weber. Both share the same procedure of conceptually varying one factor after another, taking the remaining factors as given, and then deducing the corresponding spatial patterns that economic activities will assume. However Engländer has to a greater extent than Weber couched his analysis in terms of familiar economic concepts, particularly those of marginal demand and the substitution principle. This is evident in the two basic generalizations he advances, from which most of the rest of his analysis is derived. These two generalizations may be stated as follows:

(a) *Given:* the place of *production;* the outermost spatial bounds of the consuming population are defined by the line at which the price a consumer would pay for any single unit out of a supply of a given good is equal to the price he would be willing to pay for a last (marginal) unit of that good. Beyond this line the transportation costs impose a higher price than that which the consumer is willing to pay for a last unit of the good.[68]

(b) *Given:* the place of *consumption;* the furthermost distance at which production of a given good will be carried on is at that point where the income an entrepreneur derives from the marketing of his good sufficiently outweighs the costs of producing and

[66] *Ibid.*, p. 77.

[67] Oskar Engländer, "Kritisches und Positives zu einer allgemeinen reinen Lehre vom Standort," *Zeitschrift für Volkswirtschaft und Sozialpolitik,* 5 (n.s.): 435–505 (1926), p. 494.

[68] Engländer, "Standort," in *Handwörterbuch der Staatswissenschaften,* 4th edition (Jena: 1926), p. 857.

transporting it as to exceed the income obtainable from any alternative source of income the entrepreneur might derive from his efforts.[69]

The first of these generalizations obviously rests upon the principles of diminishing utility and marginal demand, the latter upon the substitution principle. The rest of Engländer's analysis consists of deducing from these two basic generalizations how economic activities would locate under each of the many logically possible permutations and combinations of locational factors. This he does through conceptually manipulating, one by one, the variables constituting his system, viz., size of market, cost of product at place of production, fixedness or ubiquity of raw materials, cost of transportation, etc.[70] Like all the methodological rationalists Engländer fully appreciates that real land use patterns have many diseconomic features[71] which lie beyond the purview of his pure theory. But, true to his theoretical position, he contends that such real patterns only conceal the latent processes which the pure theory brings out.

Among the other methodological rationalists only the name of Andreas Predöhl is outstanding enough to bear notice.[72] His main point is that economic activity locates in terms of all the spatially contingent means of production so as to achieve whatever ratio of costs as between these productive means will comport with a minimum total cost. This, Predöhl indicates, follows from the substitution principle, according to which no productive means will long be applied to an end which yields less net returns than would another end. Apart from this stress upon the substitution principle Predöhl's theory differs little from the essential features of Weber's system.

Most of the assumptions which underlie the methodologically rationalistic position have been set forth rather clearly by its proponents. The strictly economizing character of social systems

[69] *Ibid.*, p. 860.

[70] *Ibid., passim.*

[71] See especially Engländer, "Kritisches und Positives zu einer allgemeinen reinen Lehre vom Standort," *op. cit.*, pp. 487–493.

[72] Andreas Predöhl, "The Theory of Location in its Relation to General Economics," *Journal of Political Economy*, 36: 371–390 (June, 1928). This article is a condensation of his "Das Standortsproblem in der Wirtschaftstheorie," *Weltwirtschaftliches Archiv*, 21: 294–321 (April, 1925).

and the purely impedimentive significance of space as a costful thing are deliberately set down as heuristic assumptions. The fundamental economic ideas of substitution, diminishing utility, and least cost combination make up the principal referential categories for the whole deductive system. Clearly an appraisal of these theories must have a somewhat different purpose than would one of a descriptive theory. No array of facts can prove such theories to be "wrong," for their validity or invalidity rests upon a different basis than one of descriptive accuracy. The only proper objective for an empirical examination of the methodologically rationalistic theories is to test their explanatory adequacy. With this in view we shall present in Part II some pertinent data that may help us to judge the value of these theories.

Emergence of the Problem. If we reflect upon the three groupings of ecological theory just outlined we can readily see the common denominator that runs through them all. This common denominator we have already called "ecological determinism." The determinism rests on two implicit premises that pervade all three types of ecological theory. They may be stated as follows: (a) Physical space is a self-given phenomenon, and its qualities are wholly independent of cultural values; (b) social systems are passive adapters to spatial distance and have no further role than one of compliance. These are but a more general way of stating the two premises which underlie the rationalistic theories, concerning the strictly costful character of space, and the strictly economizing nature of social systems. In their present form they apply as well to the idealized descriptive schemes. On the basis of these two premises the only possible relationship that social systems may bear to physical space is an "intrinsic" one, i.e., one in which the nexi are the component ends of the system itself, as a disparate unit.[73] And the only possible relationship that

[73] This usage of the term "intrinsic," a concept advanced by Parsons, is essentially the same as his. Our conception of the intrinsic relationship, by identifying it with the very constitutive ends of the system itself, reduces ultimately to the criterion of maintenance-of-a-system's-identity. That of Parsons', on the other hand, equates the intrinsic relationship with "appropriateness according to a logico-experimental standard." The difference is clearly not one of substance but rather of point of emphasis; ours stresses the terminating state of affairs while Parsons' stresses the process. See Parsons, *op. cit.*, pp. 210–211.

physical space may bear to social systems is that of an impediment to the achievement of the system's ends and hence to its maintenance of identity. Space being a given it is presumably an independent variable to which social systems must passively comply. And social systems, being accountable to no other ends than those which constitute them, can only comply in terms of the single criterion of minimizing cost.

Now we may ask: is this the only possible kind of relationship that social systems may bear to physical space? Or is there a logical alternative to the "intrinsic" society-space relationship? And, if there is such an alternative, does it actually show up in real spatial adaptation?

That there is a logical alternative to the deterministic scheme is shown by a number of propositions advanced by sociologists who have approached spatial adaptation from a different point of view than most ecologists. Regarding the properties of space, for instance, Sorokin has pointed out that physical space, when considered apart from the culturally defined meanings pertaining to it, may be quite irrelevant to social interaction. In his words: "Geometric space, 'bleached of all the sociocultural qualities,' is not only not identical with sociocultural space but does not touch it at all." [74]

Likewise Simmel suggests that the very conception of space may be but a subjective construct. He writes: ". . . der Raum überhaupt nur eine Tätigkeit der Seele ist, nur die menschliche Art, an sich unverbundene Sinnesaffektionen zu einheitlichen Anschauungen zu verbinden." [75]

Both of these writers, and others, point out the important properties that space may acquire through cultural definition. [76] Such an insight of course contradicts the view that space is strictly a natural *donné* whose only bearing upon social interaction is that of a hindrance.

As for the nature of social systems too, there is a logical alternative to regarding them as agents which locate only in response

---

[74] Sorokin, *Sociocultural Causality Space Time*, p. 121.

[75] Georg Simmel, "Der Raum und die räumlichen Ordnungen der Gesellschaft," *Soziologie*, 3rd edition (München: 1923), p. 461.

[76] See also René Maunier, *L'Origine et la Fonction Économique des Villes* (Paris: 1910), p. 213 and *passim*.

to economic considerations. Sombart, for instance, suggests that: "Es gibt 'Vorteile' die an einem Orte haften und sich nicht in Kostenvorteile auflösen lassen. Alle 'Fühlungsvorteile' zum Beispiel." [77] The existence of such *Fühlungsvorteile* means that social systems, in seeking locations, may be guided by other ends than those which make them up. These ends must have their being in a broader, larger kind of system. For if they were nothing but elements of a disparate system they would, along with *Kostenvorteile*, be wholly reducible to economic analysis — this, because any thwarting of them would compromise the system's maintenance of identity and would thus represent a cost to the system. Such a *reductio* would simply assimilate them into the deterministic scheme. *Fühlungsvorteile*, then, must be regarded as ends which have their being in a broader, larger kind of system than mere disparate agents.[78] To such an inclusive system we have applied the term "cultural system." [79] In this connection it is important to realize that the very contingency between social systems and physical space is a matter of cultural definition. Only when space becomes defined as an objectifier for a cultural system does spatial placement have any significance for social interaction. In the absence of such definition social systems may have a complete autonomy of physical space.[80]

What all this means for ecological theory is clear. If space gets its socially relevant qualities through cultural definition, and if social systems (when contingent upon space at all) may locate in terms of social values there is obviously far more to the society-space relationship than an intrinsic nexus. A satisfactory ecological theory must somehow conceptualize this "non-intrinsic" nexus and integrate it with the propositions applying to intrinsic

[77] Werner Sombart, "Einige Anmerkungen zur Lehre vom Standort der Industrien," *Archiv für Sozialwissenschaft und Sozialpolitik*, 33: 748–758 (May, 1910), p. 755.

[78] For further substantiation of this postulate, see Parsons, *op. cit.*, pp. 254, 391, 718–719.

[79] By "social system" we mean the *organization* of particular, concrete persons and groups into regularized interaction. By "cultural system" we mean the *integration* of ends and meanings with respect to generalized types of persons and non-human externalities.

[80] Sorokin, *Sociocultural Causality Space Time*, pp. 119, 138 n. 56; Simmel, *op. cit.*, pp. 460–461.

spatial adaptation. To that task the present study is addressed.

In order that the reader may foresee our viewpoint and will be able then to evaluate our reasoning and demonstrations it may be well to indicate here what we think the "non-intrinsic" society-space nexus consists of. It is what may be called the "symbolic" relationship. In such a relationship the characteristics of space are not those belonging to it as a natural object of the physical world but rather are those which result from its being a symbol for a cultural system. Along with this, the ends by which social systems choose locations ultimately derive from just such a cultural system. So let us define the symbolic society-space relationship as one in which the properties attaching to physical space and the ends by which a social system orients itself to space have their being in a cultural system.[81] In contrast to this, an intrinsic society-space relationship would be one in which the properties of space were natural givens and in which the ends orienting a social system to space had their only being in the system itself, as a lone, disparate unit seeking maintenance of identity. Ends which make up a cultural system we shall call "values"; the subjective state orienting social systems which act upon values we shall call "volitional." On the other hand, ends comprising only disparate social systems we shall call "interests," and the subjective orientation of such systems will be called "rational." "Value" is thus the noun for "volitional," and "interest" is the noun for "rational."

With these concepts in mind we should be able to glimpse some of the implications of our alternative to the deterministic scheme. Such questions as the following immediately arise: What locational processes may we look for in lieu of those described by the deterministic theories? Can we expect to find any idealized descriptive patterns? Indeed, will there be any uniformities discernible at all in symbolic spatial adaptation? There is only one way to solve these problems, and that is through an empirical study of data which has been selected in the light of a systematized

---

[81] In this conception of the symbolic relationship we have only restated what has become a well established principle of sociology. See particularly: Alfred Schütz, *Der Sinnhafte Aufbau der Sozialen Welt* (Wien: 1932), pp. 133–134 and *circ.;* Parsons, *op. cit.,* pp. 210–211, 258, 416; Sorokin, *Sociocultural Causality Space Time,* pp. 4, 12–13; and Sorokin, *Social and Cultural Dynamics* (New York: 1941), IV, 11–19.

hypothesis. Our first task then must be to present such an hypothesis. Following that we may briefly outline the nature of our research and indicate the kind of data upon which we shall rest our case.

The hypothesis may be stated in two general propositions, with their respective corollaries, as follows:

I. Values (volitional adaptation) comprise one of the criteria by which certain social systems choose locations. Some values become explicitly linked with a spatial area so that fetishistic symbolism results. In this phenomenon social systems which share in the values will seek identification with the spatial area as an end in itself. Locational patterns thus emerge which are meaningfully consistent with the spatially referred values. In the same manner values which express primarily the identity or solidarity of a small cultural system may acquire spatial articulation. In this process space becomes a sort of symbol for the identity of that cultural system. As a result, social systems which embody that cultural system will assume meaningfully congruent locational patterns.

II. Interests (rational adaptation) dominate the spatial adaptation of certain social systems but these interests themselves come indirectly from broader and larger cultural systems; hence they cannot be viewed as self-given ends. To be sure, the resulting locational patterns represent an intrinsic society-space relationship in that, from the point of view of the social systems seeking location space appears as a given which must be passively complied with. However, the specific nature of spatial givenness and the specific form of compliance on the part of social systems are both manifestations of particular cultural systems. Frequently the land use patterns that arise in response to interests conflict with, and supersede, those arising out of values. In such cases the older patterns may nonetheless exert a selective force upon the newly locating social systems.

Corresponding to these two propositions we have grouped our supporting evidence into two parts, viz., Part I, dealing with "The Role of Social Values in Nonrational Adaptation to Space," and Part II, dealing with "The Cultural Context of Rational Adaptation to Space."

Part I begins with a chapter on the variability of social adaptation to space. In this chapter we shall outline the history and present layout of land uses in Boston with a view to evaluating the adequacy of the idealized descriptive schemes. Our data will, we think, point up a number of faults in these schemes which a satisfactory ecological theory must eliminate. The succeeding chapter is based upon material on Beacon Hill. This district, for nearly a century and a half one of Boston's fashionable residential districts, has acquired during its long history a number of sentimental associations which are a very real attraction to certain people seeking residences. Thus we have in Beacon Hill a case of fetishism, where the symbolic attributes of a spatial area have become end-values in themselves. In the next chapter we shall show how certain venerable sites in central Boston, though not devoted to any "rational" use, have nonetheless maintained their locations in the face of competing economic uses. This persistence seems to correlate with certain values that people in Boston have attached to these sites. The final chapter in Part I will describe locational trends in the North End, a homogeneous Italian ghetto in central Boston. Despite its overcrowded and deteriorated character this district has come to symbolize, to a certain portion of the Italian population, the identity of their ethos. As a result there have emerged certain population tendencies which can only be explained through the values which these people have regarding their ethnic solidarity. Space has here become an incidental symbol to the identity of a cultural system.

In Part II we shall first describe the expansion of the retail center of Boston, in order to demonstrate our hypothesis about the relativity of rational adaptation with respect to a particular culture. The next chapter, following logically upon the earlier one, will point out what has happened as a result of the commercial invasion of a fashionable residential district, the Back Bay of Boston. Here the "persistence of reputation" as a selective force upon newer land uses will be seen, and some idea will be had as to the processes arising out of a conflict between rational and volitional adaptation to space. Finally, in our last empirical chapter, an analysis will be made of the South End, a socially disorganized rooming-house district of Boston. Our purpose will be to show the relativity of the rooming-house phenomenon, and the land use patterns arising from it, to culturally unique kinship and occupational values.

It may be noted that each of the areas selected for analysis corresponds to a particular item in the twofold hypothesis outlined above. Moreover, in a general way the arrangement of chapters corresponds to the classification of ecological theories outlined on page 6. Chapter II confronts the idealized descriptive schemes with certain "refractory" data; chapters III, IV, and V are critically oriented toward the premises of spatial givenness and adaptive passivity, which are so characteristic of the empirically rationalistic theories; and chapters VI, VII, and VIII present material that challenges the explanatory adequacy of any theory which, like the methodologically rationalistic theories, omits from its deductive scheme the cultural or volitional element. In addition to this logical coherence the areas discussed have a certain empirical coherence through the fact that they all occupy the central portion of the city and have therefore been subjected to a number of common influences. (See figure 1.)[82] Furthermore, each of the areas has at some time in the evolution of Boston been a preferred residential district. For these reasons it is hoped that the study may have some historical value as a unified study of land use in central Boston. However its primary objective remains the one of critically evaluating ecological theory in terms of factual data and of constructing in terms of these data an alternative ecological theory.

In a general way our method might be described as one of indicating affinities between behavioral phenomena and subjective phenomena. Indeed, the very nature of the hypothesis dictates such a method If we are to make out a case for the role of values in man's use of land it will be necessary to impute meanings to the actions of persons and other social systems that are seeking location. We shall further have to demonstrate that these meanings are more congruent with observable behavioral phenomena such as population movements and changes in land use than are the factors of cognition and efficiency which the rationalistic ecologists would stress. This will be no simple mat-

[82] The method of delineating these areas will be set forth in the respective chapters dealing with them.

ter. However, in order to avoid the insoluble epistemological problems inherent in an observer's imputation of meaning to another ego we shall have to lay down as a premise that it is possible to infer meanings from meaning-expressions — i.e., from oral and written statements. That actual meanings often diverge

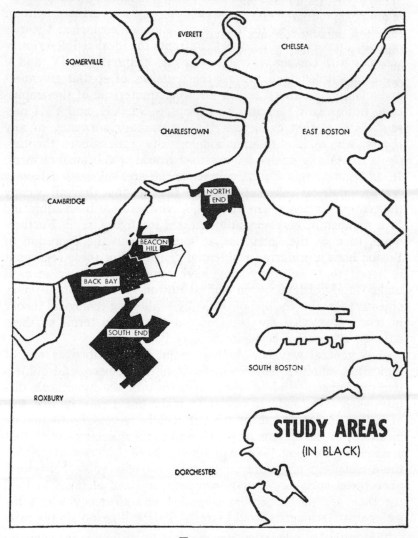

FIGURE I

from meaning-expressions cannot be doubted.[83] However, we shall adhere to the logico-meaningful postulate that meaning-expressions, when they show a consonance and fittedness to the over-all cultural context, may be taken as valid indices of another ego's subjective state.[84] Accordingly our procedure will consist in large part, though varying with the immediate problem at hand, of adducing verbatim statements that people have made regarding their locationally relevant activities, and of tallying the meanings that may be inferred from these statements with objective data on population distribution and land use changes, as disclosed by census materials and our own tabulations from directories, public listings, private registers, etc. Additional evidence will be submitted to show that our asserted correlation between meanings (more generally, values) and locational processes is more cogent than one between purely rationalistic elements and the given locational processes.

Let us turn then to our empirical analysis, beginning with a resume of the history and present arrangement of land uses in Boston. Our purpose will be to indicate how variable may be the spatial arrangements that social systems assume and, in terms of this variability, to evaluate the explanatory adequacy of the idealized descriptive schemes as generalized ecological theories.

[83] On this problem see Schütz, *op. cit.*, p. 17.

[84] The logico-meaningful method, formulated and developed by Sorokin, is described in his *Social and Cultural Dynamics*, I, 22–39.

PART I

THE ROLE OF SOCIAL VALUES IN NONRATIONAL
ADAPTATION TO SPACE

CHAPTER II

THE VARIABILITY OF SOCIAL ADAPTATION TO SPACE

IN THIS CHAPTER we shall outline the historical development and present layout of certain features of land use in Boston. Our purpose will be to confront the idealized descriptive schemes with data selected in terms of the main principles of these schemes. If the Burgess or Hoyt theories are valid we may expect to find territorial arrangements which conform to a concentric or sector pattern, or perhaps both. Any significant departure in actual land use from such idealized patterns will call into question the explanatory adequacy of the Burgess and Hoyt theories.

The arrangement of materials has been governed by two main problems: (1) Does the territorial migration of any particular type of social system, say upper class families, follow along a single sector as argued by Hoyt or expand by gradual concentric spreading as suggested by Burgess, or does it proceed in a wholly different way? (2) Does the territorial distribution at a given time of any particular class of social systems resemble a concentric or sector pattern? In accordance with these problems it has seemed advisable to arrange our data into two parts, one dealing with the historical differentiation and succession of land uses in Boston, the other describing the present arrangement of these land uses. In this way we will be able to show up both the dynamic processes out of which present land uses have developed and the layout of these present uses as now constituted, in the meantime comparing these with the processes and patterns formulated by the idealized descriptive schemes.

Historical Differentiation and Succession of Land Uses. Perhaps the most obvious fact about Boston's spatial development is that land uses have become increasingly differentiated, with the result that homogeneous areas, each put to a different use, have gradually emerged. Pioneer Boston had but a rudimentary spatial differentiation, the principal one being that between the store-keepers and townspeople who lived right in the heart of the settle-

ment at what is now the head of State street, and the majority of
the settlers, who were distributed along the shoreline north and
south of this center.[1] Dock square, as the town's landing place,
became the main produce market. Here the fish and corn markets
were located and here imports were received and stored. On
nearby State street there were established retail shops, a merchant's exchange, a postoffice, and the town house.[2] Extending
away from this center, but avoiding the steep slopes of Beacon
Hill, Copp's Hill, and Fort Hill which lay to the interior, the bulk
of the settlers located their homesteads. These homesteads were
scattered about more or less indiscriminately, and there was very
little territorial differentiation in terms of affluence or prestige.

But after 1685, with the change from a colonial to a crown
government, there arrived in Boston a new and more class conscious group of people. The English governor, his officials and
assistants, as well as shrewd entrepreneurs seeking wealth and
prominence, all introduced a class differentiation into colonial
Boston which showed itself in a corresponding spatial differentiation of residences. With the erection of the governor's mansion
on Charter street the North End became the "court end" of town
and a number of fashionable families located there. North square,
then known as Clark's square, became the social center of Boston
and nearby were built Christ Church and the Old North Church
to serve the well-to-do English families residing nearby.[3] Other
prominent families located toward the northern ends of what are
now Washington and Tremont streets and at Pemberton square.
But the area below here was "so near the extreme south end of
the town as to be socially out of the world.[4]

What little industry there was in colonial Boston was centered
mainly around the Mill Pond — a body of tidewater situated in
the vicinity of present day North Station. Here was a lumber
mill, a grain mill, a chocolate mill, and some distilleries.[5] Ship-
yards were located at the base of Copp's Hill in the North End,

---

[1] Justin Winsor, *The Memorial History of Boston* (Boston: 1880–81), I,
531.

[2] *Ibid.*, I, 539.

[3] *Ibid.*, I, 550; Robert A. Woods, *Americans in Process* (Boston: 1903),
pp. 19–24.

[4] Winsor, *op. cit.*, I, 543.

[5] *Ibid.*, II, 447; IV, 79.

and in Charlestown.[6] Beyond the settlement lay the "fields," some owned by the town and some by a few men some of whose names even now survive in the Boston aristocracy — Phillips, Leverett, Russell, Staniford, Chambers, Lynde, and Allen. The Common was at this time a cow pasture and waste land.[7]

This early differentiation of land uses is of course too vague to warrant its being compared with the concentric sector patterns outlined in the idealized descriptive schemes. It is enough now to appreciate the role of volition that was manifest in the development of a distinct fashionable residential district in the North End. This spatial differentiation, corresponding to and symbolizing a new class differentiation, is only too clearly the expression of a cultural factor, namely, the rise of a governing and mercantile class out of a hitherto democratic community of pioneer settlers. Let us see, however, if the later differentiation of spatial areas in early Boston proceeded along the simple sector or concentric lines described by Hoyt and Burgess.

The first definite shift of the preferred residential districts occurred in the middle 1700's with the gradual development of the western part of the town. By 1740 a few fine mansions were located on Cotton Hill, one of the three peaks that then comprised Beacon Hill. Bowling Green, now known as Bowdoin square, likewise became a favorite residential neighborhood and was destined to remain so for nearly a century.[8] Another fashionable area appeared at the opposite end of town from the North End and from the Beacon Hill-Bowdoin square vicinity, for by 1780 there was a pronounced shift of the elite to the Fort Hill and Pearl street districts near the present South Station. Other streets lying to the south end of town also became lined with expensive mansions — particularly Summer, Winter, Franklin, and High streets.[9] Of course this new southward movement was not as yet at the expense of the other aristocratic areas, with the result that by 1780 there were fully three fashionable residential areas: the North End, the Beacon Hill-Bowdoin square area, and

---

[6] *Ibid.*, II, 443; and Woods, *Americans in Process*, p. 27.

[7] Winsor, *op. cit.*, I, 533–537, 552; and Woods, *Americans in Process*, pp. 21–22.

[8] Woods, *Americans in Process*, p. 28.

[9] Winsor, *op. cit.*, II, 513; IV, 63–64; and Thomas W. Tucker, *Bannisters Lane, 1708–1899* (Boston: 1899), p. 16.

the Fort Hill and Pearl street vicinity, all lying on opposite sides
of the business center. Lower class districts apparently occupied
the back streets and interstitial areas although very little descriptive material is available on that point until the post-Revolution-
ary period.

Thus at the time of the Revolution the upper class residential
districts had become well differentiated into definite preferred
areas. The sequence of their development had been roughly from
north to west and then from west to south, following no consistent
sector outward and expanding in no peripheral concentric fashion.
Moreover, when viewed statically, the arrangement of these residential districts conformed to no concentric or sector pattern.
Upper class homes were located on three different sides of the
commercial portion of the city and were of varying proximities to
this center. The Fort Hill and Pearl street vicinity was close to
the commercial center and lay to the south; the North End was
likewise close to the center and lay to the north; Beacon Hill
was then remote and lay to the west. To look for simple patterns
of land use in this arrangement seems rather futile. Let us, however, defer our full judgment of the idealized descriptive schemes
until later, for we shall presently encounter data that will render
the problem a little less simple than it now appears.

With the outbreak of the Revolution Boston suffered an enormous loss of population. Most of the crown officials and a large
share of the upper classes in general had left the town with the
British evacuation. In their place there appeared a new class of
commercial people who came into Boston to capitalize on the
economic possibilities opening up as a result of the Revolution.[10]
These changes in the class composition of the community were
accompanied by certain shifts in the spatial distribution of upper
class families. These shifts were all at the expense of the North
End. The new aristocracy which had been bred by the Revolution
desired more palatial homes than were available in the North End.
That district had become well built up with dwellings, generally
small, close together, and ill suited to the tastes of the time. Consequently the nouveaus looked elsewhere for their residences and
those of the old aristocracy who came back to Boston generally

[10] Woods, *Americans in Process*, p. 32; and Charles Phillips Huse, *The
Financial History of Boston* (Cambridge: 1916), pp. 3–4.

did not return to their former homes in the North End. Gradually
the district became occupied by skilled workers and small entrepreneurs. A few "substantial families" did remain until as late
as 1840, particularly along Sheafe street with its old rear gardens.[11] But the early transformation of North street, then close to
the waterfront, into an area of ill repute catering to the demands
of sailors and other transients, gradually destroyed the entire
area's reputability.[12] Over the course of time the North End
became a definitely lower class district and with the advent of
the Irish in the 1850's it was established as a distinctly immigrant
community.

It was to the then rural and out-of-the-way Beacon Hill district
that upper class families turned after the Revolution. Apart
from a few mansions located on Cotton Hill this vicinity had so
far undergone but little settlement.[13] But with the construction
of the New State House on Beacon street, in 1795, the Beacon
Hill area acquired a high degree of desirability.[14] Hancock,
himself a nouveau, soon afterwards built his gubernatorial mansion on Beacon street and thereby furthered the new movement
of upper class families toward the Hill. It will pay us to look at
this development in a little detail, for the case brings into somewhat clearer focus the real scope of volition in spatial adaptation,
as against the inevitability that is postulated by the idealized
descriptive schemes.

The development of Beacon Hill as a fashionable residential
district, far from being inevitable, was to a considerable e .tent
the result of deliberate promotion. Of course, no one is now in a
position to say whether or not the fashionable character of the
Hill might have been acquired in the absence of the promotion.
We can only demonstrate that the actual laying out and settling
of the Hill was brought about by men who deliberately planned
the neighborhood as a fashionable residential district. The construction of the New State House came at a propitious time, when

---

[11] Woods, *Americans in Process*, pp. 33–34.
[12] *Loc. cit.;* and T. R. Sullivan, *Boston New and Old* (Boston: 1912), p. 19.
[13] Abbie Farwell Brown, *The Lights of Beacon Hill* (Boston, 1922), p. 8.
[14] Robert Means Lawrence, *Old Park Street and its Vicinity* (Boston:
1922), p. 13; and Allen Chamberlain, *Beacon Hill, its Ancient Pastures and
Early Mansions* (Boston: 1925), pp. 5–6.

upper class people, many of recently acquired wealth, were seeking a "proper" place in which to live. The New State House
apparently lent an appropriate distinction to the Beacon Hill
vicinity. In 1795, the very year of the State House's construction,
a syndicate known as the Mount Vernon Proprietors was organized for the purpose of buying up land on Beacon Hill and laying
out an appropriate arrangement of streets and lots.[15] The members of this syndicate, consisting of Jonathan Mason, Harrison
Gray Otis, and Charles Bulfinch, were all socially prominent, and
Mason and Otis themselves built mansions on the Hill for their
families. Thus a proper character to the Hill was set. To further
establish the fashionable character of the projected district an
elaborate plan was drawn up by Withington, calling for residences
all of strictly mansion type, each surrounded by large estates, and
with streets so designed as to minimize north-south traffic.[16]
This latter feature had a purpose rather obvious to one who
knows modern Beacon Hill, for then as now the northern slope
of the Hill was occupied by lower class families. The Mount
Vernon Proprietors wished to ensure the upper class character of
the southern slope and achieved this through minimizing north-
south movement and through stipulating a certain standard of
mansion construction, thereby restricting that slope to families
of some means.

The whole venture was speculative and in the opinion of some
writers was by no means foreordained to success. The first advertisements pointing out the desirability of the Hill appeared in the
Columbian Centinel of August 3, 1796, but it was not until 1802,
following the erection of Otis' and Mason's own mansions, that
other wealthy people began moving to the neighborhood.[17] A
wave of financial prosperity, by expanding the fortunes of many
families, further aided the syndicate and after the turn of the
century the Hill underwent a rapid settlement.[18] Mount Vernon,

---

[15] Chamberlain, "The Beacon Hill of the Forefathers," in *Old Days on
Beacon Hill, 1824–1924*, issued by the Women's Municipal League (Boston:
1924), pp. 6–9, 18.
[16] Chamberlain, *Beacon Hill, its Ancient Pastures and Early Mansions*, pp.
45–46.
[17] *Ibid.*, pp. 45–46.
[18] *Ibid.*, pp. 61–62.

Chestnut, and Walnut streets were the first to develop, but by 1804 the higher portions of the Hill, on Pinckney and Myrtle streets, likewise became occupied by upper class families.[19] The subsequent history of Beacon Hill is largely one of alternate expansion and neglect, correlating with the successive waves of prosperity and depression affecting the American economy. From 1814 to 1820 the Hill lost many of its families following the ruin inflicted upon wealthy people by the federal embargo against foreign trade. After 1820 the Hill underwent another burst of building, only to be checked by the 1829 panic which ruined many Boston families. In the 1830's residential development was resumed only to be again interrupted by the 1837 panic.[20] But by this time the Hill had been substantially built up and its later fluctuations in residential occupancy attended other causes that will concern us more directly in chapter III. None of these fluctuations at any time jeopardized the status of Beacon Hill as a fashionable residential neighborhood, though significant recessions and revivals have taken place that will engage us at the proper place.

It is interesting to realize that the entire development of Beacon Hill proper was, from its very beginning, directly contiguous to an area containing, as one writer of the nineteenth century put it, "the most miserable huts in the city." [21] This area, occupying the north slope of the Hill, is more generally referred to as part of the West End. From the time of the Revolution down to the present day this slope has been occupied by lower class families and has been but little influenced by its direct contiguity with the fashionable south slope, Beacon Hill proper. After 1789, when Massachusetts legally abolished slavery within the state, a large Negro population appeared in Boston and gradually took over the cheap dwellings around the north end of Joy street and the adjoining portion of Cambridge street, from there spreading over the entire north slope.[22] Here the Negroes lived in extreme poverty and dis-

[19] Woods, *Americans in Process*, p. 33.

[20] Chamberlain, *Beacon Hill, its Ancient Pastures and Early Mansions*, pp. 45–46.

[21] Cited in "A Century Ago: 60,000 Citizens, Cobbled Streets," *Boston Transcript*, July 24, 1930.

[22] Cited in "A Century Ago: 60,000 Citizens, Cobbled Streets," *Boston Transcript*, July 24, 1930; and Woods, *Americans in Process*, p. 37; and J.

organization. The area was notorious for its disreputable houses, its vice, and its riots. An entry in the police reports for July 14, 1826 reads: "— July 14. A riot on Negro Hill; several houses pulled down." [23] By the time of the Civil War this slope had become a sanctuary for escaped slaves and a terminus of the "underground railway." [24] Further toward the Charles River a population of skilled workers and seamen was more predominant. However, toward the 1870's and 1880's the north slope underwent a new development. By this time thousands of immigrants from southern and eastern Europe were seeking cheap quarters in Boston and real estate speculators were quick to see their opportunity. In a relatively short span of time the old wooden shacks and single family dwellings were razed and in their place arose the solid brick fronts of tenements lining the streets up and down the steep hillside.[25] Into these new quarters moved the Irish and, more extensively, the Jewish immigrants from Russia and Poland. It is these latter, interspersed with some Italians, who now dominate the north slope of Beacon Hill.

Thus within the Beacon Hill area, considered as a geographical unit, there have been, for a century and a half, two contiguous areas sharply set off from one another in terms of prestige value and class status, each maintaining its "reputation" through all the vicissitudes that have accompanied Boston's growth. The reasons for this "persistence of reputation" will engage us more fully at a later point. Our principal concern now is in the general arrangement of land uses, particularly as they pertain to the hypotheses of the idealized descriptive schemes. Certainly the sharp demarcation of Beacon Hill into an upper class area and a lower class area presents a phenomenon that does not fit in very well with the Burgess-Hoyt theories. By itself, to be sure, it is not a refutation of those theories but, when added to other evidence, its implications become fairly significant. For one thing, both

---

Ross McKeever, "The Beacon Hill District" (M.S.), Master's Thesis, Massachusetts Institute of Technology, 1935, p. 22.

[23] Cited in William Marshall Warren, "Beacon Hill and Boston University," *Bostonia, the Boston University Alumni Magazine,* 4: 3–21 (November, 1930), p. 8.

[24] McKeever, *op. cit.*, p. 22.

[25] Chamberlain, *Beacon Hill, its Ancient Pastures and Early Mansions,* pp. 42–43.

sides of the Hill lie within the same concentric zone — the "area of transition" in Burgess' terminology. Yet their ecological characteristics are vastly different. For another thing, even if we drew sectors in such a way as to put the south side of the Hill, Beacon Hill proper, into one sector and the north side into another sector, the pattern would hardly reconcile with the Hoyt hypothesis that adjoining sectors represent a gradation rather than a contrast; in our case the two sides of the Hill are actually polar opposites, whether viewed in terms of rent, housing standards, or the class status of occupants. It is quite evident that further factors have to be invoked if we are to explain this spatially objectified class differentiation which is so sharply delineated within the Beacon Hill vicinity.

Behind the State House, on Hancock, Temple, and Bowdoin streets were additional upper class families — this in spite of the northerly exposure of the position. To the north of here, in the West End proper, lived families of apparently middle class status, occupying Chambers, Staniford, Lynde, and Leverett streets. Allen and McLean streets, also in the West End, seem to have enjoyed a somewhat more exclusive character than the adjoining streets.[26] However the West End did not endure long as a middle class district. Gradually it lost its families, and the dwellings were taken over by landladies who rented out rooms to single men employed in the city. This rooming-house phase of the West End's history was terminated at the same time that the lower class north slope of Beacon Hill underwent its architectural transformation, and for the same reason. The influx of immigrants during the last quarter of the nineteenth century made tenements a more profitable real estate venture than rooming houses. As a result the West End was converted into a tenement quarter and has remained one to the present time.

There is one additional development in the western portion of Boston that merits attention. As early as 1811 extensive topographical alterations had been made on Beacon Hill in the form of reducing its summit to the level of the State House foundation.[27] The operation was so successful, from the real estate

[26] Woods, *Americans in Process*, pp. 36–37.

[27] William W. Wheildon, *Sentry, or Beacon Hill; the Beacon and the Monument of 1635 and 1790* (Concord: 1877), pp. 96–97.

standpoint, that it was applied in 1835 to the complete obliteration of Cotton Hill, one of the old summits of Beacon Hill. The
promoter of this venture, Patrick Jackson, then proceeded to
develop the area now known as Pemberton square into a magnificent residential neighborhood. Expensive mansions were built,
grounds were terraced, and by the late 1830's Pemberton square
constituted one of the exclusive residential quarters of Boston.[28]

A recapitulation of the upper class portions of Boston as they
were distributed in the late 1830's reveals no real sector or concentric pattern at all. To the west and northwest lay Beacon Hill,
Pemberton square, Bowdoin square, and Temple place. Slightly
to the south was Tremont street (between West street and Boylston street). Then, to the south and southeast were Fort Hill and
the adjoining portions of Pearl and Franklin streets.[29] The upper
class districts thus embraced fully two points of the compass, only
the northeast and east being unrepresented owing to the deterioration of the North End and the existence of the harbor on the east.
The discovery of any sector of upper class residential distribution
from such an arrangement appears to be quite impossible. Perhaps the concentric hypothesis may make some sort of case for
itself, in view of the fact that all of the districts in question lay
within rough walking distance of the city's business center.[30] It
should, however, be borne in mind that within this very same
radius were located a middle class district in the West End and
the working class districts in the North End and on the northern
slope of Beacon Hill. Surely to point out an equidistance of upper
class districts from the city center can have little explanatory
value when middle and lower class areas lie in the very same concentric band. To avoid any unfairness in our criticism it is only

[28] Alexander S. Porter, "Changes of Values in Real Estate in Boston the
Past One Hundred Years," Collections of the Bostonian Society, 1: 57–74
(1888), p. 67; Chamberlain, Beacon Hill, its Ancient Pastures and Early
Mansions, p. 32.
[29] Cited in "A Century Ago: 60,000 Citizens, Cobbled Streets," Boston
Transcript, July 24, 1930.
[30] By this time Beacon Hill was less isolated than it had been in 1796 when
first opened for development. Business itself had migrated in a southerly
and westerly direction, as will be shown later, and the intervening areas had
become fully settled, so that Beacon Hill was no longer a remote rural district.

right to point out that Burgess himself acknowledges certain variations within his concentric zones, as his own Chicago data clearly indicate. Our only purpose is to raise a question as to the explanatory adequacy of any theory which so idealizes land use patterns as to assign to a given zone social systems of very different and indeed sharply contrasting character. It seems as though such a procedure explains what least needs explaining and leaves unexplained that which most requires explanation. Some issue might be raised as to possible "lags" in natural succession which have enabled us to include as upper class neighborhoods areas that were presently fated to decay, thereby making an unfair case for ourselves. It is true that some of the districts noted above did later deteriorate in prestige value. Indeed, all but one of them was eventually displaced by other land uses so that only Beacon Hill survived as a fashionable residential quarter. However, there is certainly nothing wrong in selecting a given moment of history, as we have done with the late 1830's, and observing how at that time social systems of a given character (upper class families) were spatially distributed. Land uses are always changing; no one can say which are "lags" and which are not. If the Burgess-Hoyt theories are to claim any validity they must have a reasonable descriptive accuracy for any given period of land use history. Let us however maintain suspended judgment of the idealized descriptive schemes until we have finished our historical analysis and have described existing spatial patterns in some detail.

As the population of Boston increased, rising from 93,383 in 1840 to 136,881 in 1850, its spatial expansion took the only direction open to it, namely, the southwest. To the north and east lay waterways and the harbor; to the south was the "Neck," a narrow isthmus of land which could only be occupied following extensive filling-in operations. This southwesterly growth of Boston was manifested by a corresponding shift of upper class families, in this respect representing a radial or sector extension much like that postulated by the Hoyt theory. How real a sector this is we shall consider at the appropriate place.

One of the first signs of the southwesterly shift was a slow but steady removal of elite from the Fort Hill vicinity. Business had gradually extended down Pearl street toward the Hill, and one by one mercantile "blocks" expanded into adjoining streets, displacing the old mansions.[31] Nevertheless Fort Hill held out for a long time so that even by 1858 there were several socially prominent families in residence there.[32] But during the next few years the district deteriorated rapidly. The mansions became tenement dwellings for immigrant families, and around the base of the Hill were built large granite warehouses. So dilapidated did the dwellings become during the next decade and a half that there existed a positive health menace on the Hill, as manifested by a plague which had its locus there. For this reason as well as in the interests of commercial expansion the tenements were razed and the entire Hill was dug out and removed, the operation being completed in 1872. Many of the working class people resisted the demolition of their houses and some stayed on "until the roofs were taken off, and their rooms laid open to the sky."[33] By this time all the surrounding area to the southeast of the city center had become a commercial section or was occupied by working class families.

In the meantime a good many families who had left the Fort Hill vicinity were building themselves new homes on the opposite side of the Common from Beacon Hill, directly in line with the southwesterly expansion of the city as a whole. One result of this development was the pretentious line of mansions known as "Colonnade Row," extending along Tremont street from Temple place to Mason street. Here too was the estate of Amos Lawrence, a wealthy merchant, on the corner of Tremont and West streets, with a rear garden extending halfway to Washington street.[34] The whole length of Tremont street, as well as the nearby sections of Winter, Summer, Bedford, and Washington streets was occupied by upper class families.

Perhaps a fuller understanding of the way in which this area became developed for upper class occupancy will be had if we consider just one of its portions, the Temple place vicinity. Through this consideration we may realize that areas devoted to a particular land use, in our case fashionable residential occu-

[31] Lawrence, op. cit., p. 131.
[32] George E. Ellis, Bacon's Dictionary of Boston (Boston: 1886), p. 160.
[33] Huse, op. cit., p. 127; Winsor, op. cit., III, 272, IV, 46.
[34] Tucker, op. cit., pp. 8–9.

pancy, do not expand automatically or impersonally in the passive manner depicted by the idealized descriptive schemes. Rather their territorial trends are the result of positive human volition, expressed in the form of purposes, sentiments, and values. Whether or not this volition is but epiphenomenal to supposedly more basic deterministic factors is a problem that will concern us later on. At present we wish only to demonstrate the realness of this volition and its *modus operandi*. To the extent that our analysis is valid we shall have pointed up a variable that entirely escapes analysis in the idealized descriptive schemes, and which by its operation might introduce variations away from the concentric or sector patterns postulated by those theories. In the case of Temple place there happens to be detailed historical information that bears upon the problem. The street had apparently been little developed prior to 1833 when Colonel Thomas H. Perkins, a distinguished Boston business man, decided to leave his Pearl street estate and build a new home for himself on Temple place. This move attracted a great deal of attention, owing partly to the social prominence of the man and partly to the new development that the whole southeast side of the Common was beginning to experience. The result was that several other families followed Perkins by leaving Pearl street and locating on Temple place or on parallel West street. Among these families were a number of friends, relatives, and business associates of Perkins, such as Josiah Bradley, prominent merchant and old-time neighbor of Perkins on Pearl street, Samuel Cabot, Robert B. Forbes, T. G. Cary, Thomas Lee, and several others. A large proportion of these families were natives of Cape Cod who had come to Boston and had become wealthy and distinguished. Indeed, so conspicuous was this common origin that the vicinity became popularly known as "Cape Cod Row." [35] Thus in the development of Temple place, as one small portion of the larger upper class area lying to the southeast of the Common, there was something more than the impersonal, automatic, "natural trend" such as is postulated in the Hoyt theory. Regardless of the problem of causal priority, a matter that will concern us in the next chapter, there can be little doubt that, at least in the case of Temple place, the actual effecting of the upper class residential

[35] Tucker, *op. cit.*, pp. 28–31.

trend was through strictly cultural factors. To eliminate such factors from ecology seems therefore to be an omission of an important variable in spatial adaptation.

The whole elite area lying to the southeast of the Common retained its fashionable character up to the Civil War. Temple place, Tremont street, Winter street, and adjoining streets were all pervaded by a "quiet, homelike atmosphere." [36] Further away from the Common, however, there were evidences of lowering prestige; Summer street, with its termination in the warehouse district, was being invaded by stores and other businesses and this process was presently to extend into the rest of the district. In the meantime such areas as Pemberton square, Park street, and Beacon Hill continued to enjoy high residential prestige.[37] Indeed the latter had by now extended down its western slope and had embraced much of Charles street, hitherto a section of stables, foundries, and stoneyards.[38] One important trend that was eventually to completely alter the territorial distribution of residential areas in Boston was just becoming discernible in the 1840's. This was the suburban drift of the population. The principal factor in this new trend was the steam railway. By 1847 there were eight railway stations in Boston, the main terminal being one at Haymarket square. Through this means of transportation an ever-growing number of people working in Boston found it possible to live outside of the city, their number by 1852 being approximately 3,000.[39] Roxbury, Dorchester, Cambridge, Newton, Malden, and Chelsea seem to have been the principal beneficiaries.[40] No evidence is available as to class differentials in this trend, so we shall have to leave the matter as it stands for the present.

A summary picture of upper class locational patterns at this

[36] Lawrence, *op. cit.*, pp. 113–114.

[37] Thomas Wentworth Higginson, "Other Days and Ways in Boston and Cambridge," in William S. Rossiter (ed.), *Days and Ways in Old Boston* (Boston: 1915), p. 35; Sullivan, *op. cit.*, p. 21; Lawrence, *op. cit.*, pp. 98–103.

[38] Sullivan, *op. cit.*, p. 26. However, to the west of Charles street these older land uses persisted right up to the present century, when they were finally superseded by an interesting rejuvenation of Beacon Hill which far overran the original bounds of the "respectable" part of the Hill.

[39] Huse, *op. cit.*, pp. 96–97.

[40] *Ibid.*, and Joseph Edgar Chamberlin, *The Boston Transcript, a History of its First Hundred Years* (Boston: 1930), p. 111.

period may be afforded by the use of a map showing the distribution of well-to-do families. Although there were no social registers published at the time there was issued, in 1846, a somewhat comparable publication known as *"Our First Men": a Calendar of Wealth, Fashion and Gentility*. This pamphlet lists all persons in Boston and its suburbs who were worth $100,000 or more. By checking each of these names with the *Boston City Directory* for the same year it was possible to obtain the addresses of all the persons listed and to plot these addresses on a map.[41] The result is an approximate picture of the territorial layout of upper class families as it was before the Civil War. To be sure, wealth is not at all a satisfactory measure of class status, least of all in Boston where "family" and antecedents are so important. By and large, however, there is a rough correlation between the two, particularly during the period in question when most of Boston's "Brahmans" were on the make. Furthermore, it is unlikely that even the nouveaus would have lived in very different areas than those occupied by the older elite. With reasonable care we cannot go far wrong if we rely upon these data, supplemented by the descriptive material already presented, for a visual image of upper class spatial patterns as they were in 1846.

These patterns are portrayed in figure 2. On their basis it would be difficult indeed to make much of a case for an idealized descriptive scheme. About all one could say is that most of the wealthy families resided south and west of the business district, on the two sides of the Common. But this is in no sense a concentric or sector arrangement. The spatial distribution of upper class families is apparently more variable than the Burgess-Hoyt theories appreciate. Whatever forces are responsible for it must be sought in less simple and tangible factors than those of inevitable radial extension or inevitable ringlike expansion.

Our discussion has so far made but a few allusions to commercial locational trends; yet these allusions have undoubtedly raised questions in the reader's mind that must be answered. Let us then digress briefly from our main preoccupation to consider how business had become distributed since the colonial period, when the juncture of State and Washington streets constituted the town's retail center. Although the analysis will not bear directly

[41] Adjustments were made for a few changes in street names.

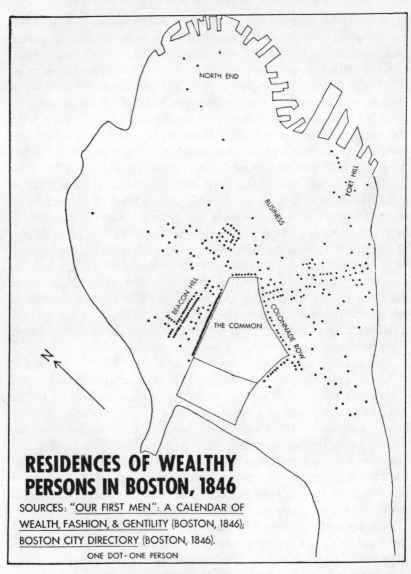

RESIDENCES OF WEALTHY
PERSONS IN BOSTON, 1846

SOURCES: "OUR FIRST MEN": A CALENDAR OF
WEALTH, FASHION, & GENTILITY (BOSTON, 1846);
BOSTON CITY DIRECTORY (BOSTON, 1846).

ONE DOT = ONE PERSON

FIGURE 2

upon the issue of idealized ecological patterns it is nonetheless indispensable to the completeness of our historical data. In chapter IV we shall consider, in the context of a different theoretical problem, the dynamic factors responsible for commercial locational trends. For the present we shall merely portray them in a descriptive manner. Once again the analysis may be more comprehensible if it is made in terms of a map, or series of maps. In figure 3 we have portrayed the overall expansion of commercial Boston since 1805, parallel with the changing contours of the

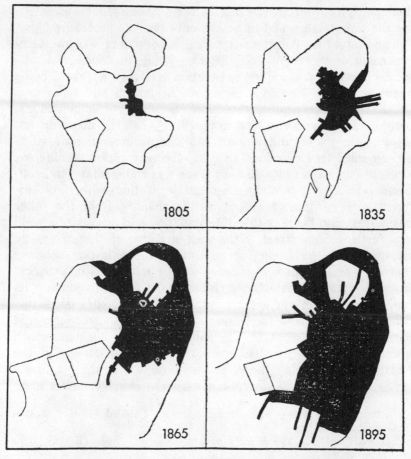

FIGURE 3. BOSTON'S COMMERCIAL EXPANSION

city's shoreline as a result of fill-in operations. The maps lay no claim to precision in detail but were constructed with as much accuracy as source material permitted. This source material consisted of a large number of isolated statements collected from pamphlets, books, and other documents, in which some sort of reference was made to business locations. To supplement this evidence recourse was had to contemporaneous city directories. Note was made of streets which, for a given year, received frequent listing as the address of business establishments; such streets were then drawn on the appropriate map as being predominantly commercial streets. In the absence of land use maps for the time this seemed to be the only feasible procedure.

The maps thus constructed reveal a consistent southwesterly expansion of the commercial district. This, of course, was the same direction in which the population was growing, there being no other course open to it owing to the harbor and waterways which lay in every other direction. Secondary commercial expansion to the north is also apparent. What the maps do not show is the gradual differentiation of the business district which accompanied its expansion. In 1805 the segregation of different kinds of enterprises into distinct areas was rudimentary and consisted primarily in a wholesale-retail separation, with some differentiation of inns, markets, and exchanges from the other businesses. But by 1835 this differentiation had proceeded a good deal further. State street, to the west of Kilby street, had become known as "The Exchange" because of the concentration of banks there.[42] The Faneuil Hall vicinity was by then a distinct market section. Upper Washington street and the area surrounding its juncture with Hanover street was a predominantly dry goods district. To the south of the business district were warehouses and hardware establishments.[43] The shoe and leather business, which became prominent in 1830, centered at Fulton street, in the North End.[44] During the 1840's and thereafter the retail dry goods stores migrated southward from the Hanover street area,

---

[42] Cited in "A Century Ago: 60,000 Citizens, Cobbled Streets," *Boston Transcript*, July 24, 1930.

[43] C. F. Hovey Co., *The History of the House of Hovey* (Boston: *circa* 1920), no paging.

[44] Richard Herndon, *Boston of To-day* (Boston: 1892), p. 8.

along Washington street, and the shoe and leather establishments shifted to the Fort Hill vicinity. With the removal of this hill between 1866 and 1872 the way was open for construction of the huge granite warehouses required by the rapidly growing cotton and wool industries of New England. The entire southeastern portion of the Hub became the locus of warehouses, hardware stores, textile establishments, and other wholesale businesses and has remained so to the present day.[45] The "shopping district" as we know it today is a relatively recent phenomenon, contingent upon rather unique socio-economic values.[46] Its antecedents may nonetheless be seen at least as far back as the 1830's when small stores — dry goods shops, groceries, and other establishments serving the short-term needs of residents — occupied Hanover street and the area adjacent to its juncture with Washington street. During succeeding decades these services gradually migrated down Washington street. By 1847 a dry goods store had located as far south as Winter street and in the next few years other establishments followed suit.[47] As of 1860, however, the shopping center still lay to the north of Franklin street.[48] But its consistent southward trend gradually brought it nearer to the Common, displacing the old mansions on Colonnade Row, Summer street, and adjoining streets. By 1886 this trend had so far advanced that Tremont and Washington streets had become shopping streets as far south as Boylston street, and the adjoining portions of Winter, Summer, and other cross streets were devoted to the same use.[49] Meanwhile the market area and the financial district had remained where they were in 1835, each expanding somewhat but undergoing none of the progressive shifts that characterized the retail and wholesale areas.[50]

With business encroaching upon their homes residents of the area lying south of the business district began to look elsewhere

[45] Chamberlin, *op. cit.,* p. 111.

[46] This problem will form the theme of chap. 6.

[47] Tucker, *op. cit.,* pp. 20–22.

[48] Clifton Joseph Furness, "Walt Whitman Looks at Boston," *The New England Quarterly,* 1: 353–370 (July, 1928); also, Rossiter, "The Year Eighteen Forty Seven," in Rossiter (ed.), *Days and Ways in Old Boston* (Boston: 1915), pp. 14–15.

[49] Ellis, *op. cit.,* p. 405.

[50] *Ibid.,* pp. 405–406.

for places in which to live. Many moved to the suburbs. Others looked to South Boston. A writer in the *Boston Almanac* for 1853 wrote: "South Boston from present appearance is predestined to be the magnificent section of the city in respect to costly residences, fashionable society, and the influence of wealth." [51]

In the meantime the population of Boston was increasing steadily; in 1840 it was 93,383; in 1850, 136,881; and in 1860, 177,992. This population growth only aggravated the housing problem which confronted the city and rendered imperative the opening up of new districts. Such a course would, owing to the semi-insular character of the Hub, require extensive fill-in operations at the "neck lands" to the south. These lands had been partially improved and offered for sale by the city as early as 1823. At that time they were regarded only as a resource for the reduction of the municipal debt, not as an outlet for surplus population.[52] But under the threat of losing all its wealthy families to the suburbs the city undertook a more systematic development of its neck lands. In 1833 the South Cove Corporation was chartered to fill in and develop some seventy acres of the area.[53] Additional contracts for filling-in and development were made during succeeding years, so that by 1850 much of the present South End had been filled in as far as Northampton street.[54]

But actual settlement of the South End came slowly. Worcester square, for instance, was laid out in 1834 but was not actually built on until 1851, after which it became a very attractive upper class residential street.[55] A Dr. Giles Lodge built a brownstone mansion on Pelham and Washington streets, in 1846; a little south of here Peter Parker, a wealthy merchant, built what was then the finest home in Boston, in 1848.[56] But for the most part the city had great difficulty in selling its properties at the high prices which it had set to ensure upper class occupancy. Settlement was further hampered by the area's remoteness from the

[51] Quoted in Woods, *The City Wilderness* (Boston: 1898), pp. 29–31.

[52] Huse, *op. cit.*, p. 30 and pp. 46–47.

[53] Porter, *op. cit.*

[54] State Street Trust Co., *Boston's Growth* (Boston: 1910), pp. 37–38.

[55] Albert J. Kennedy, "The South End," *Our Boston*, 2: 13–19 (December, 1926), p. 17.

[56] *Ibid.*, pp. 14–15.

city proper. As late as 1854 Mayor Smith complained that "there is nothing now but a wide waste of neglected territory." [57]

What finally assured fashionable occupancy of the South End was the construction in 1856 of a horse-railroad which connected the district with the city center and rendered it more accessible.[58] Following this there set in a pronounced movement of upper class families to the South End. Union Park, Chester Park, Franklin square, Worcester square, and Rutland square became particularly favorite locations.[59] Most of these squares were built co-operatively by the persons who owned abutting property and their upkeep was a private concern.[60] The reminiscences of an elderly lady who had grown up in the South End give some insight into the character of the district during its period of fashionability:

One can hardly imagine from the present surroundings of that part of the South End, the once beautiful enclosure of the Chester Square of my childhood. Among the many delightful memories of my early life in this street was the view from our front windows of the beautiful park with a circular basin of water having an ornamental fountain in the center, and we who lived in the houses about the enclosure had, as our special privilege, the right to unlock any of the four gates, and to go beyond the tall iron fence which marked the boundary for those who had no keys.[61]

A contemporary wrote of "the wide streets and open spaces and parks," with their "many expensive and beautiful residences." [62] From 1860 to 1870 the South End was the distinctly preferred residential district of the city. Beacon Hill continued to enjoy prestige, but the area lying to the east of the Common — Colonnade Row, Summer street, and Temple place — became converted to business uses within a very short span of time.

[57] *The Inaugural Addresses of the Mayors of Boston* (Boston: 1896), II, 57.

[58] Winsor, *op. cit.*, IV, 63, n. 3.

[59] Woods, *The City Wilderness* (Boston: 1898), pp. 29–31.

[60] Albert Benedict Wolfe, *The Lodging House Problem in Boston* (Cambridge: 1913), p. 22; Herndon, *op. cit.*, p. 74.

[61] A Miss Howes, quoted in Kennedy, *op. cit.*, p. 18.

[62] Letter of Joseph M. Wightman, quoted in George H. Snelling, *Memorial, with Remarks and Letters, in Favor of a Modification of the Back Bay Plan* (Boston: 1860), p. 35.

An epitome of upper class residential distribution as of 1865 would show two distinct concentrations: one at Beacon Hill, the other at the South End. Neither lies contiguous to the other. One lies to the west, the other to the south, of the business district. One is close to the city center, the other is relatively remote. In short, there is discernible neither a sector pattern nor a concentric pattern. To be sure, there was a direct linear succession outward from Colonnade Row to the South End, which might confirm this dynamic aspect of Hoyt's theory. His theory, it will be recalled, postulates a steady radial extension of fashionable areas into directly contiguous territory. However this detail can in no sense be regarded as an adequate validation of the theory. After all, residential expansion in Boston could not possibly have taken any other direction at the time than a southward one, owing to the peculiar configuration of Boston's shoreline. Filling in and settlement of the South End was a necessary preliminary to any subsequent filling in and settlement such as was to shortly take place in the Back Bay. This situation is in no sense typical of American cities and Hoyt does not mean to rest his case on such geographically determined processes. Evidence presently to be considered will show, furthermore, that the later expansion of upper class areas was not to the south but first to the northwest, then to the southwest.[63] It is probably true that volition[64] entered into the development of the South End less than it had in some of the other districts we have been considering. The imperious necessity of finding new land for residential

[63] It is worth noting that Hoyt's crude sketch maps of fashionable residential succession in Boston begin as of 1900, thus entirely omitting the period of South End dominance. His maps consequently give the impression of a consistent drift of upper class families to the west. Actually, as we shall presently indicate, the movement since 1900 has been more nearly to the southwest, with important extensions in several other directions which are minimized by Hoyt. Furthermore, his maps indicate a complete exodus of upper class families from the central portions of the city, whereas Beacon Hill and the Back Bay today actually account for one-third of Boston's *Social Registerites*. His maps thus give a wholly inaccurate picture of fashionable residential trends in Boston. See Homer Hoyt, *The Structure and Growth of Residential Neighborhoods in American Cities* (Washington: 1939), figure 40, p. 115.

[64] In the sense of willing a course of action which would not of itself have been inevitable.

expansion made the South End the only possible direction of growth. But this is not the kind of "determinacy" to which Hoyt would himself attribute his asserted radial extensions of land uses. His explanation is of a very different sort, laying primary emphasis upon the supposition that lower class areas always occupy both sides of the upper class sector and that therefore the latter has no alternative but to expand outward.[65] In the case of Boston this is not the explanation for the radial extension into the South End. Such an hypothesis, moreover, is wholly at variance with the fashionable residential trends that we have previously described, in which no upper class sector was manifest at all and in which no consistency appeared as to the kind of land uses which adjoined the upper class areas.

There is one feature of Hoyt's theory which calls for further comment. In explaining why the area lying just beyond existing upper class occupancy becomes converted to upper class use rather than lower class or non-residential uses Hoyt indicates that the holders of these lands, anticipating the greater profit that would attend fashionable residential construction, deliberately inflate land prices so as to discourage the cheaper uses.[66] We have already seen that this process did indeed operate in the development of the South End. The city set its prices so high that for years the South End remained essentially unoccupied, and only the construction of the horse-railroad rendered the lands salable. Apparently, however, even this did not expedite sales rapidly enough to suit city officials. In 1855 Mayor Smith actually recommended departure from the policy of restricting South End settlement to people of wealth. He urged that: "mechanics of limited means, who have not the potent faculty of establishing a large credit on small resources, have a direct claim to indulgence beyond all others."[67] From this he reasoned that the lands should be sold "for what they will bring, to the best bidder."[68] Acting upon this the city established more favorable loan terms and began to sell its lands at auction, thereby preparing the way for lower class invasion of the South End. This

[65] Hoyt, *op. cit.*, p. 116.
[66] *Loc. cit.*
[67] *The Inaugural Addresses of the Mayors of Boston*, II, 73.
[68] *Ibid.*, p. 75.

deflation of prices, be it noted, was an act of volition on the part
of the city; it was a deliberate, non-necessitous choice of one
course of action in preference to others. Its result was a complete
deterioration in the South End's prestige value.

Thus, Columbus avenue, laid out in 1870, was from the beginning built up with cheaper dwellings than those typical of earlier
South End construction.[69] The same was true of the "New York
streets area," bounded by Albany street, Harrison avenue, Seneca
street, and Troy street.[70] These and other portions of the South
End became middle class and lower class neighborhoods. Their
lower prestige value spread to other parts of the district. Property
values, generally an indicator of residential desirability, began to
depreciate throughout the South End. The panic of 1873 led to
foreclosures on many of the cheaper dwellings, which had been
heavily mortgaged, and these properties were dumped on the real
estate market for whatever they would command.[71] Inevitably
the purchasers were people of lower income than befitted a fashionable district. Beginning in 1870, and progressing more rapidly
during the succeeding years, an exodus of the elite set in.[72] By
1885 the South End had become wholly transformed into a rooming house area, with all the problems of disorganization that are
characteristic of such areas.[73] Many years later there was to
take place an abortive revival attempt, but our discussion of this
will be more appropriate in chapter VIII where we shall consider
the present ecological characteristics of that district.

Whether the South End's demise was inevitable or not is a
problem that need not concern us. What is of theoretical significance about it is the volitional, non-inevitable character of the
pecuniary valuation that is put upon land which is anticipated to
become fashionable for residential purposes. It was not an ecological necessity that the city inflate the prices of its newly filled
neck lands, and it was not an ecological necessity that it even-

[69] Wolfe, *op. cit.*, p. 14.

[70] Boston City Planning Board, *Building a Better Boston* (Boston: 1941),
p. 41.

[71] Wolfe, *op. cit.*, p. 14.

[72] For a novelistic portrayal of this exodus see William D. Howells, *The
Rise of Silas Lapham* (Boston: 1884), chap. ii, and John Marquand, *The
Late George Apley* (New York: 1940), chap. iii.

[73] Wolfe, *op. cit.*, p. 14.

tually deflate those prices so as to increase sales, thereby precipitating the South End's invasion by lower class families. To the extent that Hoyt relies upon this variable in his theory, then, he is unwittingly intruding a volitional element which in its logical implications completely vitiates the determinacy of his scheme. For once granting that volition can, through price manipulation, alter the occupancy of a given territory, the whole logic as to the inevitable outward extension of upper class areas along a sector disappears. There is nothing to prevent such areas from growing sideways or from leaping across adjacent territory devoted to different uses. Spatial adaptation is much more variable and random than the idealized descriptive schemes appreciate.

With the deterioration in residential desirability of the South End one would infer from the Burgess-Hoyt theories that the next fashionable area would lie farther out from the city. But the facts belie this supposition. Rather than continuing in a southward direction the upper class trend shifted to the northwest, to the newly filled Back Bay lands.[74] Filling of this area had begun in 1856 but no comprehensive plan for its laying out was made until 1864, after which the Back Bay underwent rather rapid development. Most of the district lying east of Fairfield street was developed by the Commonwealth;[75] that lying north of the old mill dam along Beacon street was filled by the Boston and Roxbury Mill Corporation; and all that lying south and west of the Commonwealth's territory was filled by the Boston Water Power Company.[76] These agencies agreed on a plan then in vogue for fashionable areas, consisting of long, broad avenues lined with trees and terminating in a park.[77] The magnificence of the plan led its opponents to decry the Back Bay as a "scene of stupendous illusions." [78] Some idea of these stupendous illusions may be

[74] It does not seem necessary for the problem at hand to go into the complicated legal, sanitary, and political circumstances which accompanied the Back Bay filling.

[75] The Commonwealth's territory was bounded on the north by Beacon street, on the east by Arlington street, on the south by both sides of Boylston street for most of the way, and on the west by an irregular line lying between Exeter and Fairfield streets. See Snelling, *op. cit.*, map.

[76] Ellis, *op. cit.*, p. 32.

[77] Hoyt, *op. cit.*, p. 120.

[78] Snelling, *op. cit.*, p. 49.

gained from the proposals that were made as the filling proceeded. In 1859 a Committee of Associated Institutions of Science and Art was organized to memorialize the legislature in favor of a "collocation of Institutions" that would comprise a cultural reservation.[79] The proposal called for setting aside a large tract in the Back Bay to be devoted solely to institutions of an educational, scientific, and artistic character. After two years of wrangling in the legislature a much diluted concession was made to the Committee, whereby one block was reserved for the Boston Society of Natural History and the Massachusetts Institute of Technology.[80] But the effort had impressed other institutions as to the possibilities presented by such a cultural reservation. During succeeding years one institution after another moved out of the Hub and into the new Back Bay lands. The Museum of Fine Arts, the Public Library, the Harvard Medical School, the Algonquin Club and other such exclusive organizations, not to speak of several preparatory schools, churches, lodges, and the like, erected magnificent edifices in the new lands. There were other ambitious plans for the Back Bay. One of these called for a large expanse of fresh water in the middle of the district.[81] Yet another proposal was for the area's conversion to a business and manufacturing district, with wharves and yards along the Charles river.[82] Apart from this last proposal most of the plans looked to the development of a sumptuous residential district occupied by the city's finest institutions and its wealthiest families.

The manner in which these plans became realized will shed further light upon the theoretical problem which concerns us in this chapter, namely, the variability or invariability of land use patterns. As the land in the Back Bay became filled and improved it was offered on the market at fixed minimum prices high enough to discourage cheap land uses and thus ensure upper class occupancy. The lots on Arlington street, fronting the Public Garden,

[79] M. D. Ross, *Estimate of the Financial Effect of the Proposed Reservation of Back-Bay Lands* (Boston: 1861), pp. 3–5; and Snelling, *op. cit.*, pp. iii–iv.

[80] James L. Bruce, "The Rogers Building and Huntington Hall," *Proceedings of the Bostonian Society* (1941), pp. 35–36.

[81] Snelling, *op. cit., passim*.

[82] Robert Morris Copeland, *Essay and Plan for the Improvement of the City of Boston* (Boston: 1872), pp. 14–15.

were naturally the first to be improved and they sold at good prices. But as the land lying west of Arlington street became improved the Commissioners entrusted with its disposal found increasing difficulty in making sales.[83] In the words of a contemporaneous analyst of Back Bay real estate:

So little confidence had yet been gained as to the value of the territory westward that, notwithstanding the known decision as to the extension and improvement of the Public Garden, they (the Commissioners) were unable to make any further sales for a period of some fourteen months. Persons who were inclined to purchase lots for their own use, influenced by this distrust, preferred waiting for others to make the first move; and thus all held back from investments in this quarter.[84]

Once again, as had been the case with the South End, the land owners, this time the Commonwealth, were faced with a problem of choice. To deflate prices, as had been done in the South End, would have precipitated lower class invasion of the Back Bay. Yet, a maintenance of inflated prices when upper class people did not have confidence in the area as a place for homes would have indefinitely postponed sale of the land. Here was clearly a problem of choosing between alternatives. To think therefore that fashionable occupancy of the Back Bay was an inevitable, necessitous development hardly seems justified. What the Commissioners finally resorted to was a bargain. Early in 1860 "several gentlemen" offered to purchase lots on Commonwealth avenue for their own occupancy, on condition that by virtue of "their risk as pioneers" they be favored with prices below the minimum fixed by the Commissioners.[85] These "gentlemen" were all socially prominent men and their precedent was deemed so important that the Commissioners agreed to the terms.[86]

[83] Ross, *op. cit.*, p. 19.
[84] *Ibid.*, p. 19.
[85] *Ibid.*, pp. 19–20.
[86] Among them were A. Lawrence, H. Saltonstall, G. T. Bigelow, L. M. Standish, S. F. Dana, and B. S. Rotch. For a complete list of their names see: Map, in *Catalogue of 38 Lots of Land on the Back Bay, Belonging to the Commonwealth of Massachusetts, fronting upon Commonwealth Avenue and Marlborough Street, to be Sold by Public Auction on Thursday, April 9, 1863*, N. A. Thompson and Co. (Boston: 1863).

The good effect of these sales in creating confidence in the progress of improvement in this district, and attracting the best class of purchasers to it, is well shown by the auction sales of October 24, where a great advance of prices was obtained.[87]

These details are important, for they reveal the ecological significance of precedent, respectability, and confidence — all things of a meaningful, valuative nature. Nor can such factors be regarded as mere epiphenomena, as mere byproducts of supposedly more basic forces that would have foreordained the Back Bay to fashionable occupancy anyway. For through them the Back Bay was probably spared the fate that befell the South End, where volition led to the choice of a different alternative. Values, it may be inferred, are independent causative variables in spatial adaptation. Their effect is inevitably to create a variability in land use patterns. Under such circumstances it is hardly justifiable to postulate such "natural" or "almost necessary" locational patterns or processes as the idealized descriptive schemes have advanced.

Following upper class "legitimizing" of the Back Bay there ensued a rapid building up and settlement of the district. Hundreds of families deserted their South End homes, often sacrificing them at great monetary loss, in order to partake of the prestige that now attached to the Back Bay. Within a few years this area had become the truly aristocratic section of Boston. Indeed it even threatened the hegemony of Beacon Hill; many old Hill families, attracted by the magnificence and prestige of the new lands, abandoned their historic neighborhood and settled in the Back Bay.[88] Some of the values and sentiments which had become identified with this area are revealed in the following contemporaneous description:

Grand, wide streets have been laid out — notably Commonwealth Avenue, two hundred feet in width, with a park running its entire length — and hundreds of the most magnificent dwellings have been erected thereon by opulent merchants of Boston. Practically, a new city has arisen, almost magically, and the Back Bay (or new West

[87] Ross, *op. cit.*, p. 20.
[88] Chamberlain, *Beacon Hill, its Ancient Pastures and Early Mansions,* p. 47.

End, as it is now commonly being termed) rivals in magnificence the most sumptuous quarters of the cities of the Old World.[89]

Much concern was manifest as to a befitting name for the district. The term "Back Bay" had acquired a bad connotation to Bostonians because of its long association with the odorous tidal flats which had once comprised the area. Such sobriquets as "New West End," "Far West End," and "the New Land," were proposed as more suitable names. But none of these endured and the area retained its original name "Back Bay," which in time lost its earlier objectionable connotations.

Eventually the Back Bay filling extended to Stony Brook and led to the development of the Fens area. Much of this section, particularly around the juncture of Longwood and Huntington avenues, had been deteriorating into a slum.[90] But with plans laid for a great park development in the Fenway this trend was reversed. A number of cultural institutions made known their plans to locate in the Fenway, notably the Museum of Fine Arts (which had previously been in the Back Bay proper, at Copley square), the Harvard Medical School, the Gardner Museum, Simmons College, and others.[91] A contemporary of the period wrote:

There can be no question as to the fact that this redemption of a quarter of the city which was distinctly tending towards the slums has been effected solely by the establishment of the Fens. It is an interesting illustration of the influence of park lands upon the neighborhood, in a real estate point of view.[92]

His point is a significant one. The supposition of the idealized descriptive schemes has been that the outward extension of land uses is not only inevitable but is irreversible. Slums in particular have been considered as terminating phases in a unilinear cycle of residential land use, the outcome of which can only be commercial or industrial occupation.[93] In point of fact this uniformity

[89] Dexter Smith, *Cyclopedia of Boston and Vicinity* (Boston: 1886), p. 105.
[90] William Howe Downes, "The Future of the Fens," the *Boston Transcript*, July 2, 1902.
[91] *Loc. cit.*
[92] *Loc. cit.*
[93] José Luis Sert, *Can Our Cities Survive?* (Cambridge: 1942), pp. 20 and 30–31; Hoyt, *op. cit.*, p. 108; Ernest W. Burgess, "The Growth of the City:

has probably existed in most American cities during their period of expansion, but it can hardly be viewed as anything more than an historically relative rule of thumb. Uniformities of this kind are not the material out of which a systematic ecological science can be built. Not only do they have exceptions, as our Fens case illustrates, but they are not stated in terms of variables that belong to a unified and logically closed frame of reference. So far as our immediate problem is concerned we have in the Fens one more instance of the variability of spatial adaptation. The failure of the idealized descriptive schemes to account for this variability cannot but qualify their explanatory adequacy.

By 1910 the Back Bay had reached the apogee of its development. Hundreds of Boston's most exclusive families made it their home, and most of the city's finest churches, schools, libraries, and other cultural institutions were located there. No other neighborhood either within the city or in its environs could claim equal distinction. But in the meantime another locational process was manifesting itself; this was the suburban drift of population. We have already had occasion to note this trend, which had become apparent as early as the 1840's. Despite the South End and Back Bay developments, which were in part designed to arrest the trend, the suburbanward exodus of families continued throughout the nineteenth century and indeed has shown no abatement during the present century. The gradual extension of transit facilities and, most important of all, the advent of the automobile, put within commuting distance of the Hub, towns that had hitherto been rural hamlets. Dorchester, which in 1880 had been a sparsely settled farming district,[94] became settled with middle class and some upper class families by the end of the century. Brighton, West Roxbury, and Hyde Park were likewise built up during this period. In Roxbury, Jamaica Plain developed into a fashionable upper class neighborhood. Meanwhile the older portions of the city — the North End, the West End, Charlestown, and East Boston — showed absolute declines in population by 1920 and have continued to lose ever since. Outside of Boston

an Introduction to a Research Project," in Robert E. Park (ed.), *The City* (Chicago: 1925), p. 50.

[94] Elisabeth M. Herlihy (ed.), *Fifty Years of Boston* (Boston: 1932), pp. 62–63.

proper the centrifugal trend was even more pronounced. Towns like Milton, Westwood, and Needham, which had long enjoyed prestige as the summer abodes of Boston's elite — with great estates and relatively sparse populations — began to experience an invasion of year-round home seekers, most of them upper class families. In some neighborhoods the trend was expedited by real estate promotional ventures. Other towns, such as Melrose, Medford, and Arlington evolved into middle class commuters' towns. Everett, Chelsea, Revere, Watertown, and Quincy became predominantly working class communities. Quantitative evidence of

TABLE 1

NUMBER OF PERSONS IN BOSTON AND IN THIRTY-ONE SUBURBS, BY DECADES

	1890	1900	1910	1920	1930	1940
Boston..........	448,477	560,892	670,585	748,060	781,188	770,816
Suburbs.........	402,293	558,763	695,722	853,740	1,069,144	1,096,412

Source: Eleventh to Sixteenth Censuses of the United States, inclusive.

this suburban drift of population is afforded by decennial census figures since 1890. By summing up the populations of the thirty-one towns surrounding Boston, for each decade, we find that the aggregate figures for the suburbs show a gradual and uninterrupted rise to the present time (see Table 1). In contrast the population of Boston reveals a somewhat slower rate of increase up to 1930, after which it underwent an actual decline.

Since our principal concern in the present chapter has been with upper class locational patterns and processes it is interesting to compare these with the trend for the population as a whole. We wish to know whether people of means and distinction have moved to the suburbs at as great or greater a rate than the rest of the population. To arrive at a quantitative measure of upper class locational shifts since 1890 recourse was had to the Boston *Social Register*.[95] This is an annual directory of families which are considered "socially acceptable." The names are almost wholly old stock Yankee names, with practically none of Irish or other "alien" extraction. The *Social Register* is not, as such, a listing of wealthy persons, for some of its entries represent fami-

[95] *Social Register, Boston* (New York, annual).

lies of quite modest means whose forebears, however, had been well-to-do or otherwise prominent. Furthermore, there are many of the *nouveau riche* in Boston, both old stock as well as Irish and Jewish who are not listed. Finally, not a few traditional elite families have allowed their memberships to lapse and are consequently not listed. In spite of all these deficiencies the *Social Register* does provide a reasonably adequate index of upper class status. Listing in it is a coveted thing which confers status and recognition upon any family; its members have a self-conception of upper class standing; and, lastly, no one of plebeian status, judged by any accepted norm of class position, will be found in it. For these reasons we cannot go far wrong in relying upon it for an estimate of upper class locational processes. Our procedure was to take the *Social Register* for 1894, 1905, 1914, 1929, and 1943, and tabulate the frequency of addresses by various neighborhoods within Boston and by suburbs surrounding the city.[96] The results of this tabulation are set forth in Table 2. As the figures indicate, the number of upper class families living outside

TABLE 2

NUMBER OF UPPER CLASS FAMILIES IN BOSTON AND IN SUBURBAN TOWNS, FOR CERTAIN YEARS

	1894	1905	1914	1929	1943
Total in Boston	1519	1635	1559	1364	962
Total in suburbs	403	807	1049	1345	1993
Brookline	137	300	348	355	372
Newton	38	89	90	164	247
Cambridge	77	142	147	223	257
Milton	37	71	1c6	131	202
Dedham	8	29	48	69	99
Other towns	106	176	310	403	816
Totals	1922	2442	2608	2709	2955

Tabulated from *Social Register, Boston.*

of Boston has nearly quintupled since 1894. Meanwhile the number of such families within Boston has dropped abruptly and uninterruptedly since 1905, this in spite of the larger number of listings in each successive edition of the *Social Register*. It is evident that well-to-do and socially prominent persons are leaving

[96] In cases where more than one address was given for a name, the Boston address was the one tabulated.

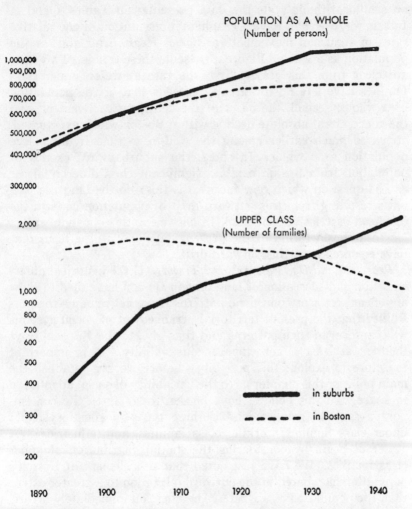

2,000,000

POPULATION AS A WHOLE
(Number of persons)

1,000,000
900,000
800,000
700,000
600,000

500,000

400,000

300,000

2,000

UPPER CLASS
(Number of families)

1,000
900
800
700
600

500

400

in suburbs

300

in Boston

200

1890   1900   1910   1920   1930   1940

FIGURE 4. CLASS DIFFERENTIAL POPULATION TRENDS WITHIN
BOSTON AND IN SUBURBS

Boston at a pronounced rate. To bring out the differential character of this suburbanward exodus by social class we may plot on semilogarithmic scale the data presented in Tables 1 and 2. In this way we shall have a graphic representation of the relative rates of suburban movement for *Social Registerites* and for the population as a whole. Figure 4 presents these trends. Two facts are clear from this graph: first, the rate at which upper class families have left Boston greatly exceeds that of the population as a whole; second, the onset of the centrifugal movement, and the concomitant absolute decline within Boston which eventuated, appeared much earlier among the well-to-do than it did in the population as a whole. In short, the suburbanward exodus of population from Boston exhibits significant class differentials.

The question which now faces us is this: do the land use patterns resulting from this outward drift of population confirm the idealized descriptive schemes? In answering this question we are led to a consideration of the present day land use patterns that have emerged from this outward drift.

Present Land Use Patterns and Trends. If the historical differentiation and succession of land uses in Boston has failed to show any clear sector or concentric patterns there yet remains the possibility that the present territorial arrangement of social systems will conform to such patterns and thus give to the Burgess-Hoyt theories at least a contemporaneous validity. It is important therefore to explore this possibility before we can establish the main point of this chapter as to the variability of social adaptation to space. To this end we have chosen to set forth the contemporary spatial arrangements of three types of social systems: upper class families, working class families, and industries.

Let us begin by considering the spatial distribution of upper class families. We have just noted that this element of Boston's population has shared in the outward migration to a greater extent than the population as a whole. The question immediately arises: is this not a partial confirmation of the Burgess concentric theory? Does this not prove that upper class families in the main tend to locate just where the Burgess theory supposes them to be, viz., in the outer zones of the metropolitan area? The surest way of determining this point is to portray on a map the percentages of the total upper class population which are located in the various

portions of Boston and its suburbs. Then we can observe directly
how real a concentric zone may be made up of upper class families. For this purpose we may once again make use of the *Social
Register* data. The basis for the percentages is the total number
of families in the *Social Register* for 1943 who lived within a

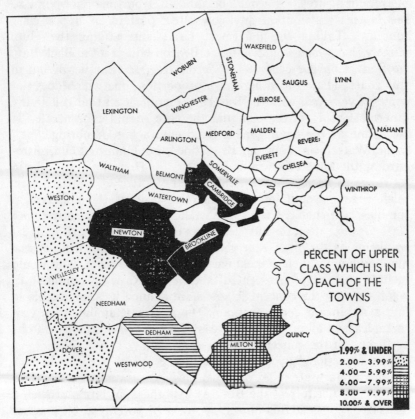

FIGURE 5

mapped out area that may be thought of as fairly integrated into
Boston's routine upper class social interaction. Entries with remoter addresses in Massachusetts, as well as those out of the
state, were not counted in this tabulation. This eliminates 526 of
the families recorded in Table 2 — families living too far from
Boston proper to be considered as effective participants in its "so-

ciety life." The results of the operation are portrayed in figure 5.[97] Within the bounds of the towns and cities represented on this map are 2,429 *Social Register* families. Of these, 39.59 per cent are within the corporate limits of Boston. The remainder are distributed throughout the outlying towns and cities of the metropolitan area. It would be difficult from any viewpoint to see in this distribution any concentric pattern of upper class families. Taking the innermost circle surrounding the Hub, namely that which would embrace Beacon Hill and the Back Bay, we find 36.66 per cent of the *Social Register* families living in this zone. That is a rather large proportion, one which does not comport very well with the Burgess generalization that it is in the outermost zones of the city that the elite should concentrate. If we define as the outer zone a band embracing Cambridge, Belmont, Watertown, Newton, Brookline, and Jamaica Plain, disregarding the remoter towns as being too far from the Hub to be in its range of upper class interaction, the outcome is little better. Such a zone would include 38.26 per cent of the upper class families. On such a basis there would be almost as many upper class families near the city center as on its periphery. Finally, if we define as the outer zone the remotest towns appearing on the map, adding up their percentages, we find that such a band would include only 23.39 per cent of the *Social Register* families. In whatever way the concentric zones are defined it is impossible to find a significant concentration of upper class families in any of them, least of all in the outer areas where they are supposed to be according to the concentric theory.

The objection may be raised that the *Social Register* listings are not an accurate index of upper class status and that therefore it is not proper to test the Burgess hypothesis in terms of such a measure. To meet this objection we have portrayed on another map, figure 6, the median estimated or contracted monthly rent in all cities and towns for which such data are available, as well as for census tracts within the city of Boston.[98] Rent being the most

[97] The absolute numbers and percentages are presented in Appendix I, as well as the towns embraced within the mapped out area.

[98] Data on median rentals for outlying towns and cities are from: *Housing, Second Series, General Characteristics, Massachusetts,* Sixteenth Census of the United States, 1940, Table 24; census tract rentals are from: *Population*

frequently used index of class status in ecological studies it should be interesting to see how strong a case can be made on its basis for the concentric theory. An examination of the map shows a rather random distribution of rental classes, at least so far as any concentric bands are concerned. The innermost zone includes the highest rental class in the whole metropolitan area (Beacon Hill, Back Bay, and the lower Fenway) and it also includes the lowest rental class (Charlestown, part of East Boston, the North End, the West End, the South End, and South Boston). Similarly the outermost zone ranges from such low rental cities as Lynn, Woburn, and Quincy, to high rental towns like Wellesley and Milton. Not a single concentric zone reveals any homogeneity in its rental classes. In terms of such evidence the Burgess hypothesis must be considered inadequate for the generalized description of upper class locational patterns in Boston.

If now the two maps are examined from a different perspective, with a view to discovering any possible sectors that might confirm the Hoyt sector theory, the outcome is not so completely negative. The most obvious feature of figure 5 is the relative absence of upper class families to the north of the city. There is, of course, a scattering of such families in some of these northern towns but their number is so negligible that it fails to show up in the statistical class-intervals necessary for graphic presentation. The real concentrations of *Social Register* families lie to the west, southwest, and south of Boston. In a certain sense a very real sector may be discerned here, running southwesterly from Beacon Hill, and including the Back Bay, Brookline, Newton, Wellesley, Weston, and perhaps Dedham. Much depends of course upon how wide an angle one will grant Hoyt in delineating sectors. Moreover, it should be borne in mind that about one-third of Boston's circumference is automatically eliminated for residential occupancy by the existence of the harbor to the east. Nonetheless the general westerly and southerly concentration of *Social Register* families is unmistakable. Does this constitute a validation of the Hoyt sector theory? In answering this question it is important to recall the reasoning which Hoyt adduces as accounting for the sector patterns into which residential areas supposedly fall. His

and Housing, Statistics for Census Tracts, Boston, Massachusetts, Sixteenth Census of the United States, 1940, Table 5.

explanation, briefly, is that upper class areas must necessarily expand outward because they are bordered on both sides by lower class neighborhoods. Consequently there is a more or less continuous radial extension from the most centrally located upper class district to the periphery. The result is the appearance, on a map, of a sector or segments of a sector. Now the actual development of upper class suburban towns does not altogether conform to this analysis. Brookline, for instance, was a fashionable upper class town before the Back Bay was ever filled in, yet it lies farther out from the Hub than the Back Bay.[99] So it is really something of an accident that, when the Back Bay was filled in and developed for upper class use, a sector pattern emerged. Much the same is true of the towns lying further out. Such towns as Dedham, Dover, and Weston (also Needham and Westwood) were once the summer resorts for Boston's upper class. Many elite families owned great rural estates in these towns and it was they who gave to the area its "fashionable" reputation. Then, when the extension of trolley lines and mass automobile transportation put these towns within commuting distance of Boston it was only natural that upper class families seeking suburban homes would move to the towns in which they already owned property or which already connoted a certain distinction. These areas were fashionable long before any continuous radius had ever emerged connecting them with the Boston Hub via Brookline and the Back Bay. In only one district does the Hoyt formula seem to apply.[100] The development of Chestnut Hill, in that portion of Newton which adjoins Brookline, was more nearly contingent upon the proximity of Brookline, which already enjoyed social distinction.

The objection may still be made that, however wrong Hoyt's own explanation of the sector phenomenon may be, there is nonetheless a definite upper class sector which would at least confirm his general description of residential land use patterns. Now it is

[99] See John Gould Curtis, *History of the Town of Brookline, Massachusetts* (Boston: 1933), pp. 210–213.

[100] In fairness to Hoyt it is necessary to indicate that many of his own general observations on urban residential patterns deviate from the simple sector pattern. His presentation is in no sense a doctrinaire one. Nonetheless the scientific adequacy of his idealized scheme may legitimately be evaluated and criticized.

true that almost three-fourths of the *Social Register* families, the exact percentage depending upon how one draws the sector's boundaries, live in a band extending southwesterly from Beacon Hill. Superficially this would seem to be more than enough proof in favor of the sector theory. But such an inference would overlook one highly important fact: the radial band within which these upper class families concentrate is not homogeneous. Thus, only a small portion of the city of Cambridge is occupied by upper class families, and this area lies in the western half of the city; between it and the Beacon Hill–Back Bay district there is no continuity of fashionable occupancy at all, but rather a heterogeneous area of working class homes and industrial plants. The fashionable Brattle street district of Cambridge is not in any sense a radial extension from downtown Boston, but is rather an isolated "island" dependent in some measure upon the proximity of Harvard University. Similarly between the fashionable portion of Brookline and the Back Bay–Fenway district is a rather deteriorated working class area, running entirely across Brookline from northeast to west along the railroad tracks. Dedham, too, if one includes it in the rough sector being considered, is inhabited not only by *Social Registerites* but also by a rather large working class population. Even though the sector lying southwest of Boston has a higher proportion of upper class families than have other parts of the metropolitan area, the fact still remains that that sector is not homogeneous in its characteristics. Within it are to be found other land uses very different in prestige character from that of upper class occupancy. It is a prime requirement of any scientific theory that in ascribing a given effect to a cause it must avoid ascribing very different and contrary effects to one and the same cause. The sector theory fails to meet this requirement. Within the supposed upper class sector are to be found non-upper class residential uses; and outside of that sector are to be found a good many upper class areas. On logical grounds the sector theory cannot be seriously entertained as a systematic ecological theory.

This conclusion is not altered if we base our reasoning upon the index of residential class status which Hoyt himself uses, viz., median monthly rentals. Figure 6 does show, as did the map of *Social Register* families, an identifiable southwesterly band of fairly high rentals. But within that band may be found low rentals. And outside of that band — to the south, in Milton, and to the northwest, in Belmont and Winchester — are to be found fairly high rentals. This lack of consistency in the cause-effect relationship postulated by the sector theory renders it quite un-

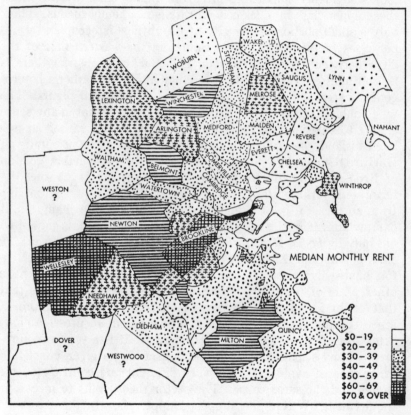

FIGURE 6

satisfactory as a scientific system for the analysis of land use. There is no need to reject the theory as being wholly "wrong"; for certain immediate, common-sense purposes there may be some practical usefulness to it. But as a logically tenable and systematic theory there can be little place for it in ecology.

Before rendering a final judgment on the idealized descriptive schemes it will be well to consider two further lines of evidence: the distribution of working class families, and the distribution of industries. Regarding the former, both Burgess and Hoyt have set down certain territorial patterns assumed to be typical of American cities. In Burgess' analysis the working class area is

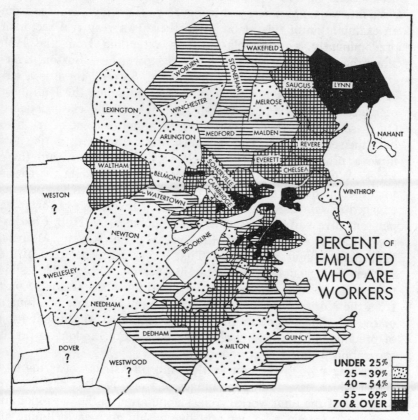

FIGURE 7

supposed to lie just outside the "zone of transition," forming a concentric band near the city center. According to Hoyt's formula the working class area should form sectors radiating outward from the city center. To test these hypotheses we have plotted in figure 7 the percentage of gainfully employed persons in each city and town outside of Boston and Cambridge,[101] and in each census tract within Boston and Cambridge, who fall into distinctly working class occupations. For this purpose the census categories of: craftsmen and foremen, operatives, service workers (excluding domestic service), and laborers, were considered working class occupations.[102] The resulting percentages, grouped by statistical class-intervals, are portrayed in figure 7. Two facts emerge from an examination of this map. First, there is a very real sector of predominantly working class towns extending from the Hub along the North Shore, through Charlestown, East Boston, Everett, Chelsea, Revere, Saugus, and Lynn. Second, there is a circular band of towns and census tracts surrounding the Hub most of which have very high percentages of working class persons. On these grounds there might seem to be an element of truth to both the sector and the concentric theories. But let us notice how large a proportion of working class persons falls within these zones. Within the area shown on the map (excluding the towns for which no data are available) there is a total of 316,840 persons engaged in working class occupations. Of these, 84,654, or 26.72 per cent, live within the sector which includes the Hub, Charlestown, East Boston, Everett, Chelsea, Malden, Revere, Melrose, Wakefield, Saugus, and Lynn. That leaves 73.28 per cent of the workers living outside the sector in question. Nor is it possible to see in the map any other clear working class sector. Apart from the North Shore sector, which accounts for only one-fourth of the laboring people in the metropolitan area, the distribution of predominantly working class towns is quite random so far as geographical patterns are concerned.

Turning now to the concentric band of districts near the city center which have high percentages of working class persons, we find that of the total working class population in the metropolitan area, 126,111, or 39.80 per cent live within an area including all of Charlestown, Somerville, Everett, Chelsea, East Boston, East Cambridge,[103] the Hub of Boston, the Back Bay, the lower Fen-

[101] Data not available for Nahant, Weston, Dover, or Westwood.

[102] Data from: *Population, Second Series, Characteristics of the Population, Massachusetts,* Sixteenth Census of the United States, 1940, Tables 33 and 42.

[103] The portions of Cambridge included were census tracts 1, 2, 3, 4, 5, 6, 7, 8, 9, 10, 11, 12, 13, 14, 15, and 18.

way, the South End, South Boston, north Dorchester, and north Roxbury.[104] Thus, even by a rather generous delineation of the supposed working class zone surrounding the city center we find only two-fifths of the laboring people living within that zone. Entirely outside this concentric band, and separated from it by intervening areas which are occupied by other occupational types, are such distinctly working class areas as Hyde Park (in southern Boston), North Cambridge, portions of Quincy,[105] Watertown, Waltham, Somerville, and Medford. Even such well-to-do towns as Newton and Dedham have considerable working class populations concentrated in certain districts. Furthermore, even within the concentric working class band which can be discerned surrounding the Hub there are districts with very small percentages of laboring people. Indeed Beacon Hill and the Back Bay, both of which lie wholly within the area that "should" be devoted to working class occupancy, have next to the lowest percentages of working class people in the entire metropolitan area.[106] In the light of these findings it is reasonable to conclude that neither of the idealized descriptive schemes satisfactorily explains the distribution of working class families. To be sure, sectors and concentric bands can be found in the land use maps that we have examined; they are just tangible enough to lend a superficial plausibility to descriptive "cartographic" theories. But closer analysis reveals that such theories account for only a part of the phenomena which they are supposed to explain. The remaining portion lies wholly outside the scope of these theories. Non-

[104] The portions of Dorchester and Roxbury included were census tracts P1A, P1B, P1C, P2, P3, P4, P5, P6, Q1, Q2, Q3, Q4, Q5, R1, R2, R3, S1, T1, T2, T3A, T3B, U1, U2, and U3.

[105] In interpreting the percentage distributions on the map it should be borne in mind that, except for Cambridge and Boston, data are available only for towns *as a whole*. Consequently such cities as Quincy, with large working class populations, do not appear particularly outstanding on the map because there are also considerable middle and upper class populations in these cities. Only for the census tract distributions of Cambridge and Boston is there any real occupational homogeneity within the area represented by a given percentage.

[106] Beacon Hill is 18 per cent working class (census tract K2); the Back Bay is 13 and 22 per cent (census tracts K3 and K5, respectively). Only the Aberdeen district in Brighton (census tract Y5C), with 17 per cent of its employed persons in the working class, has a smaller laboring population.

working class districts lie within the supposed working class zone; and working class districts are to be found outside this supposed working class zone. As Davie found in his ecological study of New Haven, simplified geographical patterns obscure the real significance of data as they are actually distributed over space.

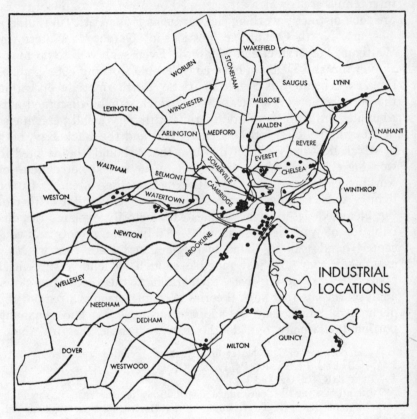

FIGURE 8

Though vague concentric and sector patterns are apparent in certain types of land use, the more important fact is the variation of land use within these zones.[107] Land use is apparently too vari-

[107] Maurice R. Davie, "The Pattern of Urban Growth," in *Studies in the Science of Society,* ed. by George Peter Murdock (New Haven: 1937), pp. 138–142.

able to be conceived of in terms of two-dimensional cartographic generalizations.

Much the same conclusion follows from a study of the territorial distribution of industries in the metropolitan area. For this material recourse was had to the *Directory of the Larger Manufacturers, Boston Industrial Area,* a pamphlet issued by the Bureau of Commercial and Industrial Affairs, Boston Chamber of Commerce.[108] Only those industrial plants employing 250 or more wage earners were included in our tabulation. The addresses of these factories were copied and a spot map made on their basis. In figure 8 the resulting distribution is portrayed upon a background of the principal railway lines. According to the Burgess concentric theory, industries will be found concentrated in a band lying just outside the wholesale and transitional areas surrounding the business center. In the case of Boston this should put most industries in an area embracing eastern Cambridge, eastern Somerville, Charlestown, East Boston, the North End, South Boston, the South End, and the Back Bay. Now by actual count there are in these districts from 49 to 57 industries, depending on how one delineates the concentric zone. These represent less than one-half of the 123 industrial plants depicted on the map. The remaining industries have locations which cannot be explained by the concentric theory. In this connection Hoyt's strictures on the concentric hypothesis are well taken. He indicates that manufacturing areas, rather than concentrating in a circular belt surrounding the city center, tend to cluster along shorelines, river valleys and belt line railroads. Hence there are no simple territorial uniformities in industrial location.[109] An examination of figure 8 shows that nearly all the industrial conurbations are on main railway lines or near railway intersection points: in Waltham, Watertown, Hyde Park, East Cambridge, Jamaica Plain, Roxbury Crossing, South Boston, Quincy, Everett, and Lynn. Really the only industries not so located are those in the Hub itself, and most of these are adjacent to dock facilities. Consequently the pattern of industrial location is in large measure a function of railroad and docking facilities. Whatever configuration it assumes is thus dependent upon the layout of transportation routes and is

[108] (Boston: 1940).
[109] Hoyt, *op. cit.*, chap. ii.

likely to be quite variable and "fortuitous" so far as the idealized descriptive schemes are concerned.

Whatever the line of evidence one follows, the outcome is always the same. Neither past nor present land uses in Boston conform to the idealized descriptive schemes. There are, to be sure, some rough cartographic patterns to be found now and then in land uses, which are just tangible enough to make the concentric-sector theories plausible. Indeed, if there were not, it would be something of a mystery how such theories had ever come to be formulated. Perhaps there is even some pragmatic value for real estate men and others in visualizing urban land uses as extending ever outward in sectors, or expanding ringlike in successive concentric bands. But it would be a very unwise investor or speculator who took such patterns at all literally. And for the scientific purpose of generalizing basic uniformities in spatial adaptation there is little to justify the idealized descriptive schemes. Even when regular patterns can be glimpsed in land use maps, the variations within each of the zones are more conspicuous than the uniformities. And wholly outside the zones are land uses whose location remains quite inexplicable. The arrangements which land uses assume are much too variable to be embraced in simple descriptive generalizations. This finding, negative and eclectic as it may be, is the one sure fact to which the data examined in this chapter consistently point.

CHAPTER III

THE INFLUENCE OF SPATIALLY REFERRED
VALUES UPON LAND USE: BEACON HILL

HAVING SEEN the variability which land use patterns may assume
we must not conclude that we have thereby vitiated all of ecological determinism. The idealized descriptive schemes, after all,
represent only one type of deterministic theory. Within the deterministic framework there yet remain alternative theoretical positions. Spatial patterns may be ever so variable on a map, as our
foregoing analysis would suggest, and yet in no way represent
a variation away from the intrinsic society-space relationship.
None of the data thus far considered would in any way refute the
rationalistic claim that in the last analysis land use is rather invariant and that the seeming operation of social values is but a
"cover," an epiphenomenon to more basic and deterministic locational processes.

Our next task, then, must be to demonstrate that social values
are real and self sufficient ecological forces. To this end we must
show that values may endow space with qualities quite extraneous
to it as a physical phenomenon. Further we must establish the
point that values may enter into the ends by which social systems
choose locations and may thus lead to non-intrinsic society-space
relationships.

In short, we shall have to substantiate our hypothesis that
space may possess symbolic qualities, and that these qualities
really exert an influence upon land use. Only then may we question the two rationalistic premises regarding the purely impeditive
nature of space and the strictly economizing orientation of social
systems seeking location.

For the investigation of these problems we have chosen to
begin with a survey of locational trends on Beacon Hill. This
neighborhood, located some five minutes' walking distance from
the city's retail center, has for nearly a century and a half kept
its reputation as a preferred upper class residential district. Associated with this persistence of the Hill's reputation is the ex-

istence of certain spatially referred values that are shared by residents of the neighborhood. These values, articulated in and symbolized by Beacon Hill, seem to be a genuine attractive force to certain old families of Boston. Following its initial development, outlined in the previous chapter, Beacon Hill became the favorite residential quarter for novelists, poets, historians, statesmen, and other notables for which Boston was at one time famous. Throughout the nineteenth century and right down to the present, while other fashionable areas arose and then declined — Fort Hill, Colonnade Row and the Summer-Winter street area, the South End, the Back Bay, and Jamaica Plain — through all of this Beacon Hill consistently maintained its fashionable character. Directly contiguous to it, occupying the northerly slope of the Hill and extending across Cambridge street to North Station, is the West End. No sharper contrast in physical appearance, economic well-being, or social prestige could be imagined than exists between Beacon Hill proper — occupying the south slope — and the West End. What Josiah Curtis said of the district in 1860 is as pertinent today: "This region is inhabited by many of our most opulent, as well as many of our more indigent citizens." [1] This social dichotomy between two directly contiguous neighborhoods has prevailed since the original development of the Hill. Today the north slope is a heterogeneous area of Jewish and Italian immigrants, transient roomers, and activities that are morally ostracized by the rest of the community. Owing to the anomie and anonymity of the neighborhood prostitution and other vicious activities flourish on this side of the Hill. Morally emancipated persons who crave a bohemian pattern of life have settled in portions of the area, sometimes developing their own private courts extending off the main streets. No more than three minutes away, over the summit of the Hill, one finds dwellings occupied by some of the oldest and most respected families in Boston. Of this slope it has been written:

Beacon Hill, the height of exclusiveness, the citadel of aristocracy, all this it has long been, as if its being a hill aided in giving it literal

---

[1] Letter of March 2, 1860 to George H. Snelling, reprinted in latter's *Memorial, with Remarks and Letters, in Favor of a Modification of the Back Bay Plan* (Boston: 1860), p. 18.

unapproachableness. It still retains its prideful poise, in its outward and visible signs of perfectly cared-for houses and correctness of dress and manners and equipage.[2]

This slope is the traditional center of Boston's upper class. Thus, of the 335 families listed in the *Social Register* for 1943 as having Beacon Hill addresses, 311 lived on the south slope and only 24 on the north slope.[3] Median monthly rentals bear out the same differential. On the south slope — Beacon Hill proper — the median contract or estimated monthly rent is $70.59, compared with $32.66 for the north slope of the Hill. The corresponding figure for the city as a whole is $29.91.[4] Likewise the working class population on the "proper" side of Beacon Hill is rather small. If one excludes the domestic service workers and the clerical workers, the proportion of employed persons who fall into distinctly working class occupations is 17.75 per cent on the south slope, compared with 35.47 per cent on the north slope.[5] These differentials reveal rather clearly the dichotomy that exists between the two slopes of the Hill.

Formulation of the Hypothesis and Method. A "common sense" explanation of this spatial dichotomy between social classes, one which might seem also to account for the remarkable persistence of fashionable occupancy on the south slope, would be a deterministic one. According to such an explanation the reason that "proper" Beacon Hill never extended to the north slope is because of the latter's northerly exposure. And the reason the south slope has enjoyed such prolonged prestige is that its eleva-

[2] Robert Shackleton, *The Book of Boston* (Philadelphia: 1916), p. 28.

[3] Tabulated from the *Social Register, Boston* (New York: 1943).

[4] *Population and Housing—Statistics for Census Tracts, Boston, Mass.,* Sixteenth Census of the United States, 1940, Table 5.

[5] Although domestic service is a laboring occupation it possesses a peculiar significance on Beacon Hill because so large a proportion of the upper class families engage maids, nurses, and other household attendants. To include them in the statistics on working class population would therefore completely obscure the significance of the occupational make-up on Beacon Hill. The clerical workers, who are quite numerous on both slopes of the Hill, present a special problem which will be considered later. They consist for the most part of young married couples and single girls who are working in downtown offices. In terms of their parents' class, or in terms of their self-conception, they cannot be classed with the "laboring" population.

tion confers a desirable isolation from traffic and noise while its southerly exposure assures an abundance of sunshine through the winter. Now undoubtedly the original layout planned by the Mount Vernon Proprietors in 1796 must have reckoned with these externalistic factors. Knowing the rigor of Boston winters the Proprietors apparently confined their plans to the south slope and thus set the matrix for the social dichotomy that has ever since prevailed between the two slopes of the Hill. The planned paucity of north-south streets and the steep grades of what streets there are all conferred a further immunity to the Hill from commercial and lower class encroachment. But it would not do to lay too much stress upon these geographical factors. In the first place, we need only recall that to the east of Joy street, behind the State House and extending over to Pemberton Square, is an area that once enjoyed fully as much prestige as the southern slope—yet it had a northerly exposure. At best this factor is to be considered a deterrent but by no means a barrier to upper class occupancy of the northern slope of Beacon Hill. Such geographical factors can influence land use only indirectly through the element of values. It should further be recognized that the isolation which accompanies elevation does not always ensure fashionable residential use to an area. After all there have been two other elevated portions of Boston which were once upper class areas but which eventually succumbed to lower class invasion, viz., Copps' Hill in the North End, and Fort Hill. If elevation *per se* guaranteed upper class occupancy to an area it would be difficult to explain why these neighborhoods and not Beacon Hill eventually declined in prestige value. No causal theory which ascribes to a given variable phenomena that follow wholly different developmental courses can be seriously entertained in ecology. Clearly some other factor is operative on Beacon Hill which was not operative on the other hills. Our task is to ferret out this variable and indicate its precise role in conditioning land use on the Hill. There is no need to deny, of course, that geographical factors such as elevation do play a genuine part in land use, but their significance is always conditional and mediate. How they influence spatial adaptation depends upon the meanings that are attached to them. In the words of Maunier: "L'action des facteurs geographiques est ainsi *conditionelle:* ce sont des particularités du milieu social qui mettent en valeur telle ou telle propriété du sol aux dépens des autres." [6]

Let us then inquire into the nature of these *particularités du milieu social* insofar as they bear upon spatial adaptation. There are two possibilities. On the one hand they may consist of a rational orientation which in the final analysis regresses to their being epiphenomena to space as an impediment. On the other hand they may consist of a volitional orientation which expresses culturally defined society-space relationships. Consider what is implied in the first of these possibilities.

On the basis of a strictly rational orientation Beacon Hill "should" be occupied by social systems which have chosen their location with a high degree of rationality — i.e., with the intention of keeping down overall cost. Moreover, the locations finally arrived at by the several social systems that are supposedly competing for least costful sites should be so allocated that in severalty they have devolved to those social systems that make them yield the greatest surplus of income over expenditure; in other words, each location should have devolved to that social system which can make the most economic use of it. Thus a locational pattern should arise that would further both the maximum utility of the neighborhood (or community) and that of the individual social systems located there. Now it is indeed true that such high rent paying social systems as business establishments and exclusive apartment-hotels have repeatedly sought to locate on Beacon Hill. Had they succeeded in this purpose the rationalistic premises would to that extent have been confirmed. But they did not succeed. Through the operation of certain non-rationalistic forces these high rent paying social systems have consistently been barred from the Hill. Along with this, the social systems which actually are on the Hill have not chosen their locations with the primary object of minimizing overall cost. Neither are the land use patterns that have emerged from this spatial adaptation the least costful ones for the individual social systems or for the community as a whole. As data presently to be submitted will show, the rationalistic premises are not adequate to describing the real locational processes on Beacon Hill.

[6] René Maunier, "La Distribution Géographique des Industries," *Revue Internationale de Sociologie*, 7 (July, 1908), p. 27.

We must look then to the second of the alternatives mentioned above. It is our hypothesis that Beacon Hill, looked upon as an elevated piece of ground, has through nothing intrinsic to it at all, acquired an affective "halo" which attracts and retains certain upper class families who would not otherwise live there. This affective significance comes from the Hill's being a symbol for certain cultural values borne by those families with respect to family lineage, neighborhood traditions, and local antiquities. Acting upon these values a large number of families have sought to be identified with the Hill. Such identification in part *expresses* the values which these families have, and in part *designates* the cultural system of which these families are a part.[7] The land use patterns which result show a meaningful consonance with the values symbolized by Beacon Hill and are quite irrelevant to the impediment-economizing emphasis of the empirically rationalistic schemes.

The best source material for these spatially referred values is afforded by the innumerable pamphlets and articles which have been written by residents of the Hill. In these publications there appear many statements about the sacredness, charm, antiquity, and tradition of the Hill. From such statements it is possible to infer probable states of mind and thus impute values to the persons who have made the statements. This procedure admittedly gives rise to difficulties. In the first place, speech reactions are very prone to diverge from actual states of mind. Secondly, even when there is a correspondence between what a person says and what he means to say, there remains the possibility of a disparity between the true subjective state of that person, as he envisions it, and the subjective state which the external observer imputes to him on the basis of a common familiarity with conventional linguistic symbols.

There is no sure method of resolving these difficulties, for the

---

[7] This twofold function of symbolism has been described by Schütz as follows: "Die übliche Rede, Zeichen sei immer 'Zeichen für,' ist doppeldeutig. Das Zeichen ist einmal 'Zeichen für' die Zeichenbedeutung, nämlich das, was es *bezeichnet* (*Bedeutungsfunktion des Zeichens*), das Zeichen ist aber auch 'Zeichen für' das, was es *ausdrückt*, nämlich die Bewusztseinserlebnisse dessen der das Zeichen gesetzt hat." Alfred Schütz, *Der Sinnhafte Aufbau der Sozialen Welt* (Wien: 1932), p. 133. The significance of these two functions will be developed in the course of the subsequent discussion.

reason that objective phenomena have no necessary one-to-one correspondence with subjective phenomena.[8] An attempt has been made by Chapple to solve the problem by denying the scientific knowability of states of mind and substituting statistical correlations between: (a) speech reaction viewed externally and irrespective of their meaningful connotations to the observer, and (b) the objective behavioral context in which these speech reactions have been made.[9] We have rejected this procedure partly because it is not a very workable technique, but principally because of its methodological premises. These in effect deny the legitimacy of values as a scientific variable. It is the whole purpose of this study to show that, so far as spatial adaptation is concerned, social action cannot be properly understood unless values are made central to ecological theory. Without the component of values, social activities become either chance concatenations or mechanistic associations, neither of which truly typifies human behavior — at least as it shows up in land use.[10]

Another proposal for the scientific handling of verbal material has been advanced by Malinowski. His procedure, though not truly behavioristic, does postulate (at least for heuristic purposes) the priority of behavior over meaning. In this respect it comes close to denying the analytical independence of meanings. By his definition ". . . meaning is equal to the function of words within the context of situation . . ." [11] The actual method proposed by Malinowski, "the contextual specification of meaning," consists of attaching meaning to words in the light of the behavioral and situational context in which they are uttered.[12] This method is an adaptation to the problem which Malinowski faced of ascertaining the meanings of words belonging to a wholly different language — one into which the observer had not himself been socialized. In

[8] Pitirim A. Sorokin, *Contemporary Sociological Theories* (New York: 1928), pp. 650–651.

[9] Eliot D. Chapple, "Measuring Human Relations: an Introduction to the Study of the Interaction of Individuals," *Genetic Psychology Monographs*, 22: 3–147 (1940), chap. vii.

[10] Sorokin, *Sociocultural Causality, Space, Time* (Durham: 1943), pp. 43–78.

[11] Bronislaw Malinowski, *Coral Gardens and their Magic* (New York: 1935), II, 223.

[12] *Ibid.,* pp. 37–45.

such a situation one must necessarily work from what is known to what is unknown — i.e., from observable behavior and verbalization to subjective states. Such a method suffers from a certain ambiguity since, as stated, it is neither clearly subjectivistic nor behavioristic. The precise latitude permitted the observer in deciding what is the contextual reference of a word is not well defined and perhaps could not be for the order of problems facing the ethnographer. In the present study the problem is a much simpler one, since it is possible to assume a reasonable similarity in the socialization by which observer, reader, and quoted subject have all acquired meaningful speech.

We have chosen to resolve this problem of attaching meaning to words through recourse to a frankly subjectivistic method — that which Cooley called the method of "sympathetic insight." [13] This method allows an observer to directly apprehend from what others say the true states of mind which have prompted those utterances. By virtue of his own participation in the culture of which his subjects are members, an observer is able to internalize "the role of the other" in his own mind and to view the conditions of action confronting his subjects in much the same way as they do themselves. The genetic problem of how such a convergence between "the ego" and "the other" develops obviously lies beyond the purview of the present study. It is enough to indicate that to the extent that the linguistic symbols used by an ego have elicited the action of others which was anticipated by the ego, to that extent the ego has had genuine insight into the meanings which the other attaches to those symbols. Subsequently, when the other uses similar linguistic symbols in a similar context, the ego is able to attach the same meaning to those symbols that he himself had in mind when previously conveying them to the other, thereby achieving a subjective rapport with the other. In this way there arises a correspondence between the meanings which a communicator attaches to certain verbal symbols and the meanings which the recipient of the communication attaches to those symbols. It is for this reason that an observer, on hearing or reading certain speech reactions, may properly impute values to the person uttering those verbalizations. In much the same way it is possible to

[13] Charles Horton Cooley, *Human Nature and the Social Order* (New York: 1922), chap. iv.

discern discrepancies between speech reactions and true subjective states. Hypocrisy or dissimulation is itself a subjective state which has its own standardized and universally understood (within a given culture) verbal and gestural symbols.

Spatially Referred Values and their Integration. The presentation of statements, then, and the inference from them of states of mind, and the accompanying imputation of values, seems therefore to be a methodologically sound procedure. Let us then consider some of the statements which residents have made about Beacon Hill. There are, to begin with, expressions of aesthetic values. One writer puts his feelings in this way:

The dignified beauty, mellow refinement, and air of comfort are felt by all who come to the hill. A sense of everything well placed, well tended, and presenting an indescribable air of breeding and quality is sensed rather than perceived.[14]

In another pamphlet we find the following sentiments with regard to Louisburg Square, one of the particularly favored portions of Beacon Hill:

It seems almost incredible that in the heart of a city there can be found so quiet and lovely a spot as Louisburg Square. It is the one unspoiled, undefiled section of Boston which has withstood the March of Progress and still clings to its age-old quaintness and charm . . . . The ancient and dignified mansions which surround it are the homes of gentle and cultured people, now as well as in the old days. There is a mellow light that seems to linger only in this place, and the atmosphere suggests peace and contentment and rest.[15]

Henry James, the author, called Mount Vernon street "the happiest street-scene the country could show." [16] Lowell referred to that "exquisite something called style" which pervades Beacon Hill.[17] A leaflet issued by the Beacon Hill Association eulogizes

[14] John R. Shultz, *Beacon Hill and the Carol Singers* (Boston: 1923), p. 11.
[15] Josephine Samson, *Celebrities of Louisburg Square* (Greenfield, Massachusetts: 1924), no paging.
[16] Quoted in Abbie Farwell Brown, *The Lights of Beacon Hill* (Boston: 1922), p. 11.
[17] Quoted in Shultz, *op. cit.*, p. 11.

the "noble profile" of the Hill and the "dignity" of its ancient dwellings.[18] A lady living on Beacon street, and a member of the Cabot family, remarked on her own and her late husband's pleasure in their home: "We always enjoyed it here overlooking the Common." [19]

All these aesthetic values merge imperceptibly into the literary tradition that is associated with Beacon Hill. Such illustrious litterateurs as William H. Prescott, Francis Parkman, George Bancroft, George Ticknor, James T. Fields, Harriet Beecher Stowe, William E. Channing, Louisa May Alcott, William Dean Howells, Thomas Bailey Aldrich have all at one time or another lived on the Hill. The list could be extended at length to include such statesmen as John Quincy Adams, Charles Francis Adams, and many others.[20] It is little wonder that one writer asserts: "Louisburg Square lays its claim to fame on the celebrities who have dwelt in it," [21] and another observes of Chestnut street that: "To some who remember the past it is full of memories of that time when Boston was the Mecca for every literary aspirant, every admirer of genius." [22] And a popular woman's magazine says of Pinckney street:

Surrounded by the literary atmosphere of Old Boston, which still persists after so many years, the quarter where once lived famous literati, offers abundant inspiration to all who seek sanctuary there.[23]

After mentioning the various notables who have lived on Beacon Hill one resident concludes: "Indeed, nearly every house on the Hill has some precious association with letters or art." [24] That

[18] Zoning Defence Committee of the Beacon Hill Association, "The Menace to Beacon Hill" (Boston: 1927).

[19] Mrs. Mary C. Briggs, of Beacon street.

[20] Abram English Brown, "Beacon Hill," *The New England Magazine*, 28: n.s. 631–650 (August, 1903), pp. 634–635.

[21] Samson, *op. cit.*, no paging.

[22] Charlotte Greene, *While on the Hill; a Stroll Down Chestnut Street* (Boston: 1930), p. 10.

[23] Harriet Sisson Gillespie, "Reclaiming Colonial Landmarks," *The House Beautiful*, 58: 239–241 *et seq.* (September, 1925).

[24] Abbie Farwell Brown, "Beacons Still on Beacon Hill," *Christian Science Monitor*, December 23, 1922.

these are genuine expressions of sentiments, which truly enter into the motivation of certain people to seek residence on the Hill, is disclosed in remarks made by a few of the older residents. Generally these persons do not "wear their hearts upon their sleeves" and frank, affective statements are not easy to get. One lady, prominent in the Beacon Hill Association, and whose forebears as well as some contemporary relatives also lived on the Hill, spoke with pride of the rooms she occupied. In her words: "I like living here for I like to think that a great deal of historic interest has happened here in this room." [25] Other residents pointed with pride to their Bulfinch staircases, or to their faded purple window panes,[26] and in other ways revealed the values which they attach to their homes. In a very real sense such values are "motives" which have, along with other considerations, prompted the people who share them to maintain residence on Beacon Hill. The expressive function of living in a symbolically significant area is particularly evident in cases of this sort.

It is a point of pride to a Beacon Hill resident if he can boast that he was born on the Hill or at least grew up there. An even greater prestige attaches to a continuity of family residence in the neighborhood. Even today several descendants of the families who originally developed the Hill continue to live there.[27] E. Sohier Welch, a prominent member of the neighborhood, is the great grandson of Francis Welch who located on Beacon Hill in 1836. On Chestnut street there lives Miss Elizabeth Bartol, great granddaughter of Mrs. James Swan, one of the original Mount Vernon Proprietors of 1796.[28] The Lymans, the Wheelwrights,

[25] Miss Marian C. Nichols, of Mount Vernon street.

[26] These purple panes possess a special significance, since they were made of glass shipped from England early in the 1800's. Owing to defects the glass turned purple in the course of a few years. These purple panes have become symbols of the venerability of certain houses and are a point of pride to the occupants of those dwellings. Some residents have put artificial purple panes in their windows, but these are known to all old residents and antiquarians for what they are and they possess none of the symbolic significance of the "real" purple panes. The phenomenon, trivial as it may seem, reveals rather well the purely symbolic, non-intrinsic character of the meanings which certain aspects of Beacon Hill and its residences possess.

[27] Allen Chamberlain, *Beacon Hill, its Ancient Pastures and Early Mansions* (Boston: 1925), p. 5.

[28] *Ibid.*, pp. 168–169.

and several others have had a similar continuity of family residence in the district.[29]

Not only do several residents of the Hill thus have a continuity of local pedigree, but many of the dwellings have their own "pedigrees," and this is a matter of great pride to the occupants of such houses. As one writer puts it: "Hardly a site but has its legend, whether it be a stately mansion with courtyard and fountain, or a drab boarding-house soon to be reclaimed."[30] This is no fortuitous phenomenon confined to Beacon Hill but is part of a pattern typical of upper class Yankee families elsewhere in New England. In a study of Newburyport, Massachusetts, Warner and Lunt found that certain dwellings, occupied by upper class families and symbolizing the status of their occupants, possessed their own "lineages." Such houses were pervaded by "the spiritual presence of the ancestors" and as such linked their occupants with sacred traditions and memories of the past.[31] A very large proportion of Beacon Hill houses possess such lineages, and they bestow a corresponding status upon whatever families currently live in them. One house is known as the Otis House, another as the Charles Francis Adams House, another as the Alcott House — not that families having those names now reside in them, but simply that the memory of earlier notables has become identified with and symbolized by the houses they once occupied. What Simmel had to say about the ecological significance of named houses, as distinct from numbered ones, may quite properly be applied as well to these old Beacon Hill houses:

Durch den Namen, der mit der Vorstellung des Hauses assoziiert war, bildet dieses vielmehr eine für sich seiende, individuell gefärbte Existenz, es hat für das Gefühl eine höhere Art von Einzigkeit.[32]

The values which attach to these houses amount to something more than just ideas; they actually become motives to action. In

---

[29] *Ibid.*, pp. 154–158, and the *Boston Transcript*, October 9, 1929.

[30] Abbie Farwell Brown, *The Lights of Beacon Hill*, p. 11.

[31] W. Lloyd Warner and Paul S. Lunt, *The Social Life of a Modern Community* (New Haven: 1941), p. 107.

[32] Georg Simmel, "Der Raum und die räumliche Ordnungen der Gesellschaft," *Soziologie*, 3rd edition (München: 1923), p. 476.

other words, people not only appreciate the pedigrees of such dwellings, but they want to be identified with them. For such people residence in a venerable old house is an expression of sentiments. The number of families whose residence on Beacon Hill so directly expresses emotional feelings toward particular houses cannot be estimated. It is very likely rather small. But in a very large proportion of the other residents such feelings have in some degree entered into the scale of criteria by which a home has been chosen.

The majority of upper class families on Beacon Hill live there for both rational and volitional [33] considerations. One family, more properly in the "nouveau" category but ambitious for social recognition, bought a home on Beacon street for the deliberate purpose of helping to "place" their subdebutante daughters. Not only was the neighborhood accessible to the functions generally engaged in by upper class girls, but it was a "proper" place in which to live. The element of affect toward Beacon Hill was negligible with this family. To them residence in the neighborhood served primarily a designative function; it was a bid for the status which residence in the neighborhood symbolized. As such it is another manifestation of the locational significance of spatially referred values. Sometimes young couples of good family but for the time being living on a shoestring will rent moderately priced apartments in converted Beacon Hill houses. Thus, without too great expense to themselves they are able to live in a socially acceptable neighborhood and thereby symbolize their class position. The designative function of living in a symbolically significant area is quite apparent in this kind of motive. Apart from these types of residents there are not a few elderly spinsters, frequently living on depleted patrimonies, who maintain residence on Beacon Hill primarily because their home was a part of their inheritance and they could ill afford to live anywhere else. Yet another group of upper class families use their Beacon Hill homes only as winter domiciles, spending the rest of the year on their suburban or country estates. Finally, as we have already indicated, there is on Beacon Hill a large population of clerical workers, both single and newly married. Such people are above all in-

---

[33] The reader will recall that we attach a special and narrow meaning to this term "volitional." See *supra,* Chap. I.

terested in inexpensive living quarters that are accessible to their places of work. Rational considerations thus preponderate in their choice of a neighborhood in which to live. Yet, even among this group there is a surprisingly real appreciation of the "reputation" enjoyed by Beacon Hill. As one young married woman observed: "For young people who are working it's quite the thing to live on Beacon Hill—especially for girls." Office girls who reside on the Hill feel a certain distinction through living there. They are also able to enhance their popularity on such occasions as the Christmas Eve Carols when they may hold open house for their friends.

These latter types of motivation for living on Beacon Hill might at first glance appear rather unrelated to the sentimental values which we have stressed as being central to locational processes in the district. Nouveaus who locate on the Hill to place their daughters are indeed acting rationally, just as are young upper class couples getting their start and desirous of inexpensive quarters. Does not this element of rationality in some measure qualify the force of our thesis? We think not. To support this point we shall have to recall certain principles which concern the modes of relationship between social values. It is by now an established principle in sociology that the relationships which exist between social ends are not mere concatenations nor simple statistically probable recurrences. Rather they are meaningful "coherences." Their togetherness follows from their mutual referability to a broader and larger value system.[34] Whether a value is integrated with another value depends upon their mutual congruence in terms of a more inclusive *system* of values. It is possible to distinguish four subtypes of such logico-meaningful integration:

1. *Logical implication,* in which every value in a set of values may be deduced by logical syllogism from the others when viewed as major and minor premises.

2. *Identical reference,* in which a number of associated values, though not subject to syllogistic deduction, all pertain to a single ultimate or maximally inclusive value.

3. *Mutual compatibility,* in which certain coexisting values in no way

[34] Talcott Parsons, *The Structure of Social Action* (New York: 1937), pp. 254, 400, 391–392, 667–668; Sorokin, *Social and Cultural Dynamics* (New York: 1937, 1941), I, 23, 65–66; IV, 17–18, 39.

contradict one another nor entail conflicting behavior, but are otherwise mutually irrelevant.

4. *Congeries,* in which a number of values coexist but comprise a mere aggregation whose components sometimes conflict, sometimes comport with one another.[35]

These subtypes may be viewed as positions on a continuum, the scale being degrees of logico-meaningful integration. The first of the subtypes, logical implication, represents the maximum of integration. So far as spatial adaptation is concerned it is shown in zoning ordinances and deed restrictions and in the judicial decisions made on their basis with respect to particular cases. This type of logico-meaningful integration is not of primary significance in ecological theory, but it will engage us to some extent in Chapter VII, in connection with an analysis of the conflict between social values (as expressed in deed restrictions) and rational interests. The third and fourth subtypes apply to a wide range of land use situations and it is here that rationality has its *point d'entrée*. The highly rational orientation of isolated social systems seeking least costful locations — which is a very real process if its cultural context is specified [36] — is a manifestation of the third and fourth subtypes. It is the second subtype, however, which is most pertinent to the problem now at hand. In terms of it the relationship between: (a) value-oriented choice of residence, and (b) interest-oriented (i.e., rational) choice of residence, on Beacon Hill, becomes clear. The latter type of choice represents a bid for the status which Beacon Hill symbolizes. But Beacon Hill would not symbolize this status were it not for the prior existence of the values which endow the Hill with its symbolic quality. If these values were not rooted in the personal ends of a good many residents the Hill would lose its upper class character. Thus the rational orientation of some families could not function as it does were it not for the volitional orientation of other families.[37]

---

[35] This typology is but a variation upon the analysis of sociocultural integration made by Sorokin, *ibid.*, vol. I, chap. i.

[36] A problem to be taken up throughout Part II of this book.

[37] The theoretical significance of this point, that others' subjective states actually constitute an externality or condition to one's own subjective states (more specifically, to their actualization), is developed by Parsons, *op. cit.*, p. 235.

The relationship of these two kinds of orientation is a logico-meaningful one, owing to their sharing an *identical reference*, viz., the aesthetic-historical-genealogical meaning of Beacon Hill. Unlike the rationalism postulated by the empirically rationalistic theories, this kind of rationalism is not directed to a physically-given spatial milieu, nor is it given in the very properties of social systems. Rather it assumes the prior existence of spatially referred values which define the very conditions and means of the action which it directs. Such a rationalism has nothing in common with that of the empirically rationalistic theories. Its very effectiveness derives from a strictly cultural element in spatial adaptation—a factor that is missing in those theories.

The upshot of all this is that, however diverse may be the actual ends which motivate families to live on Beacon Hill, the fact still remains that spatially referred values are behind most of the locational processes in that neighborhood; for these values are really at the core of a constellation of ends all meaningfully integrated with one another through their identical reference.[38] It follows, then, that there exists with reference to Beacon Hill a "cultural system" in the strict sense of the term.[39] Far from making up just a bunch of unrelated sentiments, the values that have their focus in Beacon Hill form an integrated system with its core being an aesthetic-historical-genealogical complex. Needless to say, such an integration is a purely subjective thing and the component ends would lose their togetherness if people ceased holding to the value system in question.

Neighborhood Organization in Terms of Spatially Referred Values. The foregoing analysis has possibly made a case for the reality of spatially referred values and for the fact that diverse concrete ends can truly become meaningfully integrated into a system. Perhaps too it has shown how such values may really enter into the motivation of individuals. Nevertheless there still remains the problem: are these values borne by anything more than a number of separate families who, more or less independently of one another, have located on Beacon Hill in response to

[38] On the way in which intrinsically disparate ends may become integrated see Sorokin, *Social and Cultural Dynamics*, vol. I, chap. i; Vilfredo Pareto, *Mind and Society* (New York: 1935), paragraph 994.

[39] See our definition in Chap. I.

them? If such values, however real, are borne only by disparate families their ecological significance is less than if they were borne by a larger group. We face here the problem of the organization of values in contradistinction to their integration.[40] The question is no longer one of the meaningful integration of ends. Rather it becomes one of the organization of persons and groups toward one another in terms of a value system which they all share. The problem, in short, reduces to this: is there a "social system" on Beacon Hill of greater inclusiveness than individual families, which is organized in terms of the spatially referred values we have been discussing? Is Beacon Hill a *real* community or is it merely a *nominal* one, in the technical sense of these terms? [41]

The problem can be best approached by noting, first, who live on Beacon Hill, and second, how they have become organized. To begin with, the dominant class on the Hill, though not the most numerous — is the old stock Yankee aristocracy. Membership in this class is primarily a matter of birth, and presupposes several generations of upper class forebears in one's family. Despite the displacements following upon the rise of Irish and of non-Bostonian Yankee elements, the old families — the Lowells, Amorys, Frothinghams, Forbeses, Hemenways, Adams', Coolidges, etc. — still retain positions of authority in financial, educational, artistic, and welfare organizations.[42] Among them wealth is not of primary significance, and there is a goodly number of Beacon Hill elite who are in straitened financial circumstances. The principal function of wealth for them is one of facilitating the actions deemed proper to one of upper class standing.[43] Immediately below this upper stratum of the social pyramid is a sizable population of *nouveaus* — families of respectable qualities and financial affluence, but lacking in proper genealogical quali-

[40] This is a distinction made by Sorokin. The difference pertains to the level of analysis; "integration" is a cultural phenomenon while "organization" is a social phenomenon. Both are analytical concepts which form inseparable facets of a unitary phenomenon.

[41] For the establishment and analysis of these concepts see Carle C. Zimmerman, *The Changing Community* (New York: 1938), Prologue and chaps. i, vii.

[42] Lucius Beebe, *Boston and the Boston Legend* (New York: 1935), p. 256.

[43] Cf. Warner and Lunt, *op. cit.*, pp. 82–83, 98–99.

fications. Together these two strata comprise the "center of gravity" for the values attaching to Beacon Hill.

The upper class thus defined has certain important demographic characteristics which condition the nature of its neighborhood organization. These are as follows: (a) a sex ratio that is unbalanced on the female side; (b) an atypically middle aged population, with a paucity of children; and (c) a large proportion of unmarried women.[44] The first two of these characteristics are to some extent revealed in the age-sex population pyramid of census tract K-2, which corresponds almost exactly to the south slope of Beacon Hill. In interpreting these data, however, it is necessary to bear in mind that they include not only the upper class population, which is of most interest to us, but also the maids, chauffeurs, and other domestic *attachés* as well as the numerous clerical workers living on the Hill. Consequently the strictly upper class population make-up is somewhat obscured. In the absence of any other sources, however, it will be necessary to utilize such material as is available.[45] Figure 9 portrays these data in graphic form. The negligible child population is rather clear from this figure. Only 4.85 per cent of the total population on the Hill is under 15 years of age, compared with 21.38 per cent for Boston as a whole. Equally clear is the preponderance of females at every single age group, the ratio as a whole being 184 women per 100 men. A point not quite so evident without some explanation is the middle age character of the population. To anyone who is familiar with Beacon Hill it will be obvious that the large proportion of persons between 20 and 29 years of age is attributable to the clerical population. Were it not for them the middle age character of the upper class population would be even more evident than it is on the graph. Regarding the third demographic characteristic in question there are unfortunately no statistical data available on the marital status of the upper class population of Beacon Hill. There is only the commonplace ob-

[44] *Ibid.*, pp. 422–423, on the generality of these characteristics in the upper class Yankee stock.

[45] Percentages computed from data on census tract K-2, in Table 2, *Population and Housing — Statistics for Census Tracts, Boston, Massachusetts*, Sixteenth Census of the United States, 1940.

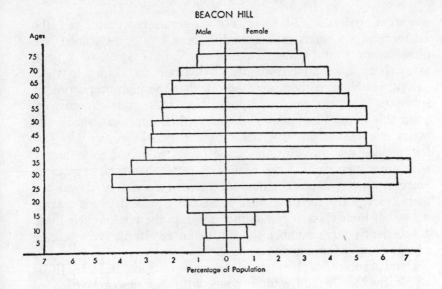

BEACON HILL

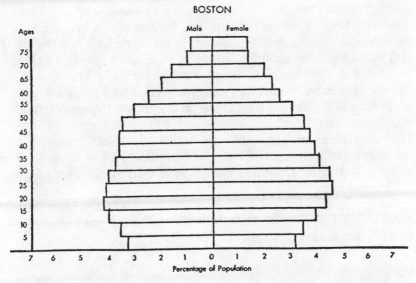

BOSTON

FIGURE 9. POPULATION COMPOSITION, BEACON HILL AND BOSTON

servation, well testified by direct observations, that "half the aristocratic old maids in Boston live here." [46] Spinsterhood is a phenomenon that typifies upper class Yankee stock in a good many New England communities. Warner and Lunt, in their analysis of Newburyport, pointed out that the high proportion of spinsters in the upper class population there was directly attributable to norms of class endogamy. The upper class man can marry a woman of lower social standing without in any way forfeiting his position. But the upper class woman has to marry within her own class if she wishes to retain her social standing. Since, however, a certain number of men do marry downward there is left a residue of women who must choose between marrying out of their class or remaining spinsters the rest of their lives. A sufficiently large number choose the latter alternative to create a large group of unmarried women. [47]

Demographically, then, the dominant group on Beacon Hill is atypically female and middle aged, with a large proportion of childless families and unmarried women. Such a population composition cannot but have its effects upon the nature of neighborhood activities. Perhaps it is not too far fetched to suggest that the strength of the affect which certain residents have toward the Hill reflects a sublimation of emotions that have not found their usual release through marriage and child-rearing. There is a decidedly "feminine" character to organized neighborhood activities on Beacon Hill, if by such a hazy term one means the expectations which generally attach to the woman's role in American culture. It is something that can hardly be verified by scientific methods, but which has been painted with artistic subtlety by such novelists as John Marquand and Anna Farquhar in their stories about Boston's upper class. [48]

Occupationally the population of Beacon Hill falls into vocations which carry social prestige. The following data show the relative occupational make-up of Beacon Hill and of Boston as a

[46] Eleanor Early, *And This is Boston!* (Boston: 1938), p. 53.
[47] Warner and Lunt, *op. cit.*, p. 102.
[48] See John P. Marquand, *The Late George Apley* (New York: 1940) or *H. M. Pulham, esquire* (Boston: 1941); Anna Farquhar, *Her Boston Experiences* (Boston: 1900).

whole.[49] The most striking feature of this make-up is of course the prominence of professional workers on the Hill. A good many of these are lawyers who have specialized in investment banking, corporation law, and the administration of trusts and estates. Some of them have nearly a full time job in handling their own inherited investments. All these positions carry with them authority and prestige and are considered proper callings for upper class men on Beacon Hill and elsewhere in Boston. No less evident from Table 3 is the negligible proportion of workers on Beacon Hill — whether craftsmen and foremen, or operatives and

TABLE 3

PERCENTAGE DISTRIBUTION OF EMPLOYED PERSONS ON BEACON HILL AND IN BOSTON, 1940, BY OCCUPATIONS

Occupations	Boston			Beacon Hill		
	Total	Male	Female	Total	Male	Female
Total employed...............	100.00	66.14	33.86	100.00	40.24	59.76
Professional workers...........	8.82	4.04	4.78	23.00	9.85	13.15,
Semi-professional workers......	1.40	0.93	0.47	1.83	0.72	1.11
Proprietors, managers, officials..	7.70	6.88	0.82	10.92	8.73	2.19
Clericals and like workers......	26.95	13.98	12.97	26.81	10.74	16.07
Craftsmen, foremen, etc........	12.71	12.23	0.48	2.98	2.33	0.65
Operatives and like workers....	18.67	12.76	5.91	2.70	1.80	0.90
Domestic service workers......	3.19	0.25	2.94	19.29	0.97	18.32
Service workers (exc. dom.)....	14.53	9.47	5.06	11.75	4.78	6.97
Laborers.....................	5.24	5.11	0.13	0.32	0.28	0.04
Occupation not reported......	0.79	0.49	0.30	0.40	0.04	0.36

Computed from Sixteenth Census of the United States, 1940.

laborers. The only exception to this, and it is a conspicuous one, is the high proportion of domestic service workers, almost all women. As indicated earlier in this chapter, these domestic workers are generally attached to family households and their residence on Beacon Hill is thus a consequence of their identification with the upper class.

With these demographic and occupational data in mind it is possible now to consider the extent to which this population has become organized in terms of the spatially referred values de-

[49] Computed from data in Table 3, *Population and Housing — Statistics for Census Tracts, Boston, Massachusetts*, Sixteenth Census of the United States, 1940.

scribed earlier. Insofar as there is any organizational activity which gives to the neighborhood the character of a "social fact," with an identity and uniqueness of its own, it is possible to call Beacon Hill a real community. To the extent that these are absent Beacon Hill is but a nominal community — an aggregate of families who are acting solely upon disparate ends and who have no collective sharing of those ends.[50] We shall endeavor to show that Beacon Hill does indeed approach the pole of real community, though not by any means conforming to the ideal type. It reveals a definite "conceptual *Gestalt*" [51] which is the social counterpart of its integrated value system. Moreover it has an historical theme which, in the very minds of the residents themselves, has a continuity of its own. All of this makes it possible to view Beacon Hill not as just a territorial area which is occupied by a number of families, but as a social system and *un être moral*.[52]

Two types of organizations may be distinguished: the informal, and the formal. The difference between them lies in the fact that a formal organization is staffed by personnel having rights and duties belonging strictly to formalized offices within the organization. These offices have a duration outlasting the tenure of particular incumbents. The rights and duties pertaining to such offices devolve upon a person only in his capacity as an official and do not extend to his non-official activities.[53]

The informal organizations on Beacon Hill center mainly around kinship ties and visiting relationships. Long inbreeding within Boston's upper class has led to a complex network of blood relationships by which each person is related to almost every other person in the class. These kinship ties go far to determine one's choice of a mate, one's occupation,[54] the schools one attends,

[50] The other elements of a community, as analyzed by Zimmerman, are of course present in Beacon Hill, viz., limited area and association. See Zimmerman, *op. cit.*, pp. 15 *et seq.*

[51] *Ibid.*, p. 144.

[52] Pierre Lavedan, *Qu'est-ce que l'Urbanisme?* (Paris: 1926), p. 2.

[53] Talcott Parsons, "The Professions and Social Structure," *Social Forces*, 17: 457–467 (May, 1939).

[54] Consider the expectations which must be imposed upon young men of such families as the Homans' and the Cheevers, who have each had four generations of physicians in their families, the Shattucks, who have had five

the clubs to which one can gain admittance, and many other aspects of one's life. Needless to say these relationships are not confined to Beacon Hill; this neighborhood is but one locale for "proper" families, and kinship ties extend over the whole Boston metropolitan area. Nonetheless Beacon Hill is the home base for a good many of these families and nearly every member of the upper class will have some relative living on the Hill. Visiting relationships not primarily familial in nature are based upon years of friendship, commonly extending back to childhood. In the past years more so than today they were routinized in the form of afternoon teas, neighbor-clubs, and the like. Even today among some of the older people these observances still hold. Somewhat more formal than the kinship and visiting relationships, but still of a functionally diffuse character, are the exclusive clubs. The Somerset Club, the Union Club, the Puritan Club, and the Algonquin Club are Boston's most exclusive "social" clubs and membership in them is confined to men in upper class families. Again, these organizations go beyond the limited area of Beacon Hill, but nonetheless they are foci for Beacon Hill social interaction and they really do manifest that area's organizational activity.

Of a less routine and intimate nature, but nonetheless comprising informal organizational activities are certain annual ceremonies on Beacon Hill. The principal one of these is[55] the annual Christmas eve candle-lighting and caroling ceremony. This old Beacon Hill custom had lapsed during the Civil War and did not reappear until the present century.[56] Individual families had, to be sure, followed the observance of placing candles in their windows for many years but the practice had had no community-wide significance. Then, in 1907 a group of families on Chestnut street, who had been celebrating a Christmas eve party, decided on an impulse to go into the streets, following English custom, and sing some Christmas carols. The venture apparently appealed to

generations of physicians, and the Porters, who have had physicians in their family ever since the seventeenth century. "Boston Proud of its Surgical Hierarchy," *Boston Transcript*, July 24, 1930.

[55] Or was, until 1940, when the custom was suspended for at least the duration of the war.

[56] Shultz, *op. cit.*, p. 16.

many local residents. The next year a typewritten invitation was circulated from door to door requesting families to put lighted candles in their windows on Christmas eve. The idea was again a success and was repeated the next year. On these occasions groups of families, with their guests, would go around the streets of the Hill singing Christmas carols.[57] The ceremony eventually became known over the whole city, and thousands of people would converge upon Beacon Hill every Christmas eve to observe and participate in it. In 1939, for instance, an estimated 75,000 persons participated in the carol singing, and nearly all the dwellings on the Hill displayed lighted candles.[58] This annual ceremony is of genuine communal significance. As Durkheim has pointed out, ritual ceremony has the function of "revivifying" in the minds of individuals the value system ("collective conscience") which gives them their collective identity. In his words:

> Through it the group periodically renews the sentiment which it has of itself and of its unity; at the same time, individuals are strengthened in their social natures.[59]

Evidence of the nearly transcendental reference of the carol-singing ceremony may be had from such statements as the following:

> As the lights begin to twinkle, time and space vanish before enthralling romance. Enchantment and charm go hand in hand. Another world persists, a world without barriers of time or distance. We have left the world behind and are in a realm half real, half touched by fancy and radiantly beautiful.[60]

Another ceremony, which accompanies the annual Christmas eve caroling and candle-lighting custom, is hand bell ringing. This ceremony is confined to two small groups of friends known as the

---

[57] Richard Bowland Kimball, *Christmas Eve on Beacon Hill* (Boston: 1918); Chamberlain, "Beacon Hill Christmas Candles," *Old-Time New England*, 26: 69–73 (October, 1935).

[58] *Back Bay Ledger and Beacon Hill Times,* December 28, 1939.

[59] Emile Durkheim, *The Elementary Forms of the Religious Life* (London: 1915), p. 375.

[60] Shultz, *op. cit.,* p. 16.

Beacon Hill Handbell Ringers, organized by Mrs. Arthur Shurcliff in 1925.[61] Mrs. Shurcliff had inherited several sets of English
bells from her father — a collector of bells and a student of the
highly skilled art of bell ringing. She and a group of her friends
are today recognized over the whole Hill for their practice of this
art during the Christmas eve caroling ceremonies.

One more ceremony, much more secularized than the preceding
ones, is the May Day festival. This was begun by Mrs. Dorothy
Barbour, proprietor of a Chestnut street shop called "The Unusual." The festival was organized "as a means of furthering
good will and neighborliness in the district." [62] For the most part
it is confined to lower Beacon Hill — that portion lying below
Charles street. In 1940 it was used as a means for getting funds
for the new music shell on the Esplanade. On that occasion
schools and colleges on the Hill collaborated in arranging for the
festivities, which included strolling street-singers, dances, flower-
selling, etc.[63]

These examples reveal rather well the character of informal
neighborhood organization on Beacon Hill. On their basis the
residents of the Hill are truly organized into a social system, a real
community. Moreover, the referent of these ceremonies is the
integrated and spatially referred value system centering around
the aesthetic-historical-genealogical complex.

Turning to formal organization we find only one association
which represents the more specialized interests of Beacon Hill
residents as a whole. This is the Beacon Hill Association. Formed
on December 5, 1922, the declared object of this organization is
"to keep undesirable business and living conditions from affecting
the hill district." [64] Its membership is for the most part confined
to property owners on the Hill, and its officers have all been
prominent citizens of the neighborhood. The activities of the Association have had profound implications for land use on the Hill
and will engage us in some detail in the next section of this
chapter.

[61] Chamberlain, "Beacon Hill Christmas Candles," *Old-Time New England,*
26: 69–73 (October, 1935).
[62] *Back Bay Ledger and Beacon Hill Times,* May 2, 1940.
[63] *Back Bay Ledger and Beacon Hill Times,* May 2, 1940.
[64] *Boston Transcript,* December 6, 1922.

In addition to the Beacon Hill Association there is the smaller association of Louisburg Square proprietors, consisting of the owners of property abutting Louisburg Square. This association dates from 1844, when the property owners of the Square decided to enlarge and ornament the oval plot in front of their houses and agreed mutually to bear the necessary expenses. Later the association assumed the task of perpetuating the proprietors' collective legal rights to the Square by prohibiting public trespass. In this way it aimed at preventing the establishment of public rights to the Square through uncontested use.[65] The proprietors employ a caretaker to tend the Square and hold annual meetings for the purpose of electing officers. All purchasers of Louisburg Square property are bound by contract to share in the expenses of upkeep and maintenance. A majority vote of those present at any duly summoned meeting is binding upon all the owners.[66]

These organizations, both formal and informal, make of Beacon Hill something more than an aggregate of disparate families. Through them the neighborhood becomes a real community having an identity of its own. This communal reality is indeed explicit in the minds of the residents themselves. The following quotation reveals this community self-consciousness, and its referability to a value system, rather well. Speaking of the Hill one resident writes:

It has a tradition all its own, that begins in the hospitality of a book-lover, and has never lost that flavor. Yes, our streets are inconvenient, steep and slippery. The corners are abrupt, the contours perverse. . . . It may well be that the gibes of our envious neighbors have a foundation and that these dear crooked lanes of ours were indeed traced in ancestral mud by absent-minded kine.[67]

Another writer observes that:

While the city surges round them, the dwellers on the Hill cling tenaciously to the traditions of a neighborhood and maintain them with an earnestness unmatched in most communities. They have their own

[65] Chamberlain, *Beacon Hill, its Ancient Pastures and Early Mansions*, pp. 191–200.
[66] *Ibid.*, p. 193.
[67] Abbie Farwell Brown, *The Lights of Beacon Hill*, p. 4.

pleasant manners and customs, their neighbor-parties and neighbor-clubs.[68]

As a real community Beacon Hill is a spatially adaptive unit in its own right. The resulting locational processes are referable directly to it and not primarily to lesser social systems—families, enterprises, etc.

At this point it will be well to recapitulate the findings thus far made and to relate them very briefly to the theoretical problem of this chapter. Four main conclusions follow from the data thus far submitted: (1) There are definite spatially referred values on Beacon Hill. By virtue of these values the territory embraced within the Hill has a symbolic quality which is in no way given in its physical nature. Space, thus, can have more than an impedi-tive, cost-imposing relation to social activities. (2) These spatially referred values are truly rooted into the motivation of individual families living on Beacon Hill. Such families, viewed as social systems, are thus acting upon something more than the ends which constitute them as disparate systems. Their spatial adaptation is therefore not wholly economizing in character, since the ends upon which they act have their being in a broader cultural system and are therefore immune from "fiscal" budgeting. (3) The ends which make up this cultural system are not randomly related to one another but are meaningfully integrated. Hence the locational activities of the social systems acting upon those ends are not at all "biotic" or sub-cultural; rather they manifest a volitional, non-deterministic factor in spatial adaptation. (4) The various social systems seeking location on Beacon Hill are not wholly independent beings whose sole relationship to one another is the competitive one of bargaining for a limited supply of space. Instead, they are organized into a larger solidary *social* system which expresses a *cultural* system of spatially referred values.

Locational Effects of Spatially Referred Values. If these conclusions have been adequately demonstrated, as we think they have, it follows that the two basic premises of empirically rationalistic ecology, and some of the deductions made from them, are factually wrong. They are wrong because they have omitted an

[68] T. R. Sullivan, *Boston New and Old* (Boston: 1912), p. 86.

important variable in spatial adaptation, viz., the element of values. However, the most important question, practically speaking, remains unanswered: have these values any influence upon land use? If they have not, the empirically rationalistic theories, however ill founded in their premises, could at least claim a pragmatic validity. In that respect they might pretend to some justification for omitting from their conceptual scheme the cultural component.

This problem may be approached directly. It is possible to distinguish three modes of influence exerted upon locational processes by the values articulated in Beacon Hill. These are the retentive, recuperative, and resistive influences. Such a classification is for the purely heuristic purpose of arranging materials and is not intended to have any theoretical significance.

It will be simplest to begin with the retentive influence. Here the main fact which presents itself is the capacity of Beacon Hill to retain its fashionable reputation and a large share of Boston's upper class families for one and a half centuries, while other fashionable areas have risen to favor and then declined. Beacon Hill was well established as a preferred residential neighborhood by 1805. Today it still has the same preferred character. In the meantime fully six other areas in Boston have been developed as fashionable neighborhoods, have enjoyed favor for a while, and have then declined. Fort Hill, which rose to popularity almost contemporaneously with Beacon Hill, had become a slum by 1855. Pemberton square, developed slightly after Beacon Hill, was converted to public and business uses by the Civil War. Temple Place, Colonnade Row, and the Summer-Winter street area, once comprising the largest fashionable district in point of numbers, lasted little more than a generation. The South End's fashionable reputation was of even shorter duration, extending approximately from 1850 to 1865. The Back Bay and Jamaica Plain present a slightly different situation. Both of these neighborhoods retain even today some of their fashionable character. Their prestige is waning rapidly however. The Back Bay in particular, though still surpassing in numbers any other single neighborhood, has undergone a steady invasion of apartment buildings, rooming houses, and business establishments which are destroying its aristocratic character. Jamaica Plain, on the other hand, has undergone what might be called a succession of elites. While the old stock Yankee elite have been gradually deserting the neighborhood, the "lace curtain" Irish, consisting of professionals, building contractors, public officials, and the like, have been replacing them. It is not quite accurate, then, to compare Jamaica Plain's decline with that of the other districts since in all strictness there has been only a change in fashionable occupancy. The fact remains, however, that through all these successions of land use only one neighborhood, namely, Beacon Hill, has consistently retained the kind of land use with which it originally began. In the meantime the city of Boston has grown entirely around it, a slum directly abuts it to the north, and business has threatened two of its sides. Here is presumptive evidence, at least, that Beacon Hill owes its survival as an upper class neighborhood to some factor which is unique to it — a factor absent in the other neighborhoods. Tentatively we have identified this factor as consisting of certain spatially referred values.

It is possible to show in quantitative terms the real extent of the retentive influence exerted by these spatially referred values. For this purpose we may have recourse to our tabulations, by place of residence, of all the families listed in the Boston *Social Register* for the years 1894, 1905, 1914, 1929, and 1943. In Table 4 we have presented tabulations for the upper class population living within Boston by districts of concentration, and for that living in the suburbs. Figure 10 portrays these trends in graphic form.

TABLE 4

NUMBER OF UPPER CLASS FAMILIES IN BOSTON, BY DISTRICTS OF CONCENTRATION, FOR CERTAIN YEARS

	1894	1905	1914	1929	1943
Within Boston					
Beacon Hill	280	242	279	362	335
Back Bay	867	1166	1102	880	556
Jamaica Plain	56	66	64	36	30
Other districts	316	161	114	86	41
Total in Boston	1519	1635	1559	1364	962
Total in Suburbs	403	807	1049	1345	1993
Totals	1922	2442	2608	2709	2955

Tabulated from *Social Register, Boston.*

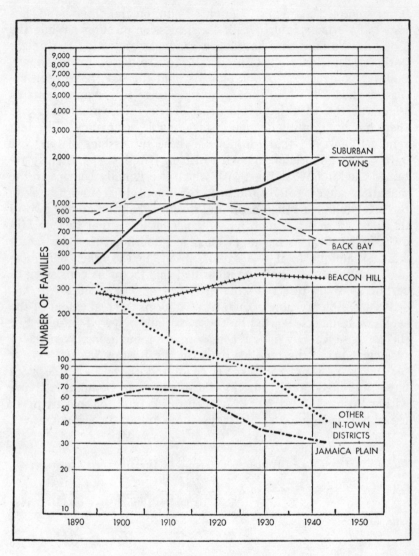

FIGURE 10. NUMBER OF UPPER CLASS FAMILIES IN BOSTON, BY
AREAS OF CONCENTRATION, AND IN SUBURBS, FOR CERTAIN YEARS

The most apparent feature of these data is, of course, the consistent increase of upper class families in the suburban towns and the marked decrease (since 1905) of those living within Boston. This outward movement is a trend that has already been analyzed and it need not engage us further at this point. What is striking about the data is the relative stability of Beacon Hill. It is the only in-town upper class neighborhood that today has more upper class families than it had in 1894. Its relative position among in-town neighborhoods is higher today than it was half a century ago. Moreover, from 1905 to 1929, while other in-town areas were losing upper class families Beacon Hill actually gained some, and at a rate nearly equal to that of the suburbs. Since 1929 Beacon Hill has undergone a slight decline, but this decline is nowhere near so precipitous as that of the other in-town neighborhoods.

A satisfying explanation of these differentials is not afforded by the empirically rationalistic theories. The causal factors which they posit have no consistent, uniform connection with the given locational processes. The fact of altitude, considered as a cost-imposing impediment, is associated not only with Beacon Hill's retentive capacity but also with Fort Hill's and Copps' Hill's decline. Obviously it cannot be considered an adequate cause. Spatial proximity to the city center, likewise viewed as an impeditive factor, is true not only of Beacon Hill but also of the South End and the Back Bay. It too is not consistently correlated with a given effect. Whatever causal factor is selected as the one adequate to explain the retentive capacity of Beacon Hill must be a variable to which the retentive capacity is *uniquely* connected, and whose absence is accompanied by the lack of retentive capacity. Such a factor seems to be found in the values which are symbolized by Beacon Hill.

Complications begin to arise, however, upon a closer inspection of the curve for Beacon Hill in figure 10. There it will be noted that between 1894 and 1905 Beacon Hill lost thirty-eight of its upper class families. At the same time Back Bay and Jamaica Plain — the other in-town neighborhoods devoted to fashionable occupancy — showed increases in their upper class populations. If, as we have argued, spatially referred values are the main causal factor in Beacon Hill's land use history this variation from

later locational trends calls for some explanation. To sustain our
hypothesis it becomes necessary to show that during Beacon Hill's
recession there was an atrophy in the intensity of the values pertaining to the Hill, or at least that the Back Bay and Jamaica
Plain gained in relative prestige value. Fortunately there is fairly
good source material that bears upon this problem and further
clarifies the ecological significance of values.

The facts show that the development of the Back Bay lands
put Beacon Hill into a relative disfavor. The magnificence and
sumptuousness of the new Back Bay, with its straight wide avenues and its green parkways appealed to many upper class families and drew some of them away from their ancestral homes on
Beacon Hill.[69] Somewhere between 1875 and 1880 the emigration
of upper class families from Beacon Hill set in. As this exodus
progressed the usual harbinger of residential deterioration appeared, viz., the rooming house. Such streets as Revere, Myrtle,
and Pinckney became largely rooming house streets occupied by a
transient population. The blight even extended as far down the
Hill as Chestnut and Beacon streets.[70] Not only rooming houses,
but stores and clubs as well began to invade the neighborhood.
This incursion of business was most pronounced on Beacon street,
where the first floors of a number of dwellings were converted
into shops.[71] A quasi-fictional writer of the time makes reference
to: ". . . the one block of Beacon Street on the hill where certain
families honourably continue their ancestral line, though hemmed
in disagreeably by tailor shops and a club house." [72] Several large
apartment houses were also erected, replacing the old colonial
homes for which the Hill had become famous.[73] A number of
private boys' and girls' schools preëmpted other old dwellings.[74]
Property values, reflecting the decline in prestige value of the
Hill, dropped steadily. Thus, dwelling number 13, on Louisburg

[69] Chamberlain, *Beacon Hill, its Ancient Pastures and Early Mansions,*
p. 47.
[70] Albert Benedict Wolfe, *The Lodging House Problem in Boston* (Cambridge: 1913), p. 24.
[71] Sullivan, *op. cit.,* pp. 75–77.
[72] Farquhar, *op. cit.,* p. 108.
[73] See the *Boston Transcript,* December 13, 1902.
[74] Greene, *op. cit.,* pp. 27–29.

Square, underwent the following changes in assessed valuation:

$$1840-\$12,000$$
$$1860-\ 18,000$$
$$1880-\ 14,500^{75}$$

Variations of this magnitude can hardly be ascribed to intrinsic property depreciation, especially considering the soundness of construction of most structures on Beacon Hill. The result of all these heterogeneous incursions was that "most of the fine old houses, some of them dating from Colonial days, were elbowed by dirty and unsanitary shacks." [76] In a very real sense Beacon Hill was losing its symbolic significance. What is important about this loss is its purely subjective character. Nothing intrinsic to the Hill or its physical aspect had altered. People merely lost some of their affective attachment to it. Durkheim's point in regard to sacred objects applies with equal force to Beacon Hill:

> Sacred beings exist only when they are represented as such in the mind. When we cease to believe in them, it is as though they did not exist. Even those which have a material form and are given by sensible experience depend upon the thought of the worshippers who adore them; for the sacred character which makes them objects of the cult is not given by their natural constitution; it is added to them by belief.[77]

Nonetheless a number of upper class families clung to the Hill. Even in 1905, when the Hill had reached its lowest ebb, there were 242 *Social Registerites* maintaining residence in the neighborhood. In that very year a noted architect, Frank A. Bourne by name, moved from his Back Bay home to a deteriorated one-time colonial dwelling on Mount Vernon street. Bourne was a close friend of the Codmans and certain other families who had remained on the Hill and who had been seeking for some years to effect its revival. After purchasing the property Bourne made extensive renovations in it, leaving the colonial exterior intact but improving the interior in accordance with more modern living re-

---

[75] Direct source mislaid. Original data available from tax assessors' lists.
[76] "The Regeneration of Beacon Hill: How Boston Goes About Civic Improvement," *The Craftsman*, 16: 92–95 (April, 1909), p. 92.
[77] Durkheim, *op. cit.*, p. 345.

quirements. In this way was begun the regeneration of Beacon
Hill as a preferred residential district. The details of this regeneration are illustrative of the recuperative influence that spatially
referred sentiments may exert upon land use. It will be well
therefore to analyze it in a little detail.

Throughout the period of Beacon Hill's slump Mr. William
Coombs Codman, whose family had lived on the Hill for several
generations, had made repeated attempts to stimulate a revival.
Early in the present century he purchased two houses, made improvements in them, and sold them at a small profit. It was
shortly afterwards that Mr. Bourne, the architect, moved to the
Hill and renovated an old dilapidated house. Codman thereupon
intensified his efforts, interesting his friends and business ac-
quaintances in purchasing and improving properties for their own
use as well as for sale. The revival was not a typical real estate
boom, for it lacked the extensive publicity and speculation which
typically accompanies such ventures. Rather it represented the
efforts of a few friends and real estate men working on one property at a time — buying, improving, and selling or occupying for
personal use. Always the improvements left intact the colonial
exteriors of the buildings.[78] Occasionally neighbors would get together to plan jointly their adjoining properties, thus achieving an
architectural consonance.[79] The nature of the Hill's appeal, and
the kind of persons attracted, may be gathered from the following
popular write-up:

To salvage the quaint charm of Colonial Architecture on Beacon
Hill, Boston, is the object of a well-defined movement among writers
and professional folk that promises the most delightful opportunities for
the home seeker of moderate means and conservative tastes. Because
men of discernment were able to visualize the possibilities presented
by these architectural landmarks, and have undertaken the gracious
task of restoring them to their former glory, this historic quarter of old
Boston, once the centre of literary culture, is coming into its own.[80]

[78] *The Beacon Hill District: Similar to the Washington Square Greenwich
Village Section;* no author, publisher, or publication date indicated. Pamphlet
available in the Landscape Architecture Library, Harvard University.
[79] "The Regeneration of Beacon Hill: How Boston Goes About Civic Improvement," *The Craftsman,* 16: 92–95 (April, 1909), p. 92.
[80] Gillespie, *op. cit.*

So intense was the revival that it extended across Charles street, down to the river — an area that had previously been inhabited by the servants and attendants of Hill residents — and also across the summit and down the north slope. Below Charles street the tenements, stables, and workshops were gradually displaced by homes, antique shops, and apartment buildings. Over the summit, and down the north slope, a number of families in quest of a quasi-bohemian life with a touch of "culture" located in privately developed colonies. Thus Primus avenue, extending off Phillips street, formerly a dirty obscure alley notorious for its vice, crime, and frequent police raids, was reconstructed and terraced by Mr. Elliott Henderson. It was designed for "tenants who appreciate something out of the ordinary." [81] Champny place, lying off Anderson street, was another such development. In addition to these collective projects a number of individuals, particularly artists and actors, bought up what were known as "rat houses"; typically they abutted squalid tenements and were in dilapidated condition. Here the inhabitants could enjoy the "cultural atmosphere" of Beacon Hill as well as the *demi-monde* bohemian flavor of the north slope. Little drama colonies, exclusive clubs, radical political groups, and exotic tea rooms appeared all over the Hill.[82] In the words of one resident: "The Hill is swarming with youthful dreamers. Young Poetry, Art, and Music are 'at home' here tonight, or wandering bright-eyed with the singers." [83] Between these "cultural" groups and the literary and artistic traditions so long associated with Beacon Hill there is a very real meaningful affinity, so that this influx of intelligentsia may quite properly be considered as a locational consequence of the values articulated in Beacon Hill.

However, the older aristocratic families did not look upon this exotic development with unqualified approval. One real estate woman in business on the Hill wrote the following letter to the editor of a Boston newspaper:

. . . Beacon Hill has acquired a reputation for "atmosphere" and quaintness in its quiet old-world streets which attracts those who are

[81] Elmer F. Murch, "A Reclaimed Beacon Hill—Primus Avenue, et al.," *Boston Transcript*, August 21, 1926.

[82] Beebe, *op. cit.*, pp. 303–305, and chap. xxix; Kimball, *op. cit.*

[83] Abbie Farwell Brown, *The Lights of Beacon Hill* (Boston: 1922), p. 11.

seeking for cozy, artistic, and unusual surroundings, but Beacon Hill
is not and never can be temperamental, and those seeking to find or
create there a second Greenwich Village will meet with obstacles in the
shape of an old residence aristocracy whose ancestors have had their
entries and exits through those charming old doorways for generations.
More and more, as the world of progress and change has surged about
and beat upon the bulwarks of the hill, have those who dwell there
drawn together for self-defence. Here as nowhere else in Boston has
the community spirit developed, which opens itself to the best in the
new, while fostering with determination all that is fine and worth keeping in the old.[84]

On the whole the revival did consist primarily of a return of conservative upper class families to the Hill. As the data in Table 4
and figure 10 indicate, there was a gain of fully 120 *Social Register* families on Beacon Hill between 1905 and 1929. The return
of these predominantly well-to-do people, and the physical renovation of many of the old dwellings, led to an increase in assessed
property values. Viewed as a whole assessed valuations on Beacon Hill increased by 24 per cent from 1919 to 1924 and by another 25 per cent from 1924 to 1929.[85] Assessed valuations for a
sample site, number 13 Louisburg Square, show the following
trend:

$$1901-\$14,800$$
$$1920-\ 24,000$$
$$1931-\ 34,000^{86}$$

To be sure, a great deal of caution must be used in interpreting
these assessment data. Owing to stringency in municipal finances
the assessment rates of Boston, particularly those in the central
portions of the city, have for some time been far in excess of
actual market valuations. Undoubtedly a large part of the increase shown in the above data reflects this artificial inflation of
property values by the assessors. However, this is not so true of
the data for 1920 and earlier, so that much of the rise between

[84] Elizabeth W. Schermerhorn, letter to editor, *Boston Herald,* September
16, 1923.
[85] *Boston Transcript,* April 12, 1930.
[86] *Assessed Values of Real Estate in Boston,* issued in 1901 by Real Estate
Publishing Co.; issued in 1920 and 1931 by the Boston Real Estate Exchange
(Boston, 1901, 1920, 1931).

1901 and 1920 can with reasonable assurance be ascribed to the enhanced value attending the fashionable revival and structural renovation on Beacon Hill. In any case we need not rest our case too heavily upon this line of evidence; it is only supplementary to our historical and *Social Register* material.

Not only did the class structure remain essentially unchanged after the Hill's revival, despite the influx of young artists and "intellectuals," but the territorial locus of the upper class continued to be primarily on the south slope. The extension across Charles street was the only wholly new addition to the old-time bounds of "proper" Beacon Hill. The little colonies and novel "rat houses" on the north slope did not attract many upper class families and only a few are listed in the *Social Register* as living there today. Apparently the room layouts and construction standards of the cheap tenements on the north slope were such as to obstruct any large scale upper class invasion of that area.[87] Today, as before, the streets nearest the Common denote the greatest status: Beacon street, described by Oliver Wendell Holmes as "the sunny street that holds the sifted few," enjoys the greatest prestige; Chestnut street has the wealthiest families and was able to maintain its exclusive character during the 1880–1905 recession somewhat better than the other streets; Mount Vernon street, though it has a high proportion of old families, is more impoverished and is not "kept up" so well. Pinckney street presents all extremes, ranging from Italian and Jewish tenements to the homes of old Yankee families. Figure 11a portrays the distribution, by blocks, of mean monthly rentals on Beacon Hill, as of 1940, and figure 11b the addresses of *Social Register* families on the Hill as of 1943. The rental data is obtained from census materials[88] and the spot map from our own tabulations of *Social Register* addresses. Even a cursory inspection will reveal the high correlation which exists between the density of upper class families on the Hill and the mean monthly rentals. It seems

[87] See J. Ross McKeever, "The Beacon Hill District," (MS.), Master's thesis on deposit at the Massachusetts Institute of Technology Library of Architecture (Cambridge: 1935), pp. 26–27.

[88] Table 3, *Housing; Supplement to the First Series, Housing Bulletin for Massachusetts; Boston; Block Statistics*, Sixteenth Census of the United States, 1940.

reasonable, then, to attribute the enhanced values of Beacon Hill
following its recuperation, not to the exotic, quasi-bohemian colonies near the summit and down the north slope, but rather to the
"solid," well-to-do upper class families in whom are borne the
values which the Hill symbolizes.

At this point a critical question arises. On what basis can we
say that it is really the upper class which most fully bears the
spatially referred values stressed throughout this analysis? We
have, of course, already pointed out that nearly all the written
expressions of such sentiments have been issued by upper class
persons and we may therefore infer with some justification that it

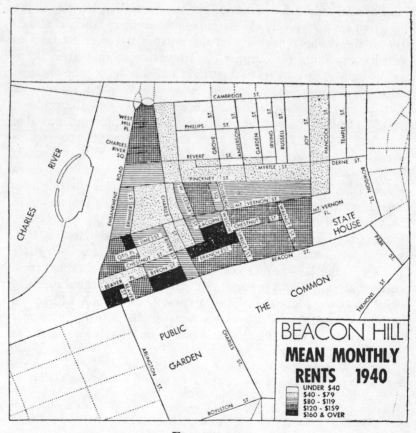

FIGURE 11a

is in such persons that the spatially referred values are found. But there is another line of evidence by which the assumption may be tested. The evidence consists of the relative rates of population turnover on Beacon Hill as between upper class persons and "non-upper class" persons. If it can be shown that upper class persons have a lower rate of turnover than the remainder of the population there is reason to believe that those are the persons who are the bearers of the values symbolized by Beacon Hill. To be sure, it is not a certain proof, since alternative explanations for such a differential turnover might be adduced. To the extent, however, that it fits in with other lines of evidence it can be used as evidence for our hypothesis. The procedure consisted, first, of

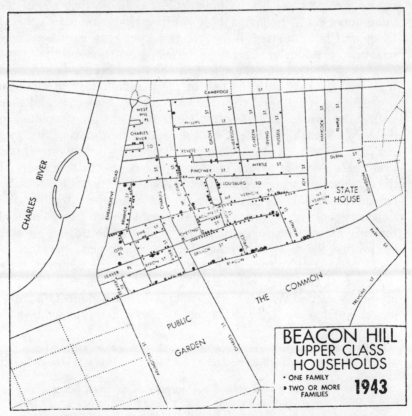

FIGURE 11b

selecting a sample street on Beacon Hill, viz., Chestnut street, and copying down from the Boston *Police Lists*[89] for 1943 the names of all persons twenty years of age and over living on that street. A total of 530 names was thus procured. Each of these names was then checked with the *Social Register* for the same year to ascertain which could be considered upper class persons. Of the 530 persons on Chestnut street 113 were found listed in the *Social Register*.[90] The next step consisted of taking the *Police Lists* for the previous year, 1942, and checking those names copied from the 1943 lists which were found also in the 1942 lists. It was discovered that 100 of the 113 upper class families living on Chestnut street in 1943 had been there (at same addresses) one year before, i.e., 88.5 per cent. Similarly it was found that 260 of the "non-upper class" persons (those not listed in the *Social Register*) living on Chestnut street in 1943, or 62.3 per cent, had been there one year previously. Clearly a larger proportion of the upper class persons living on the street in 1943 had been there in 1942 than was the case with the rest of the population. The identical procedure was followed with the *Police Lists* for 1937, and then with those for 1932. The complete tabulations are presented in Table 5. From this table it can be seen that whereas fully 37.2 per cent of the 1943 upper class population on Chestnut street had been there 11 years before, only 10.6 per cent of the remainder of the population had been there then. The reader may be struck by the unaccountably large turnover in the non-upper class population between 1937 and 1942. No sure explanation can be offered for this except the suggestion that perhaps the advent of war diminished the rate of turnover for non-upper class persons between 1942 and 1943 and that consequently the figure of 62.3 per cent of the 1943 population having been there in 1942 is atypically large. Whatever the explanation the immediate problem at hand seems adequately met by the differentials shown in

[89] The *Police Lists* include the names of all persons 20 years of age and over. Full title: City of Boston, *List of Residents 20 Years of Age and Over as of January 1, 1943.*

[90] It should be noted that this is the number of *persons*, not of *families*. Hence the discrepancy between this figure and the number of dots on Chestnut street as indicated in figure 11b, which portrays the number of *families* listed in the *Social Register*.

TABLE 5

DIFFERENTIAL POPULATION TURNOVER ON CHESTNUT STREET BETWEEN
UPPER CLASS AND NON-UPPER CLASS PERSONS, FOR CERTAIN YEARS

	Number of Persons, 1-1-43	Number of Persons, 1-1-42	Number of Persons, 1-1-37	Number of Persons, 1-1-32
Upper Class				
Number.................	113	100	61	42
Per Cent................	100.00	88.5	54.0	37.2
Non-Upper Class				
Number.................	417	260	80	44
Per Cent................	100.00	62.3	19.2	10.6

Computed on basis of tabulations from *Social Register, Boston,* and *Police Lists.*

the table. There can be little doubt that persons listed in the
Social Register constitute what Sorokin has called the "center of
gravity" for the values which Beacon Hill symbolizes. If these
data are recombined so as to bring out the percentage which the
present upper class population bears to the total population, by
years, the point becomes even more evident. As Table 6 indicates,
the proportion which the 1943 upper class population bears to the

TABLE 6

PROPORTION BORNE BY THE 1943 UPPER CLASS POPULATION ON CHESTNUT STREET
TO THE TOTAL POPULATION OF CERTAIN PRECEDING YEARS

	1943	1942	1937	1932
Total Numbers of the 1943 Population at Same Address in Previous Years.........	530	360	141	86
Percentage of Total Numbers of the 1943 Population Comprised by Upper Class...	21.3	27.8	43.3	48.8

Computed on basis of tabulations from *Social Register, Boston,* and *Police Lists.*

total population of the preceding years becomes progressively
greater. In other words, the upper class represents the constant
element of the Chestnut street population — the least varying
segment of the population. These findings seem to justify our
supposition that the upper class population is the one which most
fully shares in the spatially referred values on Beacon Hill and is
therefore the most inclined to live in the neighborhood. For this
reason it seems clear that the recuperative capacity of Beacon

Hill resides in the upper class population rather than in the bohemian artists, actors, and pseudo-intelligentsia seeking novelty
and "atmosphere."

There is a third kind of influence which spatially referred
values may exert upon land use and which is well illustrated by
Beacon Hill. This is the resistive influence. Now and then an
area having sentimental significance to certain persons and groups
will be threatened by rival social systems. In many cases this
threat induces the residents to rouse themselves and resist the
imminent invasion. Sometimes the result is to prevent more economic land uses from occupying territory that is best suited to
them. Consequently land that might yield a greater profit if
opened up to these other uses is put to a "dis-economic" use. Such
an outcome remains a mystery if we look to the empirically rationalistic theories. For it means that land has actually remained
in a symbolic use when it might have been put to a more profitable
use. It means too that social systems have chosen locations, not
to minimize cost, but to satisfy certain sentiments. So far as the
rationalistic theory is concerned then, the two premises regarding
the strictly costful character of space and the purely economic
orientation of social systems would not tally with actual locational
processes. It is important therefore to discover just how social
systems, acting in response to sentiments, will resist the incursions
of other social systems that are incompatible with their values.

Very shortly after the fashionable revival of Beacon Hill a
number of residents and antiquarian groups expressed concern
over the destruction or reconversion of some of the dwellings.
There developed an increased interest in maintaining the typical
colonial appearance of the Hill as a whole. Thus when it became
known that a certain Beacon street house had been offered for
sale some concern was expressed by a Boston antiquarian journal
as to the possible fate of the property. In an article dealing with
the matter the editor wrote as follows:

This is an event of more than usual importance, for on the fate of
this house may depend the future character of Beacon street on the
hill. . . . While it is quite possible that someone may wish to buy
this estate for a home, it seems to us more likely that it will be bought
for apartment house purposes, implying the demolition of the present

building or its destruction through ruinous remodelling. . . . Such a calamity, for it would be nothing less, is not to be thought of for a moment. The problem is how to prevent it.[91]

Another instance of the growing concern over possible threats to the Hill was the fracas over the repaving of Mount Vernon street with brick. The residents of that street registered their vigorous objections to any such plan, contending that brick paving would present an appearance incongruous to the street's colonial architecture and would impair its distinctive appearance.[92]

These and other threats to the integrity of the Hill finally led residents of the neighborhood to organize the Beacon Hill Association, on December 5, 1922. This organization was at first headed by Frank A. Bourne, William C. Codman, Allan Forbes, Romney Spring, Marian C. Nichols, and Grace Minns — persons all prominent in the Hill's revival some years earlier.[93] At the time of the Association's organization the city of Boston was preparing a new and comprehensive zoning program and the time was propitious for Beacon Hill residents to have their plans for the Hill embodied in the final zoning law. A list of recommendations concerning height limits (to restrict apartment houses and thus protect old residences), and the confinement of business to certain specified streets, was submitted to the City Planning Board in 1923. Only a few of these recommendations were embodied in the zoning ordinance of 1924. So there ensued a ten-year battle on the part of the Beacon Hill Association to have the zoning areas revised in accordance with its recommendations. Its object was to ensure the Hill as a restricted residential district, free from undesirable businesses and apartment houses.[94]

The first endeavor of the Association was to have Phillips street, on the north slope, rezoned from local business uses back to residential uses. The hearing was held on February 13, 1925 and a decision in favor of the Association was passed.[95] In 1927

[91] "The Parker-Inches-Emery House, 40 Beacon Street, Boston," *Bulletin of the Society for the Preservation of New England Antiquities,* 4: 2–11 (August, 1913), pp. 2–3.
[92] *Boston Transcript,* October 27, 1920.
[93] *Boston Transcript,* December 6, 1922.
[94] *Boston Globe,* April 27, 1923.
[95] From records of the Building Department, City of Boston.

the first major challenge to Beacon Hill appeared in the form of a petition filed by a building organization with the Board of Zoning Adjustment to have the height limits in a specified portion of the Hill raised from 65 feet to 155 feet. This was to permit the construction of a four million dollar apartment hotel. Proponents of the venture pointed out that erection of the building would stimulate the construction of additional such apartment hotels, all of which would enhance property values and be a source of gain to Beacon Hill property owners. Building Commissioner L. K. Rourke announced that he knew of an additional twenty million dollars worth of apartment hotels which would locate on Beacon street and vicinity if the zoning law were altered in accordance with the petition.[96] The Beacon Hill Association was roused to action. Immediately it organized a zoning defense committee which circularized the neighborhood to protest the project. At the hearings on January 7 some 500 persons, mostly women, were present to decry the petition.[97] The Association took the position that "if this increase in height were permitted, it would completely destroy the consistent character of the Beacon Hill district. . . ."[98] Subsequent deliberations were held and a final decision was rendered in favor of the Association.[99] Sentiment had prevailed over economic advantage. The case sheds some doubt upon the validity of Wirth's generalization that:

> The more fundamental of these (ecological) factors is probably that of economic values, for the sentiments of the people tend ultimately to bow before this criterion which is the expression of the competitive process.[100]

In 1930 the Association, continuing its campaign to secure for Beacon Hill more immunity against apartment hotel construction, petitioned for a reduction of the height limits on Beacon street, from the State House to Charles street, and on part of Joy street,

[96] Murch, "Four-Million-Dollar Apartment House Awaits Zoning Decision," *Boston Transcript*, January 29, 1927.

[97] *Boston Transcript*, January 7, 1927.

[98] Zoning Defense Committee, Beacon Hill Association, "The Menace to Beacon Hill" (leaflet, 1927).

[99] *Boston Transcript*, March 18, 1933.

[100] Louis Wirth, *The Ghetto* (Chicago: 1928), p. 285.

from 80 feet to 65 feet.[101] Circulars were sent out, and the indispensable support of the Briggses, who owned important business property on the corner of Beacon and Charles streets, was obtained. At the hearings considerable opposition was encountered by the Association. Romney Spring, president of the Association, was criticized as being "a rank sentimentalist who desired to keep Boston a village." [102] However the petition was granted and the height limits were reduced to 65 feet on the streets in question.[103] This brought nearly the whole Hill under the 65-foot limit and assured a uniform architectural appearance to the neighborhood.

But the very next year a petition was brought by William P. Homans and Elliott Henderson to alter the zoning restrictions on Beacon street, from the State House to Charles street, so as to permit the location there of "high-grade stores." The Association again organized an opposition, 34 persons wrote letters of protest, and President Romney Spring declared that acceptance of the petition would mean invasion of the Hill by cheap stores and gaudy signs. The petitioners argued that wealthy persons were gradually leaving their single-family dwellings and were moving into near-by apartments and hotels, hence permission should be granted for businesses of a high grade to locate in the vicinity. At the hearings some 36 persons opposed the petition and only 5 favored it. The Board of Zoning Adjustment rejected it unanimously and the threat of business encroachment on the Hill was again removed.[104] It is quite evident in this case that an economically superior land use was defeated by an economically inferior one. Certainly the high-grade stores and specialty shops that sought in vain to locate on the Hill would have represented a fuller capitalization on potential property values than do residences. In all likelihood the attending increase in real estate prices would not only have benefited individual property holders but would have so enhanced the value of adjoining properties as to compensate for whatever depreciation other portions of the Hill might have suffered. The dynamic force behind this resistance to an economically superior land use lies wholly outside the

[101] *Boston Post*, April 6, 1930.
[102] *Boston Transcript*, April 12, 1930.
[103] *Boston Transcript*, May 16, 1930.
[104] *Boston Transcript*, January 10, 1931 and January 29, 1931.

scope of rationalistic ecology. It consists of a non-rational orientation to space, one that reflects the values which Beacon Hill symbolizes. Failure to include such a variable in the theoretical system of social ecology removes from our understanding an important locational process.

In 1933 the Beacon Hill Association undertook a campaign to reduce height limits on the one portion of the Hill which was not yet under the 65-foot limit, viz., that segment of Beacon street which extends from Charles street to Embankment road. A petition with 300 signatures was submitted to the Board of Zoning Adjustment and, after some opposition in which the residents of the Hill were characterized as "staid Victorian sentimentalists," [105] the petition was accepted.[106] Later activities of the Association have been on a smaller scale, having to do with such matters as subduing rowdyism at the Christmas Eve caroling ceremony, protesting exorbitant assessed valuations, etc.

All of these examples illustrate the power of spatially referred values to resist social systems which might violate the symbolic quality of an area. Nor is it necessary to restrict ourselves to Beacon Hill. Abundant evidence of similar locational processes can be found in such cities as Philadelphia, New Orleans, Baltimore, and even in such newer cities as Chicago, Detroit, and others whose land use history has lain wholly within a highly commercialistic era. In the older portions of Philadelphia, for instance, there are a good many islands of fashionable residential areas, consisting of short streets leading off from business thoroughfares or from tenement and apartment house districts. Delancey street, between 18th and 21st streets, is occupied by some of the most respectable upper class families in the city, yet it is but four blocks from Market street, a physically deteriorated district of second-rate stores. Between Delancey street and Market street is a mixed tenement and apartment house area. Despite the proximity of such radically different land uses the residents of Delancey street, commonly known as "the cave dwellers," stubbornly resist alien incursions and have preferred to allow single family residences to remain vacant and boarded up rather than permit their conversion to apartment house purposes. A

[105] Arthur W. Stevens, quoted in the *Boston Transcript,* April 8, 1933.
[106] *Boston Transcript,* April 7, April 8, and April 20, 1933.

recent ecological study of New Orleans has described the persist-ence of the French Quarter and other spatial patterns there in the face of competing land uses.[107] Further studies of this sort should clarify even further the resistive capacity of spatially referred values in urban spatial dynamics.

There are, then, three demonstrable kinds of influence which values may exert upon land use: the retentive, the recuperative, and the resistive. In the case of Beacon Hill it is the symbolic quality of the area, not its impeditive or cost-imposing character, that most clearly accounts for these trends. And it is the dynamic force of spatially referred values, rather than considerations of economy, which explains why certain upper class families prefer to live on Beacon Hill rather than in the suburbs or in other in-town districts. From these tested findings we may conclude that values are indeed self-sufficient ecological forces and that they have a very real causative influence upon land use. Far from being mere epiphenomena to some more basic determinism, values may be formulated as an independent variable in ecological theory. Omission of this variable renders any ecological theory both logically and empirically inadequate. Nor is it quite enough to concede the existence of an "arbitrary control which custom and consensus imposes upon the natural social order," [108] or of "historical inertia," [109] and "cultural biases" [110] in land use. Such expressions imply a certain fortuity and unnaturalness about the causativeness of social values. Only when values are posited as an autonomous and independently causative variable can loca-tional processes such as we have described be fully understood.

There remains one further land use trend on Beacon Hill which must be briefly considered. As the curve in figure 10 reveals there are 27 fewer upper class families residing on Beacon Hill in 1943 than there were in 1929. Such a drop, while not large, demands some explanation. All the evidence points to two factors as being

[107] H. W. Gilmore, "The Old New Orleans and the New: a Case for Ecology," *American Sociological Review*, 9: 385–394 (August, 1944).

[108] Robert E. Park, "Human Ecology," *American Journal of Sociology*, 42: 1–15 (July, 1936), p. 13.

[109] James A. Quinn, "The Burgess Zonal Hypothesis and its Critics," *American Sociological Review*, 5: 210–218 (April, 1940), p. 216.

[110] Quinn, "The Hypothesis of Median Location," *American Sociological Review*, 8: 148–156 (April, 1943), p. 156.

responsible for this decline: first, the depression following 1929 seriously reduced the incomes of many residents, particularly those of elderly women whose sustenance so largely depended upon securities; second, the over-assessment of property on Beacon Hill has become so exorbitant that residence in the neighborhood is disproportionately expensive relative to the satisfaction of living there.[111] The combination of these factors, balanced against the motives, both volitional and rational, which prompt people to live in the neighborhood, has apparently been strong enough to induce some families to move elsewhere. Actually the significant fact is not that Beacon Hill has undergone a slight decline since 1929 but rather that, in the face of such powerful economic deterrents to living there, it has so nearly held its own. In contrast with Beacon Hill the other in-town upper class districts show precipitous rates of decline.

One adjustment to the increasing costs of living on Beacon Hill has been the movement away from single family dwellings to small apartment houses — generally old dwellings reconverted for the purpose. This is especially characteristic of the older women. By living in a comfortable apartment, with all the distinction and satisfaction of living on the Hill but free from the expense of a large household with maids, butlers, and other appurtenances, an elderly upper class woman can easily reconcile her sentiments with her budget.

As a result of this drift to apartment houses there exists a distinct bimodal distribution of families by type of dwelling. Table 7 shows this distribution rather well. It shows that the largest number of families falls in the single family attached type of dwelling and in the 5–19 family apartment type of dwelling.[112] In short, one might say that there are two kinds of residents on Beacon Hill: those who live in single family dwellings, and those who live in apartment houses with 5–19 families; there are few who fall in between these two poles. What effect these trends

[111] In 67 sales of Beacon Hill properties between 1935 and 1939 the total of the selling prices (i.e., actual market value) was only 58 per cent of the total assessed values. Urban Land Institute, *A Survey in Respect to the Decentralization of the Boston Central Business District* (Boston: 1940), p. 18.

[112] Table 6, *Population and Housing — Statistics for Census Tracts, Boston, Massachusetts*, Sixteenth Census of the United States, 1940.

TABLE 7

DWELLINGS ON BEACON HILL BY TYPE OF OCCUPANCY, 1940

Type of Dwelling	Number
All dwelling units	1,675
1 family detached	68
1 family attached	369
2 family side by side	6
2 family other	82
3 family	93
4 family	192
1–4 family with business	38
5–9 family	370
10–19 family	325
20 family or more	120
Other dwelling places	12

Source: Sixteenth Census of the United States, 1940.

will have upon the eventual retentive and resistive capacity of Beacon Hill cannot be foreseen. It is enough for our immediate problem to recognize that the symbolic quality of Beacon Hill will survive only so long as people continue to share and act upon the values which it symbolizes. If the upper class should eventually lose its affective attachment to the Hill there would probably be a displacement of existing land uses by those of a more economic character.

CHAPTER IV

PLACE AS A FETISH:
BOSTON COMMON AND OTHER HISTORIC SITES

OUR ANALYSIS of land use on Beacon Hill came to the conclusion
that space is not always put to its most economic use. But it has
not in any way shown that space may be put to wholly non-
economic uses. After all, Beacon Hill does yield income, though
evidently not as much as it might. From a certain standpoint,
therefore, the area can still be viewed as a productive agent. As
such it is subject to certain "virtual movements" comprehensible
in terms of marginal utility analysis, even though its real use does
not follow the principle of substitution. Hence, while the actual
use of land on Beacon Hill has to be explained through principles
lying outside of economics, yet some *aspects* of those land uses
admittedly can be understood only through economic analysis.
Now it is not the purpose of this chapter, nor of those which
follow, to question this. All social interaction which involves the
use of scarce means has an economic aspect which can be analytically set apart and fitted into a rationalistic scheme. Since space
obviously has the property of scarcity — along with other properties — it always presents a rational aspect which lends itself
to economic treatment. But it is still a possibility that space can
be put to uses which yield no income at all. In other words, perhaps land can become an end value in itself to the extent that
it is not a productive agent at all.[1] This is a problem which cannot be solved in terms of our Beacon Hill data, for the reason
that the Hill is, after all, being put to some sort of productive use.
It will be necessary to look to other areas for evidence that bears
upon this problem. There happen to be in central Boston a number of sites or "places" that are devoted to no productive use at
all, though there is no "necessary," intrinsic reason why they
are not. That their productive possibilities have never been

---

[1] Not to deny, of course, that it has the potentiality of being a productive
agent.

capitalized upon poses a neat test case for the problem of this chapter.

The places in question are the Boston Common, the Granary Burying-ground, King's Chapel Burying-ground, the Old South Meeting-house, Park Street Church, and the Old State House. Several others, such as Faneuil Hall, the Old North Church, King's Chapel, and others might also be added, though they do not put into such clear relief the main aspects of the problem. A few additional sites which at first glance seem to contradict our hypothesis will also be considered, notably the Hancock House, destroyed in 1864, and the Central Burying-ground, partially violated late in the nineteenth century.[2] In our analysis of these areas we shall be concerned with the problem: why have they been put to no productive use? A clue to our answer lies in the theoretical conclusion which came out of the Beacon Hill analysis. There it was found that values may endow space with symbolic qualities which in turn lead to meaningfully congruent land uses. Incompatible land uses, no matter how intrinsically appropriate they may be, are barred from such areas. Consequently values become self-sufficient causal factors in spatial adaptation.

In the present chapter this insight will be pursued further. If space can, through cultural definition, be wholly divested of its productive character, becoming an end value in itself, it is necessary to explain what this means for the functioning of a community as a social system. Surely no community would deprive itself of a productive agent like land unless some sort of "utility" accrued to it. Our task is to find out what this "utility" consists of, and in that way explain why space may sometimes be put to uses that are not economically productive at all. To do this we shall have to note briefly the rather unique position of Boston as an American metropolis. Unlike most American cities which developed during the highly commercialistic nineteenth century, Boston began in an era when religion and education rivalled trading as important community building forces. Under

[2] It will be noted that these spatial areas differ in one respect from those comprised in Beacon Hill, the North End, the Back Bay, and the South End. The latter are distinct neighborhood communities, whereas the areas dealt with in the present chapter "belong to" all of Boston and, for that matter, to the entire American nation.

the influence of a Calvinistic ethic, which in some ways has persisted right down to the present in the form of Irish Catholic
puritanism, Boston has possessed a distinct and coherent value
system. Through this value system the city, viewed as a social
system, has manifested a certain indifference to "the logic of
economy." This outlook has led to some rather important locational consequences which bear upon our problem of the "utility"
of "wasted" space.

The Functional Significance of Spatial Symbols. We may approach this problem first in terms of the Boston Common and,
as before, develop our theory *pari passu* with our factual survey.
The Common is a 48.5 acre tract of ground which has survived
to the present from colonial days when it was used as a common
pasture and training field. Such plots of ground, which are so
typical a feature of New England settlements,[3] have their beginnings in the antiquity of western community formation. But in
New England they have always been guarded with particular care
from private usurpation. Thus on March 30, 1640 the townspeople voted as follows:

> Also agreed upon that henceforth there shalbe noe land granted
> eyther for houseplott or garden to any person out of the open ground
> or Comon Feild Which is left betweene the Centry Hill & Mr. Col-
> brons end.[4]

For over three centuries since that decree the Common has remained largely intact, though the city has grown entirely around
and beyond it. Today it is an economically useless tract of land
wedged directly into the heart of the business district. On three
of its five sides are women's apparel shops, department stores,
theaters, and other high-rent business establishments. On the
fourth side is Beacon street, extending alongside Beacon Hill.
Only the activities of Hill residents have prevented business from
invading that side. The fifth side is occupied by the Public Gar-

[3] Lois Kimball Mathews, *The Expansion of New England* (Boston: 1909),
p. 17.
[4] Quoted in M. A. De Wolfe Howe, *Boston Common, Scenes from Four
Centuries* (Cambridge: 1910), pp. 5–6.

den, an extension of the Common dating from 1824. Intrinsically the area would be admirably suited to commercial use, and, as we shall presently see, there have been several attempts to convert it to some such purpose. That such attempts have not succeeded, and that the Common has remained economically unexploited, should rather embarrass the empirically rationalistic theories.

To understand how so valuable a productive agent could ever get removed from the economic process we must see what values have become attached to the place and what functional significance these values have for the community. Like Beacon Hill, the Common has become invested with an affective quality. It has become a symbol for some very strong community sentiments. It has been the locale of historic events that pertain to early nationhood, civic origins, family genealogies, and the like. On it were mustered the forces which engaged in the first skirmishes of the Revolution. Here camped the British troops which held Boston in subjugation during the first years of the Revolution and whose evacuation left such an impress upon civic self-consciousness. This has been the arena for great civic celebrations, with all their solidarizing significance, ever since the Revolution: the celebration of Cornwallis' surrender, the Bunker Hill Procession for Lafayette, the Railroad Jubilee, and innumerable political, religious, and anti-slavery observances.[5]

The conjunction of such great events with a distinct locality was bound to engender certain sentiments toward that locality. Simmel has observed this tendency for space to become an objective reminder of important events rather clearly:

Für die Erinnerung entfaltet der Ort, weil er das sinnlich Anschaulichere ist, gewöhnlich eine stärkere assoziative Kraft als die Zeit; so dasz, insbesondere wo es sich um einmalige und gefühlsstarke Wechselbeziehung handelte, für die Erinnerung gerade er sich mit dieser unlöslich zu verbinden pflegt und so, da dies gegenseitig geschieht, der Ort noch weiterhin der Drehpunkt bleibt, um den herum das Erinnern die Individuen in nun ideell gewordene Korrelation einspinnt.[6]

[5] Joshua H. Jones, Jr., "Happenings on Boston Common," *Our Boston*, 2: 9–15 (January, 1927), *passim*.
[6] Georg Simmel, "Der Raum und die räumliche Ordnungen der Gesellschaft," *Soziologie*, 3rd edition (München: 1923), pp. 475–476.

This associative process by which emotions become linked to a spatial area is but a special case of the more general rule that meanings necessarily fix upon symbols for their communication between agents.[7] What is unique about it, however, in contrast to the more general process, is its "fetishistic" character; almost invariably the events which the spatial area symbolizes recede into the background and it becomes an end value in itself.[8] The idea of the symbol comes to usurp the idea for which the symbol originally stood.[9] And this idea in turn becomes the nucleus for a constellation of emotions which often have little or no relation to the events originally denoted by the symbol. The result is that the spatial area becomes the symbol for a variegated pattern of values, intrinsically unrelated, but meaningfully integrated through their common articulation around the symbol. In people's minds these diverse values belong together and are fitting to the events which the area originally symbolized. Hence, as Parsons has indicated, "from this point of view the fact of their empirical heterogeneity may not matter; the unity and order may lie in the things symbolized, not in the symbols."[10]

Just such a fetishistic process has taken place with the Common. The dramatic events which lent to the Common its original affective significance, while by no means absent from people's consciousness today, are less apparent in the imagery which it elicits than are other more generalized sentimental responses. Evidence of this can be found in the meaning expressions which are made from time to time about the Common. These fall into two rough classes: (1) those whose reference is mainly to social systems (the nation; the city); (2) those whose reference is mainly to cultural systems ("principles," "ideals," "moral forces"). Needless to say there is no such clear separation as this in the minds of the persons who have made the expressions.

[7] Emile Durkheim, *The Elementary Forms of the Religious Life* (London: 1915), p. 220.

[8] Pitirim A. Sorokin, *Social and Cultural Dynamics* (New York: 1941), IV, 43, n. 39.

[9] Durkheim, *op. cit.*, pp. 230–231.

[10] Talcott Parsons, *The Structure of Social Action* (New York: 1937), p. 416.

It is only by inference that we can thus differentiate the vague reference which characterizes most affectively toned expressions.

Among the meaning expressions falling in the first class are those which have a nation-wide reference. Illustrative of these is the following:

The Common, with its intermingling of tragedy and comedy, carries in its soil such a story of human progress and development that it no longer belongs to Boston alone, but to the entire world. Events that occurred on or near Boston Common have so indelibly impressed themselves on our government and country that history will never allow them to be forgotten, or this spot to become less sacred and hallowed. Boston Common may be said to be the very foundation of our government, as from it have come the Town Meetings, and through these our picturesque little red schoolhouses, and much of our whole educational system.[11]

More common are the values which pertain to municipal self-consciousness. One citizen, writing to the editor of a Boston newspaper, declares that:

I, for one, am glad that we, here in Boston and neighboring towns, cling to those sacred places which are historic. The more modern cities are more than jealous of the great background of which Boston boasts. We of Boston should hold dear those things and places which the whole world knows us by.[12]

Another resident regards the Common and its immediate vicinity as forming:

the best impression and embodiment of our civic life and consciousness. This is our acropolis; and one does not sell those things—at least not without spiritual loss.[13]

At a public meeting sponsored for the purpose of saving the Old South Meeting-house one speaker, generalizing his sentiments somewhat from the topic, exclaimed:

[11] Jones, *op. cit.*, p. 9.
[12] D. L. Houghton, letter to editor, *Boston Herald*, November 20, 1930.
[13] Joseph Lee, letter to editor, *Boston Transcript*, January 5, 1903.

Yet there stands Boston Common just where and just what it was —
no larger, and thank heaven! as yet no smaller (loud applause) than
it was fifty years ago.[14]

One writer, in a more regretful vein, observes that:

We have little left to remind us of our fathers and their early
struggles, but let us hold fast to what we have. . . . They serve ever
to remind us of the heroic period in the history of our native city, and
as such ought to be preserved for the benefit of our children and future
generations. Our landmarks we must preserve. . . . — they are historical monuments and mementos of Boston's past progress, patriotism,
and glory, that should never be effaced.[15]

Behind these expressions lay the kind of values to which every
group owes its solidarity. Without such values social systems
would have no more solidarity than they could win through furthering the maximum self-interest of their members. Solidarity
of that sort is precarious and is ever prone to disintegration. It
is only when the members of a social system share certain common and emotionally toned values that the latent tendency of all
social systems toward disintegration can be arrested. Most pertinent to our immediate problem, of course, is the symbolization
of these values by a tangible place, so that the sight of that place
evokes in people's minds the values which underly the social system. In this fact lies the clue to the question raised earlier in this
chapter, concerning the "utility" which accrues to a social system
through withholding productive land from intrinsically appropriate use. The "utility" consists of the solidarizing function
which symbols can have. Thus, although the Common is but a
tract of waste land so far as economic utility is concerned, it
nonetheless has a very real function in renewing and revitalizing
the sentiments of communal solidarity. These sentiments, be it
noted, do not pertain to the dramatic events which originally gave
the Common its symbolic character. It is not the recollection of

[14] Speech by Joseph S. Ropes, reprinted in *Proceedings of a Public Meeting
held at Faneuil Hall, June 7, 1876* (Boston: 1876), p. 7.

[15] Alexander S. Porter, "Changes of Values in Real Estate in Boston the
Past One Hundred Years," *Collections of the Bostonian Society,* 1: 57–74
(1888), p. 71.

Cornwallis' surrender or of the British evacuation which comes to people's minds in the presence of the Common. These ideas have receded into the background and the Common, already established as a symbol and having become an end value in its own right, now serves as the focus of a vague cluster of sentiments referring to national and civic identity. Its presence serves ever to elicit the values which a person has toward these social systems. In this way it binds him more closely with other persons and thereby contributes to maintaining the identity of the respective systems. That is the functional significance of fetishism.

But the process goes even further. Not only does the Common, as a symbol, serve to solidarize the person with various social systems but it serves also to integrate him with broader cultural systems. It performs this integrative function in the same way that it performs the solidarizing one: by renewing and revitalizing those ends of the person which link him with the larger systems. Examples of the integrative function which the Common plays may be found in such meaning expressions as the following:

Boston Common was, is, and ever will be a source of tradition and inspiration from which the New Englanders may renew their faith, recover their moral force, and strengthen their ability to grow and achieve.[16]

Similarly one orator appeals to:

the great principle exemplified in the preservation of the Common. Thank Heaven, the tide of money-making must break and go around that.[17]

An antiquarian writer, commenting on the mutilation which the Common has experienced during its long history, remarks that:

Here, in short, are all our accumulated memories, intimate, public, private.[18]

[16] Jones, *op. cit.*, p. 15.
[17] Speech of Dr. William Everett, quoted in the *Boston Transcript*, March 7, 1903.
[18] T. R. Sullivan, *Boston New and Old* (Boston: 1912), pp. 45–46.

And another writer observes of the Common that:

Standing practically untouched and unbroken, in the very heart of the city, it represents the permanence of ideals.[19]

Expressions like these reveal rather well the genuine moral influence which the Common can exert upon those who share the values it symbolizes. In this respect the Common illustrates the general principle which Durkheim saw when he observed that men's moral conscience could not long endure without the aid of external reminders. The "collective conscience" goes through continual variations in intensity, so that it would be liable to extinction during its weaker phases unless there were something more enduring to summon it back into being. This need is met by symbols.[20] Moreover, such is the nature of conscience that it cannot be distinctly felt or acted upon without the aid of symbols — what Durkheim calls "totems." [21] This arises out of the "contagious" nature of moral values, by which "the idea of a thing and the idea of its symbol are closely united in our minds; the result is that the emotions provoked by the one extend contagiously to the other." [22] Hence the experiencing of a moral value becomes all bound up with the perception of the symbol by which it has been objectified. In this way symbols have a genuine functional significance for the values, moral and otherwise, which make up a cultural system. Spatial areas like the Boston Common are no exception to the rule. By means of the Common certain values, comprising altogether a cultural system, are periodically renewed and reinvigorated. This system, to be sure, is but weakly integrated. For some persons the Common signifies the Puritan heritage of New England; for others, the republican form of government; for others, religious freedom, etc. But all of these fuse together in the minds of most persons, so that there is a meaningful integration real enough to make of the whole a cultural system. The objective representation of this system is one of the functions of the Common.

[19] Robert Shackleton, *The Book of Boston* (Philadelphia: 1916), p. 5.
[20] Durkheim, *op. cit.*, pp. 230–231.
[21] *Ibid.*, p. 211.
[22] *Ibid.*, p. 219.

Because of its sentimental significance the Common has become buttressed up with several legal guarantees. These may be viewed as an institutionalized crystallization of the more nebulous sentiments attaching to the Common. Thus, the city charter of Boston, first drawn up in 1822, contains a clause still in force which forbids the city from ever disposing of the Common or any part of it.[23] In one of the earliest decisions passed by the State Supreme Court on a matter involving the Common it was declared that: "The city holds the Common for the public benefit, and not for its emolument, or as a source of revenue." [24] By various legislative enactments the city is forbidden to lease the Common[25] and is limited as to what it can build upon it.[26] Likewise the city is barred from laying out roadways over the Common.[27] Another court decision declares that:

Except in the exercise of the right of eminent domain, the Common could not be appropriated to a public use entirely inconsistent with the general character of the use originally intended.[28]

In this same decision the general nature of the city's rights and obligations with respect to the Common was summarized. The court declared that Boston "is in a kind of trust relation to the people for whose use the property was provided." [29] In addition to these statutory guarantees the Common enjoys a further immunity. By accepting the bequest of one George F. Parkman, in 1908, amounting to over five million dollars, the city incurred the obligation to maintain the Common, and certain other parks, in their present outlines.[30] In his will Parkman expressed the hope that: "the Boston Common shall never be diverted from its present use as a public park for the benefit and enjoyment of its citizens." [31] All of these legal norms gain their strength from the

---

[23] Moses King, *The Back Bay District and the Vendome* (Boston: 1881), p. 25.

[24] *Steele* v. *Boston,* 128 Mass. 583.

[25] Leg. st. 1854, c. 448, paragraph 39.

[26] Pub. sts. c. 54, paragraph 16; c. 27, paragraph 50.

[27] Pub. sts. c. 54, paragraph 13.

[28] *Codman* v. *Crocker,* 203 Mass. 146.

[29] *Codman* v. *Crocker,* 203 Mass. 146.

[30] Howe, *op. cit.,* p. 79.

[31] *Loc. cit.*

values which underly them. They show rather clearly how complete has been the removal of the Common from the economic
process and its devotion to a use that cannot be "justified" in
terms of a rational social economy. As a real situation, however,
such a disposal of a potential productive agent has to be explained. The empirically rationalistic theories, predicated as they
are upon marginal utility analysis, cannot explain this situation.
Only by invoking the cultural element in spatial adaptation is it
possible to understand why an area like the Boston Common
becomes invested with symbolic properties which render it immune from rational use and which nonetheless perform definite
real functions for the community.

Another instance of fetishism is to be found in the old burying-
grounds of central Boston. There are four of these cemeteries,
three of which occupy commercially valuable land. The Granary
Burying-ground, located on Tremont street beside Park Street
Church, dates from 1660.[32] Today it fronts on one of Boston's
principal downtown business streets and is lined on two of its
sides by buildings ranging in height from five to ten stories.
King's Chapel Burying-ground, also located on downtown Tremont street, is the oldest of Boston's cemeteries, dating from
1630.[33] It too occupies commercially valuable land. The contrast
that is presented by ten-story office buildings reared up beside
this quiet cemetery affords visible evidence of the conflict between
"sacred" and "profane" that has operated in Boston's ecological
pattern. The Central Burying-ground, at the corner of two of
Boston's busiest downtown thoroughfares, Boylston and Tremont
streets, dates from 1756.[34] Although it is generally identified with
the Boston Common the land it occupies was never a part of the
original Common and its development must therefore be treated
separately. Finally there is Copp's Hill Burying-ground, located
in the North End, and dating from early in the seventeenth century.[35] Isolated as it is from the commercial portion of central
Boston its survival does not present as significant a problem as

[32] Robert Means Lawrence, *Old Park Street and its Vicinity* (Boston:
1922), p. 47.
[33] George E. Ellis, *Bacon's Dictionary of Boston* (Boston: 1886), p. 277.
[34] *Ibid.*, p. 279.
[35] Justin Winsor, *The Memorial History of Boston* (Boston: 1880–1881),
I, 555.

do the other cemeteries and for that reason it need not receive the same analysis.

Even more than the Common these colonial burying-grounds have become invested with a moral significance which renders them almost inviolable. To begin with, there is the usual sanctity which attaches to all cemeteries. Thus, in a case brought before the Supreme Court involving the threatened violation of a cemetery in the town of Seekonk, Massachusetts, the court observed that:

And while many ancient burial-places have been very much neglected, and left without the care which seems appropriate and becoming, we cannot doubt that their use for purposes of private profit would at all times have been regarded as incongruous and censurable. They are places devoted not only to the undisturbed repose of the dead, but to the sentiments, affections, and tender memories of the living.[36]

Moreover, in the venerable cemeteries of Boston there is an added sacredness growing out of the age of the grounds and the fact that the forebears of many of New England's most distinguished families as well as a number of colonial and Revolutionary leaders lie buried in these cemeteries. In the Granary Burying-ground alone lie the remains of eight governors, three judges, the parents of Benjamin Franklin, several Revolutionary leaders, and a number of forebears of present-day upper class families. There is thus a manifold symbolism to these old burying-grounds, pertaining to family lineage, early nationhood, civic origins, and the like, all of which have strong sentimental associations. The strength of these sentiments cannot be better expressed than they are in the following quotation. Referring to King's Chapel Burying-ground a nineteenth century writer reflects thus:

But there are few persons who would be willing to see this ground, where are the sepulchres of the fathers, disturbed. It is almost the sole visible memorial which remains of them. Their homes have crumbled, the churches in which they worshipped have been replaced by more recent structures, the open hills from which they looked out on the sea and the forest have been discrowned and almost levelled into the valleys, and the winding pathways of the new settlement have become

[36] *Commonwealth* v. *Viall*, 84 Mass. 512.

the streets of an overcrowded city. Since the earlier monuments were erected, successive generations have come and gone. . . . Nothing remains the same, but the burial-places of the dead.[37]

In such meaning expressions as this one can readily discern the integrating function which cemeteries, as spatial symbols, may exert. Even more than the Common they renew and intensify the values which a person has with respect to the cultural system of which he is a bearer. As the writer just quoted has so well said:

> The burial-place of the dead, so far as it has any influence, is on the side of virtue and religion. It is associated with hallowed and affectionate memories. Its voice is one of perpetual rebuke to folly and sin. It warns men to serve God in lives of usefulness and righteousness and piety, while it directs the thoughts to that tribunal before which each man shall give account of the deeds done in the body.[38]

The moralizing significance of cemeteries is thus a genuine one.[39] So it is little wonder that "the ancient burying-grounds . . . are cared for, maintained, and respected as historic landmarks which it would be sacrilege to disturb." [40] Despite the challenges of more rational land uses, some of which will soon be described, these spatial areas have remained intact to the present day. The explanation for their survival lies wholly outside the empirically rationalistic scheme. It is to be found in the symbolic character of burying-grounds as fetishes. They are end values in themselves, and they are venerated for their own sake. Any confounding of them with utilitarian considerations of advantage would be inconceivable.[41] By virtue of this they have become entirely removed from the process of economic allocation.

In addition to the Common and the burying-grounds there are a number of downtown sites which, along with the buildings that occupy them, possess a fetishistic character. These places have

---

[37] Thomas Bridgman, *Memorials of the Dead in Boston* (Boston: 1853), pp. 17–18.

[38] *Ibid.*, p. 20.

[39] Georg Simmel, "Über räumliche Projektionen socialer Formen," *Zeitschrift für Sozialwissenschaft*, 6: 287–302 (1903), p. 295.

[40] Ellis, *op. cit.*, p. 81.

[41] Parsons, *op. cit.*, p. 675.

the same solidarizing and integrating functions which the other much larger spatial areas perform. Consider the following rhetorical address on the occasion of the city government's removal to the Old State House, in 1830:

> The spot on which we are convened is Patriot Ground. It was consecrated by our pious ancestors to the duties of providing for the welfare of their infant settlement, and for a long series of years was occupied in succession by the great and good men whom Providence raised up to establish the institutions and liberties of their country.[42]

Such a statement constitutes an expression of genuine sentiment and patriotism toward city and country. More than that, it cannot help but arouse in the minds of its hearers, who have been reared in the same value system, corresponding emotions of pride and respect toward city and country. In this way it revitalizes and maintains that value system as a functioning unity. Without the tangible spatial locale and physical structure of the Old State House to serve as a symbol these sentiments would tend in time to atrophy. There would be no occasion to utter such expressions as those of Harrison Gray Otis; and if any such expressions were made they would fall upon unresponsive ears. But, symbolized by a distinct place and building the values gain a certain "immortality" which ever gives rise to appropriate verbal expressions and is ever roused to further vitality by those very verbal expressions.

The Old State House is not the only such fetish in central Boston. Thus, speaking of the Park Street Church, a local clergyman said:

> I love to stop before the beautiful Park Street Church spire . . . , a spire that speaks still of the old residential Beacon Street, and of the days when its bell called across the Common to its congregation to gather in their meeting-house, to worship the God of their Pilgrim Fathers.[43]

[42] Harrison Gray Otis, *An Address to the Members of the City Council on the Removal of the Municipal Government to the Old State House* (Boston: 1830), p. 3.

[43] Rev. J. Edgar Park, in sermon to New Old South Church, June 7, 1920, quoted in Lawrence, *op. cit.*, p. 121.

Of such a place Simmel has indicated that it "stellt den Gesell-
schaftsgedanken dar, indem es ihn lokalisiert." [44] This localization
of the values which comprise a social or cultural system is one
way of objectifying them and thus of renewing and strengthening
their vitality. A similar function is performed by other historic
landmarks in central Boston — the Old South Meeting-house,
King's Chapel, Old North Church, etc. These represent something
more than just economically useless sites. For they exert a positive influence upon social and cultural processes. To regard them
as ecological "sports" — as chance departures from the "natural"
competitive process — would be a factual error. More than that,
it would represent a faulty scientific interpretation of spatial
adaptation. Only insofar as all the properties of space, and not
merely the impeditive ones, are properly conceptualized in a systematic theory can ecology have explanatory adequacy for land
use.

Disfunctional Consequences of Fetishism. Spatial fetishes thus
have a positive function for society. They have, in other words,
a "utility." At this point an objection of crucial theoretical significance may be raised: how does such a conclusion reconcile with
the serious strains and maladjustments which are present in the
land use pattern of central Boston? Any number of economic
indices can be cited which reveal the "disutility" and cost which
accrues to the people of Boston through withholding all this exploitable land from the productive process. Do not these indices
completely vitiate our foregoing conclusions? This is a problem
of considerable theoretical import and must receive a careful
analysis. Let us therefore consider some of the economic indices
of the cost which results from turning potential productive agents
to purely symbolic ends.

The most visible index of such "disutility" is that of congestion.
Throughout its history Boston has suffered from land shortage.
Much of this arose out of the semi-insular character of the Hub,
but part of it is attributable to the existence of so much "wasted"
land in the city. More than most cities Boston has had unusually
high real estate values throughout the nineteenth and twentieth
centuries, even during the depression phases of business cycles.
The result has been an extraordinary crowding of dwellings in

44 Simmel, *op. cit.*, p. 294.

the older residential quarters, and the construction of business buildings without any regard to light or exposure.[45] Much was done in the way of filling-in on the East Cove, the Mill Pond, South Cove, and of course the South End and Back Bay districts, but even this failed to relieve the land shortage. What all this has meant for the spatial development of Boston's retail center is clear from the present character of that district. Few cities of comparable size have so small a retail district in point of area. Unlike the spacious department stores of most cities, those in Boston are frequently compressed within narrow confines and have had to extend in devious patterns through rear and adjoining buildings. Most of the buildings are old and are rapidly depreciating in value. Yet exorbitant assessed valuations, far beyond the market value of such properties, have deterred any efforts at renovation. These exorbitant assessed valuations are themselves the result of a tax base which is inadequate for maintaining municipal functions. There is not the space in downtown Boston for the businesses which could profitably locate there and thus enlarge the tax base. As one writer on city planning has indicated: "The city must forever be hampered by its voluntary acceptance of the central island of undigested landscape, the Common." [46]

Traffic congestion provides another index of the disfunctional consequences of spatial fetishism. Traffic in downtown Boston has literally reached the saturation point, owing partly to the narrow one-way streets but mainly to the lack of sufficient arterials leading into and out of the Hub.[47] The American Road Builders Association has estimated that there is a loss of $81,000 per day in Boston as a result of traffic delay. These losses ramify out to merchants, manufacturers, commuters, and many other interests.[48] The extension of a single arterial across the Common would have gone far to relieve the congestion on Tremont and

[45] John C. Kiley, "Changes in Realty Values in the Nineteenth and Twentieth Centuries," *Bulletin of the Business Historical Society*, 15 (June, 1941), p. 36.

[46] Frank Chouteau Brown, "Boston's Growing Pains," *Our Boston*, 1 (November, 1926), p. 12.

[47] See Elisabeth M. Herlihy (ed.), *Fifty Years of Boston* (Boston: 1932), p. 53.

[48] *Ibid.*, pp. 53–54.

Beacon streets, the two main in-town arterials.[49] Proposals of that sort have indeed been made but, as we shall presently see, they have been consistently vetoed by public sentiment.

Further difficulties have arisen from the rapid southwesterly extension of the business district during the past two decades.[50] With the Common lying directly in the path of this extension the business district has had to stretch around it in an elongated fashion. As a result businesses of a given type may be found scattered over a distance much too great for the average shopper who is interested in comparing similar merchandise at different places. There is unfortunately no quantitative measure of the disutility which arises from such a commercial pattern, but the inconvenience to buyers and the consequent loss to businesses is all too obvious.

Most of these indices of "disutility" are attributable in large part to the Common. But the Common is not the only obstacle to an economic land use pattern. The three downtown cemeteries, as well as the various colonial churches and meeting houses, all occupy sites that might be put to profitable use. Moreover, the dis-economic consequences attending such a "waste" of productive land extend even further than the removal from income-yielding uses of a given amount of space. For it is a standard principle of real estate that business property derives added value if adjoining properties are occupied by other businesses.[51] Just as a single vacancy will depreciate the value of a whole block of business frontage, so a break in the continuity of stores by a cemetery or an old church damages the commercial value of surrounding properties. Such symbolic sites as the Granary Burying-ground, King's Chapel Burying-ground, Park Street Church, the Old South Meeting-house, the Old State House, and several others not only occupy commercially valuable land but they interrupt the continuity of business frontage on their streets. It is not surprising then that several of these places have been challenged at

[49] Frank Chouteau Brown, "Boston: More Growing Pains," Our Boston, 3 (February, 1927).

[50] Urban Land Institute, A Survey in Respect to the Decentralization of the Boston Central Business District (Boston: 1940), p. 15.

[51] Richard M. Hurd, Principles of City Land Values (New York: 1903), pp. 93–94.

various times by real estate and commercial interests which have sought to replace them by more profitable uses. In every case the sentiments which attach to them have resisted such threats.

From these lines of evidence it becomes clear that fetishes do have disfunctional consequences for a population. Yet our previous findings have suggested that fetishes possess a positive functional significance for the community. How do these debit and credit aspects stand to one another? Can they be added and subtracted so that a "balance" will result? And is one "natural" while the other is "irregular"? To resolve these problems it will be necessary to adumbrate upon an aspect of Pareto's theory of utility, as developed in his analysis of the social system. This matter has to do with the non-commensurability of utilities as between a social system and the component members of that system. In Pareto's terms it is necessary to distinguish between the utility *for* a community and the utility *of* a community. The former refers to the utility of the component members of a social system taken in severalty. The latter refers to the utility of the community taken as a reality *sui generis*.[52] Between these two there is no necessary correspondence except at a certain minimal point where every increase in the utility *for* the community will always entail a corresponding increase in the utility *of* the community. But at most positions on the two continua there will be a discrepancy between the two utilities, so that increases in one are accompanied by decreases in the other. Applying this significant insight to our own problem it appears that the *disutilities* which result from turning potentially productive land to symbolic uses devolve most immediately upon individual members (businesses, families, and other subsystems) of the community. And, correspondingly, the *utilities* arising out of fetishistic land uses accrue most directly to the community as a whole. In other words, the removal of land from the economic process diminishes the utility of individuals — i.e., what Pareto would call the utility *for* the community. And the devotion of such land to a symbolic function increases the utility of Boston as a social system — i.e., the utility *of* the community, in Paretan terms. This is not to say that fetishistic land uses impose no disutility whatsoever upon the

[52] Vilfredo Pareto, *Mind and Society* (New York: 1935), paragraphs 2133–2139.

community as a whole, nor is it to suggest that fetishism has no utility for disparate individuals within the community. On the contrary; the removal of land from economic productivity represents a cost to the community which has to be proportioned with its other functional requirements.[53] Similarly the devotion of land to the symbolic representation of values yields an affective utility, in the form of emotional satisfaction, to individuals within the community. The point, however, is that the direct incidence of these utilities and disutilities must be distinguished as between system and subsystem. Fetishism is most immediately a utility *of* the community, in that its solidarizing and integrating functions serve to renew and intensify the values of that community. Likewise the loss of productive land through its being turned to symbolic representation is most immediately a disutility *for* the community, in that individual businesses cannot take advantage of a potential productive agent to put it to income-yielding purposes. Clearly these utilities are heterogeneous and non-commensurable variables which must be analytically segregated. Only thus is it possible to understand why a municipality will put up with congestion, inconvenience, and unnecessary expense so as to preserve these economically useless tracts of ground.

Clearly there is no way of adding or subtracting the two utilities because they have no common denominator (except at the minimal point at which survival of the system is in question). Hence to say that Boston would be "better off" by converting the Common to business uses is a meaningless assertion. "Better off" implies position on a single continuum, whereas the actual situation involves two distinct and incommensurate continua. Following out the implications of this point it should be clear that there is no "naturalness" to one type of utility nor any "irregularity" to the other. The symbolic representation of values, so as to maintain solidarity and integration, is as real a functional requirement

---

[53] In the last chapter of this work we shall submit a highly abstract deductive definition of such proportionalization. For the present it is enough to indicate that proportionalization is always in terms of "maintenance-of-the-system's-identity," and that there is in this sense a common denominator to all utilities, whether *of* or *for* the community. Such a common denominator is, of course, wholly abstract and finds empirical expression only at a minimum point, which Pareto calls point Q.

for any social system as is economy in the allocation of scarce productive agents. Both are therefore "natural."

The Conflict between "Sacred" and "Profane" Land Uses. But the fact still remains that there are powerful strains within the spatial structure of Boston. Despite the incommensurate character of the two kinds of utility they still present conflicts which are reflected in actual locational processes. Individuals who have not been fully socialized into the values which attach to the Common, the old burying-grounds, and other fetishes, have frequently sought to violate those spatial areas. Such threats have uniformly aroused moral indignation. The ensuing disputes partake rather vividly of a conflict between "sacred" and "profane" land uses. It will pay us to consider in some detail the nature of this conflict so as to better understand the empirical ramifications of our rather abstract discussion of utility.

Beginning with the Common we find that the whole history of that tract of land has been plagued with attempts to turn it into private use or to encroach upon its boundaries. As Howe puts it, "salvations from one threatened encroachment after another have occupied many Bostonians for a generation past." [54] Not to go too far back into the early history of the Common we may begin with the permission, granted by the city government in 1869, to erect a Musical Festival auditorium on the Common. The public response to this authorization was one of moral indignation. Several citizens prepared to make an appeal to the state Supreme Court in order to forestall construction. "The popular feeling was so strong . . . that the managers of that enterprise deemed it injudicious to accept the grant, and the building was placed upon land farther south and west." [55]

During succeeding years, as the Back Bay settlement was progressing, a number of proposals and plans were made for extending Columbus avenue or Commonwealth avenue across the Common. So much agitation attended these plans that in 1875 the state legislature passed an act which prohibited the extension of streets or ways across any tract of land that had been devoted

---

[54] Howe, *op. cit.*, p. 72.

[55] Report of a Committee of Citizens, *The Public Rights in Boston Common* (Boston: 1877), p. iii; see also Howe, *op. cit.*, p. 73.

to public use as a park for twenty or more years — except as approved by the citizens in a special meeting called for the purpose.[56] In 1872 a potential threat to the Common arose from the city's authorization for merchants, whose stores had been destroyed by the great fire of that year, to build temporary structures on the Common. However, reconstruction of the burned area proceeded so rapidly that no advantage was taken of this authorization.[57] One year later, under the pressure of increasing vehicular and trolley car congestion, the Board of Aldermen voted to remove the iron fence which then bounded the Tremont street side of the Common. This was to allow the widening of Tremont street so that it might accommodate additional horse-railroad tracks. However the public protest became so strong that the fence had to be restored.[58]

In 1877 the Massachusetts Charitable Mechanics' Association requested from the city permission to erect a large exhibition building on the Common. The structure was to be a temporary one, though the hope was expressed by the Association that the exhibition might become a triennial affair, with the building being re-erected every three years. Prominent business interests supported the proposal, pointing out the increased trade and prestige that would accrue to the city through sponsoring such an exhibition.[59] The public response was instantaneous. Letters of protest appeared in the local newspapers, objections were registered by the Massachusetts Volunteer Militia and several other organizations, and a hearing was scheduled before a committee of citizens. At this hearing accusations of "vandalism" were levelled against the Association.[60] In an informal statement before the committee one speaker made the following remarks:

I am not astonished, sir, in these times, that there are societies willing, in spite of these old and sacred memories, and ready to come here and ask you to grant them a privilege which they ought not to have. . . . Grant this corporation the right to put a building upon the Common

---

[56] Report of a Committee of Citizens, *op. cit.*, pp. vi and 4.
[57] *Ibid.*, p. iv.
[58] *Ibid.*, p. v.
[59] *Ibid.*, pp. vi–ix and 31–47.
[60] Curtis Guild, in statement quoted in Report of a Committee of Citizens, *op. cit.*, p. 8.

for three months, or any given time, and it takes away the sacred character of the Common. I say sacred, because there are convictions that ought to be cherished by Bostonians.[61]

In the end the Association was denied the right to hold its exhibition on the Common.

Most of the subsequent threats to the Common have arisen from two sources: (a) the trolley and subway system, and (b) the widening of downtown streets. During the 1890's the pressure of vehicular and trolley car traffic on Tremont street became acute. Photographs of Tremont street during the rush hours show solid lines of trolley cars jammed by horse-drawn carriages.[62] Various solutions were proposed for relieving the congestion. One called for the extension of trolley tracks across the Common, in line with Columbus avenue. Another involved digging an open trench for trolley cars directly through the Common, with overhead bridges for pedestrians. Other plans merely entailed a widening of the streets abutting on the Common. However:

Aside from the inadequacy of all such plans for accomplishing the various results sought for, the controlling sentiment of the citizens of Boston, and of large numbers throughout the State, is distinctly opposed to allowing any such use of the Common.[63]

The solution finally chosen was construction of a subway to Boylston street.[64] However, this did not appease all elements of the community. A poem written at the time refers to the proposed subway in the following sarcastic vein:

> Since we must have our subway tracks,
> The forester must swing his axe, . . .
>
> Our Common's beauties we must mar
> That all may take a trolley car.[65]

[61] Arthur Pickering, in statement quoted in Report of a Committee of Citizens, *op. cit.*, p. 6.

[62] See photographs in *First Annual Report of the Boston Transit Commission* (Boston: 1895).

[63] *Ibid.*, p. 9.

[64] Howe, *op. cit.*, pp. 73–74.

[65] William Bellamy, *A Second Century of Charades* (Boston: 1896), verse CII.

In 1896 a group of eighteen citizens, led by Frederick O. Prince, filed suit in the state Supreme Court indicting the Transit Commission for tearing up the Common and the Public Garden pursuant to constructing the subway. They appealed to the statute, passed in 1875, which forbade the extension of routes or ways across any park more than 20 years old without the consent of the inhabitants of the city. The court ruled, however, that the voters of Boston had accepted the act authorizing construction of the subway and that the legislature, in a statute of 1894, had also approved its construction, thereby vitiating the force of the earlier statute.[66] For several years the matter lay rested, the subway was constructed, and the Common seemed to have remained essentially undamaged. Then, in 1909 a new extension of the subway was proposed, leading under the Common from Park street to the Charles river. In June of that year suit was brought by ten taxpayers to enjoin the Transit Commission from putting through the tunnel. Once again, however, the court ruled that the subway was not incompatible with the purposes of the Common and that "the increase of facilities for approaching the Common will be a convenience to the public in the use and enjoyment of it."[67]

The pressure for street widening has been constant and some concessions have had to be made. In 1920 the sidewalk on the Tremont street side of the Common was removed so as to permit street widening.[68] In the spring of 1930 a plan was submitted to the Traffic Commission which called for taking off slices from the Common so as to allow the widening of Park and Arlington streets.[69] However this plan was not consummated. In the following year a resident of Boston rather apologetically suggested a similar plan. He excused himself by writing that:

I know that the Common is of some interest historically, but I don't believe that our traditions or interests would suffer in the least if these suggestions were carried out. . . . My family has been in Boston for many years, and I hope that, if anybody should object to these mild measures, I shall not be accused of being a wanton iconoclast.[70]

[66] *Prince* v. *Crocker*, 166 Mass. 347.
[67] *Codman* v. *Crocker*, 203 Mass. 146.
[68] Herlihy, *op. cit.*, p. 190.
[69] *Boston Transcript*, April 14 and April 26, 1930.
[70] H. James Jones, letter to editor, *Boston Herald*, April 1, 1931.

Many lesser challenges have been made from time to time upon the Common's integrity. But for the most part they have met with general indifference or, when of a more serious character, with moral indignation. Utility *of* the community has prevailed over utility *for* the community.

In accounting for such a situation the empirically rationalistic theories are quite inadequate. To begin with, in their view the only adaptive agents in the locational process are disparate social systems. There is no recognition that some locational processes might be referable to broader, larger social systems, such as communities. In the case of the Common, however, it is clear that its functional significance is for the community of Boston as a reality *sui generis*.

For that reason the community, and not its lesser subsystems, is the real adaptive agent. Furthermore, any attempt to understand the pressures and counter-pressures that have pervaded the Common's history by resorting to the idea of competition for accessible location would be futile. Finally, the rationalistic assumption of an identity between utility of the part and utility of the whole is demonstrably untrue. The reader will recall our analysis in chapter I where it was shown that only by this hypothesis could the empirical rationalists explain how spatial order might result from the competitive struggle for space between social systems having strictly a bargaining relationship to one another. The foregoing analysis of conflict between "sacred" and "profane" land uses should demonstrate the fallacy of such an hypothesis. There is no necessary identity between utility of the part and utility of the whole. Pareto established this point deductively and we have in some degree confirmed it inductively.

This is an important finding. For it vitiates the last postulate underlying the empirically rationalistic scheme. In the previous chapter the two initial premises of rationalism were refuted. These had to do with the strictly impeditive character of space and the purely economizing character of social systems. Likewise the assumption that social systems stood to one another only in a contractual relationship was disposed of. In the present chapter the supplementary prop by which the rationalists tried to explain how orderliness might result from the competition of disparate social systems for location has been invalidated. Thus the whole deductive construct of empirically rationalistic ecology collapses.

In order to securely establish these conclusions it will be well to consider two more specific landmarks in Boston where the conflict between "sacred" and "profane" land uses is put into especially clear relief. These two landmarks are the Old South Meeting-house and the Park Street Church. Both of these buildings and the sites they occupy have been very seriously threatened, one even to the point that demolition had actually begun. The circumstances which led to their survival will help us to a real understanding of the interaction between rational and volitional adaptation to space.

The threat to the Old South Meeting-house arose as a sequel to the great Boston fire of 1872. As a result of the fire, which had slightly damaged the church, the congregation decided to hold its services elsewhere. The building was leased to the federal government for use as a post office. Four years later, in 1876, this old building, dating from the seventeenth century and representing a focus of many sentimental associations connected with the colonial and Revolutionary history of Boston, was advertised for sale. The advertisement read as follows:

THE OLD SOUTH CHURCH BUILDING

All the materials above the level of the sidewalks, except the Corner Stone and the Clock in the Tower, of this ancient and historical landmark building, which has now come under the auctioneer's hammer, and will be disposed of on Thursday, June 8, 1876, at 12 o'clock noon on the premises, on the corner of Washington and Milk streets.

The spire is covered with copper, and there is a lot of lead on roof and belfry, and the roof is covered with imported old Welch slate. 60 days will be allowed for the removal.

Terms cash.[71]

Following this notice of intended sale there were protests from all over the country. But the resistance was unorganized and ineffectual. On June 8, 1876 the building was sold at auction for $1,350, to be removed in sixty days. Demolition began immediately. The clock was taken down and some of the masonry was

[71] "Freedom and the Old South Meeting-House," *Old South Leaflets*, No. 202 (Boston: 1910).

removed. Then a prominent Boston business house, George W. Simmons and Son, bought the right to hold the building intact for seven days. On June 14 a mass meeting was held in the Old South, speeches were held, and a course of action was outlined to raise funds for repurchasing the building and preserving it. A citizens' committee made an offer to the Old South society of $400,000 in cash for the building, and the offer was accepted. Months of campaigning followed, under the name of the Old South Preservation Fund. The New England Mutual Life Insurance Company lent $225,000 on the property and took a mortgage. An initial cash payment of $75,000 was made to the Old South society. On May 4, 1877 a second mass meeting was held. The state governor delivered an opening address, poems especially written for the occasion were recited by Oliver Wendell Holmes, James Freeman Clarke, Julia Ward Howe, and other notables. In December of the same year a fair was held to raise additional funds. The decisive act was a donation by Mrs. Mary Hemenway, of Beacon Hill, to the amount of $100,000. The Old South was thus preserved and has since been used as a museum for relics of the American Revolution.[72]

The other of the landmarks, Park Street Church, is a much newer structure, dating from 1809, and is not the symbol for quite such sacred values as is the Old South. Nevertheless, owing partly to its aesthetic properties and partly to the "contagious" tendency of values, by which they readily attach to different symbols though there is no objective basis for such attachment, Park Street Church has become the focus for genuine emotional feelings. When therefore it was announced, on December 9, 1902, that a building syndicate had secured an option on the church and lot and was preparing to erect a tall office building on the site, there was a response of indignation from the community at large. The church had for some time been in financial difficulty and this had precipitated dissension within the congregation.[73] As one of the attendants is quoted as saying: "The real reason Park Street Church was sold was because of money. Some years ago the church got into difficulty; there was quarreling and religion

---

[72] *Ibid.*
[73] Committee for the Preservation of Park Street Church, *The Preservation of Park Street Church, Boston* (Boston: 1903), p. 41.

went out." [74] Additional considerations had been the church's dwindling congregation, and the desire of some of its members to remove to the then fashionable Back Bay or Fens area.[75] At first the church society had been predominantly opposed to sale of the historic building.[76] However, after a series of meetings, in which the women pew holders were barred from voting owing to a clause in the society's constitution, a majority vote in favor of sale had been obtained.[76a]

Once the fact became known a subscription fund was begun with which to endow the church and preserve it from destruction. A meeting was held on January 14, 1903 at the Beacon Hill home of Mr. William Tudor. By then $100,000 had already been pledged and a committee was elected to take whatever further steps might be necessary.[77] Prominent organizations backed the campaign to preserve the church, notably the Twentieth Century Club, the Society of Colonial Dames, and several others.[78] Eventually an offer of $350,000 was made to the church society as an endowment, on condition that the church keep and use its property at its present location. This offer was declined; the church society refused to consider anything less than $600,000.[79] Such an attitude aroused resentment in certain quarters. The church society was accused of having a mercenary attitude toward its property, the real value of which represented an unearned increment wholly creditable to the community of Boston and not to any endeavors on the part of the church. We read:

That this historic and beloved building, the property in a sentimental and most real sense of the entire community, should be ruthlessly swept away, in order that the society with which the title rests should be a great financial gainer, is a monstrous thing.[80]

[74] Quoted in the *Boston Transcript*, February 27, 1903.
[75] *Loc. cit.*
[76] *Boston Transcript*, December 15, 1902.
[76a] *Boston Globe*, June 27, 1903 and July 1, 1903.
[77] Committee for the Preservation of Park Street Church, *op. cit.*, pp. 19–20.
[78] *Boston Sunday Journal*, March 15, 1903.
[79] *Boston Globe*, June 27, 1903.
[80] *Boston Sunday Journal*, March 15, 1903.

This sentiment of indignation and resentment reveals rather well the "sacred" *versus* "profane" character of the conflict. That a church devoted to things religious should exhibit so self-seeking an attitude toward the disposition of its property was offensive to the sensibilities of some persons in the community — particularly in view of the symbolic significance of that property. The fact that legal title to the church and lot rested with the church society, and that in point of law the owners might dispose of their property as they wished, in no way mitigated the popular attitude of indignation.

The trustees of the building syndicate, who had negotiated the sale, expressed their position as follows:

This site is the most conspicuous in the whole city, and there can be no more advantageous position for a retail establishment. The reports show that nearly 11,000,000 persons entered the Park street subway station during the past year, and it is fair to presume that the same number left the subway at that station, thus showing an aggregate of 22,000,000 persons yearly brought to this point because of the subway. . . .

As to the lot itself, the light is absolutely unequalled, having the Granary Burying-Ground on the one hand, Park street and the wide expanse of the Common on the other, and Tremont street and Hamilton place in front.[81]

To the syndicate the Park Street Church was not a symbol for affectively toned values but was rather a potential productive agent — a means that should be rationally appropriated and put to its most profitable use. Among the newspapers of Boston the *Herald* was the most disposed to the church's removal. A *Herald* editorial on the Park Street Church affair, after chiding the sentimentality of "certain people," concluded with the suggestion that: "We ought to be to some extent reasonable even in our sentimentality." [82]

Following refusal of the church society to accept the offer of a $350,000 endowment the Preservation Committee sought to in-

---

[81] Henry Whitmore, of the firm of Messrs. Meredith and Grew, quoted in the *Boston Transcript*, December 15, 1902.

[82] *Boston Herald*, February 4, 1903.

terest the state in buying the property and devoting it to some appropriate public use. Several other similar plans were advanced but none ever received serious consideration. Finally the rather unexpected announcement was made that the deal had fallen through. Owing primarily to financial difficulties which precluded its living up to the terms of the contract the building syndicate had forfeited its option.[83] An editorial in the *Transcript* rejoiced that: "Park Street Church is now declared to be as good as saved." [84] But, two months later the church society again determined, by a 23 to 3 vote, to dispose of its property. Newspapermen had been barred from this meeting, owing to the church's desire to prevent any further public clamoring.[85] Deacon Wyman expressed his opinion that the society's determination to sell was a strictly church affair and should not be the concern of the public.[86] Throughout the next two years further negotiations were undertaken, one involving the lease of the lot for ninety-nine years and the construction upon it of a mammoth office and business building,[87] another involving construction of a modern commercial building and its lease to the Boston Herald Company for twenty years.[88] Neither of these was consummated. More than a year later Deacon Parker responded to queries about the church thus: "The future of the church? Well, that is hard to say." [89]

In the end the building was preserved, though its front became converted for occupancy by stores. Its survival cannot be wholly or even largely attributed to the endeavors of the Preservation Committee, acting upon spatially referred values. Rather the church society's failure to consummate negotiations resulted in the building's preservation. Nevertheless the whole affair brings out in striking detail the play of values *versus* interests and the conflict between "sacred" and "profane" land uses. What is even more important for ecological theory is the referability of the

[83] *Boston Globe,* April 2, 1903.
[84] *Boston Transcript,* editorial, April 2, 1903.
[85] *Boston Transcript,* July 1, 1903.
[86] *Boston Journal,* July 1, 1903.
[87] *Boston Globe,* June 27, 1903.
[88] *Boston Post,* June 15, 1904.
[89] Quoted in the *Boston Sunday Globe,* August 27, 1905.

values symbolized by Park Street Church. These values were borne by the community at large, or at least by a good share of it. The church society on the other hand, owner and occupier of the "sacred" property, was the very group most eager to dispose of it, as shown by the society's successive attempts to negotiate a sale. In short the preservation of Park Street Church was a "utility" to the community as a whole and, in some ways at least, was a "disutility" to certain subsystems within the community (the church society, the building syndicate, the Boston Herald Company, and others). Clearly no ecological theory can be adequate which equates two such heterogeneous utilities. Only by distinguishing between the utilities which accrue to larger social systems, like communities, from those which accrue to subsystems, like families, businesses, churches, etc., can such locational processes as we have described be understood. This presupposes a recognition that spatial adaptation involves something more than a multitude of disparate systems having only a competitive relationship to one another. It is necessary to realize that a community, viewed as a reality in its own right, is an adaptive agent. The locational processes arising from its quest for symbolic representation in fetishes correspond to a very real form of utility, one that may be quite at variance with the effort of subsystems to gain least costful locations. The empirically rationalistic theories are incapable of fitting such phenomena into their conceptual scheme. For that reason they may be considered empirically inadequate.

It should not be inferred from our analysis of Park Street Church that fetishes yield no utility to subsystems. On the contrary there are some "sacred" sites whose main representative function is for the subsystem rather than for the community as a more inclusive system. This is illustrated in the case of St. Paul's Church, on Tremont street. In 1902 a building syndicate offered $1,500,000 for the purchase of the church and its site, plus a $5,000 bonus to each proprietor of the church who voted in favor of the sale. In spite of this tempting offer the proprietors, in their annual business meeting, voted unanimously that the church was not for sale.[90] St. Paul's Church is nowhere near so old as many

[90] *Boston Transcript*, April 1, 1902.

of Boston's other landmarks, but it nonetheless represents an end value to its congregation, one that is venerated for its own sake.[91] As such its devotion to non-productive uses yielded a greater utility to the congregation than would its appropriation to some income-yielding end.

It is not always that income-yielding land uses must yield to fetishistic ones. There have been several instances where venerable landmarks were infringed upon or destroyed in response to the pressure of interests. The one violation which has been the source of greatest regret to later Bostonians was the destruction, in 1864, of the Hancock House, one-time gubernatorial residence of the first signer of the Declaration of Independence. In the words of an antiquarian journal: "the fate of this house has become a classic in the annals of vandalism." [92] When notice was given of the Hancock heirs' intention to sell the mansion, a special legislative committee was formed to arrange for its purchase by the state. Legislative authorization for its purchase was given, contingent upon acceptance by certain state officials. However, delay in getting this approval resulted in loss of the opportunity. Two wealthy citizens bought the house with the intention of razing it and erecting some modern dwellings on the site.[93] At this point the Hancock heirs offered the house as a gift to the city, provided it be removed to another location.[94] But the city passed the offer by and in the following year the mansion was razed.

Another violation of a spatial fetish was the removal, in 1895, of some 900 bodies from part of the Central Burying-ground, on Tremont and Boylston streets, so as to permit the construction of the subway. Anticipating the possibility of public indignation the city entrusted the care of the remains with Dr. Samuel A. Green

[91] See the values expressed in sermon by Rt. Rev. William Lawrence, *The Seventy-Fifth Anniversary of the Consecration of Saint Paul's Church, Boston, Sunday, May Twenty-six, 1895* (Boston: 1895), p. 35.

[92] *Bulletin of the Society for the Preservation of New England Antiquities*, I (May, 1910), p. 1.

[93] Report of Committee on the Preservation of the Hancock House, *City Document—No. 56* (Boston: 1863), pp. 8–10.

[94] *Bulletin of the Society for the Preservation of New England Antiquities*, loc. cit.

and arranged for their proper and decent reinterment. Two special memoranda were published by the Transit Commission outlining the procedure and justifying the steps that had been taken. In one of these reports the following statement was made:

It goes without saying that such action, under the guidance of your Board, would be decently and respectfully done. With that end in view I would recommend that all such traces of the human body as may be found in these excavations should be carefully gathered up and placed in proper receptacles for their reinterment in the same burying ground, where presumably repose the ashes of the kindred, and that this suggestion be carried out with the same regard for the feelings of friends . . . as was shown at the original burial, and as if each bony fragment was now fully identified with the person to whom it formerly belonged.[95]

Most of the remains were reburied in the same cemetery, although the Lowell and Tuttle families arranged for reinterment of the remains of their forebears elsewhere.[96] The whole thing was handled so tactfully that little opposition was incurred. Nonetheless the incident reveals rather well how the Transit Commission, in rational pursuit of an interest, had to reckon with certain spatially referred moral sentiments. In this case social values assumed the status of a conditional factor to the rational attainment of an end.

One more instance of the violation of a spatial fetish was the rearrangement of gravestones in several of the older burying-grounds so that they would appear symmetrical. Oliver Wendell Holmes regarded this as "the most accursed act of vandalism ever committed within my knowledge," and elaborated as follows:

I have never got over it. The bones of my own ancestors, being entombed, lie beneath their own tablet; but the upright stones have been shuffled about like chessmen, and nothing short of the Day of Judg-

---

[95] Appendix C ("Report of Dr. Samuel A. Green, on the Method to be Used in the Care of Human Remains Found under the Boylston Street Mall"), *First Annual Report of the Boston Transit Commission* (Boston: 1895), pp. 65–66.

[96] Appendix D ("Report of Dr. Samuel A. Green") in *op. cit.*, pp. 67–68.

ment will tell whose dust lies beneath any of those records, meant by affection to mark one small spot as sacred to some cherished memory. Shame! shame! shame! — that is all I can say.[97]

One local resident, in a letter to the writer, spoke of this violation of the downtown cemeteries as follows:

Bear in mind that almost all of our occupants of downtown graveyards are infidels of the Protestant faith; whereas, the custodians are almost all confirmed believers in the Roman Catholic faith. Moreover, every corpse is probably that of an Englishman or of the descendant of an Englishman; whereas, the custodians are almost all of Irish descent. I leave the rest to your imagination. At all events in the Granary and in the King's Chapel Burying-Grounds the gravestones have almost all been regimented for purposes of more easy care of the grounds. . . . The affection with which the public authorities regard our graveyards is right along this line.[98]

In all of these examples it appears that space has been divested of its role as a productive agent and has been removed from the process of rational allocation. As a result it has been put to wholly non-economic uses — uses that yield no income whatsoever. And yet, paradoxically, it has yielded "utility." But this utility is not of the sort which attends the minimization of cost. It is of a very different order, one which nevertheless has real functional significance for the larger social and cultural system. The utility consists of the symbolic representation of this larger social and cultural system and hence the fuller solidarization and integration of the individual with that system. By thus representing before people's minds the identity of the larger system to which they owe allegiance a spatial fetish renews and revitalizes the ends which attach those people to their system. In this way the latent process of atomization inherent in all systems is arrested and maintenance of the society's identity is furthered.

This is a positive function of spatial fetishes. And yet, real disfunctions result from this removal of a potential productive

---

[97] Oliver Wendell Holmes, *The Autocrat of the Breakfast Table* (Chicago: no date), pp. 263–264.

[98] Personal correspondence to writer, the authorship of which must be kept anonymous. W. F.

agent from the economic process. This fact forces us to recognize
the non-commensurable character of utilities as between the whole
and the part, the system and the subsystem. Without this distinction certain land use phenomena cannot be explained. And
yet, the recognition of this heterogeneity of utilities vitiates the
supplementary hypothesis by which the empirically rationalistic
theories have tried to explain the spontaneous orderliness of
spatial patterns. In this way the last logical postulate of empirical
rationalism is rendered inadequate to the describing of locational
processes. The reconstruction of ecological theory must start
from wholly different premises. One of these is that space may be
a symbol for social values.

CHAPTER V

THE INFLUENCE OF LOCALIZED SOCIAL SOLIDARITY
UPON LAND USE: THE NORTH END

So FAR we have established two main points. We have, to begin with, shown that there is more to the society-space relationship than an intrinsic nexus. Apparently space may be not only an impediment (or, viewed positively, a productive agent),[1] but may also be a symbol. Secondly, we have shown that social systems choose locations not only in response to interests but also in response to values. These values derive from a broader, larger cultural system which has found articulation in a spatial area. If these two points are granted, it follows that values are independently causative factors in land use. For it is they that endow space with its symbolic quality and it is they that instill themselves in the end-repertoires of social systems, thus guiding the latter in their adaptation to space. This has been found to be true of the locational processes on both Beacon Hill and the numerous historic sites scattered throughout central Boston. At this point, however, the question may arise: just how much causal power can be imputed to values on the basis of two sets of data in both of which there were no serious physical obstructions to volitional land use? In the case of Beacon Hill, the Common, the burying-grounds and the historic landmarks, the geographical and architectural layout of the areas did not present any serious barriers to such an orientation. Might not the efficacy of values be much less in other cases where geographical and physical fac-

[1] From our point of view a productive agent simply represents one pole upon a continuum of "impeditiveness," that pole being characterized by alterability and amenability to manipulation by the actor or human agent. But it is nonetheless a very real impediment, abstractly speaking, for it mediates and qualifies the attainment of ends. The opposite pole is characterized by unalterability and "giveness." The whole productive process consists of the manipulation of more alterable impediments *vis-à-vis* less alterable impediments.

tors were such that only a rationalistic theory could describe the resulting locational processes?

The question thus raised cannot, of course, provide a refuge for the empirically rationalistic theories. So long as values have *any* significant causal efficacy in land use it follows that the empirically rationalistic theories fall short of describing at least some locational processes. And that has been our principal claim.[2] Nonetheless it may be profitable to pursue the question that has been raised with a view to estimating just how causative social values may be. In the face of physical resistances how great a causal power may they possess? If it can be shown that this power is considerable we shall have made an even more convincing case for the necessity of reorganizing ecological theory so as to incorporate the cultural component as a central variable.

Physical Deterrents to Volitional Adaptation. There are a number of courses open to us for the solution of this problem, of which we have chosen one. We have selected for detailed analysis a residential neighborhood in central Boston whose physical characteristics present a number of deterrents to people seeking homes. Our specific problem will be to explain, not why people live there at all, but why people having certain ethnic and demographic characteristics show a greater tendency to live there than people not having those characteristics. The area thus selected is the North End, a physically deteriorated and congested residential neighborhood lying between the wholesale market section and the railroad terminus at North Station.[3] This district, almost wholly Italian in population, has been called "Boston's classic land of poverty."[4] The aptness of this characterization is disclosed by a number of indices of housing and other physical conditions, all of which class the North End as being the least

---

[2] In Part II of this study we shall, of course, go further and indicate that rational adaptation is itself contingent upon a particular cultural system. This, however, is not the immediate point at issue.

[3] For purposes of this study the North End has been defined as that area bounded on the west by Washington Street North, on the north and east by Commercial street, on the southeast and south by North street, and on the southwest by Mechanic-Hanover-Morton-Endicott-Stillman streets. Within this area 50 per cent or more of the persons listed in the *Boston City Directory* for 1942 have Italian names.

[4] Robert A. Woods (ed.), *Americans in Process* (Boston: 1903), p. 5.

desirable of Boston's residential districts from any physical stand-point. Thus fully 16.46 per cent of the dwelling units in the North End are defined by the census as being in need of major repairs.[5] This compares with 9.32 per cent for Boston as a whole.[6] The reason for this structural deterioration lies in the age of the dwell-ings. Sixty per cent of the buildings in the North End are forty or more years old, and 18 per cent of them are eighty or more years old. Only eleven new structures were built in the North End between 1930 and 1940.[7] Indicative of the dilapidated char-acter of many buildings is the recent sale of a 20-room apartment building for only $500. Not only are the houses substandard but they are overcrowded. Indeed the North End is by far the most congested residential quarter of Boston, having a population den-sity of 924.3 persons per acre; the next most densely populated neighborhood is the West End, with 369.7 persons per acre.[8] The congestion of the North End relative to that of other portions of Boston is brought out clearly by the data in Table 8, which show, by health and welfare areas, the number of persons per in-habited acre and the percentage of households having more than 1.5 persons per room.[9] From these data it can be seen that hardly any district of Boston even approaches the North End in degree of congestion. It is not surprising then to find that the area has declined in population from 21,111 in 1930 to 17,598 in 1940.[10]

[5] In using census data we have delineated the North End so as to include census tracts F1, F2, F4, and F5. The area thus bounded corresponds almost perfectly with the area which embraces all streets of whose occupants 50 per cent or more have Italian names, as calculated from the *Boston City Direc-tory,* 1942.

[6] Computed from census tract data in *Population and Housing — Statistics for Census Tracts, Boston, Massachusetts,* Sixteenth Census of the United States, 1940, Table 6.

[7] The Finance Commission of the City of Boston, *A Study of Certain of the Effects of Decentralization on Boston and some Neighboring Cities and Towns* (Boston: 1941), p. 11.

[8] Greater Boston Community Council, Research Bureau, Community Studies, *The People of Boston and Its Fifteen Health and Welfare Areas* (Boston: 1944, mimeographed bulletin), Table 3.

[9] Greater Boston Community Council, *loc. cit.*

[10] Aggregate populations of census tracts F1, F2, F4, F5. 1930 data are from *Census Tract Data, 1930 Census,* Table 1; unpublished material from the Fifteenth Census of the United States, 1930, tabulated especially for the

TABLE 8

PERSONS PER INHABITED ACRE AND PER CENT OF HOUSEHOLDS HAVING MORE
THAN 1.5 PERSONS PER ROOM, BY HEALTH AND WELFARE AREAS IN BOSTON, 1940

Health and Welfare Area	Per Cent of Households with over 1.5 Persons Per Room	Persons per Inhabited Acre
Boston as a whole	3.9	94.5
Back Bay	4.8	202.8
Brighton	3.4	72.5
Charlestown	4.1	255.1
Dorchester (north)	2.2	103.0
Dorchester (south)	1.2	69.2
East Boston	7.6	203.4
Hyde Park	3.3	31.2
Jamaica Plain	2.3	46.4
North End	*15.8*	*924.3*
Roslindale	1.1	48.4
Roxbury	3.8	147.9
South Boston	4.6	196.8
South End	6.4	349.3
West End	4.5	369.7
West Roxbury	0.6	27.8

Source: Greater Boston Community Council, *The People of Boston and Its Fifteen
Health and Welfare Areas*, 1944, Table 3.

To such a district the term "slum" may accurately be applied.[11]

In its population characteristics the North End is no less distinctive. Thirty-six per cent of the population is composed of foreign-born white persons.[12] These foreign-born are almost entirely of Italian origin, as may be seen from the below data on country of birth of foreign-born white persons in the North End.[13] Of the native white residents in the North End the overwhelming majority are second and third generation Italians — young adults

Boston Health Department. 1940 data are from *Population and Housing —
Statistics for Census Tracts, Boston, Massachusetts*, Sixteenth Census of the
United States, 1940, Table 2.

[11] See James Ford, *Slums and Housing* (Cambridge: 1936), I, 11–13, for
a rigorous definition of the term "slum."

[12] Computed from census tract data in *Population and Housing — Statistics
for Census Tracts, Boston, Massachusetts*, Sixteenth Census of the United
States, 1940, Table 1.

[13] Computed from census tract data in *Population and Housing — Statistics
for Census Tracts, Boston, Massachusetts*, Sixteenth Census of the United
States, 1940, Table 3.

TABLE 9

<small>COUNTRY OF BIRTH OF FOREIGN-BORN WHITE PERSONS IN THE NORTH END, 1940</small>

Country	Number	Percentage
Total number of foreign born......................	6335	100.00
Italy...	5940	93.77
Spain, Portugal....................................	179	2.83
Canada..	37	.58
Ireland..	36	.57
Latin America.....................................	14	.22
Other countries....................................	129	2.03

Source: Sixteenth Census of the United States, 1940.

and their children born in the United States but whose parents or grandparents immigrated to this country from Italy. These characteristics, of course, fit a pattern that is typical of immigrant slums in all large American cities. The slum is everywhere characterized by substandard housing, population congestion, declining numbers, and a population that is either of foreign origin or of extreme heterogeneity. It is in terms of these typical features that orthodox ecology — both the idealized descriptive schemes and the empirically rationalistic theories — has formulated its theory of the slum. Put most briefly this theory postulates that: "The slum is the area of minimum choice. It is the product of compulsion rather than design." [14] In other words, the slum is a residual area whose occupants live there because they have to rather than because they have voluntarily chosen to. Such a proposition renders land use in slums a completely deterministic phenomenon, for it denies that volition plays any significant role in the choice of residence. Presumably a family, in seeking a home, rationally apprehends the undesirable physical characteristics that prevail in a slum and determines to live elsewhere if it has the means. Those families which lack the income to pay the rent which more pleasant neighborhoods can command will be forced to take up residence in the slum. Inferentially such families, once they acquire sufficient means, will move to more desirable districts. Rationality thus becomes the only link between a social system and space. Now it is not our purpose to deny that

[14] R. D. McKenzie, "The Scope of Human Ecology," in Ernest W. Burgess (ed.), *The Urban Community* (Chicago: 1926), p. 180.

for most urban families this is indeed a predominant consideration in the choice of residence. Most people reject at the outset,
on very rational grounds, the thought of deliberately choosing to
live in a slum. But it does not necessarily follow that for *all*
people rationality is thus the *only* orientation to space, even in
the extreme case of residence in a slum. We have already found
such a conception to be inapplicable to fashionable residential
areas and to historic landmarks. It should therefore be a significant finding if the same can be said of immigrant slums, where
there is every objective deterrent to residence, once a person is
aware of the whole range of living conditions possible in American cities.

At first glance there would seem to be little or no evidence
whatsoever for the influence of volition upon locational processes
in the slum. The total population in the North End has shown an
actual decline in numbers, the district is familiar to every Bostonian as a squalid tenement quarter, and every social service
agency knows it as an area of poverty, unemployment, juvenile
delinquency, and many other welfare problems. And most important of all, the Italian residents themselves fully recognize the
district for what it is. Evidence that there is no deficiency in the
awareness that residents have of the North End's physical characteristics may be found in the following statement:

Non per colpa degli Italiani, ma per l'antichità relativa del luogo, il
North End è il quartiere meno decente cella città. I casamenti si ac-
catastano quali gabbie immani per tutte le vie: si stringono in ogni
lembo di terra disponibile, sì che nel North End, quartiere populare,
si fanno pagare pigioni elevate come nei quartieri aristocratici.[15]

The elected representatives of the North End in the city council
and in the state legislature are constantly pleading for more play-

[15] "Not through the fault of the Italians, but because of the relative age
of the place, the North End is the least attractive quarter of the city. The
large dwellings are almost like cages for everyone in them; they squeeze
people into every bit of available ground, so that in the North End, a lower-
class quarter, rents are as high as in the aristocratic quarter." *Venticinque
Anni di Missione fra gl'Immigrati Italiani di Boston, Mass., 1888–1913*
(Milano: 1913), p. 59.

fields and open air spaces, and this issue always finds a place in the political platform of local candidates. Ignorance of better places in which to live cannot by itself account for why some persons maintain residence in the North End.

The Hypothesis of Space as an Instrumentality. It would seem almost futile to look for any retentive influence by the North End upon its population, or for any attachment on the part of persons and groups toward the area. And yet, a study of certain migration differentials in the North End brings out a real congruence between Italian social structure and locational processes. Specifically it reveals a selective incidence of the gross population decline upon local residents, a selectivity which corresponds to varying degrees of identification with Italian values. Thus residence within an immigrant slum becomes more than a matter of spatial placement; it signifies as well the acceptance of immigrant values and participation in immigrant associations. This arises from the fact that spatial nearness is easily construed as identification with a given group, for it shows a willingness to be "available" and "on hand" for the routine interactions that are possible only when persons are spatially near to one another. Hence, for immigrants sharing certain common values and participating in common associations, the physical undesirability of a slum may be far outweighed as a criterion for selecting a place of residence by the status and recognition which goes with residence with their fellow nationals.

In this phenomenon there is a society-space relationship that is partly intrinsic and partly symbolic, yet which is not identical with either. Thus, it is undoubtedly true that one reason spatial proximity is so commonly construed as acceptance of a group's values is that nearness is a necessary precondition to continuousness of interaction. This follows from the impeditive character of space, by which the loss of time involved in traversing distance reduces the possible duration and continuousness of interaction between persons. But this impeditive quality is not by itself enough to explain why social systems attach the particular meanings which they do to spatial proximity. For it is a fact that many forms of spatial proximity, such as living in hotels and rooming houses, imply no necessary identification whatsoever with the persons involved.[16] Clearly it is necessary to look to the meanings which people attach to spatial proximity. In other words, spatial proximity may have a symbolic significance for certain kinds of social systems.

And yet, this symbolic quality is quite different from the fetishism which was found on Beacon Hill, and in the historic landmarks of central Boston. Unlike fetishism, where place becomes an end value in itself, the symbolism involved in spatial proximity is but an instrumentality or means. It is not the object of veneration or respect at all. Nevertheless it comes to articulate and objectify the identity of a group. Through this it gives rise to locational processes that are incomprehensible in terms of the area's purely physical properties. In other words, the locational significance of spatial symbolism is not limited to its fetishistic qualities. For it has the added potentiality of being what we shall call an "instrumentality."

The general nature of this instrumental property of space may be noted at this point, by way of formulating the specific hypothesis of this chapter. A suggestive approach to the problem has been made by Simmel in his analysis of space as an element of group persistence. According to Simmel there are four elements or bases of group persistence: (a) permanence of locality; (b) gradual change of membership; (c) objectification of group unity in symbols; and (d) concentration of group unity in a specialized "organ." [17] From a logical standpoint this classification suffers from an eclecticism and overlapping of items. This, however, can be remedied by translating its items into a more simple scheme. Thus permanence of locality is not as such a basis of group persistence since a good many groups, notably nomads and gypsies, maintain solidarity without it. Actually it is but an external condition which, by virtue of its bearing upon social interaction, peculiarly lends itself to the symbolic representation of group

---

[16] In some hotels, to be sure, there is a class symbolism involved in one's choice of place. But this sort of identification is not inherent in the fact of spatial proximity as such.

[17] Georg Simmel, "The Persistence of Social Groups," *American Journal of Sociology*, 3: 662–698 (March, 1898); 3: 829–836 (May, 1898); 4: 35–50 (July, 1898).

unity. It may thus be viewed as a subtype of Simmel's third element, objectification of group unity in symbols. Similarly gradual change of membership and concentration of unity in a specialized organ may be regarded as coördinate preconditions to group persistence inhering in the make-up of the agents which constitute the group.

For our purposes, then, it will be useful to revise the elements of group persistence (maintenance of a social system's identity) into the following classification:

(a) Consensus about certain values, deriving from a *cultural* system, in terms of which a particular *social* system has its being.

(b) Objectification of these values in instrumental symbols, of which space is frequently an appropriate one.

(c) Gradual change of membership, and concentration of unity in special subsystem having a coördinative function.

Between the three items of this classification there is a functional relationship of such a nature that changes in one entail corresponding changes in the other. Thus, insofar as space becomes a symbol for the values shared by the members of a group, any significant change in the degree of consensus which the members of that group have toward those values will change the status of space as a symbol so that people will distribute themselves differently than they did before. Such alterations Simmel views as "räumliche Projektionen der funktionellen Änderung." [18] A reverse relationship may also operate, to be sure. Once space becomes a symbol for a social system's identity it tends to strengthen the consensus which that system has with respect to its values.[19] However, this reverse influence, by which spatial proximity reinforces social solidarity, will not be of major interest to us in the present chapter, since its significance has already been described in our analysis of Beacon Hill.

What is most important now about this functional relationship between solidarity and symbolism is its non-explicit character.

[18] Simmel, "Über räumliche Projektionen socialer Formen," *Zeitschrift für Sozialwissenschaft,* 6: 287–302 (1903), p. 293.

[19] Simmel, "Der Raum und die räumliche Ordnungen der Gesellschaft," *Soziologie* (München: 1923), p. 467. See also: René Maunier, *L'Origine et la Fonction Économique des Villes* (Paris: 1910), p. 211.

Space in this case is not the conscious object of veneration. Rather it is but a neutral instrumentality of the values about which the members of a social system have consensus. Defining this relationship more carefully, we may say that a spatial area becomes an instrumentality when a social system defines location within that area as a gesture or expression of integration with the values which its members share. This definition excludes applying the term "instrumentality" to the causal influence which spatial proximity may have upon social solidarity. It is only in the sense of a "denoter" or "designator" that the term "instrumentality" is to be understood in the present study.

Applying this to the North End the reader will recall that the Italians who live there have no apparent affective attachment to the neighborhood as a spatial area. Indeed, for at least some of them the area has a negative emotional significance. In no sense of the word can the North End be regarded as a fetish for the people who inhabit it. And yet, as will presently be shown, residence in the district is commonly construed by persons of Italian origin as denoting identification with the Italian community and with its distinctive values in regard to occupation, family, choice of friends, group membership, etc. As a result of this definition put upon the North End, persons who share Italian values show a greater tendency to live there than those who do not. Thus some fairly significant migration differentials appear which cannot be explained through the empirically rationalistic view of the slum as an "area of minimum choice" or as "the product of compulsion rather than design." Only by invoking once again the cultural component in spatial adaptation can these locational processes be understood. For it is through the cultural component that space acquires its symbolic property as an instrumentality of value-consensus. Thus, even in the face of such physical resistances as are found in slums, social values will be found to have a very real causal influence upon land use. The necessity of incorporating them, along with other variables, into a systematic ecological theory becomes all the more evident.

Italian Community Organization. The North End is the one distinctly Italian community of Boston. In it are to be found most of the main Italian associations of the metropolitan area: Italian markets, Italian churches, Italian benevolent orders, Italian doctors and lawyers, etc. Ninety-four per cent of its foreign-born residents are of Italian origin and an overwhelming majority of its native-born residents have Italian antecedents. Within its limited expanse are to be found 18.82 per cent of all Italian-born persons in Boston. The dominant position of the North End in

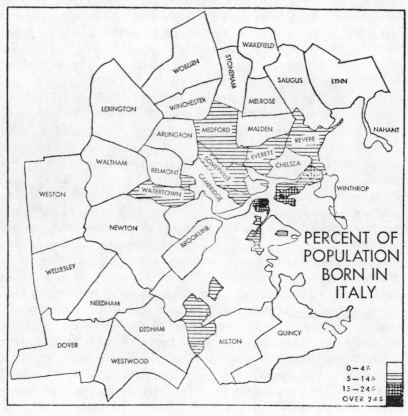

FIGURE 12

the overall distribution of foreign-born Italians in Boston is revealed in figure 12. From the map it can be seen that the North End far exceeds any other neighborhood in its proportion of Italian-born persons. In a sense it constitutes a population reservoir from which Italians have overflowed into East Boston, the

West End, East Cambridge, and various scattered clusters throughout the towns of Revere, Everett, Medford, and Somerville.

However, the North End has not always been an Italian district. Between 1850 and 1880 it was a predominantly Irish neighborhood, and it is only with the beginning of the present century that Italians have come to dominate the district. Thus, in 1880 there were only 1,277 Italians in all of Boston,[20] and a good many of these lived elsewhere in the city. However during succeeding years the Italian population underwent a very rapid growth. Every year hundreds of new immigrants docked at the Charlestown pier where they were met by friends who had paid their steerage across and who then set them up in rooms in the North End. The Stabile Bank, an important financial institution in the North End, used to have a regular tallyho which brought newly arrived Italian immigrants directly from the docks to the North End.[21] Thus by 1905 the North End had become the principal area for Italian settlement in Boston; in that year the district contained 7,700 Italians, 6,800 Irish, and 6,200 Jews.[22] At first the Italians were forced to occupy the least desirable portions of the North End, along North street and the adjoining alleys. Evidence of this is disclosed by the Tenement House Census of Boston, made in 1891. Among other things this census grouped nationalities according to the percentage of their numbers, by wards and precincts, which lived in tenements defined as "poor and bad" in at least one respect. Thus, in Wards 6 and 7, which embraced the North End and part of the West End, 56.23 per cent of the Italians lived in tenements that were "poor and bad," whereas only 39.65 per cent of the Jews and 27.15 per cent of the Irish lived in such tenements.[23] Gradually, however, as their numbers increased, the Italians expanded along North street, then

[20] Frederick A. Bushee, "Italian Immigrants in Boston," *The Arena*, 17: 722–734 (April, 1897), p. 723.

[21] *Italian News*, September 1, 1944.

[22] William Foote Whyte, "Race Conflicts in the North End of Boston," *The New England Quarterly*, 12: 623–642 (December, 1939), p. 624.

[23] Frederick A. Bushee, *Ethnic Factors in the Population of Boston*, Publications of the American Economic Association (New York: 1903), Table 7, p. 33, based on the Tenement House Census of Boston, 1891.

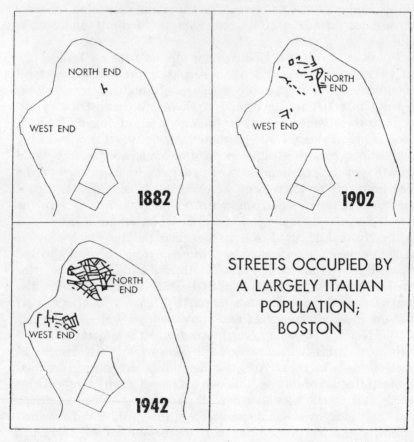

FIGURE 13

moved into North Bennet street, and eventually preëmpted the entire North End. In figure 13 we have portrayed this territorial expansion of the Italians, for 1882, 1902, and 1942.[24]

The associational activities of the first Italians were to a large extent dictated by their demographic and occupational character-

---

[24] The 1882 map is based on the findings of Whyte, *op. cit.*, p. 630; the 1902 map is adapted from Woods, *op. cit.*, maps opposite pp. 41 and 47, and indicates streets of whose inhabitants 50 per cent or more have Italian names; the 1942 map is based on our own tabulations of streets of whose inhabitants 50 per cent or more have Italian names, as indicated by street listings in the *Boston City Directory* for that year.

istics. Most of the early immigrants were men who came as "birds of passage" with the object of making money, accumulating savings, and then returning to their homeland. Even as late as 1901, 79 per cent of the Italian immigrants were men.[25] Nearly all were illiterate peasants who possessed no skills and were easy prey for employment agents, loan sharks, and other exploiters.[26] Under these circumstances the first associations formed by the Italians were mutual aid societies. Sometimes these were co-operatives, sometimes they were organized by the church or by non-Italian organizations. Another early form of association was the *paesani* group, an informal organization composed of Italians who had come from the same village or locality in Italy. Fellow *paesani* rendered a great many mutual services to one another, ranging all the way from invitations to dinner and other forms of hospitality to making loans, helping establish new arrivals, etc. As the number of Italians increased and as it became apparent that many of them would remain in this country permanently the proportion of women among the immigrants rose, and in time the sex ratio became more nearly equal.[27] This enabled a more normal domestic life for Italian immigrants and reëstablished the preëminent position of the family in Italian social organization.

Present-day social structure in the North End derives in large part from these three patterns of association: the mutual aid societies, the *paesani,* and the extended family. In addition to these there is of course the church, as well as the less obvious political and extralegal organizations which have considerable significance in the North End. By virtue of all these associations and interaction patterns the North End possesses a "community life organization" which endows it with a reality.[28] Only by conceptualizing this reality within a system of ecological variables can the locational processes of the North End be understood. To hold to the mechanistic premise of the empirically rationalistic

[25] Bushee, *Ethnic Factors in the Population of Boston,* p. 18, based on the Tenement House Census of Boston, 1891.

[26] This was not so characteristic of the Genoese and other northern Italian immigrants.

[27] Today there are 89.04 women per 100 men. Among the foreign-born there are 79.28 women per 100 men, showing thus a slightly greater inequality.

[28] See Carle C. Zimmerman, *The Changing Community* (New York: 1938), p. 154.

theories and say with Park, in regard to community organization, that "the ties which hold it together are physical and vital rather than customary and moral" [29] entirely obscures such locational processes as prevail in the North End. Just as with Beacon Hill, so in the North End, the community as a reality *per se* is a spatially adaptive unit, and the territorial patterns which result from its adaptive processes cannot be attributed to disparate social systems seeking location through the mechanisms of competitive bargaining.

Undoubtedly the most important institution in Italian community organization is the family. The proportion of married adults in the North End is slightly greater than that for the general population of Boston. Thus 56.78 per cent of the North End population aged fifteen or more years is married; the corresponding figure for the population of Boston as a whole is 50.46 per cent married.[30] Not only do the majority of adult Italians marry, but most of them have large families. As a result the North End ranks near the top among health and welfare areas of Boston in regard to the average number of children per household who are under 18 years of age. Table 10 shows that only East Boston, which is an Italian neighborhood of second-generation settlement, exceeds the North End in this respect; Hyde Park, another Italian district, and Charlestown and South Boston, both of which are Irish neighborhoods, have ratios that are equal to that of the North End.[31]

These figures do not, however, disclose the real significance of kinship for Italian social structure. Even those adults who never marry, and those who marry but have no children, generally participate in a well defined kinship organization. This organiza-

[29] Robert E. Park, "Human Ecology," *American Journal of Sociology*, 42: 1–15 (July, 1936), p. 15.

[30] North End percentage tabulated from *Census Tract Data, 1930 Census,* Table 7, unpublished material from the Fifteenth Census of the United States, 1930, tabulated especially for the Boston Health Department. Boston percentage tabulated from *Abstract of the Fifteenth Census of the United States,* 1930, Table 121 in "Population" section.

[31] Greater Boston Community Council, Research Bureau, Community Studies, *The People of Boston and Its Fifteen Health and Welfare Areas* (Boston: 1944, mimeographed bulletin), Table 1, based on Sixteenth Census of the United States, 1940.

TABLE 10

AVERAGE NUMBER OF CHILDREN UNDER 18 YEARS OF AGE PER HOUSEHOLD,
BY HEALTH AND WELFARE AREAS IN BOSTON, 1940

Health and Welfare Area	Number of Children
Boston as a whole	1.0
Back Bay	0.2
Brighton	0.8
Charlestown	1.3
Dorchester (north)	1.2
Dorchester (south)	1.1
East Boston	1.4
Hyde Park	1.3
Jamaica Plain	1.1
North End	*1.3*
Roslindale	1.0
Roxbury	1.1
South Boston	1.3
South End	0.7
West End	0.8
West Roxbury	1.1

Source: Greater Boston Community Council, *The People of Boston and Its Fifteen Health and Welfare Areas*, 1944, Table 1.

tion is built along consanguine lines so that the solidary unit completely transcends individual conjugal households. Between the members of this extended kinship structure there is a genuine in-group feeling and solidarity which is manifested by reciprocal services, sharing of meals, visiting, and other overt activities. The titular head of this unit is the eldest male; his authority is paramount and respected, even by children who have matured, married, and set up their own households. An editorial in the *Italian News*, a weekly newspaper printed and published in the North End, eulogizes "Italian Home Life" as follows:

Amidst the turmoil of modernity and the wide chasm ever widening between the parents, the solidarity of the Italian family is a redeeming phenomenon. Loyalty, respect and honor still hold the fort as the priceless ingredients of family harmony in spite of the assaults of modern looseness and cynicism.[32]

In a certain sense the larger family extends even beyond the blood tie. Thus, a man who has particular regard for a close friend of

[32] *Italian News*, February 4, 1944.

his may become a *compari* of that friend; he will serve as god-father to his friend's children and in that way will become a very real member of the latter's family. Women may enter into similar relationships by declaring themselves *commari*.[33] The solidarizing and integrating function of the Italian family lies in its providing the individual with an arena of appreciation and reward for distinctly Italian traits. It offers the individual "a great deal of social satisfaction almost entirely within the framework of Italian culture."[34] In this way it cultivates and perpetuates Italian values and maintains the community's separateness from the larger society. In many homes it is a point of pride to converse only in the Italian language. Indeed many of the older women know very little English; all their friends and associates are Italian, and their whole world is encompassed by the bounds of the immigrant community in which they live.[35] To a striking extent the status which an individual Italian has in the North End community is contingent upon his position in the kinship structure and the completeness with which he identifies himself with it. Status in the North End is in very large degree the "status of ascription" rather than the "status of achievement."[36] Hospitality to friends and relatives is the ceremonial expression of this status. A family is rated according to its hospitality and good taste in inviting friends to the Sunday meal. To be able to serve a large dinner, with all the wine that guests can take, is a sign of respectability.[37] It is status of this sort — within the extended kinship group — that matters most to the Italian who is fully integrated with the local value system.

Next in importance as a solidarizing and integrating factor in the North End community are the *paesani* groups. These groups, consisting of immigrants who came to the North End from the same villages or provinces in Italy, are generally the most important non-familial organizations to which the older Italian belongs. They range all the way from such informal "clubs" as

[33] Mr. Norman A. Franzeim, boys' worker, North Bennet Street Industrial School.
[34] Irvin L. Child, *Italian or American?* (New Haven: 1943), p. 60.
[35] Jerre Mangione, *Mount Allegro* (Boston: 1943), pp. 51–53, 59.
[36] Ralph Linton, *The Study of Man* (New York: 1936), pp. 115 ff.
[37] John Manfredi, Department of Sociology, Harvard University.

that which a group of men on Sheafe street, all of whom came from the province of Avellino, have recently formed,[38] to somewhat more formal organizations like the Torrese Club, which is made up of natives of Torre le Nocelle, also in the province of Avellino.[39] Sometimes these *paesani* groups form small sub-neighborhoods within the North End. Thus, on Sheafe street there are some twenty families from Avellino. Around Fleet and Commercial streets there is a concentration of Calabrians and Sicilians. Other such localized *paesani* groupings exist in the North End, although with the passage of time their distinctness is being rapidly obliterated.[40] The functions of the *paesani* groups are partly secular and partly religious in character. Thus the Italian who wishes a funeral for some close relative generally goes to the undertaker of his *paesani*. Any *paesani* group which is at all large will have its own undertaker, generally a socially prominent individual who assiduously cultivates active relations with his fellow *paesani*.[41] Until the outbreak of the present war each group of *paesani* in the North End held an annual *festa* in honor of its patron saint. These *festas*, accompanied by parades, special masses, costumes, oratory, and family reunions, were potent solidarizing and integrating factors in the Italian community.[42] They had the additional function of associating in the minds of Italians the identity of their nationality group with the North End as a territorial locus.

Within the North End may be found a number of other clubs, lodges, and benefit societies. There are over fifty mutual aid societies alone in the community.[43] In all of these associations, just as in the extended families and in the *paesani* groupings, Italian values are at a premium. The net result is a fuller internalization of these values in the individual's personality and his more complete integration into the cultural system which they comprise. At the same time, through the selective association which they entail, by which Italians associate with other Italians,

[38] Mr. Norman A. Franzeim.
[39] *Italian News*, January 7, 1944.
[40] Whyte, "Race Conflicts in the North End of Boston."
[41] Whyte, *Street Corner Society* (Chicago: 1943), pp. 201–202.
[42] *Ibid.*, pp. 269–272.
[43] Mr. D. E. Lucozzi, realtor, Salem street.

these groups bring about a solidarization of their members with the Italian community. The significance of the Italian churches, so far as their community-building influence is concerned, lies in much the same direction. There are two distinctly Italian churches in the North End: The Church of the Sacred Heart, at North square, and St. Leonard's of Port Maurice, on Prince street. In addition to these there are three other Catholic churches in the North End, though these are preponderantly Irish — despite the fact that that nationality has entirely left the North End. The influence of the Italian churches is nowhere near so paramount as it is among certain other Roman Catholic minorities, notably the Irish and the French Canadians. Nonetheless by their use of the Italian language, their sanctification of Italian marriages, and their sponsorship of many secular Italian clubs and affairs, they contribute to the formation of a localistic solidarity among North End Italians.

Finally there are the political and extralegal organizations which constitute so pervasive a feature of North End life. The Italians have been slow to take to politics. Even today less than half of the first generation Italians in the North End are naturalized citizens, though most of them have been in this country for twenty or thirty years.[44] Furthermore, as of 1930, fully 39.08 per cent of the foreign-born persons in the North End are illiterate and could not possibly participate in political affairs.[45] Among the fifteen health and welfare areas of Boston the North End ranks lowest in the median number of school years completed by persons 25 years of age and over; its median of 6.3 years compares with 8.9 for Boston as a whole.[46] Nonetheless, in spite of these disabilities, the North End has developed a considerable

[44] Exactly 44.90 per cent of the foreign-born in the North End are naturalized citizens. Computed from census tract data in *Population and Housing — Statistics for Census Tracts, Boston, Massachusetts,* Sixteenth Census of the United States, 1940, Table 3.

[45] Calculated from census tract data in *Census Tract Data, 1930 Census,* Table 6; unpublished material from the Fifteenth Census of the United States, 1930, tabulated especially for the Boston Health Department.

[46] Greater Boston Community Council, Research Bureau, Community Studies, *The People of Boston and its Fifteen Health and Welfare Areas* (Boston: 1944, mimeographed bulletin), Table 4.

degree of ethnic solidarity about political matters — a solidarity which reinforces its self-conception as a community. Owing to the American system of territorial representation, by which a minority can gain political recognition only if it dominates a definite spatial unit, like a ward, such ethnic groups as the Italians can elect their own members to office only if they are territorially contiguous. As a result, ethnic solidarity becomes objectified in terms of spatial localization. Actually it has only been since 1934 that the North End Italians have had political representation through one of their own nationality. In that year Edward P. Bacigalupo won the contest for the office of state representative by beating the powerful Hendricks Club, an Irish political machine that had heretofore dominated Ward 3, in which the North End is situated. Five years later, in 1939, the North End won representation on the city council for the first time by the election of Joseph Russo as city councilor.[47] Through these victories the Italians have been able to gain for themselves certain political favors which had heretofore been much less accessible. The distinctly ethnic basis of this political solidarity appears in the political advertisements distributed by Italian candidates. Thus, in the 1943 campaign for reëlection Joseph Russo used the following appeal:

BEWARE!
ITALO-AMERICAN VOTERS
OF WARD 3, BOSTON
It took a life-time to be represented by
one of our own in the City
Council
Don't Lose What Belongs to Us!
Keep the Office in our Ranks!
Beware of False Italo-Americans!
Vote For and Reelect a Genuine
American of Italian Extraction
Joseph Russo [48]

[47] Whyte, "Race Conflicts in the North End of Boston," pp. 639–640.
[48] Political advertisement in *Italian News*, October 29, 1943. Russo won 81 per cent of the votes cast for city councilor in precincts 1, 2, 12, 13, and 14, comprising the North End portion of Ward 3. *Italian News*, November 12, 1943.

During the same campaign the editor of the local *Italian News* recommended that: "We're all supposed to be Americans, but remember, we must draw racial lines, just as other racial denominations do. When they quit doing it, then we'll quit." [49] Ethnic solidarity upon political matters goes even further than this. Very frequently a group of *paesani* will pledge their votes *en bloc* to a single candidate. For this reason politically ambitious North Enders are careful to maintain and cultivate their *paesani* affiliations.

Closely coördinated with this political organization are certain extralegal activities. A good many local residents directly or indirectly participate in various activities such as the purchase of "numbers" and the trafficking of liquor. Small businessmen who act as "bookies," individuals who regularly buy "numbers," and higher-up organizers who head these activities are integrally bound up with politicians for protection and reciprocal services. Because of the strictly local character of their political representation and hence of their protection in activities which outsiders might threaten, the Italians who organize such activities tend to concentrate in the North End. In this way the solidarity attendant upon extralegal organization is a very real community-building factor.

Through all these associations and interaction patterns the North End Italians have developed a genuine solidarity and ingroup consciousness. Outsiders frequently comment upon the smugness and self-sufficient demeanor of Italians. The subjective counterpart to such overt traits is a very real "consciousness of kind." Italians make constant reference to "our people," "our colony," and "sticking together." Outsiders are the object of suspicion and distrust. The editor of the *Italian News*, in a personal column, writes as follows: "Joe, when you purchase anything, especially in the North End where there are altogether too darn many non-Italian establishments, insist on a receipt for your purchase." [50] Among the older Italians the term "Americanate" symbolizes the "quintessence of foolishness." [51] Toward

---

[49] *Italian News*, October 29, 1943.

[50] *Italian News*, November 19, 1943.

[51] Enrico C. Sartorio, *Social and Religious Life of Italians in America* (Boston: 1918), p. 80.

Italy, their motherland, there is a strong affective attachment which manifests itself in a certain romanticization of that country and a militant concern for its welfare. Headlines in the *Italian News* read:

"A TENDER TRIBUTE TO PATHETIC ITALY" [52]

"U. S. PREPARING ANTI-CATHOLICS TO GOVERN CATHOLIC ITALY" [53]

"SEES ANARCHY IN ITALY IF ANTI-CATHOLICS RULE" [54]

Such identification with the motherland renews and revitalizes the Italians' ethnic self-consciousness and thus further contributes to their communal identity.

Participation in all these associations and interaction patterns is greatest among the immigrant Italians. The second generation, born and raised in the North End, is not so completely identified with them nor with the distinctly Italian values of the older generation. Three broad reaction patterns may be discerned among the younger Italians: (a) the in-group reaction; (b) the rebel reaction; and (c) the apathetic reaction.[55] Those who fall into the first category have largely identified themselves with Italian groups and conform their personal aspirations with distinctly Italian prestige criteria. For them there is defined a life pattern that is almost wholly embraced within the family and the *paesani*. The "rebels," on the other hand, in one degree or another repudiate Italian values and seek identification with American groups. They stop turning over their earnings to their fathers, they adopt courtship and marriage patterns which are morally reprehensible by Italian norms, they seek companionship outside the narrowly circumscribed family and *paesani* lines, and they develop occupational interests that are quite at variance with what their immigrant parents respect.[56] Those second-generation Italians who adopt the apathetic reaction manifest typically

[52] *Italian News*, December 10, 1943.
[53] *Italian News*, August 13, 1943.
[54] *Italian News*, September 3, 1943.
[55] Child, *op. cit.*, chaps. iv–vi.
[56] *Loc. cit.*

neurotic tendencies, with considerable repression. They avoid discussing their nationality and in other ways endeavor to retreat from a situation of conflict. Each of these reaction patterns has an appropriate significance for the maintenance of Italian communal identity in the North End. The in-group reaction tends to perpetuate this identity; the rebel reaction tends to obliterate it; and the apathetic reaction tends to atomize it. The spatial corollaries of these alterations in communal identity are most instructive for the problem which we must now take up, viz., the influence of localized solidarity, and its atomization, upon land use patterns.

The North End as an Instrumentality of Italian Community Organization. The foregoing analysis of associational and interactional patterns of North End Italians indicates that there is a genuine ethnic solidarity which is founded upon a number of groupings — the family, the *paesani*, the lodges, clubs, and other benefit societies, and finally the political and extralegal organizations. Each of these establishes a selective association by which Italians associate with other Italians more than they do with non-Italians. Furthermore, there is a "multimodal" character to such in-group association which contrasts with the strictly special purpose interaction between Italians and outsiders.[57] It is in this way that a distinct communal identity appears. Out of the composite network of family, *paesani*, club, and political interactions which engage the North End Italians there emerges a social system having a greater inclusiveness than any of these lesser systems and having a reality *sui generis*. This social system is what may be called the North End community. The system thus constituted has its being not by virtue of its summing up, in arithmetic fashion, a number of disparate lesser social systems, but rather by virtue of its being the bearer of a cultural system for which all these lesser systems are likewise bearers. About this cultural system and its component values there is a consensus. It is through this consensus about major life values on the part

[57] On these distinctions see Pitirim A. Sorokin, Charles J. Galpin, and Carle C. Zimmerman, *A Systematic Source Book in Rural Sociology* (Minneapolis: 1930), I, 308–321; also Pitirim A. Sorokin, "Systematic Sociology," *forthcoming.*

of individual Italians in the North End that there comes into being a real community.

However, such consensus about values is only one element of community identity. For any social system to maintain identity there must be an additional element, viz., an objectification of its values by some instrumental symbol.[58] Now, the *differentium specificum* of the community as a distinct type of social system lies in the fact that for it the instrumental symbol is a spatial area rather than a costume or badge or some other such vehicle. That is the reason why communal identity presupposes not only consensus about certain values, but also the added factor of localism. It is only insofar as consensus becomes localized, so that its values are instrumentalized by a limited spatial area, that a social system can properly be called a community.[59] For this reason it is incumbent upon us, before describing the locational effects of Italian ethnic solidarity in the North End, to show that that solidarity is indeed localized — i.e., that it is instrumentalized by space.

In general it may be said that Italian associations do put a premium upon residence within the North End. There is, for instance, a pronounced tendency for members of the same extended family to live near one another. This kinship localism manifests itself in a number of ways. It is not uncommon to find a single tenement entirely occupied by a single extended family: elderly parents, matured children with their mates, and grandchildren. There are instances where such a family has overflowed one tenement and has expanded into an adjoining one, breaking out the partitions for doorways.[60] Most frequently the matured children who live with their parents are daughters. This conforms to the institutionally expected concern which an Italian mother has for the welfare of her newly married daughter. The ideal pattern is for the daughter to continue living in her mother's house, with she and her husband being assigned certain rooms which they are supposed to furnish themselves. Over the course of time the young couple is expected to accumulate savings and

[58] See *supra*, p. 178.
[59] Zimmerman, *op. cit.*, p. 15.
[60] Mr. Harland Lewis, former boys' worker, Roxbury Neighborhood House.

buy their own home, preferably not far away.[61] The hold of parents upon their children is often surprisingly strong. Whyte, in his study of North End gang life, cites the case of Tony Cataldo (fictitious name) who decided to move away from the North End because his son had reached the age when he was playing with neighbors' children and was learning "bad language." However "in deference to the wishes of his mother and father" he remained in the community, though he forbade his son to play with the neighbors' children any longer.[62] Another manifestation of the localizing effects of Italian kinship solidarity is preferential renting, by which an Italian who owns a tenement will let apartments to his relatives at a lower rental. Frequently this pattern of preferential renting extends to close family friends.

Paesani and other friendship solidarities likewise assume a decided localism. As already indicated, fellow *paesani* show considerable tendency to live near one another, sometimes occupying much of a single street or court.[63] Such proximity, or at least common residence in the North End, greatly facilitates participation in the *paesani* and other informal functions which are so important to the first generation Italian. Moreover, it is in the North End that the *festas*, anniversaries, and other old world occasions are held, and such is their frequency that residence in the North End is almost indispensable to regular participation. The social relationships comprised by these groupings, as well as the benefit orders, secret societies, and religious organizations, are thus strongly localistic in character. One second generation Italian, when asked if his immigrant parents ever contemplated leaving their North End tenement, replied: "No, because all their friends are there, their relatives. They know everyone around there."[64] The very compactness of the North End is conducive to chatting and frequent outdoor visiting. On warm days the old ladies can sit on their doorsteps and visit with their neighbors; they are with people who "understand" them, who are their own kind. Outside of the North End they would be away from their

---

[61] John Manfredi.
[62] Whyte, *Street Corner Society*, p. 148.
[63] See *supra*, p. 187; Whyte, *Street Corner Society*, p. xix; Child, *op. cit.*, p. 45; Sartorio, *op. cit.*, p. 18.
[64] Mr. Magano, of Cambridge.

friends and fellow *paesani;* their neighbors would be "aliens" who could not appreciate their language, their clothes, and their manners.

Finally, the political and extralegal organizations of the North End exert a localizing influence through making residence in the community a prerequisite to receiving political protection, public office, and other favors. As indicated earlier, a territorial system of political representation means that such minority groups as the Italians can put their own men into office only insofar as they are spatially contiguous and solidary. A consequence of this is that an Italian who wants some political or public works job or who wishes to receive special relief consideration is practically obliged to live in the North End.[65] Conversely too, the politically ambitious Italian must maintain residence in the North End if he is ever to be elected to office. Thus:

> Politics, far more than any other interest, gives dignity to the larger social life in these wards. The man who succeeds in business moves away into pleasanter surroundings; the man who succeeds in politics must, in effect at least, remain. Politics lifts and localizes at the same time.[66]

The businessman who sells "numbers" or deals in liquor is likewise under pressure to maintain residence in the North End. If he is to receive "protection" in his activities he must put the politicians under some obligation to him, and that necessitates his getting votes for those politicians. To be a vote-getter such a businessman must have the friendship of the local population, and an invaluable aid to winning such friendship is local residence. For the same reason the young man desirous of getting a job in organizations of this kind will increase his chances if he lives in the community and has status in one of the informal North End gangs.[67]

In this way the North End, as a spatial area, becomes an instrumentality of Italian community solidarity. Residence

[65] In some other communities, to be sure, particularly in Revere and Somerville, the Italians have become sufficiently numerous to elect some of their own to public office.

[66] Woods, *Americans in Process*, pp. 176–177.

[67] Cf. Whyte, *Street Corner Society*, chap. iv.

within it is construed by Italians as identification with them and as acceptance of the values which they share. Departure from it is in some degree construed as rejection of them and their values. To be sure, such a judgment varies with the emigrant's particular relationship to friends in the North End and the circumstances of his leaving. Many emigrants continue to enjoy standing and recognition within the North End for years after their departure. In their generalizations, however, the North Enders do put a negative interpretation upon emigration from the community. One Italian writes of an emigrant from the North End as follows:

> I still remember with regret the vain smile of superiority that appeared on his face when I told him that I lived at the North End of Boston. "Io non vado fra quella plebaglia." (I do not go among those plebeians.) [68]

Referring to another such emigrant a politically prominent woman in the North End is quoted as saying: "He was born down here, but he moved out long ago. He had nothing to do with the people here, and they had nothing to do with him." [69] This instrumental symbolism of the North End is clearly of a very different order from the fetishistic symbolism found in Beacon Hill and in the various historic landmarks of central Boston. In no sense of the word is there any affect toward the area as such. As one North End real estate man commented:

> Most of the older people take the North End for granted. When they first came it was the only place they could go to. After they were here for a while they discovered that Americans didn't live that way and the younger ones desired to move to the suburbs where they could have a yard. But the older ones won't move. They have their friends here, the markets are close, . . . [70]

This expression, that the older Italians "take the North End for granted," typifies the attitude which they have toward the area.

[68] Sartorio, *op. cit.*, pp. 43–44.
[69] Whyte, *Street Corner Society*, pp. 231–232.
[70] D. E. Lucozzi.

Yet, along with this affectively neutral orientation there is a very real symbolic quality attached to the North End — a quality which comes from its objective representation of Italian community solidarity.

Locational Effects of Spatial Instrumentalism. As a result of the symbolic quality which attaches to the North End there have developed certain unmistakable differentials in the rate of emigration from the district — differentials which correspond closely to varying degrees of identification with the Italian community. In the light of these differentials residence in the North End is seen to be a spatial corollary to integration with Italian values.

To get at the emigration differentials in the North End two entirely different statistical procedures have been followed. One of these consists of estimating emigration through the use of life expectancy tables — calculating the difference between the actual population in 1940 and that which one would expect to exist as a residue of the 1930 population (given probable survival rates) and then attributing that difference to emigration. The other procedure involves taking a sample list of residents for one year, finding which of these were no longer at the same address one year later, eliminating those which are recorded as dead, and considering the remainder as emigrants. Neither of these procedures, taken alone, is completely satisfactory as a precise measure of emigration differentials. Each rests upon certain assumptions of probability, and, worse yet, each suffers from certain inaccuracies inherent in our source material. They are, however, the only methods available and we shall have to do the best we can with them. Provided that they are used with proper reservations and are constantly referred to a context of case material and first hand knowledge they are not likely to mislead us. Moreover, the striking agreement on results which the two methods yield is somewhat reassuring as to their essential reliability.

Let us begin with the first of the methods described, that which involves the use of life tables.[71] Applied to our North End data, the technique consists of comparing the actual 1940 population with the residue of the 1930 population which probably survived

[71] This technique is outlined in C. Warren Thornthwaite, *Internal Migration in the United States* (Philadelphia: 1934), pp. 19–21.

to 1940 according to survival rates for Massachusetts.[72] Whatever deficit the actual 1940 population may show from the estimated 1940 population is a measure of "effective emigration." It is not a measure of the actual volume of emigration, since no deduction is made for the amount of immigration *into* the district between 1930 and 1940.[73] Effective emigration simply indicates the extent of population decline which is attributable to emigration rather than to death. Such a measure necessarily suffers from a number of deficiencies: (a) It tells us nothing at all about the absolute volume of emigration. It is strictly a measure of population decline after the element of death has been eliminated. Its significance lies in its revealing what elements of an area's population are being lost to it to the greatest extent. (b) The index of effective emigration is probably not so accurate for small populations, such as districts within a city, as for large populations, such as states or national regions. The reason for this lies in the elementary statistical principle that small populations are more subject to unique variations away from typical rates than are large populations. (c) Closely related to this defect is another one: the application of a state-wide survival rate, based upon rural as well as urban areas and upon upper class populations as well as lower class populations, to a restricted urban slum area such as the North End opens the way to serious possibilities of error. This is because the health and welfare conditions which prevail in a slum are certainly not representative of those for the state as a whole and are likely to create atypical survival rates. However, in the absence of survival rates for such small areas as the North End there is no alternative to using whatever data are available, and qualifying all our interpretations with suitable reservations. As a matter of fact, in the present case the amount of error that has been introduced into our estimates of effective emigration through the use of a state-wide survival rate is not so great as one might

[72] Survival rates for Massachusetts were computed from state life tables in National Resources Committee, *Population Statistics, 2. State Data* (Washington: 1937), Part C, p. 38.

[73] By use of *Police Lists* for two different years a count was made of immigration into a sample precinct of the North End (precinct 13). The figure (61) reveals so small a volume of immigration that any use of it to compute actual emigration by age groups would have introduced statistical unreliability into the estimates.

expect. This point is established by recourse to survival rates which happen to be available for Negroes in Ohio. That group, being a highly urbanized and slum-dwelling minority, may be presumed to typify survival rates under such living conditions. Applying the rates of that group to the North End showed a very negligible difference in emigration differentials from those which had been calculated on the basis of Massachusetts survival rates. Moreover, that difference, small as it was, actually emphasized even further the emigration differential which is most pertinent to our hypothesis. This is attributable to the higher-than-average mortality in the younger age groups which characterizes slums, a fact which causes some of the younger-age emigration to be "concealed" when state-wide survival rates are applied to a slum. Thus the true differential age-group migration that prevails if young persons are really leaving at a greater rate than older persons is minimized by such a procedure as we have followed. Consequently the differentials which are presently to be described are more likely to be an understatement rather than an overstatement of the real emigration differentials that prevail in the North End. (d) Finally, among the defects attaching to effective emigration as a measure of differential migration trends are two possible sources of error inherent in the source material. First, there is the well known fact that in industrialized areas there is very frequently an underenumeration of people in the 50 and over age group, owing to the practice of older wage-earners' falsifying their age with a view to protecting themselves in their jobs. Secondly, there is an even more common underenumeration of population in the 0–5 age group. Since this group obviously falls in the 10–15 age interval ten years later, the latter age group will show an unaccountably large population relative to that which it had ten years previously when it constituted the 0–5 age group. The effect of this is to spuriously reduce the amount of emigration that has actually taken place in the younger age groups.

With these deficiencies constantly in mind, but with the realization that another procedure is presently to be followed by which all our interpretations can be checked, let us turn to the findings. Two types of emigration differentials are disclosed by our data: (a) that between immigrant Italians and second-generation Italians; (b) that between the younger age-groups and the older age-groups. The differentials by nativity are set forth in Table 11. From the table it is clear that American-born Italians account for a much greater share of the effective emigration from the North

TABLE 11

Effective Emigration from the North End, Boston, 1930 to 1940, by Nativity

Nativity	1930 Population	Per Cent of 1930 Pop. in Each Nativity Group	Effective Emigration 1930–1940	Per Cent of Emigration Accounted for by Each Nativity Group
American-born (2nd generation)...	12,553	59.46	3,399	76.42
Italian-born (1st generation)......	8,557	40.54	1,049	23.58
Totals........................	21,110	100.00	4,448	100.00

Computed from census tract data and survival rates.

End than do the Italian-born Italians. Thus the former, the second generation, comprised but 59.46 per cent of the 1930 population, yet they contributed 76.42 per cent of the effective emigration. The first generation on the other hand accounted for much less than its "due" share of the emigration. If we calculate the relative loss to each of the nativity groups we find the following: where the effective emigration of second generation Italians represents 27.08 per cent of their number in 1930, that of the first generation represents only 12.26 per cent of their number in 1930.[74] Obviously the American-born Italians in the North End are declining at a more rapid rate than the Italian-born Italians.

Equally clear differentials appear in effective emigration by age groups. If we compare the difference between the percentage which each age group at the modal age of migration contributes to the effective emigration, and the percentage which each age group comprised of the 1930 population, we find that the age groups 20–29 account for much more than their share of effective emigration; the age groups 40–69 account for much less than their share.[75] In Table 12 the figures preceded by a plus sign

[74] Since there is no sampling involved in these data it is unnecessary and indeed impossible to apply any statistical tests of reliability.

[75] "Modal age of migration" refers to that age group which is midway between the group in which its members fell five years earlier and that in

indicate "excess" emigration; those preceded by a minus sign indicate "deficit" emigration. It is evident that only the younger age groups contribute an "excess" emigration; the older age

TABLE 12

DIFFERENCE BETWEEN PERCENTAGE CONTRIBUTED BY EACH AGE GROUP TO
EFFECTIVE EMIGRATION AND PERCENTAGE IT COMPRISED OF 1930 POPULATION

Model Age of Emigration	Differences between Percentages	
	Male	Female
5–9	−1.70	−0.33
10–14	+0.38	+0.04
15–19	+0.21	+2.66
20–24	+4.18	+3.01
25–29	+2.04	+2.35
30–39	−0.97	−0.07
40–49	−2.31	−1.09
50–59	−1.43	−1.17
60 69	−2.29	−1.19
70–79	−1.13	−0.59

Computed from census tract data and survival rates.

groups are all in the "deficit" category. One interesting disclosure made by the table is that young women tend to leave at an earlier age than young men. Presumably this reflects the earlier marriage age of Italian girls relative to that of men. The slight "excess" of emigration in the age group 10–14 is not by itself significant. It is to be tallied with the very slight "deficit" emigration of the age group 30–39 which is the probable parent generation. In all likelihood the "deficit" emigration of this latter age group is just so slight — i.e., just near enough to "excess" — that its children are sufficiently numerous to fall into the "excess" category. All in all the pattern of age group emigration differentials as

which its members will fall five years later. It is the probable age group in which most of the migrants fell *at the time of their migration.* The reasoning behind this supposition is as follows: The 1930 age group 0–4 becomes 10–14 by 1940. We cannot assume that all the mobility was while the members were still in the 0–4 group. Neither can we assume that it took place while they were in the 10–14 group, to which they belonged ten years later. So, we assume that each year-age group contributes equally to the mobility and that each year-age group contains about the same number of members. Then we find that: the greatest number of moves is in the period 5–9, because all members pass through this age-group, while only one-fifth of the members pass through the extreme high and low ages of 15 and 1.

portrayed in these calculations is most plausible. It shows that the North End is losing its young people to a much greater extent than its older people.

Before attempting to interpret these findings let us turn to the other of our two methods for estimating emigration differentials. This method is somewhat more orthodox and has the reassuring aspect that it is based upon a list of actual emigrants from the North End during a one-year period. Moreover, since the names, ages, sex, and domestic status of the emigrants are known, this method permits of more varied applications than the one based upon survival rates. We shall therefore be able to glimpse a little more fully just who are leaving the North End, and what are their characteristics. The procedure was a simple one. Precinct 13, within Ward 3, was selected as a typical sample area of the North End. The *Police Lists* of that precinct for two years, January 1, 1938 and January 1, 1939, were then examined, and every name appearing in the lists for 1938 which was not recorded as being at the same address in the lists for 1939 was copied down, along with the age and sex of the person in question.[76] The next step was to eliminate those names whose absence in the 1939 lists was due to death. This was done by referring to the state *Registry of Deaths*, in which are recorded the names of all deceased persons and the dates of their demise.[77] Following this it was necessary to eliminate the names of those persons who had not really moved out of the North End but had merely changed their addresses within the community. For this purpose the *Boston City Directory* for 1939, the listings of which are as of July 1, was consulted. Every name in our own list was looked up in the *Directory* and note made as to whether the person's move was merely to another address in the North End or to some other neighborhood within Boston. If the name was not listed in the *Directory* at all it was assumed that the person had moved to some city or town

---

[76] The years 1938 and 1939 were deliberately chosen because they were pre-war years and would not suffer from the disruption caused in 1940 by the draft of young men. The *Police Lists* have as their full title: City of Boston, *List of Residents 20 Years of Age and over as of January 1, 1938*, and the same for succeeding years.

[77] The *Registry of Deaths* is a series of bound volumes available in the Department of Vital Statistics, State House, Boston.

outside of Boston. Inasmuch as the *Directory* is supposed to list all residents of Boston such an assumption is reasonably justified. Omitting thus all the persons who had merely relocated within the North End there remained a list of 258 persons who had left precinct 13 in the North End between January 1, 1938 and January 1, 1939. Of these emigrants the age and sex was known, as well as the probable domestic status[78] and the general destination.[79] With such material it becomes possible to analyze differential emigration from the North End in considerable detail.

Before considering the results of this analysis it will be well to once again take note of the deficiencies in our data. There are many of these though only one of them is really serious. (a) To begin with, there is some falsification of legal residence. Politically active persons who live in the suburbs but who have a stake in North End politics sometimes get themselves declared as residents at some address in the North End and their names are accordingly registered on the *Police Lists.* Such falsification, however, is not sufficiently widespread to seriously affect the reliability of a large sample such as ours. (b) The *Police Lists* are frequently inaccurate on details of spelling and age. Italians themselves, particularly the elderly and illiterate ones, vary the spelling of their own names from year to year; "Giuseppe Morello" in 1938 may become "Joseph Morelli" the next year. Such variations and errors in spelling made it necessary when consulting the *Registry of Deaths* and the *City Directory* to look up every conceivable way of spelling a given name when it could not

[78] Persons with the same family name, same former address, and who were of opposite sex and of approximately equal age were presumed to be husband and wife if living alone. If, however, such persons were living with older couples having the same family name there was no way of distinguishing husband-wife couples from brother-sister couples. For this reason our data on marital status does not segregate spouses from siblings (of opposite sex). Whole-family moves were obtained by noting migrants having a common family name, identical former address, and an age-sex distribution that indicated obvious parent-child and sibling relationships. Of course the *Police Lists* include only persons 20 years of age and over; hence the children which our material revealed were all matured adults who were still living with their parents.

[79] "Destination" is known for all districts within Boston. For moves to communities outside of Boston there is no way of ascertaining the specific destination and it is possible only to use the blanket term "outside Boston."

be found under its first form. Every effort was made to properly identify every person, but a few errors have undoubtedly crept in. (c) Certain Italian names are very common — e.g., "Joseph Rossi." Consequently in identifying names in the *City Directory* it was often difficult to know which "Joseph Rossi" was the one corresponding to our list compiled from the *Police Lists*. This problem was generally solved by consulting earlier issues of the *City Directory* and noting which of all the "Joseph Rossis" had *not* had the earlier North End address; whichever "Joseph Rossi" remained was obviously the one who had moved from the North End to the new address in question. However, some errors may have entered at this point. (d) The *City Directory* is not always accurate. Sometimes it will list as the address of a person one that is a year or more old. Moreover, it apparently omits at times the names of aged persons living with matured children. The principal effect of such errors is to spuriously "increase" the number of migrants who have been classed as going "outside Boston"; for we, finding no listing of a name in the *City Directory*, have uniformly classified it as being "outside Boston." However, we shall not make too much of our data on the destination of emigrants, hence no serious inaccuracy accrues to our differential emigration rates through the errors of the *City Directory*. One other effect of inaccuracies in the *City Directory* is to make it difficult sometimes to know whether a given person has merely relocated at another address in the North End or has moved out of the district. Our procedure in such cases was to consult later issues of the *Directory* on the supposition that by then the change in address had been duly made. Such a procedure of course carries with it the danger of including second moves of a family in with the original move. However, even in such cases the fact of departure from the North End would remain the outstanding feature and hence no serious damage to our hypothesis would have been suffered. (e) The *Police Lists* include only persons 20 years of age and over. Consequently no emigration data on children can be computed from these data. (f) Finally, and most seriously, the data for females becomes progressively inaccurate with younger age groups. The reason for this lies in the fact that a woman listed as "Rose Cavarielli" in the 1938 *Police Lists* might have become married during the course of the year and by

1939 would appear under a wholly different family name. Naturally there was no way of identifying such persons except when they remained at the same address in the North End (which was quite frequent), in which case the woman could be detected with reasonable certainty through her first name and through her age. For the others there was no feasible and economic method of correcting the error, which is surely of some magnitude. Fortunately, however, the early age of marriage for most Italian girls makes it probable that the error thus introduced applies only to the female age group 20–29 years. Moreover, the net effect of such an error is of course to spuriously magnify female emigration. Now it happens that, even in spite of this magnification of female emigration, male emigration appears higher by our data for every single age group. Consequently the sex differentials in emigration which result from our procedure are an understatement rather than an overstatement of the actual sex differentials in emigration. For this reason we can make use of these data with perfect confidence, knowing that they err on the side of conservatism rather than rashness. The true sex differentials in emigration are unquestionably much greater than those disclosed by our data.

So, with all these qualifications and precautions in mind, let us consider the findings. In Table 13 we have presented the age and sex composition of the emigrants covered by our sample. From

TABLE 13

NUMBER OF PERSONS 20 YEARS OF AGE AND OVER IN WARD 3, PRECINCT 13,
BOSTON, ON JANUARY 1, 1938, WHO LEFT THE NORTH END BY
JANUARY 1, 1939, BY AGE AND SEX

Age Groups	Total Emigrants	Male	Female
20–29	103	58	45
30–39	47	28	19
40–49	51	36	15
50–59	28	20	8
60–69	18	15	3
70 and over	11	7	4
Totals	258	164	94

Tabulated from *Police Lists.*

the table it is clear at a glance that the greatest number of emigrants fall in the age group 20–29. Beyond the age of 60 the number of emigrants is rather negligible. Fully 150 of the 258 emigrants are under 40 years of age. Equally clear is the sex differential. At every single age group the number of male emigrants exceeds the number of female emigrants. In view of the error attending our "overenumeration" of female emigrants, for reasons described above, the actual sex differential is considerably greater than the table indicates, particularly in the younger age groups when women are marrying at the greatest rate.

A proper interpretation of these data cannot, however, be made until they are compared with the age and sex distribution of the population from which the migrants have come. For a preponderance of younger age groups in emigration means one thing if the population from which those migrants have come is predominantly youthful; it means an entirely different thing if that population is predominantly middle-aged or elderly. In the case of the former, for instance, one would on chance alone expect the migrants of younger age groups to outnumber those of older age groups. So, too, sex differentials among emigrants do not mean very much until they are compared with sex differentials among the total population from which the migrants have come. Only when relative proportions are compared, as between emigrants and the population from which those emigrants have come, can the true emigration differentials be brought out. For this purpose a check list was made of the total population of precinct 13, in ward 3, on the basis of the *Police Lists* for January 1, 1938. The entire population of this precinct was classified by age and sex groups comparable to those of the emigrating population. A total of 2,257 persons 20 years of age and over was thus recorded — certainly a statistically adequate sample. The next step was to compare *relative* rates of emigration by age and sex groups, thus adjusting to the unequal numbers within each of the age and sex groups of the total population. Following this the statistical significance of the difference between these rates was calculated to see if it was a reliable one or whether it was so small that the random error attending sampling procedure might account for it. Through these calculations we find in Table 14 the proportions in regard to age differentials in emigration. Thus, where 13.41 per cent of the population under 40 years of age left the North End during 1938, only 9.49 per cent of the population 40 years of age and over thus emigrated. The difference between these rates is

TABLE 14

NUMBER AND PROPORTION OF EACH AGE GROUP RESIDENT IN WARD 3, PRECINCT 13,
BOSTON, WHICH EMIGRATED FROM THE NORTH END IN 1938

Age Groups	Total Population in Each Age Group	Number Emigrating in Each Age Group	Per Cent of Each Age Group Emigrating
20–39..................	1119	150	13.41
40 and over.............	1138	108	9.49
Totals.................	2257	258	11.43

Tabulated from *Police Lists.*

3.92 per cent, which is exactly 2.93 times the standard error of the difference between these rates ($\sigma = 1.338$ per cent). This is a statistically reliable difference and cannot be attributed to chance error attending the procedure of sampling. Indeed, by reference to a probability table it can be shown that there are only about $3\frac{1}{2}$ chances in a thousand that the difference between the rates of emigration by age groups is a chance difference due to sampling.[80] It is evident from this that young adults are leaving the North End at a greater rate than older adults. If the data are grouped in another way we find that, of the population which remained at the same addresses in the North End during 1938, 48.47 per cent were under 40 years of age. In contrast, of the population which left the North End during 1938, fully 58.13 per cent were under 40 years of age. Here again the difference between the two rates is statistically reliable, being 2.92 times the standard error of the difference (actual difference = 9.66 per cent; $\sigma = 3.308$ per cent). Clearly the younger age groups loom larger in the emigrating population than they do in the non-emigrating population.

Sex differentials in emigration appear equally significant. As may be seen from Table 15, 13.40 per cent of the male population left the North End during 1938, while only 9.10 per cent of the female population thus emigrated. The difference between the two rates is 4.30 per cent, which is 3.20 times the standard error of the difference between these rates ($\sigma = 1.344$ per cent). In other words, there are only 1 1/3 chances in a thousand that the

[80] See Herbert Arkin and Raymond R. Colton, *An Outline of Statistical Methods,* 4th edition (New York: 1939), Table 32a, p. 118.

TABLE 15

NUMBER AND PROPORTION OF EACH SEX RESIDENT IN WARD 3, PRECINCT 13,
BOSTON, WHICH EMIGRATED FROM THE NORTH END IN 1938

Sex	Number in Each Sex	Number of Each Sex Emigrating	Per Cent of Each Sex Emigrating
Male	1224	164	13.40
Female	1033	94	9.10
Totals	2257	258	11.43

Tabulated from *Police Lists*.

difference between the sex emigration rates is a chance difference
due to sampling. On this basis it is clear that the exodus of men
from the North End exceeds the exodus of women.

Two additional aspects of the differential emigration from the
North End call for comment. First of all, the number of emigrants who are single or widowed slightly exceeds the number
who are married or are brothers and sisters. But more significant
than this are the variations by age groups in the proportion who
are single or widowed. Table 16 presents these variations con-
cisely. The age group variations in the proportion single or widowed are striking. The great majority of emigrants in the 20–29
age group are single. But the proportion changes with the next
age group. A somewhat larger number of emigrants in their
thirties are married (or are living with sibling of opposite sex)

TABLE 16

NUMBER OF PERSONS, BY MARITAL OR BROTHER-SISTER RELATIONSHIP, RESIDENT IN
WARD 3, PRECINCT 13, BOSTON, WHO EMIGRATED FROM THE NORTH END IN 1938

Age Groups	Husband-Wife or Brother-Sister	Single or Widowed
20–29	32	71*
30–39	28	19
40–49	24	27
50–59	14	14
50–69	4	14
70 and over	4	7
Total	106	152

Tabulated from *Police Lists*.
* Of these 71 single or widowed persons aged 20–29, 9 left with their parents, as
members of a family unit. In their cases the real emigrants were obviously the parents rather than the young persons.

than are single or widowed. With the older emigrants — those
aged 60 or more years — the number of single or widowed persons again exceeds the number who are married. These variations
are instructive about the circumstances which typically underlie
the emigration of each of the age groups. The youngest migrants
are apparently leaving home on their own, to make their way in
some other part of Boston or in another city. In this respect they
conform to LePlay's particularist type of family, in which matured children try to win their status independently of family
connections. These young migrants are breaking away from the
kinship and associational solidarities of the North End and are
seeking identification with very different American patterns. To
them, residence in the North End is distasteful, partly because of
the physical undesirability of the neighborhood but primarily because of its status connotations. On the other hand residence in
the "American" suburbs is viewed as a symbol of "success." The
attitude of these emigrants is well expressed by the statement of
one young Italian, a student at college, who is eager to move away
from the North End. When asked why young people were leaving
the North End so rapidly he replied: "Oh, they just get absolutely disgusted with it and vow they'll leave as soon as they're
able to. . . . I know I wouldn't stay there — not any longer than
I had to." [81] Much the same motivation characterizes the emigrants who fall into the 30–39 age group, the principal difference
being that such persons are more often married. Most of these
young married couples had remained in the North End while their
children were still very small. But as their children began to grow
up they looked to the suburbs for a more suitable environment in
which to raise their families. Generally they are American-born
themselves and are sufficiently identified with American family
and associational patterns to desire that their children grow up
in an "American" neighborhood. The older emigrants — those
over 60 years of age — generally leave the North End for very
different reasons. As the table shows, most of them are single or
widowed, the latter undoubtedly predominating. Typically they
are elderly persons whose children have grown up and moved to
the suburbs. Perhaps they themselves remained in the North End
for several years, until their mates died. Then, finding themselves

[81] M. A. Gravallese, of Hull street.

alone, they have gone to live with their children in the suburbs. It is not uncommon to find old grandmothers who have thus moved to their sons' or daughters' homes and who have preempted many of the domestic functions while the daughter or daughter-in-law, in an effort to affect the American female role and emancipate herself from household chores, is working in an office or factory and leaving maternal duties to the grandmother.

One final aspect of differential emigration from the North End which may be briefly noted is that of destination. For reasons already explained our data on the destination of emigrants are not very reliable and too much significance should not be attached to them. For what they are worth, however, they indicate that the great majority of emigrants from the North End leave Boston for other cities. Specifically, of the 258 emigrants from the North End represented in our sample, 211 left Boston altogether; only 47 located elsewhere in the city. To the extent that this differential is a real one it appears that the Italian emigrants have moved to suburban communities where social participation is largely freed from the extended Italian family, the *paesani* groups, and the informal associations of the North End. Evidence of this is afforded by impressionistic knowledge, supported by the testimony of Italians themselves, as to the destination of emigrants from the North End. The most popular areas of second settlement have been, in just about this order: East Boston, Revere, Somerville, Everett, and Medford. East Boston, however, is inhabited by a considerable immigrant Italian population and is less clearly a second generation area. Revere was the first suburban community to enjoy the favor of American-born Italians and it probably has the greatest number of them today — outside of the North End and East Boston. However, it has undergone a considerable decline in prestige value during recent years. At present Medford seems to have the greatest prestige value for Americanized Italians and its second generation population has increased rapidly during the past ten or fifteen years.

None of the emigration differentials that are based upon our sampling procedure appear to be particularly great. However, it should be borne in mind that these differentials apply to emigration for only a single year; extended over a span of several years they would assume a considerably greater absolute magnitude than might appear from the figures for one year. That this is the case is suggested by our earlier data on effective emigration, estimated on the basis of survival rates. Those data extend over a ten-year period and disclose a very significant difference in the absolute numbers of emigrants as between younger and older Italians and American-born and Italian-born Italians. All the evidence thus points consistently to one conclusion: those elements of the North End population which are most fully solidary with Italian associations and interaction patterns, viz., the older, Italian-born persons, show a smaller rate of emigration from the community than those elements which are rebelling against the values of the North End community.[82] The sex differential lends itself to the same interpretation. The "proper" Italian girl as she reaches maturity is required to lead a very circumscribed life. Her parents jealously restrict her extra-familial activities with the result that her whole scheme of aspirations becomes oriented to traditional Italian values. For her, unlike for her brother, there is not the freedom to choose between a "rebel" reaction and an "in group" reaction; the latter is unequivocally defined as the only one for her if she is to maintain her good name and that of her family.[83] Likewise the older Italian woman is far more immersed in the confines of the North End than is the Italian man. Sartorio remarks that:

One of the greatest surprises of my life . . . is to hear from time to time, especially from Italian women who have lived in America for years, a statement like this: "I have been down to America today," meaning that they have gone a few blocks outside the district of the Italian colony.[84]

Many of the older Italian women can scarcely speak any English at all.[85] Nearly all of them dress in the solemn black garments that are expected of a respectable married Italian woman. Within the North End they are appreciated as such; outside the North End they are viewed as oddities. It is little wonder that the

[82] See *supra,* pp. 191–192, on the unequal solidarity toward the Italian community as between the first generation and second generation Italians.

[83] Mangione, *op. cit.,* chap. viii.

[84] Sartorio, *op. cit.,* p. 19.

[85] Mangione, *op. cit.,* p. 59.

women are so much less disposed to emigrate from the one community where there is respect for the values with which they have been socialized.

From all this it seems clear that there is a very real congruence between Italian community solidarity and North End locational processes. Residence in the North End is apparently a spatial corollary to integration with Italian values. Likewise emigration from the North End signifies assimilation into American values and is so construed by the people themselves. Thus, while the area is not as such the object of affective attachment, as are Beacon Hill and the Common, it nonetheless has become a symbol for Italian community solidarity. By virtue of this instrumental symbolism the area has acquired a certain retentive power over those residents who most fully share the values which prevail there. Residence within it is a bid for status within the Italian scheme of valuation. Naturally the older people and the women are the ones whose personal aspirations are most integrated with this Italian value system. They have been socialized into it; they have spent nearly the whole of their adult lives in an Italian colony, close by their relatives, *paesani,* and other intimate friends, all of whom have provided an arena for appreciation and reinforcement of this value system. It is little wonder that they show lower rates of emigration from the North End than do the second generation and the men, or that when they do leave it is typically because they are widowed and have chosen to live with their children in the suburbs.

There are three additional lines of evidence which point to the causal influence which localized social solidarity may exert upon land use in a slum. The first of these is migration *into* the district. If our hypothesis is true that residence within the North End expresses identification with Italian values, one would suppose that most of the people moving into the community would be Italians. That this is indeed the case seems to be supported by calculations made from the *Police Lists* of January 1, 1939, for Ward 3, precinct 13, in the North End. The *Police Lists* indicate, opposite the name of every entry, the place of residence of that person one year previously. From such data it is a simple matter to tabulate the number of persons who have moved into the North End from elsewhere during the course of the year. Tabulations made in this way are shown in Table 17. By summing up the last two items we find that during the year of 1938, 61 persons moved into the North End from outside the district. From the family names of each of these persons it was possible to distinguish

TABLE 17

CHANGES IN RESIDENCE DURING THE YEAR 1938, IN WARD 3,
PRECINCT 13, BOSTON

	Number of Persons
Same residence on January 1, 1938, as one year later	2101
Within North End on January 1, 1938, but at different address	162
Outside of North End on January 1, 1938, but within Boston	38
Outside of Boston on January 1, 1938	23
Total number of persons in precinct, January 1, 1939	2324

Tabulated from *Police Lists.*

Italian from non-Italian migrants. Of the 61 persons, 53 were Italians. The remaining 8 migrants consisted of four young married couples, three of which were Irish and one, Slavic. Clearly whatever attractive influence the North End exerts is a selective one in terms of ethnic affiliation. Such a selective immigration process cannot be understood except in terms of the localization of ethnic solidarity, by which residence within the North End denotes identification with distinctively Italian groups and acceptance of an Italian value system.

The second line of evidence supporting the ecological significance of spatial instrumentalism is that of population turnover. From Table 17 above, it can be seen that the turnover of population attending immigration is exceedingly small in the North End. Specifically, only 61 persons of the 2,324 residents in the North End as of January 1, 1939, had come to the district from elsewhere during the course of the previous year — i.e., 2.62 per cent. This is actually a lower rate of turnover than prevails on Beacon Hill, where the proportion of newcomers to Ward 3, precinct 4, during the year 1938 was 19.36 per cent.[86] The North End is clearly a demographically stable area. Such a stability contributes in no small measure to the perpetuation of the Italian value system. This it does partly through minimizing the number of ac-

[86] To be sure, most of this turnover on Beacon Hill is attributable to the population of clerical workers, maids, and other non-elite persons.

commodations which have to be made to a non-Italian population and partly through creating a "center of gravity" in the form of a settled population of old, Italian-born residents.[87] Conversely this very stability of population is itself a result of the Italians' localized solidarity. Thus, "aliens" who do not share Italian values cannot hope to win acceptance in the social life of the North End. As a result they are dissuaded from even considering residence in the district. On the other hand, Italians who are seeking residence in the North End fit immediately into an appropriate kinship structure and *paesani* group, with rights and obligations defined in advance and fully coördinated with the migrants' aspirations and expectations. In this way the localized solidarity of the Italians creates a selective receptivity toward migrants entering the North End.

The third and last indication of the importance of spatial instrumentalism is the trend of property ownership in the North End. Italians, more than most immigrant nationalities, attach a great deal of significance to the ownership of real estate. This attitude traces back to the quasi-servile tenant status which most of the Italian immigrants had known in their homeland. The result of this was to establish in their minds an extraordinarily high valuation of property ownership. Many of the North End Italians have regularly sent in a portion of their savings to relatives in Italy with a view to investing it in land. Others, more certain of remaining in the United States, have invested it in North End and suburban real estate. As a result the proportion of North End buildings and lots which are owned by Italians increased markedly during the first decades of Italian residence in the district. Later, however, the rate of increase diminished, particularly as younger Italians, seeking a better investment than dilapidated tenement buildings, put their money in suburban properties. Nonetheless Italian commitment to the North End in the form of property investment has increased right down to the present time.[88] Quantitative evidence of this is afforded by maps in the

[87] See *supra*, p. 178; Sorokin, *Social Mobility* (New York: 1927), pp. 533–538.

[88] The number of owner-occupied dwelling units in the North End is admittedly small, being only 6.02 per cent as based upon census tract data. However, a "dwelling unit" by census definition is any set of rooms in-

Bromley Atlas for 1902, 1922, and 1938.[89] These maps indicate, along with other data, the owner of every single building and lot in central Boston. It was a simple matter to tabulate the number of properties in the North End whose owners had Italian names and the number whose owners had non-Italian names.[90] The pro-

TABLE 18

NUMBER AND PERCENTAGE OF BUILDINGS AND LOTS IN THE NORTH END OF BOSTON OWNED BY PERSONS WITH ITALIAN NAMES*

Year	Total Number of Buildings and Lots	Number Owned by Italians	Percentage Owned by Italians
1902	1981	378	19.08
1922	1617	836	51.70
1938	1397†	810	57.98

Tabulated from *Bromley Atlas*.
* A large proportion of the non-Italian owners are banks and mortgage companies.
† This progressive diminution in the total number of buildings and lots is due to the merging of some buildings, the demolition of many, and the replacement of lots by street widenings and extensions.

portions shown in Table 18 were thus arrived at. There are unfortunately no quantitative data for the trend since 1938. However, persons familiar with recent real estate developments in the North End have noted a sharp upturn in Italian property investment within the district. Following the outbreak of the recent war with Italy the further shipment of money to that country by persons in the United States was prohibited. Consequently the Italians, barred from remitting savings to relatives in Italy, took to investing their funds in local real estate. Many of them have undertaken extensive improvements in their tenement buildings, so that the value of such property has been enhanced. Needless to

habited by a whole "family"; hence a single tenement may appear in the census as 20 or 30 dwelling units. Obviously the ownership of those 20 or 30 dwelling units can be held by only one party, even if that party resides in the tenement; hence the percentage of owner-occupied dwelling units is necessarily very small. Source of data: *Population and Housing — Statistics for Census Tracts, Boston, Massachusetts*, Sixteenth Census of the United States, 1940, Table 4.
[89] Full title: *Atlas of the City of Boston: Boston Proper and Back Bay*, published by G. W. Bromley and Co. (Philadelphia).
[90] For this purpose the North End was delineated as that area bounded by the following streets: Washington, Blackstone, North, and Commercial.

say this increased financial commitment to the North End will tend to bind the Italians even further to the district. This is particularly true in view of the fact that the increased rate of North End property investment has artificially inflated prices, so that Italians are paying more for their tenements than they are really worth. Undoubtedly these prices will drop precipitously after the war, so that Italian owners will face the alternatives of unloading their investments at a drastic loss or of holding on to them for whatever regular income they will bring. Many will undoubtedly choose the latter.[91] The localizing effects of this are obvious.

Of course, before we can be sure that our asserted affinity between localized social solidarity and the various migration differentials, turnover rates, and property trends is indeed a valid one we must consider alternative explanations. Three alternatives, all within the empirically rationalistic framework, present themselves: (a) The people who remain in the North End are those who cannot afford to live elsewhere. The second generation, having risen in economic well-being over the earlier generation, moves out of the North End because it can afford to. (b) The old people remain in the North End because they are aged, and aged people never are as mobile as younger people. (c) The Italians remain in the North End for the rational reason that the produce markets are near by.

Now it is possible to demonstrate that none of these alternative hypotheses are adequate to explain the differentials which we have described. We may begin with the first alternative. If low rent were the decisive factor determining the location of older Italians one would expect to find a high proportion of Italians wherever the rent was low. Moreover, the overall distribution of low income Italians should correlate closely with the distribution of low rental areas. Whatever cartographic pattern characterized the latter should also characterize the distribution of low income Italians. In point of fact, however, the lowest rentals are not to be found in the North End at all, but are to be found in portions of Charlestown, South Boston, and in the vicinity of "Chinatown," where there are very few Italian families.[92] To be sure,

---

[91] Mr. Bodge, real estate division, First National Bank of Boston.

[92] Moreover, in Charlestown and South Boston the proportion of foreign-born persons of all nationalities is relatively low.

the North End is one of the lower rental areas of Boston. But if low rent were both a necessary and a sufficient cause of Italian first generation residence in the district, then non-Italians too should be in the North End in the same proportion that they bear to the total population of comparable income status. But that is not the case. The North End is almost exclusively Italian. Obviously some other factor must be invoked to explain this ethnic exclusiveness of the North End. Such a factor can only be found in the cultural component, by which the North End has come to symbolize Italian solidarity, and by which residence within the North End is construed as identification with Italian values.

There can be no denying, of course, that the income level of North End Italians is on the average lower than that of Italians elsewhere in Boston. In the North End the mean monthly rent is $19.08.[93] For persons of Italian birth in Boston as a whole the mean monthly rent is $23.18.[94] Although these two figures are not strictly comparable, since the former includes both first and second generation Italians while the latter includes only first generation Italians, they do suggest that emigration out of the North End correlates with rise in income status.[95] But this by no means proves the argument that the Italians who remain in the North End do so because they are poor, or that those who leave the district do so only because they are financially able. For in a very real sense low income status is a corollary to identification with Italian values, and rise in income status is a corollary to repudiation of Italian values. Thus improved income status is not so much the "cause" of emigration from the North End; rather both of these are the results of a third variable, viz., rejection of Italian values. In the Italian value system the dutiful son either entered his father's occupation as a matter of course or prepared for one of the professions. The valuation which attached to both of these was not through their being avenues to "success" or "per-

[93] Calculated from census tract data in *Population and Housing — Statistics for Census Tracts, Boston, Massachusetts,* Sixteenth Census of the United States, 1940, Table 5.

[94] Calculated from data in *Population: Nativity and Parentage of the White Population; Country of Origin of the Foreign Stock,* based upon 5 per cent sample; Sixteenth Census of the United States, 1940, Table 16.

[95] We are assuming here that rent is a rough index of income level.

sonal advancement." They were valued for the prestige and respect which they brought to the family.[96] In the American status system, however, where prestige and respect so largely depend upon possession of the symbolic appurtenances to personal "success," the second generation Italians have had to choose between two wholly different scales of valuation, one Italian and based upon status of ascription, the other American and based upon status of achievement. A goodly proportion have chosen the latter, and have thus become oriented toward "quick paying," remunerative jobs. They have accepted the American scale of personal valuation and with it all its corollaries: striving for occupational advancement, and migrating from the North End "foreign" colony to an "American" suburb. The main factor in this entire process is identification with one or another value system. Thus we are forced back once again to the component of social values in our effort to understand the causation of locational processes in the North End. The emigration differentials in the North End apparently cannot be explained merely in terms of economic status and rent-paying ability, since those are themselves results of the cultural component in social interaction.

Turning to the second of the rationalistic alternatives for explaining North End emigration differentials we meet up with a very similar causal situation. It is not enough to attribute the age differential in emigration to such "common sense" platitudes as the fact that old people always are less mobile than young people. If age were itself a necessary and sufficient cause of low mobility then one should expect to find low rates of mobility for all old people in whatever part of the city they may be. Yet this is not the case. The transient old man of the South End is a "social type" that may be found in "homeless men's areas" of every large city — in Chicago's "Hobohemia," New York's "Bowery," Seattle's "Skidroad," etc. Biological age cannot by itself be an adequate determinant of low mobility. That old people are as a rule less mobile than young people is most directly a result of their social relationships. The old person will try to live where his friends and relatives live. They are the ones whom he needs for companionship, security, and assistance. The older Italian

---

[96] Cf. Mangione, *op. cit.*, p. 226.

who clings to the North End is but a special case of this general uniformity. His friends and relatives are Italians whose mutual companionship and assistance is most fully realized through residence in the North End. It is this localization of the older Italian's associations and friendships that explains his relative disinclination to leave the North End — not the fact of biological age. The latter is but a circumstance which increases the older Italian's dependence upon his friends and relatives, most of whom live in the North End. Thus it is the cultural component, consisting of the localization of Italian solidarity, that is the really autonomous causal factor in differential emigration by age groups.

Finally there is the third rationalistic alternative to explaining the emigration differentials which we have observed, viz., the proximity of the Italian markets. Now it is true that residents commonly give as a reason for their living in the North End the fact that the Italian markets on Blackstone street, Salem street, and many of the side streets are near by. Anyone familiar with the Italian diet, with its unique spicing and flavor, its ministrone soup, and its spaghetti, will appreciate the importance of accessibility to Italian stores where only the appropriate ingredients may be obtained. There are thus very rational grounds for Italian residence in the one district where they may purchase their unique national foods. But can the location of Italian produce markets be properly taken as the "cause" of Italian residence in the North End? There would seem to be much more reason to believe that the markets are in the district because the Italian population is near by. Evidence of this is seen in the extension of distinctly Italian produce stores into certain suburban communities where there have developed sizable Italian populations. Thus the Gloria Chain Stores, which specialize in Italian foods, have established branches in Revere, East Boston, Hyde Park, Everett, and Newton, where there are considerable numbers of Italians. Apparently the Italian produce markets comply more with the location of Italian populations, rather than vice versa. Indeed, the very existence of these Italian markets is contingent upon the persistence of Italian culinary tastes — themselves a component of the Italian value system. Were it not for the importance which attaches to food as a symbol of family status and hospitality among Italians and for the persistence among them of uniquely

Italian food preferences, the Italian markets would not take on their causal significance for locational patterns. It follows, then, that though the rational desire to be near Italian markets is indeed a consideration with many Italians in living within the North End, nonetheless this rationality operates within a value context which serves as a precondition to the exercise of rationality. This rational orientation to the North End and its markets is thus meaningfully integrated with the volitional orientation toward food and family hospitality, since both have the same *identical reference*, namely, the overall value system of Italian immigrants.[97]

All three of the rationalistic alternatives for explaining emigration differentials in the North End inevitably regress back to the variable which we have been emphasizing all along. That variable is the cultural one — namely the localization of Italian associations and interaction patterns in a particular spatial area, the North End. By virtue of such localization the North End has become an instrumental symbol for Italian ethnic solidarity. Residence within it is a token of identification with Italian groups and of integration with Italian values. Those persons who most fully identify themselves with Italian patterns tend to remain in the North End, in spite of the deteriorated, congested conditions which prevail there. Apparently the affect which attaches to "one's own kind" outweighs awareness of the slum's undesirability as a place in which to live. Social values thus have an influence upon land use which is not at all limited to areas with congenial physical and architectural characteristics. Their influence extends to districts where there are very real physical deterrents to residence, fully recognized by the inhabitants themselves. The necessity of incorporating such a variable into ecological theory becomes all the more evident.

Before concluding this analysis of land use in the North End it may be well to conceptualize a little more precisely the emigration of young people from the community. Granted that it goes along with emancipation from Italian values, what theoretical significance may it have for the relationship between social systems and physical space? Clearly it is the converse of localized solidarity. Where the first generation Italians have expressed

---

[97] See *supra*, p. 100, on the nature of such integration.

their ethnic solidarity in a territorially bound community organization, the second generation Italians, insofar as they fall into the rebel reaction,[98] have expressed their rejection of ethnic solidarity by a dispersed territorial pattern. Such spatial corollaries to alterations in the social structure have been conceived by Simmel as "räumliche Projektionen der funktionellen Änderung."[99] Let us briefly recall some of the "functional alterations" that Italian social structure has undergone through the maturation of the second generation. Our object will be to see just how these changes have been instrumentalized by the dispersed territorial pattern which the second generation is taking on. The changes in Italian social structure seem to fall into two broad classes: (a) The transition from multimodal, "diffuse" association to unimodal, "specific" association; (b) The transition from status of ascription to status of achievement. The former is most immediately a *social* change; the latter, a *cultural* change. Among younger Italians the family has lost a great deal of its "all purpose" character. The second generation Italians are not content with limiting their contacts to the extended consanguine family which is so basic to first generation society. Neither do the *paesani* groupings have the meaning for second generation Italians which they have for the immigrant Italians.[100] In place of the extended consanguine family the second generation Italians have tended to accept the American pattern of conjugal solidarity with its relative independence from the line of generation continuity. In place of the *paesani* groups and the other strictly Italian associations the second generation has tried to identify itself with uniquely American urban groupings — the occupational, fraternal, religious, and other such associations in which one's status is relatively independent of his family and other relationships. Criteria of personal evaluation have undergone an equal transformation. Where the immigrant Italian seeks prestige and respect in terms of his kinship and *paesani* affiliations, the second generation Italian seeks it in personal achievements, particularly as objectified by money, a car, and a home in the suburbs. The

---

[98] See Child, *op. cit.*, chaps. iv–vi, and *supra*, p. 191.

[99] Simmel, "Über räumliche Projektionen socialer Formen," *Zeitschrift für Sozialwissenschaft*, 6: 287–302 (1903), p. 293.

[100] Whyte, *Street Corner Society*, pp. xix–xx.

American-born Italian often looks upon his immigrant parents with mingled contempt and pity.[101] They in their turn look upon him as disrespectful, thriftless, and *Americanate*.

Both of these changes in Italian social structure are "projected" upon space in the form of altered residential patterns. Once again, it is through the cultural definitions which attach to location that these residential patterns assume their symbolic significance. *Where* a person lives "places" him in the eyes of others, because space so readily lends itself to representing social affiliations.[102] Hence a person generally wants to live in whatever neighborhood will place him well in the eyes of the ones whose estimation he cares for. The second generation Italians, in bidding for the estimation of Americans as a whole, have tended to locate in suburban areas. There they feel that they are no longer being stamped as "Italians" through living in an Italian colony. There they feel that they may be esteemed in proportion to their accomplishments or their affluence or their personal qualities, independent of family and *paesani* connections. In this respect they are conforming to the typical urban residential pattern of western society in which place of residence is an objective symbol of personal achievement rather than of in-group identity. Only in homogeneous immigrant slums such as the North End does the latter type of pattern survive. The distinction has been conceived by Simmel as that between "rational festgelegten Stadtsiedelung gegen den naturhaften Stammesgedanken." [103] In the latter space is an instrumental symbol of in-group solidarity; residence within a particular area denotes to the in-group and to the larger society that one is identifying himself with that particular group. In the former, on the other hand, space is an instrumental symbol of personal accomplishment; residence within a particular area denotes that one has achieved a corresponding measure of occupational success and class status. As one ecologist has indicated:

In an impersonal setting, such as the large city, community status does not rest on any intimate evaluation of the person. Instead, certain

---

[101] *Loc. cit.*
[102] Cf. Maunier, *op. cit.*, p. 213.
[103] Simmel, "Der Raum und die räumliche Ordnungen der Gesellschaft," pp. 477–478.

easily recognizable traits, such as possessions, become symbolic of each status class. Among the urban badges of status are areas of residence. Each residential area, then, has a status value in the eyes of the community.[104]

Among the Italians of Boston there are some rather interesting departures from this uniformity — departures which remind us once again of the pervasive causal influence which localized solidarity may exert upon land use. They indicate that emigration from the North End does not always symbolize rejection of Italian values but may at times actually create satellite localizations of ethnic solidarity. In one case an extended Sicilian family, the Alibrandis, have left the North End as a group, and have relocated around Humboldt avenue in Roxbury. Here there live several households, each in its own dwelling, but all related to one another by marriage or descent. The father still maintains his barber shop in the North End, Italian is spoken in all the homes, and traditional Italian mores are imposed upon all. In another case an Italian contractor, after years of successful business operations, decided to leave the North End and move to Framingham. There he purchased a large house for himself and several dwellings with their lots along the same street. He then rented out these houses at preferential rates to some of his close relatives, friends, and employees. There has thus developed a little "colony" centered around "the boss" who, of course, enjoys the highest status in the group. Even more common than such emigration patterns as these are the cases in which an old Italian couple, having accumulated savings over the course of years, will purchase a suburban house and invite one of their matured children, along with his or her family, to live with them. The latter is expected to support his or her elderly parents until they die, it being understood that at that time the house will go to the child who has thus supported his or her parents. Whatever other children the couple may have will fully accept this arrangement since, by agreement, they have been exempt from supporting the old couple. Such first generation emigration from the North End as this is an interesting departure from the overall differentials by age and

---

[104] Harold A. Gibbard, "The Status Factor in Residential Successions," *American Journal of Sociology*, 46: 835–842 (May, 1941), p. 836.

nativity. Nevertheless it is meaningfully congruent with Italian kinship values and family solidarity and cannot be understood apart from them.

So far as the emigration of young people is concerned it appears that the circumstances of early childhood upbringing account for which individuals will fall into the "rebel" reaction, with its spatial corollary of suburban residence, and which will fall into the "in-group" reaction, with its spatial corollary of residence in the North End. Whyte has found a clear demarcation among teen-agers in the North End as between the "corner boys" and the "college boys." The former tend to remain in the North End, the latter to leave. The corner boys conform their personal aspirations with strictly local values, they identify themselves with North End associations and interaction routines, and they tend to more fully accept Italian values. The college boys, on the other hand, are discontented with the circumscribed life of an Italian colony and are ambitious for occupational "success" according to the traditional American pattern. Typically they have been good students at the public schools, they have saved their money for an education rather than for entertaining their pals, and in other ways they have had their personal aspirations oriented toward distinctly American criteria of evaluation.[105] In such differential socialization as this are to be found the origins of the selective process by which some young people become "rebels" and others loyal Italians.

The counterpart to this differential socialization is of course to be found among all youths in contemporary American society, with its open class system.[106] In this respect the North End corner boy and the North End college boy have their equivalents in nearly every neighborhood of Boston or of any other American metropolis. Everywhere the "good student" finds his life course laid out in terms of prevailing middle class values with their norms of professional-managerial status and single-family residence in the suburbs. And everywhere the "poor student" — the athletic, rough-housing type — finds his career laid out in terms of particular friendship ties, through which he finds "a job" and

---

[105] Whyte, *Street Corner Society*, pp. 104–108.

[106] The following analysis owes its formulation to the comments and suggestions of Professor Talcott Parsons.

takes for granted the necessity of living in a low-rent working class district. What is unique about the differential socialization of youth in the North End, however, is the correspondence of the "good student" role, and its sequelae of middle class status and suburban residence, with Americanization; and, on the other side, the correspondence of the "one-of-the-gang" role, and its sequelae of working class status and tenement or three-decker residence, with Italian identification. In the North End, Americanization implies the rebel reaction; Italian identification implies the in-group reaction. It is a pure circumstance that there exists for the Italian youth an ethnic value system with its own distinctive goals and rewards with which he may identify his ego when he finds himself outside the good student–middle class avenue of personal development. For him, unlike his "American" equivalent, there is a network of preëxisting solidarities with which he may align himself by way of compensation for his exclusion from middle class groupings.

From all of this it should be evident that processes of spatial adaptation are on every hand correlative to processes of social organization. Unless these processes receive positive formulation in ecological theory there can be no comprehension of some very real and important locational phenomena. Even in an urban slum such as the North End the causal significance which social values may have for land use is apparently considerable. In spite of its physical deterioration and population congestion the slum may at times acquire definite symbolic properties. By virtue of those symbolic properties certain social systems will locate in the slum even when fully aware of its objective undesirability. There thus appears to be no justification whatsoever for the logical premises of empirically rationalistic ecology. On every count our land use analysis has consistently forced us to recognize a single *dictum*, which has been put by Sorokin as follows: "This means that any ecological study is possible only after the studied sociocultural phenomenon is located in its system of meanings in the universe of meanings." [107]

[107] Sorokin, *Sociocultural Causality Space Time* (Durham: 1943), p. 138, n. 56.

PART II

THE CULTURAL CONTEXT OF RATIONAL ADAPTATION TO SPACE

CHAPTER VI

CONTRACTUALISM AS THE MASTER PATTERN IN THE LOCATION OF COMMERCE: THE RETAIL CENTER

ECOLOGICAL RATIONALISM is apparently inadequate for the explanation of actual, concrete locational processes. But it cannot on that account be categorically dismissed as a methodological position. It is always a legitimate scientific procedure, after all, to arbitrarily specify certain premises as given, for the purposes of analytical generalization, and then to deduce from these how the unknown variables will behave, even though such conditions never present themselves to direct observation. The ecologist is therefore quite within his rights, on scientific grounds, to deliberately limit himself to the study of those locational processes which *would* operate *if* space were only an impediment and *if* social systems were only economizing agents. Whatever generalizations he may formulate, provided they are logically deduced from his initial premises and are mutually integrated with one another, will have an *eo ipso* validity. They will in other words comprise a "pure" theory, one that is applicable as well to one sociocultural regime as to another. But they will not depict empirical locational processes. They will only divulge the latent, "virtual," "as if" processes which may be presumed to exist given the specified initial premises.

This is the position which the methodologically rationalistic theories have taken. Indeed these theories have deliberately limited the scope of ecology to the study of those locational processes which pertain to space as an impediment and to social systems as economizing agents. In the words of Engländer:

Vielmehr ergibt sich der Zusammenhang der Sätze einer allgemeinen Standortslehre . . . aus ihrem Begriffe, der zugleich ihre Aufgabe darstellt, als Lehre von der örtlichen Bedingtheit in der Volkswirtschaft, die somit alle jene Erscheinungen zu erklären hat, die sich aus örtlicher

Gegebenheit von Angebot und Nachfrage im Hinblick auf die mit Raumüberwindung verbundenen Kosten ergeben.[1]

Having thus restricted themselves they proceed to build up a deductive construct, a "pure" theory, fully aware that this theory does not describe real land use. Rather it is designed to show up the latent, "virtual" processes that are never immediately apparent to the senses but which can only be deduced from initially specified premises. These premises impute a strictly cost-minimizing character to social systems in their adaptation to space and a strictly impeditive character to space in its significance for social systems. Implied in these premises is the further idea that social systems have no other orientation to space than that which inheres in their very constitutive ends. In other words, social systems are postulated as disparate entities having an autonomous existence of their own, independent from any larger context of values. Finally, if there is to be any orderliness to the spatial patterns which these disparate systems take on there is implied in the methodologically rationalistic premises the added corollary that the maximum utility of the aggregate of systems will always correspond with the maximum utility of each individual system. Such a correspondence is presumably brought about through the "substitution" process.

The Cultural Contingency of Rationalism. There is thus a point for point similarity between the methodologically rationalistic theories and the empirically rationalistic theories. The similarity may be put negatively in this way: the rationalistic theories are all alike in their exclusion of the cultural component. The only difference between them is in the fact that with the methodological rationalists this exclusion is intentional. For that reason it is impossible to criticize their theories in the same way that we have criticized the empirically rationalistic theories. It is not enough to show that social values actually do influence land use; the methodological rationalists will admit that. What is necessary now is to demonstrate that rational adaptation is itself a culturally relative phenomenon. In other words, we must show that the

[1] Oskar Engländer, "Kritisches und Positives zu einer allgemeinen reinen Lehre vom Standort," *Zeitschrift für Volkswirtschaft und Sozialpolitik,* 5 (n.s.): 435–505 (1926), p. 504.

methodological rationalists have taken as their premises factors which are not "self-givens" but which are unique properties of a particular kind of value system. Consequently the failure to give positive formulation to this value system in systematic ecological theory results either in sterility or error. As Sombart has indicated:

> Gewisz kann man eine "reine" Theorie des Standorts geben. Aber sie kann nur zweierlei sein: entweder anämisch, wenn sie nur die wirklich allen Wirtschaftsweisen gemeinsamen Elemente berücksichtigt; oder falsch, wenn sie einen wirklich starken Faktor der Wirtschaftsbildung — der doch kein historisch bedingter ist — herausgreift und mit ihm alle historischen Möglichkeiten erklären will.[2]

Weber, Engländer, and Predöhl have all posited as elements in their "pure" theory factors that are historically conditional. They presuppose a value system in which social systems have a free bargaining relationship to one another *vis-à-vis* the special-purpose end of selecting locations. They presuppose, further, a value system in which spatial sites are capable of alternative uses — i.e., in which space is a "mobile" transferable productive agent. The only reason that social systems are able to choose between alternative locations through competitive bargaining is by virtue of a congenial value context. Likewise the only reason that physical space is capable of allocation according to the principle of substitution is by virtue of just such a value context; apart from such a context space could not be a productive agent at all. From this it follows that the very disparateness of social systems, insofar as they are disparate, is of cultural definition. Similarly it follows that the very impeditiveness of space is of cultural definition, since it is only through its status as a productive agent that space has to be "dealt with" so that it imposes end-deprivation, or "cost," upon social systems.[3]

[2] Werner Sombart, "Einige Anmerkungen zur Lehre vom Standort der Industrien," *Archiv für Sozialwissenschaft und Sozialpolitik*, 30: 748–758 (May, 1910), pp. 751–752.

[3] Even at the polar extreme of unalterability, space is impeditive only because a more inclusive set of values has so defined the conditions for a social system's existence that this system has to traverse space in order to maintain its identity. This is just as true in a Robinson Crusoe economy

In brief, the rational orientation to space is a culturally contingent phenomenon.

Put more rigorously the hypothesis to be developed in this and the two succeeding chapters is as follows: The fact that a social system in its processes of maintaining identity is able to and has to deliberately seek a least costful location in terms of its own constitutive ends as a disparate system is the consequence of an historically unique value system which defines social systems as freely bargaining agents with respect to special-purpose ends and which defines physical space as a productive agent for the attainment of those ends. The subjective orientation involved in this process is what we mean by "rationalism." The value system which establishes such an orientation is what we shall call "contractualism." The methodological rationalists, in their efforts to develop a "pure" theory have thus developed only a "contractualistic" theory — or, what Sombart calls a "capitalistic" theory.[4] It describes how spatial adaptation would proceed if social systems and physical space had the characteristics which pertain to a contractualistic value system. Consequently it is not the "pure," "extra-cultural" theory that its proponents have supposed it to be.

The Role of Accessibility in Retail Location. To establish this hypothesis we have selected for analysis the retail business center of Boston. Here more than anywhere else is contractualism the master pattern of spatial adaptation. The relationship between individual businesses, viewed as social systems, comes closest to the pure and rational bargaining for special-purpose ends which is posited in the rationalistic theories. And the quality for which spatial locations are valued is most fully that of their being productive agents. Hence in the business district there should be the clearest manifestation of rationalism on the empirical level. We may therefore find in it the neatest test case as to whether or not rationalistic spatial adaptation is a culturally relative phenomenon.

---

where the ends upon which Robinson acts so as to survive (some of which entail traversing space) derive from a broader value context (largely cognitive) by which he *knows* what he must procure from nature and *how* he must go about it. Only feral man would be a truly disparate system.

[4] We have used the term "contractualism" because of its greater inclusiveness, one that transcends the strictly economic connotation of "capitalism."

Basic to all the rationalistic theories is the conception of transportation as the means through which the impeditiveness of spatial distance is reduced. Transportation is the instrument through which space is rendered "alterable." A location with poor transportation facilities will obviously present a greater obstacle to the spatially contingent ends of social systems than a location with good transportation facilities. Accessibility thus becomes the desideratum for all social systems for whom space is a condition to the achievement of ends. Within the modern western city the most important means of transportation are, of course, transit systems and automobiles. Their routings determine which portion of a city will have the greatest accessibility.[5] The relative importance of various means of transportation in Boston (prior to the war) is shown in Table 19.[6] If we sum up the 1938 figures

TABLE 19

NUMBER OF PERSONS ENTERING CENTRAL BUSINESS DISTRICT OF BOSTON DURING MONTH OF JUNE AS DETERMINED BY SUM OF DAILY SEVENTEEN-HOUR PERIODS

	1927	1938	Per Cent Change
Mass Transportation			
Rapid transit	537,263	436,402	−18.8
Subway	194,418	197,137	+1.4
Steam railway	182,940	85,448	−53.3
Street cars	50,448	19,294	−61.8
Buses	20,210	47,885	+136.9
Steamships, ferries	13,347	8,876	−33.4
Individual Transportation			
Passenger cars	332,770	488,458	+46.8
Trucks	79,519	87,538	+11.0
Horse-drawn vehicles	12,761	608	−95.2
Pedestrians	233,277	170,500	−26.9

Source: Urban Land Institute, *A Survey in Respect to the Decentralization of the Boston Central Business District*, 1944, p. 27.

for rapid transit, subway, and street cars we have a total of 652,833 persons entering the central business district of Boston

[5] We prefer the term "accessibility" to the term "nodality," proposed by one economic ecologist, because of its more evident meaning and wider familiarity. Cf. William H. Dean, Jr., *The Theory of the Geographic Location of Economic Activities* (Ann Arbor: 1938), p. 36.

[6] Copied from Urban Land Institute, *A Survey in Respect to the Decentralization of the Boston Central Business District* (Boston: 1944), p. 27.

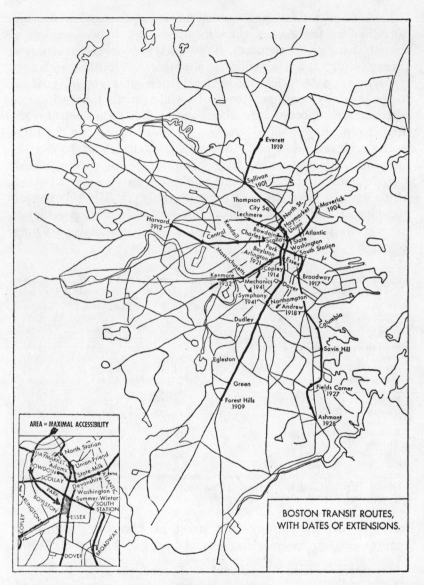

Everett
1919

Sullivan
1901

Thompson
City Sq.
Lechmere

North St.
Hoymarket
Union

Maverick
1904

Harvard
1912

Central   Kendall

Bowdoin
Scollay
Park
State
Washington
South Station

Atlantic

Charles

Boylston
Arlington
1921

Copley
1914

Essex

Dover

Broadway
1917

Massachusetts

Kenmore

Mechanics
1941

1932

Symphony
1941

Northampton
Andrew
1918

Columbia

Dudley

Savin Hill

Egleston

Green

Fields Corner
1927

Forest Hills
1909

Ashmont
1928

AREA OF MAXIMAL ACCESSIBILITY

North Station
HAYMARKET   Adams
BOWDON   Union-Friend
SCOLLAY   State-Milk
Park   Devonshire
BOYLSTON   Washington
                 Summer-Winter
                 SOUTH STATION
COPLEY
ARLINGTON   ESSEX

DOVER   BROADWAY

BOSTON TRANSIT ROUTES,
WITH DATES OF EXTENSIONS.

FIGURE 14

234

on the elevated railway system. All of this population movement is tied to fixed routes of transportation, unlike the movement of passenger cars and pedestrians which have some freedom in their choice of routes. For this reason and in view of the large volume of traffic which it bears, the elevated railway system exerts a preponderant role in determining which portions of the metropolitan area are most accessible. To be sure its importance has declined both relatively and absolutely since 1927, as shown by Table 19. This decline has had noteworthy consequences for the location of business activities. However, because of its continued importance in the total volume of passenger traffic, as well as by the spatial fixity of its routes, the elevated railway system will undoubtedly exert a paramount influence upon the relative accessibility of various portions of Boston and its environs. In figure 14 we have portrayed the network of trolley, bus, and subway routes which serve the Boston metropolitan area, along with the dates at which the various subway and elevated extensions were made.[7] From the map it is clear that all these routes converge upon a very limited portion of the territory which is served. Every day hundreds of thousands of persons are drawn from the wide hinterland and are transported to a small bit of territory in the Boston Hub. It is less costful in terms of time, fuel, maintenance, etc., to transport the whole metropolitan population to the Park street or Washington street subway stations than to any other single spot in the metropolitan area. Hence the area adjacent to Park street and the Washington-Summer street intersection is the most accessible part of Boston.

The most important result of this maximal accessibility of the Park street and Washington street areas is the enormous volume of population flow which exists at those points. Indeed, except for the outer termini of the subway system, these two entrances receive the largest number of passengers in the entire metropolitan area. They far surpass any other downtown entrance. Their relative importance in passenger flow is revealed in Table 20, which shows the fare collections made at various entrances of

[7] Adapted from "Boston Elevated Railway System Route Map." Dates of entrances obtained from Elisabeth M. Herlihy (ed.), *Fifty Years of Boston* (Boston: 1932), pp. 270–275 and from Mr. Matthews of the Public Relations Department, Boston Elevated Railway.

the subway system.[8] Of the central entrances the Washington street entrance receives the largest number of passengers, as shown by fare collections. The Park street entrance ranks second, the South Station entrance ranks third,[9] and the Boylston-Essex entrance is fourth. By noting the locations of the various entrances in Figure 14 it will be seen that the single combination of stations which has the maximum population flow within a restricted area is the Park street, Washington street, Boylston street, and Boylston-Essex streets stations. These four entrances form a rectangle which just about embraces the area of highest population flow in the city of Boston. Away from this rectangle the influx of subway and elevated passengers diminishes irregularly, though it rises again to very high figures at the outer termini of the system. However, these high figures for the terminal entrances of the subway and elevated system have quite a different significance from the figures for the central subway entrances. Thus Harvard square, Maverick square, Sullivan square, and Dudley street entrances receive many passengers who have actually entered the transit system at some remoter bus or trolley stop and, on their way to the city center, have transferred at these subway or elevated entrances where they must pay. Such passengers never leave the transit system while at the entrances in question and hence they do not constitute "population flow" for the spatial areas surrounding those entrances.

The total population served by the Boston elevated system is approximately 1,338,000.[10] Nearly one-half of this population lies outside the city limits of Boston. Moreover, as we have seen in Chapter II, the proportion of the population which dwells outside of corporate Boston has increased steadily throughout the present century. This outward drift of population has been in a westerly direction, along the Worcester and Concord turnpikes. However, most of this extension has not gone beyond a seven-mile radius

[8] From Board of Public Trustees, Boston Elevated Railway Co., Report, sheets 18 and 19 (Boston: January, 1944).

[9] The high figure for South Station entrance does not indicate true population flow in that vicinity since a large proportion of the fares collected there indicate passengers who have just left their commuting trains and have immediately boarded the subway.

[10] Herlihy, op. cit., p. 268.

TABLE 20

AMOUNT OF FARE COLLECTIONS MADE AT SUBWAY AND ELEVATED ENTRANCES OF
BOSTON FOR YEAR ENDING DECEMBER 31, 1943

	Receipts
Hub and Back Bay Entrances	
North Station (incl. West)	$ 543,901.49
Union-Friend	286,849.55
State-Milk-Devonshire	601,617.79
Washington-Summer-Winter	1,732,234.49
Boylston-Essex	813,892.43
Boylston (North and South)	562,121.16
Park Street (North, South, Under)	1,381,466.90
South Station	994,370.02
Scollay Square (plus Under)	358,710.77
Charles	187,927.57
Bowdoin	84,944.79
Canal	400,704.42
Haymarket Square	291,496.35
Adams Square	4,349.62
Kenmore	240,330.43
Massachusetts	392,387.80
Copley	401,315.94
Arlington	482,666.56
Mechanics	95,647.22
Symphony	223,473.23
Outlying Entrances	
Everett	902,506.19
Sullivan Square	1,165,132.14
Thompson Square	104,941.78
City Square	429,287.70
Dover	238,513.58
Northampton	246,642.85
Dudley	1,601,728.04
Egleston Square	510,964.13
Green Street	88,019.89
Forest Hills	763,354.93
Harvard	1,704,239.52
Central	401,389.97
Kendall	247,363.92
Broadway	129,078.75
Andrew Square	455,868.00
Columbia	105,590.83
Savin Hill	98,324.16
Fields Corner	571,215.28
Shawmut	69,032.68
Ashmont	543,894.67
Maverick	1,391,345.23
Lechmere Square	667,628.41

Source: Board of Public Trustees, Boston Elevated Railway Co., Report, sheets
18 and 19 (1944).

surrounding the State House, so that the population remains within the real functioning unit comprised by the Boston metropolitan area.[11] Such a dispersion of population naturally requires adjustments in transportation facilities so that the impediment put by greater distance upon population movement to the Hub may be cut down. One such adjustment has been the westward extension of the subway system. As may be seen from figure 14 the more recent extensions of underground transit have been the Kenmore and the Symphony entrances, built in 1932 and 1941 respectively. The net result of these extensions is a diminution in the overall costs to the metropolitan area attendant upon transporting increased populations lying to the west of Boston proper. Such changes in the transportation system cannot help but alter the relative accessibility of various points within central Boston. The automobile has likewise had a profound influence upon the location of accessible areas. Owing to the congestion which it creates in downtown streets the automobile becomes a handicap to efficient transportation in the city center, both to the owner of the vehicle and to the city as a social system. Consequently the increased use of the automobile has enhanced the accessibility of areas bordering upon the city center (such as the Back Bay sector of Massachusetts avenue) and of such satellite centers as Harvard square, Sullivan square, Maverick square, etc. This has been at the expense of the Park street, Washington street, and Boylston street centers.

The question which now arises is this: what significance has such a layout of "accessibilities," with its recent shifts resulting from transit extensions and increased use of the automobile, for the location of commercial activities viewed as social systems? What kinds of businesses will be found at the area of maximal accessibility? It seems best to approach these questions, first on a descriptive level, and then on an analytical level. To begin with, in the immediate vicinity of the four central subway entrances one finds the highest assessed land values in the entire city of Boston. The four corners of the rectangle embraced by

[11] Finance Commission of the City of Boston, *A Study of Certain of the Effects of Decentralization on Boston and Some Neighboring Cities and Towns* (Boston: 1941), pp. 4–9.

these entrances are assessed at an average value of $99.89.[12] Within the rectangle and its immediate vicinity are values even higher than this. Away from the rectangle the assessed values decline rapidly in most directions, with the exception of the rather high values extending out Boylston street. But more important than assessed values as an index of land use[13] are the kinds of social systems that are found there. On three of the four corners are the city's largest department stores: Jordan Marsh, Filene's, and Gilchrists'. On the fourth corner is the Touraine, a women's outfitting shop. Only a few steps away are such other department stores as R. H. White's, Kennedy's, C. F. Hovey, Chandler's, and R. H. Stearns. Also within this rectangular area are five-and-ten-cent stores, men's and women's clothing stores, jewelry stores, theaters, novelty shops, and coffee shops. One does not find grocery stores, furniture stores, service stations, parking lots, taverns, garages, or dance halls. Table 21 shows by actual count the number of businesses, classified according to type of service, that are located in the rectangle constituted by Washington, Tremont, Boylston, and Winter streets — the area which in terms of fare collections by the elevated railway system has maximal accessibility.[14] This classification is a purely heuristic one and without theoretical significance, although in the next section of this chapter we shall re-analyze the classification from a more analytical point of view. For the present we are only interested in finding out what kinds of businesses are found in the area of highest accessibility. From the table it can be seen that businesses engaged in the supplying of personal furnishings and personal

[12] This per square foot valuation was computed by summing the *land* valuations of all four corners of the Winter-Washington-Summer intersection, of two corners of the Winter-Tremont intersection, of one corner of the Tremont-Boylston intersection, and of all four corners of the Washington-Boylston-Essex intersection, and dividing by the respective number of square feet in all these lots. Figures obtained from Boston Real Estate Exchange, *Assessed Values of Real Estate in Boston* (Boston:1941).

[13] Particularly in view of the serious discrepancies which prevail in Boston between assessed values and real market values of property.

[14] The count includes all business establishments, regardless of the particular floor in a building they may occupy. Source: *The Boston City Directory* for 1944.

TABLE 21

BUSINESS ESTABLISHMENTS, BY TYPE, IN AREA OF CENTRAL BOSTON BOUNDED BY
WASHINGTON, TREMONT, BOYLSTON, AND WINTER STREETS, 1944

	Number of Establishments
Personal Furnishings.................................... 383	
Women's clothes, dressmaking.......................................	84
Men's clothes..	15
Hats..	15
Shoes...	35
Millinery..	29
Hosiery...	7
Tailoring..	71
Wigs, toupees...	5
Furs, linens, corsets, etc......................................	122
Personal Adornment.. 149	
Jewelry, watches..	30
Flowers...	1
Perfume...	2
Hairdressing, manicuring, etc..................................	109
Barbers...	6
Toiletries...	1
Department stores.. 6	
Clothing upkeep... 11	
Cleaners and dyers..	8
Shoe repair...	3
Recreation... 38	
Theaters..	9
Billiards..	3
Musical goods...	8
Shower baths..	1
Taverns, liquor...	4
Clubs...	13
Food... 47	
Confectionery...	14
Grocery (specialty)..	1
Coffee shops, lunch rooms.....................................	32
Household Items.. 67	
Household furnishings...	18
Dry goods...	8
Installment goods...	40
Furniture...	1
Schools.. 4	
Drugs.. 5	
Professional services..................................... 123	
Physicians..	5
Dentists..	23
Lawyers...	6
Chiropodists..	36
Podiatrists...	3
Optometrists, oculists..	34
Artists...	2
Architects..	2
Accountants..	1

TABLE 21 (Continued)

	Number of Establishments
Advertisers	3
Dermatologists	1
Hearing aids	2
Physical culture	5
Personal Items	42
Novelties	31
Photography	8
Cigars	3
Finance	25
Banks	6
Loans, credit, agents	19
Five-and-ten-cent stores	3
Tourist service	6
Telegraphing	1
Churches	2
Hotels	4
Clubs, religious organizations	8
Real Estate	7
Newspapers	2
Publishers and printers	6
Broadcasters	2
Office supplies	2
Miscellaneous	55
Wholesale clothing	16
Total Number of Establishments	1014

adornments are overwhelmingly predominant in this area. Fully 532 establishments are engaged in selling clothes,[15] shoes, hats, jewelry, flowers, and other of the usual symbols of personal propriety and acceptability. This represents 52.47 per cent of all the businesses within the area. A large proportion of the remainder consist of distinctly personal service businesses, notably coffee shops, confectionery stores, novelty shops, optometrists, and certain kinds of professional services. Most of them, however, cater to the woman shopper. The goods which these establishments sell are all characterized by standardization, brief durability, frequency of purchase, and moderate price relative to consumer's total income. Moreover they all have to do with rendering a person socially acceptable in terms of urban American symbols of respectability. The significance of these characteristics will engage us somewhat later. It is enough now to have them in mind.

[15] Including dressmakers and tailors.

Away from the maximally accessible rectangle the proportion which clothing and related stores bears to the total number of stores gradually diminishes. To the south, on both Washington and Tremont streets, are additional theaters, cinemas, and other entertainment facilities. Beyond these are furniture stores and heavy household equipment stores. To the east, toward South Station, are hardware and appliance shops. To the north is the cheap entertainment district of Scollay square, and beyond it another hardware and furniture area. Northeast of the Washington-Summer-Winter intersection is the banking and investment house district. Beyond it lie, on one side, the wholesale and storage businesses and, on the other side, the meat and produce markets. Other distinct and identifiable areas of homogeneous commercial functions are to be found in the textile and leather goods district around Essex street, the antique shops area on Charles street, the bookshops area around Ashburton place and on the northern extremity of Beacon street, etc. Figure 15b portrays fairly well the territorial differentiation and distribution of the main commercial functions in central Boston.

A comparison of the commercial land use maps for 1886 and 1943[16] (figures 15a and 15b) reveals a surprising fixity of the various specialized areas. Thus the districts devoted to finance and to wholesaling have remained essentially unchanged for 49 years. Likewise the heart of the retail district is today just where it was in 1886. However, one important locational shift is apparent in retail business which calls for some comment. As may be seen from figure 15b, there has been a very pronounced westerly drift of retail stores out Boylston street and the in-town segment of Newbury street. The stores involved in this outward movement are mostly specialty shops which feature high grade clothing, novelties, antiques, and the like. Their appeal is almost wholly to the higher income level of shoppers. As a result of this drift there has developed a new and distinctly smart shopping district at the southeastern extremity of the Back Bay. There

[16] Map for 1886 constructed from data in George E. Ellis, *Bacon's Dictionary of Boston* (Boston: 1886), pp. 405–406; 1943 map adapted and modified from map 2A in *Report on a Survey of Business and Industrial Buildings, City of Boston, 1935,* E. R. A. Project No. X2235, F2, U46 (Boston, City Planning Board, 1935).

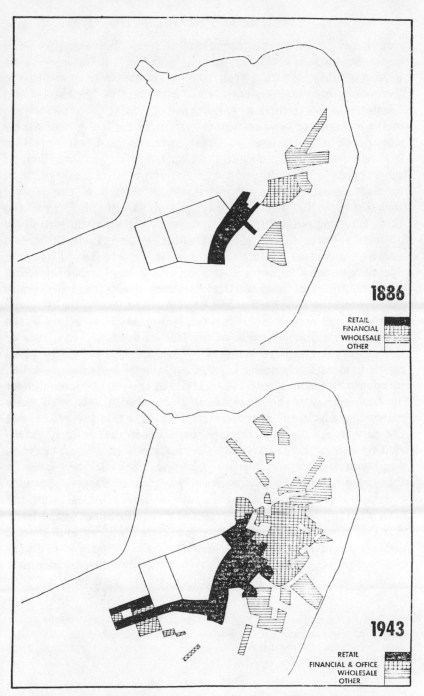

FIGURES 15a AND 15b. DOMINANT COMMERCIAL LAND USES

would seem to be a very tangible relationship between this retail expansion into the Back Bay district and the contemporary shifts in accessibility resulting from recent subway extensions to the Kenmore and Symphony entrances. Although the Park street and Washington street entrances, lying as they do at the intersections of the entire metropolitan transit system, are still the most accessible portions of Boston — at least so far as fixed transportation is concerned — their relative position has somewhat declined at the expense of the Boylston and Arlington entrances, which in turn owe most of their increased passenger flow to the general westerly extension of the subway system. All of this has put the Back Bay shopping district at an improved though still secondary position relative to the older Washington and Tremont streets district. Increased use of the automobile, greatly helped by more adequate parking facilities in the Back Bay, has further improved the accessibility of Boylston and Newbury streets and has thereby accelerated the westward trend of retail business. Finally, some degree of pull upon high class retail stores may have been exerted by the very fashionableness of the Back Bay itself. Evidence of this lies in the fact that during the "carriage days" of thirty years ago a moderate expansion of specialty shops had already taken place into Boylston street. The details of this early encroachment by business upon the fashionable Back Bay district will more fully engage us in the next chapter. Of course retail stores are not the only businesses that have participated in the westerly extension of commercial activities. Certain kinds of office buildings, notably insurance and medical buildings, have loomed large in this movement. Thus no less than three large insurance companies — the John Hancock, the Liberty Mutual, and the New England Mutual — have erected palatial edifices in the Back Bay, not to mention the Professional Arts Building and several distinct medical centers in the district.[17] This relocation of financial and professional functions has not the same significance that retail business has, and for that reason will not be considered with as much detail in the theoretical analysis which follows. It is

[17] Finance Commission of the City of Boston, *A Study of Certain of the Effects of Decentralization on Boston and Some Neighboring Cities and Towns* (Boston: 1941), p. 17.

enough to indicate that such establishments are not as dependent upon transportation accessibility as retail businesses are. Hence other factors, to be noted in the next chapter, are responsible for their drift to the Back Bay. Much the same considerations apply to such other areas as the banking and investment district around State and Devonshire streets. Accessibility to heavy population flow is not essential to the functioning of banks, investment houses, commercial lawyers, and other such social systems. Nor is convenience to the mass of people so very important, since the bulk of transactions engaged in by these systems is with large corporations. Each single transaction assumes so great a significance for a corporation that a special trip is necessary for the negotiators anyway. Hence perfect convenience is hardly a consideration. However, even though banking and investment areas do not bid for maximally accessible locations, they do tend to form distinct areas by themselves. Part of this segregation represents an accommodation to the convenience of lawyers, large investors, and corporation representatives who find proximity to one another of some material advantage. But part of it undoubtedly derives from the prestige that accrues to a lawyer, for instance, through having an office on State Street or Devonshire Street. State Street has all the prestige and meaningful connotations to Boston that Wall Street has to New York, and this undoubtedly attracts lawyers to the area.

With this idea of the relationship between commercial land use and accessibility patterns in mind, let us go on to a more theoretical analysis of the reasons for this relationship. Our task will be to show why retail business in general, and not wholesaling, residence, or manufacturing, is found at the area of maximal accessibility.[18] Further than this, we shall try to explain why cer-

---

[18] It is important to recognize that what is the maximally accessible area for one type of social system is not necessarily the maximally accessible area for every other type of social system. Obviously the optimal location for a dock will be very different from the optimal location for a department store. This point seems to have received no explicit recognition in the ecological literature and yet it is a significant one. In the present chapter we are arbitrarily limiting ourselves to the ecology of those social systems which have as their maximally accessible location the point at which population flow is greatest.

tain kinds of retail business, notably those which sell personal furnishings, succeed in getting the most accessible sites, rather than other kinds of retail business.

We may begin with three general propositions. The first of these states that, insofar as social systems have a rational orientation toward the attainment of their ends, they will seek to so conjoin the various productive agents bearing upon end-attainment as to achieve a minimal cost per unit of end-attainment — i.e., a least thwarting of other, extraneous ends.[19] Indeed this proposition is implied in our very definition of rationality. Hence for those social systems which deal with space as a productive agent, complete rationality will decree location at the point of maximal accessibility, since it is there that the least obstruction to the functioning of the system is suffered. The second general proposition which may be advanced is this: social systems are unequally contingent upon spatial distance, viewed as an impediment, for their maintenance of identity. In other words, the functioning of some social systems is more obstructed by spatial distance than is that of other social systems. At one extreme are those social systems whose functioning demands one location and no other. At the other extreme are those social systems which are relatively free of spatiality and can function about as well in one location as in another.[20] Between these two extremes most social systems range themselves according to their differential contingency upon spatial distance. The third of our general propositions states that social systems are willing to "pay" more, in the sense of suffering a qualified attainment of their ends, for highly accessible locations than they are for non-accessible locations. This is the reason that accessible locations are able to command "rent."

Granting these three propositions it logically follows that different types of social systems will show different variabilities

---

[19] In technical economic terminology this would be at the highest profit combination of inputs or productive agents. It should not be confused with the least cost combination of inputs.

[20] See Sombart, *op. cit.*, pp. 753–754; Georg Simmel, "Der Raum und die räumliche Ordnungen der Gesellschaft," *Soziologie* (München: 1923), pp. 462–463; Tord Palander, *Beiträge zur Standortstheorie* (Uppsala: 1935), p. 29.

away from their respective points of maximal accessibility. Some social systems — those which are most dependent upon "perfect" location — will have highly fixed, invariant locations. On a map they will concentrate around the point of maximal accessibility. Such social systems must have great rent-paying ability, owing to the high market value of their locations. Other social systems, to the extent that they are rational and in proportion to their contingency upon spatial distance, will seek as much accessibility as befits their respective highest-profit combinations of productive agents. They will "bid" for accessibility up to as high a rent as they can stand, and, by virtue of the increasing rent which accompanies greater accessibility, they will in the course of their bidding reach a point beyond which greater accessibility is not worth the added cost. That point is the one at which spatial location, combined with the other productive agents used by the various social systems in question, imposes a minimum overall cost for each of them. Those social systems whose functions are least contingent upon spatiality will assume relatively random locations. Thus they will show the greatest variability away from the point of maximal accessibility. The result of this differential compliance with spatial distance is a separation of land uses into the "preëmptive" and the "residual" types. Those social systems whose functioning demands an accessible location take on a preemptive role in land use. Almost invariably the land which such social systems need will devolve to their use, following the Law of First Choice as developed by Black and Black.[21] Paraphrasing their formulation of this law we may say that: "Any productive agent for which only a limited number of social systems are qualified in proportion to the need for it, will have first choice of these social systems." [22] On the other hand, those social systems whose functioning does not urgently demand accessible location tend to become residual land uses. They will locate on whatever sites are left after the preëmptive land uses have occupied the accessible areas.

That this deductive theory does tally with real locational processes in commercial land use is indicated by data on the variability

[21] John D. Black and Albert G. Black, *Production Organization* (New York: 1929), chap. vi.
[22] *Loc. cit.*

of spatial positions assumed by three kinds of business establishments: department stores, jewelry stores, and bookstores. These three types of business are alike in the general type of function which they perform, namely, that of retailing personal consumption goods which are of relatively small value. They are alike, moreover, as to the class of clientele they serve, namely, persons who are connected with families. They do not predominantly serve transients, unattached persons, nor of course do they serve non-personal social systems such as other businesses. For these reasons they all have as their "ideal" location the area of maximal accessibility as defined by transit routes. It is legitimate therefore to compare them in respect to their relative variability away from the area of maximal accessibility. Our procedure was to copy from the classified business section of the *Boston City Directory* all addresses of jewelry, book, and department stores which were located within the downtown shopping area. Businesses located in the North End, the West End, or in remoter portions of Boston were not included since such stores are mostly local-service agencies and do not really serve the larger metropolitan population. The next step was the somewhat vulnerable one of assuming that assessed land values, at least when grouped by broad statistical class-intervals, do bear some relationship to maximal accessibility. We have already noted that the highest land values are to be found within and around the Washington-Tremont-Winter-Boylston streets rectangle — the area most accessible from the subway and elevated system. To be sure, assessed values often show serious variations away from true market values, particularly in Boston where assessments are dictated largely by municipal financial stringency rather than by objective standards of real estate valuation. Perhaps it is reasonable, however, to assume that random errors in valuation (away from the consistent over-valuation which prevails in Boston) are canceled by a large enough number of individual properties such as we have tabulated. Moreover, individual assessed values cannot diverge from average assessed values for comparable property so grossly as to cover more than a single statistical class-interval of valuation figures. For these reasons it seems legitimate to use assessment data as a crude index of relative accessibility. On this assumption we have computed the per square foot assessed value of every lot

occupied by a jewelry, book, or department store in the downtown shopping area.[23] The valuations for each type of store,
grouped by statistical class-intervals, are presented in Table 22.
From the table it is evident that bookstores are most frequently

TABLE 22

DISTRIBUTION OF JEWELERS, BOOKSELLERS, AND DEPARTMENT STORES IN
DOWNTOWN BOSTON ACCORDING TO ASSESSED PER SQUARE FOOT
VALUATION OF THEIR LOTS

Assessed Per Square Foot Land Values	Booksellers No.	Per Cent	Jewelers No.	Per Cent	Department Stores No.	Per Cent
$ 0– 29	25	75.76	21	38.88		
30– 59	7	21.21	19	35.18	1	12.50
60– 89	1	3.03	5	9.26	1	12.50
90–119			5	9.26		
120–149			3	5.56	2	25.00
150–179			1	1.86	2	25.00
180–209					1	12.50
210 & over					1	12.50
Totals	33	100.00	54	100.00	8	100.00

Computed from *Boston City Directory*, 1941, and *Assessed Values of Real Estate in Boston*, 1941.

located on land of low assessed valuations. Department stores, on
the other hand, are more frequently located on land of high assessed valuations. Jewelry stores occupy an intermediary position
between these. Apparently department stores are most nearly preemptive land uses, while jewelers and even more so bookstores
are residual land uses.

The relative variability away from optimal location as between
these three types of businesses appears even more clearly when
the mean assessed valuation of the lots occupied by each of the
types is compared with the maximum assessed valuation occupied
by any of them. The most valuable lot included in our tabulation
— the one occupied by R. H. Stearns Co., on Tremont street — is
assessed at $210 per square foot. The mean assessed valuation of
lots occupied by department stores is $135 per square foot; that

[23] Assessment data obtained from Boston Real Estate Exchange, *Assessed
Values of Real Estate in Boston* (Boston: 1941). The *land* valuations for all
the lots were divided by the respective number of square feet in the lots,
thus obtaining assessed per square foot values.

for lots occupied by jewelers is $47; and that for lots occupied by booksellers is $20. Subtracting each of these means from the maximum figure we find the following distribution of variabilities away from optimal location as between the three types of businesses:

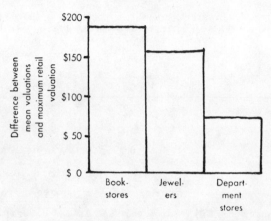

FIGURE 16. RELATIVE VARIABILITY FROM OPTIMAL LOCATION

Apparently department stores have relatively invariant locations; they must locate at the maximally accessible sites in a city or they cannot function at all. This being the case the highest-profit combination for them is found at the locations which command the highest rent. Only by virtue of their ability to pay such rent are they able to preëmpt those locations. Bookstores, on the other hand, are able to function and maintain their identity at much less desirable locations, even though an ideal location for them too would be at the point of maximal accessibility. However, because rival businesses are willing to bid higher for these ideal locations, thereby raising the rent beyond the highest-profit combination for bookstores, the latter must fall back to more residual locations. As a result they show the greatest variability away from optimal location.

Generalizing from these data it may be suggested that there is a variable autonomy for different kinds of social systems from a maximally accessible location. Retail business as a whole preempts the zone of maximum population flow surrounding the point at which transit routes converge. This is for it the area of maximal accessibility. Since the very performance of retail functions demands accessibility for shoppers it becomes economically advantageous for stores to take on the burden of high rent in return for the better patronage which comes from accessibility. The result is a concentration of retail stores at the area of maximal accessibility. Other social systems, less contingent upon spatial distance, show a more dispersed and more variable pattern of distribution — one that is inversely proportional to their contingency upon spatiality. The spatial autonomy of such social systems as wholesale businesses, schools, hospitals, and families is much greater than that of retail business, and the variability of their locational patterns is correspondingly greater. The same principle governs the relative variability of location for different kinds of retail stores. Those whose functioning is most contingent upon spatial distance preëmpt the most accessible locations. Other stores take residual locations in accordance with their relative contingency upon space. The result is a differential variability in locational patterns as between the various types of retail business. In this uniformity is to be found the explanation for the concentration of retail stores as a whole, and of department stores and personal furnishings stores in particular, at the area of maximal accessibility.

The Locational Implications of Contractualism. Throughout the foregoing analysis we have not had to invoke any cultural factors in spatial adaptation. Seemingly it has been enough to view stores as disparate social systems bargaining freely for accessible locations, and to view space as a physically given impediment to the functioning of these stores. The "necessary and sufficient" cause of the relative accessibility of various locations, and of spatial impeditiveness as a productive agent, has seemingly been transportation. This is the view which the methodological rationalists have taken as the basis of their "pure" ecological theory.[24] In their scheme they have tried to exclude whatever is culturally unique and "historical." Their aim has been to de-

---

[24] The fact that their analysis has been in terms of industries rather than retail stores does not alter the methodological status of their deductive scheme.

velop a deductive theory that is applicable to the "virtual" locational processes of any sociocultural regime. The question which confronts us now is this: Have they really done what they thought they did? Indeed, is our own analysis of the relative variability in location among different kinds of retail stores really adequate as it stands? True, we have found a genuine uniformity in the way that retail stores distribute themselves in the commercial district of a large city. But is this uniformity really "pure" or "extra-cultural"? Can the existence of retail stores be taken as self-evident, as given in their own autonomous processes of self-maintenance? Can the specific kind of obstruction which space puts upon the functioning of retail stores be taken as inherent in the very nature of space? If not, it can only be that they are predicated upon an historically relative value system. In that case the uniformities which show up in the locational processes of retail stores, as well as of all other capitalistic enterprises whose survival depends upon rational bargaining for location, are not "pure" at all. They only describe locational processes within a particular kind of value system — one that may be called a "contractualistic" value system. It is to this hypothesis that we shall now address ourselves.

A few words may first be said regarding the nature of a contractualistic value system. As formulated by Sorokin there are two primary *differentia specifica* to a contractual social relationship. These are: (a) the rationalistic "bargaining" orientation of the interacting agents, and (b) the limited number of interests or ends involved in the interaction. From these two basic characteristics follow a number of logical corollaries, notably the brief duration of interaction, the mutual bargaining character to the relationship between agents, the freedom of choice as to the alignments into which each agent will enter, and a certain degree of "strangerness" within the relationship.[25] It is this value system which has dominated western society throughout the past three centuries. And these have been the very centuries during which the distinctive features of the modern metropolis have emerged. Such a parallelism is something more than a coincidence. There appears to be a genuine functional relationship between the two,

[25] Pitirim A. Sorokin, *Social and Cultural Dynamics* (New York: 1937), III, 30–35.

such that the unique features of the modern "great city" — its *raison d'être,* its organization, and its spatial structure — can only be understood in terms of the contractualistic value system under which it has emerged. This may become clearer if we consider some of the ecological implications of a contractualistic value system. These may be divided into two classes, corresponding to the two *differentia* of contractualism that have just been indicated.

First, there are the ecological implications of a *rationalistic* orientation. Principal among these is the relegation of space to the status of a productive agent, a mere means to some remoter end. Under contractualism space tends to be divested of its symbolic qualities and becomes affectively neutralized. Its fetishistic and instrumental potentialities are outweighed by its utility as a productive agent which can be rationally allocated among various uses according to the relative profit-making ability of those uses. As a result, any social system whose functioning is contingent upon spatial distance will try to locate in such a way as to approach a highest-profit combination of productive factors (including location). Then, according to the principles developed in our preceding section, different types of social systems will segregate themselves over space in accordance with their relative dependence upon accessible location. Retail businesses, for instance — whose existence will be explained in a moment — tend to be preëmptive land uses, since the very performance of their functions depends upon accessibility to patrons. Home-seeking families, on the other hand, insofar as they locate in terms of space as a productive agent,[26] tend to be residual land uses which take over whatever locations have not already been preëmpted. Retail businesses show the smallest range of variability away from optimal location, whereas families show probably the greatest range of variability. What is important for us to recognize in this is the fact that such a segregation is not "automatic" or "extra-cultural" but is the expression of a very unique and historically relative

---

[26] We have already seen in our North End and Beacon Hill analyses that they actually locate in terms of other considerations than this. At present we are concerned only with imagining the logical implications of a pure contractualistic pattern of land use. In the succeeding chapter on the Back Bay we shall inquire more closely into the interplay between rational land use and volitional land use.

value system, namely, contractualism, by which space is divested of all its attributes except the one of impeditiveness. In the logically pure case, a contractualistic land use pattern would indeed fit the deductive theory of the methodological rationalists. But to regard such a locational process as "natural," as inherent in all spatial adaptation, would be no more justified than to regard the fetishistic symbolism found in religious cities like Mecca or Benares as the "natural" process which really governs spatial adaptation. Symbolism is just as real a quality of space as is impeditiveness. The paramount importance of the latter in modern western cities is no more inherent or inevitable than the paramount importance of fetishism in Islamic and Hindu settlements. Both are historically relative. Neither can be understood apart from the particular value systems under which they have developed. The dominant role of retail land use in the cities of western Europe and America is a very real phenomenon which cannot be neglected in ecological analysis. Retail stores are indeed the spatially preëmptive social systems of the modern metropolis. But their preëmptive character derives directly from a contractualistic value system which has rendered space a mere impediment to the functioning of social systems. Consequently every spatially contingent social system has no other criterion for choosing a location except the one of minimizing cost. And, being the most spatially contingent of a city's social systems, retail stores find their highest-profit combination at the area of maximal accessibility.

But none of this explains why there are such social systems as retail stores. Nor does it tell us the reason for the contingency of retail stores upon spatiality in the first place. To understand these questions we must turn to the second basic ecological implication of a contractualistic value system, viz., the limited-purpose, functionally specific character of contractualistic interaction. This phenomenon may be approached, first, as it manifests itself in the larger social system comprised by western society, and second, as it manifests itself in the specific market relation involved in retailing.

Above all, contractualism implies an "open" class system with a great deal of vertical mobility. Further, it implies the assignment of status to persons in terms of their achievements. This is owing to the absence of any other basis for assigning status except the one of competence in fulfilling the obligations which attach to a person's specific role. In a contractual regime there is not the kinship, ethnic, or religious cohesion out of which might emerge a rigid caste system with its status of ascription. As a result contractualism leads to a constant infiltration of upper classes by nouveaus who are eagerly seeking the symbolic trappings of higher status. This carries with it two typical features of consumption under a contractualistic regime, namely, standardization of desires and "fashion." The functional significance of these features in a highly mobile and anonymous society such as that implied by contractualism has been conceived by Zimmerman in terms of the "fixation of institutional and occupational patterns." Standardization of clothing, for instance, is almost inevitable in a highly mobile society. For in such a society nearly everyone has some hopes of climbing the social ladder. Hence nearly everyone is forever trying to emulate the costumes of the elite. The result is a practically uniform costume for all strata of the population. "Respectability" demands that one be dressed in this uniform costume.[27] Moreover the objective, impersonal evaluation of people such as takes place in contractualism is greatly facilitated by a uniform costume in which there are no distracting individual variations in garb. Sombart too has pointed out the *"Vereinheitlichung des Bedarfs"* which accompanies a capitalistic or, in our words, contractualistic value system. His emphasis is upon the leveling of tastes which accompanies an urban mode of life with its obliteration of unique local, regional, and class idiosyncrasies.[28] Along with standardization there appears "mode" or, more properly, "fashion." Once again, the anonymity and the flux which go along with contractualism lead to a constant process of change in the trappings of respectability, like clothing, style of home, model of car, etc.[29] This constant change in sym-

---

[27] Carle C. Zimmerman, *Consumption and Standards of Living* (New York: 1936), pp. 245–248.

[28] Sombart, *Der Moderne Kapitalismus* (Leipzig: 1902), first edition, II, 319–326. See also R. D. McKenzie, "The Role of Standardization," mimeographed, in J. F. Steiner (ed.), *Readings in Human Ecology* (Seattle: 1936).

[29] Zimmerman, *op. cit.*, pp. 254–256. Acknowledgment is also due Mr. George H. Grosser for suggestive comments on this point.

bolic appurtenances expresses the desire of some individuals to achieve a distinctiveness which they cannot easily get in an undifferentiated and mobile society where anonymity makes it hard to know a person's standing except as it is tangibly symbolized through clothing, dwelling, or some other such object. Of course, once a new "distinctive" style in any of these consumers' goods appears it immediately diffuses among parvenus and soon loses its initial symbolic significance, thereby offering the opportunity for a new variation in style. As Sombart has suggested, the very existence of "fashion" testifies to a strain between the democratic equality that is implied in contractualism and the urge to individual differentiation that is so rooted in human nature.[30]

Turning to the way in which contractualism manifests itself in the retailing market relationship we encounter what may be called "the shopping pattern." This pattern is a result, in part, of standardization and fashion in consumers' goods whereby clothes, jewelry, etc., lose their value in a very short time. Not only is their durability brief, but their symbolic worth is quickly superseded by some new fashion, thus requiring a constant buying of "the latest" in clothing and other status symbols by the would-be parvenu. Purchasing thus involves considerable expenditure of time and, what is even more important, it involves a rational comparison of price and quality at different markets. As a result there appears the pattern of "shopping," by which persons who are contemplating the purchase of a particular item compare various samples of that item at different establishments. This of course means walking or traveling over distance, with all the inconvenience and loss of time which that implies. Convenience, or accessibility, thus enters into the shopper's calculus of "pain and pleasure," along with quality and price of commodities, in determining the store at which he will eventually make his purchase. In all of this the relationship between buyer and seller is limited to the specialized task of arriving at an exchange that is advantageous to each party. In the logically pure case, one does not buy from the seller who is a fellow lodge-member or who stands to

[30] Fashion "eine besondere unter jenen Lebensformen darstellt, durch die man ein Kompromiss zwischen der Tendenz nach socialer Egalisierung und der nach individuellen Unterscheidungsreizen herzustellen sucht." Sombart, *op. cit.*, p. 334.

one in a particular kinship relation, but rather from the one who offers the best bargain. As a consumer one is free to buy from whomever he wishes.[31] This is indeed a unique exchange relationship which makes its appearance only with certain distinct social and cultural features all of which are presupposed in contractualism, viz., money, equality among consumers, segregation of the exchange relationship from other social relationships, multiplicity of alternative market outlets, etc.[32] More than this, however, the modern "shopping pattern" is the corollary of a unique differentiation of sex roles in the urban American family. Shopping is the specific task of the married woman. To her is entrusted the family function of spending that portion of income which goes to food, clothing, and status symbols; to her is delegated responsibility for judging what status symbols are necessary and suitable for her family and for purchasing them economically.

Out of this historically unique "standardization-fashion-shopping" complex has emerged the modern retail store. This type of market is in a sense the epitome of the contractual relationship and is the distinct product of a contractualistic value system. Without the huge volume of consumption which results from standardization and fashion, without the shopping pattern by which patrons tend to entirely divorce their relationship with the merchant from their family, occupational, religious, and other ties, and without the whole complex of money, fee simple property, private access to capital, and innumerable other features of a contractualistic value system — without all of these the retail store as a distinct type of social system would be inconceivable. The function of the retail store is to effect a conveyance of finished products to undifferentiated consumers in return for a reciprocal service represented by money, and to derive from this transaction a profit. Its functioning as a social system is predicated upon its ability to make *conveniently* available to shoppers

[31] On the concept of "functional specificity" and its contingency upon division of labor with its attendant cultural prerequisites see Talcott Parsons, "The Professions and Social Structure," *Social Forces*, 17: 457–467 (May, 1939).

[32] See Frank H. Knight, "The Ethics of Competition," in his *The Ethics of Competition and Other Essays* (New York: 1935), pp. 49–58, reprinted from *Quarterly Journal of Economics*, 37: 579–624 (1923).

goods of such a variety, quality, and price as will induce enough purchases to put the store's total income ahead of its costs. This requires an elimination of all the deterrents to patronage, among which is spatial distance. The shopper, having no other relationship to retailers except the specific one of transacting an exchange, and being eager to compare the goods of different stores in a short span of time without having to cover too much distance, will tend to buy from whatever store offers the best product for the lowest price at the most accessible location. And the retailer, having no other criterion for selecting location except the one of convenience to his customers, will strive for as much accessibility as he can profitably afford. Such an orientation is the result of cultural definition by which the acquisitive quest for profit becomes the *conditio sine qua non* to the business' survival. The referability of this orientation is not to the business as a disparate, self sufficient system but rather to the cultural context in which the business has its being and must function.[33] In this way the functioning of retail stores as a distinct type of social system becomes highly contingent upon spatiality. And among different kinds of retail stores there exist varying degrees of contingency, in direct relation to the importance of convenience to the shopper. Those stores whose goods are fairly well standardized, are highly subject to fashion, are most important as status symbols, and are most dependent upon volume of patronage, tend to require the most accessible locations since they are the ones in which "shopping" is the dominant purchasing pattern. On the other hand those stores whose goods are either wholly standardized with none of the variations attending fashion or are extremely individualized so as to appeal to a very small clientele are generally more able to function at less accessible locations.

Perhaps these general remarks will become clearer if they are considered in terms of a particular type of retail business, namely clothing stores. We have already seen that no less than 383 of all the business establishments located within the area of maximal accessibility in Boston are clothing stores. In other words, more than one-third of all the stores in the heart of downtown Boston sell nothing but clothes, hats, shoes, furs, and other personal

---

[33] Talcott Parsons, "The Motivation of Economic Activities," *The Canadian Journal of Economic and Political Science*, 6: 187–202 (May, 1940), p. 199.

furnishings. These stores for the most part deal in ready-made clothes which require only minor alterations. Now, this pattern of ready-made clothing upon which so large a share of the urban retail structure rests, is a very recent historical development. In Boston during the 1840's clothing was made almost entirely within the home by sewing women and tailors. At that time clothing was made to last for years, so that the turnover in suits, dresses, hats, etc., was very much less than it is today.[34] Ready-made garments were practically unknown. Not until the 1850's, following the invention of the sewing machine, did ready-made clothing appear on the market. In Boston it began with a sailors' outfitting establishment in the North End. Later a merchant by the name of John Simmons, in Quincy Market Hall, put ready-made clothing on a mercantile basis, following which its expansion was rapid.[35] Today between 80 and 90 per cent of men's clothing is of the ready-to-wear type. A somewhat smaller percentage of women's clothing is of this type but the proportion is nonetheless great. The stores which have grown up in response to this development are obviously predicated upon a very "novel" pattern of clothing consumption. Nor does the cultural uniqueness of the retail clothing store end with this. The peculiar importance of clothing in modern society is attributable, as we have already seen, to its symbolic significance in a highly mobile and impersonalized society where status is mainly one of achievement and where achievement tends to be symbolized by what Veblen has called "conspicuous consumption." The constant succession of styles resulting from this pattern puts a premium upon "fashionable" dress and thus establishes the demand in terms of which retail stores are able to exist and function. Considerations such as these should rather convincingly establish the cultural relativity of retail stores as distinct types of social systems. To take them as given, as beings whose existence needs no further explanation, can only lead to a narrowly contractualistic ecology; for apart from a contractualistic value system there could hardly be such a type of social system.

From this it seems evident that the methodological rationalists

[34] "Recollections of Old Boston," in William S. Rositter (ed.), *Days and Ways in Old Boston* (Boston: 1915), pp. 41–42.

[35] Richard Herndon, *Boston of To-Day* (Boston: 1892), p. 8.

have developed an ecological theory which takes for granted the existence of certain kinds of social systems and certain peculiar properties of physical space, all of which are really the products of a unique value system. They are in no way universal or "natural." Under a different value system the characteristics of social systems as spatially adaptive agents and the properties of physical space as an externality would be very different, and the resulting locational processes would entirely escape analysis in the rationalistic scheme. Sombart's strictures upon Weber's ecological theory are especially pertinent here:

Seine ganze Standortstheorie beruht doch offenbar auf der Annahme eines freiwirtschaftlichen systems, bei dem sich Preise der Produkte und Preise der Arbeitskräfte durch das "freie Spiel der wirtschaftlichen Kräfte" bilden und eine freie Bewegung der Güter und Personen erfolgt. Durchaus richtige Annahme für die "(reine) Theorie der kapitalistischen Wirtschaft"; aber für jede Wirtschaftsweise? Auch für den Sozialismus zum Beispiel? Der von ganz andern Wertvorstellungen ausgehend systematisch den Standort der Gewerbe regeln würde? [36]

From this we cannot, of course, dismiss the methodologically rationalistic theories as being "wrong," for that is quite beside the point. The truth or error of such theories can only be determined by examining the deductive consistency of their propositions with the initial premises, and then seeing whether these propositions describe at all accurately the empirical phenomena falling within their purview. Given the modern metropolis along with the cultural factors upon which it rests, there does appear to be some correspondence between real locational processes within the business district and the propositions of the methodologically rationalistic scheme. But it would be a mistake to consider such a correspondence as proving the "purity" of the rationalistic scheme. In truth the whole logical construct of methodological rationalism is a culturally relative theory. It can explain only those locational phenomena characterized by rational orientation and spatial impeditiveness, as well as the broad complex of historically unique conceptions of property, status, consumption,

[36] Sombart, "Einige Anmerkungen zur Lehre vom Standort der Industrien," p. 751.

money, etc., which lie behind these characteristics. If social ecology is to reach scientific maturity it must develop some generalizations that apply to more than just contemporary culture. To do this it will have to make the cultural component central to its theoretical system.

CHAPTER VII

THE SELECTIVE INFLUENCE OF SOCIAL VALUES UPON RATIONAL LAND USE: THE BACK BAY

RATIONAL ADAPTATION apparently dominates retail land use. This being the case one would expect to find occasions in which an expanding retail district ran up against rival land uses. In such an encounter it might seem as though retail businesses, being preemptive users of land, would invariably prevail over their rivals — whether residences, schools, churches, or whatever else. Yet our earlier analysis of Beacon Hill and the various historic sites of central Boston showed otherwise. Apparently there are occasions in which dis-economic land uses persist in the face of more economic land uses. Volitional adaptation has been found to be as real a locational process as rational adaptation.

The fact does remain, though, that in modern American cities, dis-economic land uses have generally succumbed to the more economic ones. This is rather to be expected, given the prevailing contractualistic milieu within which the modern city has arisen and must function. But it by no means follows that in such an ecological succession the more rational land use remains unaffected by the previous type of occupancy. It is quite possible that the original land use may exert a certain selectivity upon the kinds of more economic social systems which inherit an area. There may be, to paraphrase Pareto, a "persistence of reputations" with respect to an area, such that some social systems will be more meaningfully congruent and fitting to the district than others. By virtue of this meaningful congruence such social systems will enjoy a preëmptive position with respect to rival social systems which may or may not be as economic. In this interpenetration of rationality and volition in land use there lies a significant ecological problem which must now engage our attention.

Value Connotations of the Back Bay. The clearest example of this phenomenon in Boston is to be found in the Back Bay district. We have already had occasion to deal with this area, first in Chapter II where its original development was considered, and again in Chapter VI where its invasion by the retail district was noted. The precise extent of this district has been variously defined. According to the Back Bay Association it embraces the tract bounded by Beacon, Charles, and Stuart streets and Huntington and Massachusetts avenues.[1] In common usage it extends beyond Massachusetts avenue to include Bay State road and even the Fens district. So far as our immediate problem is concerned it has seemed advisable to delineate the Back Bay in terms of the area occupied by families listed in the Boston *Social Register*. For of all the residential quarters in Boston the Back Bay has been generally known as the fashionable district *par excellence*. At one time it was the home of nearly one-half the *Social Registerites* in Boston. Even today, after forty years of decline, the Back Bay accounts for one out of every five entries in the *Social Register*. Most of these upper class families live on Beacon street, Marlborough street, and Commonwealth avenue as well as on the cross streets lying between Arlington street and Charlesgate East; they also extend west of Charlesgate East, along Bay State road, as far as Granby street. Eight upper class families still reside on Newbury street, and there are six entries on Boylston street, but this portion of the Back Bay has long since fallen into disfavor as a residential quarter.[2]

Within the Back Bay proper there is a differential valuation of streets which has its origin in the very beginning of the district during the 1860's. According to Boston lore, Beacon street has been occupied by people who have both "family" and money; Marlborough has been occupied by people with "family" but no money; and Commonwealth avenue has been the choice of people with money but no "family." Further than this, the water side of Beacon street, next to the Charles river, has enjoyed much greater prestige than the south side of the street. These differences, which manifest themselves clearly in the varying architecture of the three streets, trace back to the original sale of Back Bay lands when proximity to the river and to the open park extending along Commonwealth avenue were coveted residential sections. One in-

[1] *Back Bay Ledger and Beacon Hill Times*, February 5, 1942.

[2] Most of these Boylston street entries are merely registrants at the Tennis and Racquet Club on Boylston street.

dex of the relative desirability of Back Bay streets in 1861 is the average price per square foot at which lots were sold. The following list indicates the high valuation put upon Commonwealth avenue, the lesser but considerable value of Beacon street, and the marked depreciation in value to the south, approaching the railroad tracks.[3] Arlington street lots, fronting on the Public Garden,

TABLE 23

AVERAGE PER SQUARE FOOT VALUES OF LOTS SOLD IN THE BACK BAY, BOSTON, PRIOR TO 1861

Streets	Values	
	Private Sales	Auction
Commonwealth avenue........................	$1.75	$2.33
Beacon street................................		1.50
Marlborough street..........................		1.34
St. James street.............................		0.75

Source: M. D. Ross, *Estimate of the Financial Effect of the Proposed Reservation of Back-Bay Lands.*

sold for as high as $4.00 per square foot. Southward from the Back Bay proper the prestige value of land declines abruptly. Thus the Huntington avenue lands, which lie across the railroad tracks from Back Bay proper, never have become "respectable," in spite of early efforts to develop it into a middle class area.[4] Columbus avenue too has suffered from its location across the railroad tracks as well as from its proximity to the South End. Early attempts to "legitimize" it for upper class occupancy were short-lived.[5] Much of this "sooty side of Back Bay" [6] has become semi-bohemian in character, particularly in the neighborhood of St. Botolph, Irvington, and Garrison streets. It is not surprising that sections of these and near-by streets have acquired undesirable moral connotations. St. Botolph street is distinctly a student-

[3] M. D. Ross, *Estimate of the Financial Effect of the Proposed Reservation of Back-Bay Lands* (Boston: 1861), Tables A, F, and pp. 9, 20.

[4] On these efforts see Franklin Haven, Alexander H. Rice, and Peleg W. Chandler (trustees), *A Statement in Regard to the Huntington Avenue Lands, in the City of Boston* (Boston: 1879).

[5] See Anna Farquhar, *Her Boston Experiences* (Boston: 1900), pp. 67–69.

[6] For impressionistic description and character sketches of life in this area see Ruth Ennice, "Back Bay" (MS), master's thesis, Boston University, 1941.

artist street, with light housekeeping apartments and kitchenettes being occupied by artists, musicians, college students, etc. Finally, to the west of the Back Bay there is the Fenway. Originally planned for single family residences after the Back Bay model, the Fenway has become a predominantly upper middle class apartment area. Rentals in this district are well above the average for apartments in the city of Boston. Its buildings were expressly built for apartment use and hence have undergone none of the deterioration which Bay Bay buildings have experienced through their conversion from single family occupancy to apartment purposes.

Within the bounds of these surrounding neighborhoods the Back Bay proper, despite its physical deterioration and its gradual conversion away from single family residential uses, still retains much of its one-time aura of aristocratic splendor and distinction. This persistence of reputation may be ascribed to three factors: (a) the existence of deed restrictions which tend to protect existing uses and which obstruct certain kinds of rival land uses; (b) the location of a great many religious, educational, artistic, and "cultural" associations in the area; and (c) the continued residence in the district of many upper class families.

Let us consider each of these in order. To begin with, nearly all of the properties in the Back Bay are covered by deed restrictions which govern the height and character of buildings, their setback from the street, cellar depth, and the kind of uses to which they may be put. These restrictions were designed "for the purpose of making the lots attractive to prospective purchasers and of developing 'a magnificent system of streets and squares.' . . ." [7] Thus in lots sold by the Boston Water Power Company the following restrictions were attached to every deed:

No building shall be erected on said described premises except outhouses to dwellings, the exterior walls of which shall be of any other material than brick, stone, or iron, nor shall any building erected thereon be used or occupied for a stable, either livery or public or private, for carpenters' shops, white or blacksmith shops, or for any foundry,

[7] "Special Report of the Attorney General Relative to Certain Restrictions Imposed by the Commonwealth on Certain Lands in the Back Bay District of Boston," *Massachusetts Senate Document No. 3*, 1929 (filed November 26, 1928).

mechanical or manufacturing purposes or for any other business which shall be offensive to the neighborhood for dwelling houses.[8]

Restrictions nearly identical with these applied to the whole of the Back Bay. On Commonwealth avenue there was the further prohibition of mercantile establishments.[9] The only area not covered by deed restrictions was that portion of Newbury street lying between Hereford street and Massachusetts avenue,[10] where stables and later garages located and have persisted to the present day.[11] In addition to these private restrictions upon land use in the Back Bay there have been a number of public zoning ordinances applying to the area. Thus in 1898, before any uniform zoning ordinance had been developed in regard to height limits in Boston, a special statute was enacted which limited the height of buildings near Copley square to 90 feet.[12] The purpose of this statute was to maintain the architectural homogeneity of edifices in that portion of the Back Bay surrounding the Public Library, Trinity Church, the New Old South Church, and certain buildings that have since been demolished (the old Museum of Fine Arts and the old buildings of the Massachusetts Institute of Technology). These restrictions have had two principal effects. First, they have tended to perpetuate that type of land use for which they were originally designed, namely fashionable residential occupancy. Second, the restrictions have made it impossible or inconvenient for radically incompatible land uses to locate in the Back Bay. In the case of Commonwealth avenue, for instance, commerce is expressly forbidden. On the other streets, where restrictions as to cellar depth are in force, there has been a serious deterrent to commercial land use arising out of the unavailability of storage space which is so necessary for most retail stores.[13]

---

[8] Cited in *Evans* v. *Foss*, 194 Mass. 513.

[9] "Report of Attorney General as to Advisability of Removing Certain Restrictions Imposed by the Commonwealth on Land in the Back Bay District of Boston," *Massachusetts Senate Document No. 2, 1927* (filed December 1, 1926).

[10] *Evans* v. *Foss*, 194 Mass. 513.

[11] On some other Back Bay deed restrictions see *Vorenberg* v. *Bunnell*, 257 Mass. 399; also Haven, Rice, and Chandler, *op. cit.*, p. 14.

[12] St. 1898, c. 452.

[13] "Report of Commission to Investigate the Advisability of Removing Certain Restrictions Imposed by the Commonwealth on Land in the Back Bay

The second factor in the Back Bay's prolonged prestige value is the presence of a great many social systems that are generally known as "cultural institutions." An editorial in the *Back Bay Leader* reads as follows:

The entire country knows by reputation this center of culture, the Back Bay section of Boston. Artists, musicians, writers, and others whose souls are filled with the immortal longings for fame, look forward to the time when the galleries, the salons, or the theatres of Back Bay will some day be the locale of their creations. We who live here should remember that we have at our finger tips a wealth beyond measure.[14]

Another community newspaper, the *Back Bay Ledger and Beacon Hill Times*[15] confidently asserts that: "Without a question people concede that Back Bay is the cultural center of New England."[16] In truth the Back Bay is indeed the seat of a great concatenation of religious, educational, artistic, medical, and other such associations. To begin with, some of the most expensive church buildings in the city of Boston are located there. Trinity Church, costing $750,000 and considered in its day "the finest church-edifice in New England, if not in the United States,"[17] and the New Old South Church, costing $500,000, are perhaps the most noted of the Back Bay churches. But other distinctive churches in the district are Central Church, First Church, Second Church, Arlington Street Church, Emmanuel Church, Brattle-Square Church,[18] and the Christian Science Mother Church. All of these were built during the latter part of the nineteenth century or the early part of the present century while the Back Bay was at the peak of its aristocratic development. In addition to the churches there are schools, both public and private. Some of these are Boston University, the Prince School, and in the Fenway to the west of Back Bay proper, the Harvard Medical School, Boston Latin School,

---

District in the City of Boston," *Massachusetts House Document No. 277*, 1924 (filed December 17, 1923).

[14] *Back Bay Leader*, editorial, October 19, 1939.

[15] Successor to the *Leader*.

[16] *Back Bay Ledger and Beacon Hill Times*, February 27, 1941.

[17] Moses King, *The Back Bay District and the Vendome* (Boston: 1881), pp. 12–13.

[18] *Ibid.*, pp. 10–14.

Massachusetts College of Pharmacy, Leland Powers' School for Acting, Gordon Theological College, Tufts Medical School, Northeastern University, Massachusetts Institute of Technology School of Architecture, Simmons College, Emmanuel College, and a great many private business colleges. Libraries, museums, and auditoriums are located throughout the Back Bay, notably the Boston Public Library, Symphony Hall, the Opera House, the Horticultural Hall, the Museum of Natural History, Museum of Fine Arts, and the Gardner Museum. Finally, though not located in the Back Bay proper but nonetheless connected with it through meaningful association, are the hospitals around Brookline and Longwood avenues. Principal among these are Peter Bent Brigham, Collins Memorial, Huntington Memorial, Beth Israel, and the Children's Hospital.[19]

Intrinsically perhaps there is very little in common between the functions which these different associations perform. But in terms of the values which attach to present-day occupations there is a distinct meaningful congruence between schools, churches, hospitals, and museums. This meaningful congruence arises out of the professional character of the functionaries in such associations. The clergyman, the doctor, the teacher, and the museum supervisor are all persons who have been trained to a high degree of technical competence and they have all been versed in a generalized intellectual tradition.[20] The associations which are staffed by such functionaries partake of the same prestige value that attaches to the professional role in modern society. There is thus a meaningful congruence between various associations of this character. In the case of Boston this meaningful congruence has become objectively symbolized in the form of territorial contiguity. As we have already seen in our analysis of Beacon Hill, physical space is peculiarly suited to symbolizing position upon a scale of valuation. In Maunier's words:

Ce qui confirme cette fonction de l'espace des groupes comme emblème c'est que, de même que les blasons ou les vêtements—qui ne

[19] For an ecological analysis of this Back Bay "cultural" center see Richard E. DuWors, "The Dominant Educational Area of Boston" (MS), 1937.

[20] These *differentia* of professionalism have been formulated by Professor Talcott Parsons.

sont souvent eux-mêmes que les emblèmes — servent à marquer extérieurement la hiérarchie des groupes. . . .[21]

The concentration of "cultural" associations in and around the Back Bay is a particular instance of this. The Back Bay has been especially appropriate for such social systems by virtue of its splendor and aristocratic distinction during the late nineteenth century. Such a reputation is quite consonant with the status connotations of professionalism. Both have an identical reference, in that they share a common position high upon the scale of social prestige. Hence the symbolic quality attaching to the Back Bay through aristocratic residence has readily transferred to such social systems as schools, churches, hospitals, etc., which partake of the same general status. Today, in the face of waning prestige value, the Back Bay finds itself bolstered up by the presence of distinctly professionalized social systems within its borders. Through this reinforcement it still maintains a semblance of its one-time prestige value.

In addition to the deed restrictions and the "cultural" associations of the Back Bay there is a further factor which helps to prolong the area's fashionable reputation. That is the continued residence in the district of a sizable upper class population. Table 24 indicates the total number of families listed by the *Social Register* as living in the Back Bay, along with the relative position of the district with respect to the Boston metropolitan area. The absolute and relative decline of the Back Bay in upper class population is quite evident from these data. Nonetheless the fact does remain

TABLE 24

NUMBER OF UPPER CLASS FAMILIES IN THE BACK BAY OF BOSTON AND IN THE METROPOLITAN AREA, BY YEARS

	1894	1905	1914	1929	1943
Back Bay	867	1166	1102	880	556
Metropolitan Area (incl. Back Bay)	1922	2442	2608	2709	2955
Per Cent Borne by Back Bay to Metropolitan Area	45.11	47.75	42.26	32.48	18.82

Calculations made from *Social Register* tabulations.

[21] René Maunier, *L'Origine et la Fonction Économique des Villes* (Paris: 1910), p. 213.

that nearly twenty per cent of Boston's upper class families continue to live in this one district. Old Boston names like Cabot, Sears, Sprague, Forbes, and Frothingham may still be found on Beacon street, Marlborough street, and Commonwealth avenue. In terms of occupational structure the Back Bay is unmistakably upper class. As may be seen from Table 25 the proportion of professionals and managers in the Back Bay is considerably higher than in Boston as a whole.[22] The high proportion of domestic service workers is another index to the district's aristocratic character. Finally, as may be noted by reference to Figure 6 on page 80, Back Bay rentals are the highest in the city of Boston;

TABLE 25

Percentage Distribution of Employed Persons in the Back Bay
and in Boston, 1940, by Occupations

Occupations	Boston			Back Bay		
	Total	Male	Female	Total	Male	Female
Total Employed..............	100.00	66.14	33.86	100.00	40.37	59.63
Professional workers...........	8.82	4.04	4.78	18.44	9.19	9.25
Semi-professional workers......	1.40	0.93	0.47	2.18	1.05	1.13
Proprietors, managers, officials..	7.70	6.88	0.82	11.99	9.25	2.74
Clericals and like workers......	26.95	13.98	12.97	21.95	10.29	11.66
Craftsmen, foremen, etc.........	12.71	12.23	0.48	3.10	2.64	0.46
Operatives and like workers....	18.67	12.76	5.91	2.47	1.44	1.03
Domestic service workers......	3.19	0.25	2.94	26.94	1.64	25.30
Service workers (excluding domestic)...................	14.53	9.47	5.06	11.91	4.27	7.64
Laborers....................	5.24	5.11	0.13	0.29	0.27	0.02
Occupation not reported......	0.79	0.49	0.30	0.73	0.33	0.40

Calculated from data in Sixteenth Census of the United States, 1940.

census tracts K3 and K5, which correspond very well with our delineation of Back Bay proper, have median estimated or contracted monthly rentals of $75 and $73, respectively.[23] Indices such as these testify to the persistence of spatial prestige value in the Back Bay district.

[22] Computed from data in Table 3, *Population and Housing — Statistics for Census Tracts, Boston Massachusetts*, Sixteenth Census of the United States, 1940.
[23] Computed from data in Table 5, *Population and Housing — Statistics for Census Tracts, Boston, Massachusetts*, Sixteenth Census of the United States, 1940.

Factors in Land Use Changes in the Back Bay. There can, however, be no denial that the Back Bay has changed. Today there are less than half as many upper class families in the area as there were forty years ago. The buildings themselves have considerably deteriorated; 14 per cent of them are eighty or more years old, and 68 per cent are forty or more years old.[24] Twenty-six per cent of the dwellings have become multi-family residences or rooming houses and 16 per cent of them are large apartment buildings.[25] These trends reflect the change which tastes in housing and place of residence have undergone during the past fifty years. The late nineteenth century vogue of swell-front or brownstone front houses extending continuously along tree-lined thoroughfares that lead to the city center has long since been superseded by the vogue of single-family dwellings, with yards, located in "bedroom towns" surrounding the city proper. It is little wonder that upper class families have been deserting the Back Bay and other intown districts (excepting Beacon Hill) and have relocated in fashionable suburban towns like Newton, Milton, Weston, and remoter communities.

In addition to such changes in taste as a factor in the exodus of upper class families from the Back Bay, and the steady deterioration of the district's physical structure, there is another factor which must not be overlooked. This is the general property tax. American cities are unique in the extent to which they rely upon real property for the bulk of their municipal revenues.[26] The implications of such a taxation system for urban land use are manifold and it is not our intention to consider all of them. But there is one implication which has a particular bearing upon locational trends in the Back Bay and which must be taken note of: that is the deterrent effect which assessment procedures have upon home ownership and residential stability. In most American cities — and Boston is flagrantly typical in this respect — tax assess-

---

[24] The Finance Commission of the City of Boston, *A Study of Certain of the Effects of Decentralization on Boston and Some Neighboring Cities and Towns* (Boston: 1941), p. 11.

[25] Computed from data in *loc. cit.*

[26] John M. Gries and James Ford, *Home Finance and Taxation*, vol. II in the President's Conference on Home Building and Home Ownership (Washington: 1932), pp. 103–106.

ments are vacillating, irregular, and unpredictable.[27] Sometimes
property is consistently overvalued, sometimes it is consistently
undervalued, and sometimes it is varyingly overvalued and undervalued in the same city. Overvaluation is the uniform practice
in Boston. Thus, in a study of 1,265 real estate sales made between 1935 and 1939 in central Boston, the Urban Land Institute
found that the sum total of all the selling prices was only 54.6 per
cent of the sum total of all the assessed valuations. In other
words, true market values were but half the assessed values.[28]
The discrepancy is even greater in the Back Bay. Of 299 sales of
property made in that district during the same four-year period
the sum of the selling prices was only 45.4 per cent of the sum of
the assessed valuations.[29] The reasons for this extreme over-
assessment of real estate in Boston are not hard to find. In the
first place, due to physical depreciation and lack of new construction the total assessable valuation in the city has decreased by
over half a billion dollars between 1928 and 1940.[30] At the same
time municipal expenses, particularly for welfare and relief, have
increased enormously. This means that property must be assessed
for all that it can stand. Secondly, and more importantly, 88.5
per cent of the population of Boston (occupying 78 per cent of
the area) does not pay enough in taxes to cover the costs of services rendered. The tenement and three-decker districts, which so
overwhelmingly dominate the Boston landscape, cost the city
nearly twice their return through taxes. As a result the fashionable residential areas and the retail business district must make
up the difference. They are consequently assessed far beyond
their true market values.[31] Owners of Back Bay property, as well
as the owners of Beacon Hill and downtown property, are paying
far greater taxes than they would for comparable property in the
suburbs. What this means for the retentive capacity of the Back
Bay upon its upper class population is obvious. An editorial in the
Ledger-Times reads as follows:

[27] Cf. *loc. cit.*
[28] Urban Land Institute, *A Survey in Respect to the Decentralization of the
Boston Central Business District* (Boston: 1940), p. 17.
[29] *Ibid.*, p. 18.
[30] Boston City Planning Board, *Building a Better Boston* (Boston: 1941),
pp. 8–9.
[31] *Loc. cit.*

Commonwealth avenue is a beautiful street in many ways; but it looks like a deserted village in many block lengths, where house after house has been boarded up, and the one time residents gone. Why is it that no new buildings take the place of these hollow shells of former mansions? The answer is — the assessment rates in Back Bay, and the confiscatory taxes that result from the average assessor's assumption that we will continue to stand the gaff. . . . It has been said by some citizens that Back Bay supports Boston as to municipal income. But it can't last forever.[32]

Well-to-do people have adapted to this by emigration. Not only do they leave the Back Bay but they leave the city of Boston altogether. This is shown by our data on population trends in Tables 1 and 2 (pages 71 and 72) and summarized in figure 4 (page 73). One reason for their departure from Boston may be inferred from data on relative tax rates for towns and cities in the metropolitan area. Table 26 presents these rates as of 1940.[33] The emigration of upper class families in response to these differential tax rates only aggravates the financial predicament of Boston by further reducing the tax base and leading to still higher tax rates and still greater discrepancies between true and assessed property values. From the standpoint of individual families, of course, the entire process is a rational adaptation to conditions that have become so stringent as to quite override social values. Regardless of the prestige value of the Back Bay and regardless of the district's symbolic significance, the deterrents to home ownership in the area pretty nearly exceed the limits within which values can determine place of residence. Perhaps the outcome would be different if there were as strong an emotional attachment to space as there is on Beacon Hill. But the Back Bay lacks those sentimental connotations which are such indispensable elements of fetishism. Its symbolic significance has always been in terms of splendor, sumptuousness, and aristocratic magnificence. Such connotations do not arouse the same affective attachment as do ancient historical associations. Consequently, in the "proportionalization of ends" which ultimately underlies every social system's choice of location[34] the threshold at which rationality be-

[32] *Back Bay Ledger and Beacon Hill Times*, editorial, January 11, 1940.
[33] Urban Land Institute, *op. cit.*, p. 67.
[34] Insofar as space is an objective vehicle to a system's attainment of ends.

TABLE 26

Tax Rates per $1,000 of Assessed Valuation, Boston Metropolitan Area, 1940

Chelsea	$45.40	Melrose	$33.60
Revere	44.00	Norwood	33.40
Cambridge	43.00	Hull	32.60
Saugus	42.30	Quincy	32.30
Somerville	42.30	Lexington	32.20
Medford	41.60	Winthrop	29.40
Malden	41.40	Belmont	29.20
Boston	*40.60*	Newton	29.20
Everett	37.40	Needham	27.80
Waltham	36.40	Swampscott	27.40
Canton	36.20	Winchester	27.20
Nahant	36.00	Milton	26.40
Arlington	35.80	Hingham	26.00
Lynn	35.40	Walpole	25.00
Woburn	35.40	Brookline	24.50
Dedham	35.20	Cohasset	24.20
Reading	35.20	Weymouth	24.00
Watertown	35.00	Westwood	22.00
Wakefield	34.40	Wellesley	21.90
Stoneham	34.20	Weston	21.00
Stoughton	34.20	Dover	18.30
Braintree	34.00		

Source: Urban Land Institute, *A Survey in Respect to Decentralization of Boston Central Business District*, p. 67.

comes dominant is considerably lower in the Back Bay than it is on Beacon Hill.[35]

Meaningfully Selective Succession of Land Uses in the Back Bay. The transformation which has been wrought in the Back Bay following upon the exodus of upper class families has assumed three main forms: (a) Many of the single-family dwellings have been converted into rooming houses and apartment houses, while some have been demolished to make way for more modern apartment buildings; (b) Professional men, particularly doctors and dentists, have occupied many of the one-time dwellings and newer buildings, sometimes in individual offices, sometimes in complete medical centers; (c) Specialty shops and "high class" retail stores have extended down much of Boylston and Newbury streets at their in-town ends. These are the types of land use which have been gradually succeeding the older pattern of upper

[35] In our concluding chapter we shall outline in a more systematic way the nature of this proportionalization of spatially contingent ends.

class single-family residence in the Back Bay. However unrelated
to one another and to the earlier land use pattern they may appear to be, there is a very real meaningful congruence between
them and their predecessors. As has already been suggested, this
meaningful congruence derives from the common position which
these land uses have, high upon the scale of social prestige. Perhaps the point will become clearer if we consider briefly each of
these succeeding land uses and note their meaningful affinity to
the earlier pattern of upper class single-family residence.

We may begin with a consideration of the trend toward apartment houses and rooming houses which has assumed so great a
magnitude in the Back Bay. From the very establishment of the
Back Bay as a fashionable residential quarter there appeared a
number of exclusive apartment hotels throughout the district. Indeed Marlborough street was the only street that consisted solely
of single-family dwellings during the early years of the Back
Bay's history.[36] From the exclusive apartment hotel of the 1880's
to the present day rooming house or converted brownstone front
apartment house there has been a steady gradation, not a sudden
metamorphosis. Today many of the old mansions, long a burden
upon banks and mortgage companies,[37] have been cut up into
kitchenette apartments for occupancy by young couples, childless couples, elderly persons both single and married, and single
adults who have joined together to obtain commodious living
quarters. In some cases the old structures have been demolished
and replaced by more modern apartment buildings which generally command high rentals. In other cases the fatal cycle that so
often terminates in slum conditions has manifest itself through
the letting of rooms. The pattern of leasee landlords and landladies, renting a house from the bank or mortgage company and
occupying one or more rooms on the first floor, letting out the
other rooms to single tenants, has become widespread throughout
the Back Bay. In most cases such rooming houses are still of the
"respectable" kind; commonly the tenant is expected to leave his
door open when he has visitors of the opposite sex, or he is supposed to receive them only in the parlor room. Rentals are much
higher than in the South End so that the lower class and transient

[36] Dexter Smith, *Cyclopedia of Boston and Vicinity* (Boston: 1886), p. 117.
[37] *Back Bay Ledger and Beacon Hill Times*, August 15, 1940.

type of roomer is effectively excluded from the area. But there is forever the pressure to accept any and all roomers, no questions asked, so as to increase income; maintenance of a "respectable" rooming house is never easy. Nonetheless through resisting this pressure and through making various accommodations the Back Bay has managed to remain a high rent district. Residence within it is highly desired by apartment seekers who can afford the expense. One indication of the Back Bay's residential desirability for roomers and apartment dwellers is the fact that the area has undergone an actual increase in population. Indeed the Back Bay and Beacon Hill are the only in-town residential districts of Boston which have grown in population between 1930 and 1940. Their position relative to the South End, the North End, East Boston, South Boston, and Charlestown may be seen from Table 27.[38] Such a population increase of course reflects not only the attractiveness of the Back Bay to many persons but also mani-

TABLE 27

POPULATION OF IN-TOWN NEIGHBORHOODS OF BOSTON, 1930 AND 1940, AND RATE
OF INCREASE OR DECLINE

Neighborhood	1930	1940	Percentage Change
Back Bay	7,814	8,928	+14.26
Beacon Hill	4,486	4,613	+2.83
North End	21,111	17,598	−16.64
South End	34,402	31,418	−8.67
East Boston	61,454	59,663	−2.91
Charlestown	31,663	25,587	−19.19
South Boston	34,689	31,127	−10.27

Source: Fifteenth and Sixteenth Census of the United States, 1930 and 1940.

[38] The figures for Back Bay, Beacon Hill, North End, and South End represent the sums of the census tracts embraced in those respective districts as we have delineated them in the relevant chapters of this thesis. The figures for East Boston, Charlestown, and South Boston represent, respectively, Wards 1, 2, and 6. Sources: "Census Tract Data, 1930 Census," unpublished material from Fifteenth Census of the United States, 1930, compiled by Boston Health Department, Table 1; *Population and Housing — Statistics for Census Tracts, Boston*, Sixteenth Census of the United States, 1940, Table 2; *Population*, vol. III, Part I, "Massachusetts," Fifteenth Census of the United States, 1930, Table 22; and *Population, Second Series, Characteristics of the Population, Massachusetts*, Sixteenth Census of the United States, 1940, Table 34.

fests the steady process of house partitioning which has resulted from the conversion of single family dwellings to multi-family occupancy.

The apartment house and "respectable" rooming house are known to every student of real estate as "parasites." They rarely improve the prestige value of an area but generally capitalize on preëxisting prestige value. In the words of one land use analyst:

The average apartment is not attempting to create values by its own design and arrangement, but rather is absorbing values already created by single-family and two-family dwellings. . . . Generally its location has been contingent upon the maximum possible financial return with minimum investment. It has intruded into well established and well kept residential districts.[39]

The apartment house and rooming house thus exploit the good reputation of a residential neighborhood. Only in exceptional cases will they locate at the very start in physically deteriorated portions of a city. Almost invariably they seek out reasonably fashionable districts that have just entered the transitory phase which follows upon emigration of upper class families. In this relationship lies the meaningful congruence between the apartment house–rooming house phenomenon and fashionable single family residence in an urban area. The apartment house, in contrast to the tenement house, is a unique middle class phenomenon that has developed in response to the housing needs of a mobile, conjugally solidary type of family unit. As Bartholomew has indicated:

Because of changing economic conditions, the apartment house has been growing in popularity. The increase in the number of employees of large corporations who are not permanently settled, the large number of families in which both husband and wife are employed, the smaller size of families in general, the difficulty of obtaining and the high cost of keeping efficient domestic help, the increasing tendency of elderly people to seek smaller and more convenient quarters when their children are grown, the joining of forces by several single men or women in renting apartments instead of living in rooming and lodging houses, together with the added convenience and increased facilities available

[39] Harland Bartholomew, *Urban Land Uses* (Cambridge: 1932), p. 51.

in modern apartment buildings, all have made this new type of multi-family housing unit an economic necessity.[40]

By virtue of its middle class character the apartment house has to locate in areas having an appropriate prestige value. Strictly speaking a new apartment building could be erected in the North End with no greater cost and with fully as much accessibility to the city center as one in the Back Bay. But the North End lacks the proper class connotations. The same is true of the South End. But in the Back Bay there is a "persistence of reputation" which lends a suitable prestige value to any apartment house located in the neighborhood.

Very similar considerations apply to the respectable rooming house. Given the occupational system of today, with its stress upon mobility and upon gaining a technical or business or secretarial education, and given the conjugal family system with its temporal gap between membership in the parental family and membership in the procreative family — given these cultural patterns there is bound to be in every large city a large population of single young persons ambitiously seeking an education or occupational advancement and desirous of moving freely as opportunities require. Such a population generally has had a middle class background, else it could not have had the technical, business, or secretarial training which it has. The housing requirements of such a population will not be served, on the one hand, by tenements such as prevail in the North End nor, on the other hand, will they be served by cheap rooming houses with their vice and disrepute such as prevail in the South End. Detached young people of middle class origin, however desirous they may be of economizing, will generally demand "atmosphere," cleanliness, and the presence of "respectable" fellow tenants in their rooming houses. For these reasons they will tend to locate in neighborhoods that have a good reputation. Areas such as the Back Bay, which have just begun the downward cycle of physical deterioration but which still enjoy considerable prestige value, are particularly suited to the housing needs of these people. That such has been the case in the Back Bay is strikingly revealed in the age-sex make-up of the area. As shown by figure 17 the Back Bay is

[40] *Ibid.*, p. 43.

occupied chiefly by (a) young adults, and (b) women of all ages. In the latter respect it bears a close resemblance to Beacon Hill. Undoubtedly a large proportion of the older women belong to the same Yankee upper class stock which is so characteristic of Beacon Hill. The younger adults, too, resemble their Beacon Hill counterparts; most of them are clerks, secretaries, salesmen, stenographers, etc. Altogether they represent one-fifth of the Back Bay population.[41] They are the ones who are inheriting the fashionable reputation of the Back Bay.

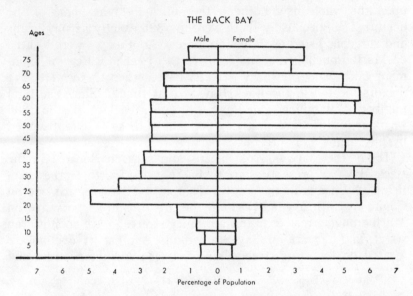

FIGURE 17. POPULATION COMPOSITION, BACK BAY

Turning to the other of the succeeding land uses in the Back Bay, namely the influx of physicians and surgeons, we find once again a close affinity between this professional occupancy of the district and previous upper class residential occupancy. Moreover we find, as with the apartment houses, that this succeeding land use is not wholly new to the Back Bay. In fact there seems to

[41] The population aged 20–29 comprises 20.46 per cent of the total Back Bay population. Population composition is for census tracts K3 and K5, as computed from: *Population and Housing — Statistics for Census Tracts, Boston, Massachusetts*, Sixteenth Census of the United States, 1940, Table 2.

be a striking consistency in the degree to which professional occupancy of an area is associated with upper class residential occupancy. In 1840, for instance, Winter street was the center of "a large number of professional men, doctors and dentists of the highest grade." [42] A glance at figure 2, page 56, reminds us that this was the very area in which a great number of Boston's aristocratic families then lived. By 1880, when the Back Bay had been built up as the most fashionable district of Boston, the doctors had drifted to Boylston street. Their presence there bestowed upon the whole neighborhood the sobriquet "the home of the doctors." [43] Specifically there were in 1886 exactly 52 physicians and surgeons listed on Boylston street. Another 42 were located on Marlborough street, and from 10 to 15 each on Beacon, Commonwealth, and Newbury streets. Altogether there were 152 doctors located in the Back Bay at that time.[44] Since the total number of "families" listed as residing in the Back Bay in 1886 was 2,074,[45] it follows that 7.33 per cent of these were represented by physicians and surgeons.

Today there are 698 physicians and surgeons located in the Back Bay,[46] representing approximately one-fourth of the practicing physicians in the city of Boston.[47] Of these, 201 are on Commonwealth avenue, 183 are on Beacon street, 105 are on Marlborough street, 4 are on Newbury street, 27 are on Boylston street, and 147 are on Bay State road. Another 31 doctors are located on the cross streets lying between Arlington street and

[42] Thomas W. Tucker, *Bannisters Lane, 1708–1899* (Boston: 1899), p. 17.

[43] King, *op. cit.*, p. 31.

[44] The listings unfortunately make no distinction between doctors' residences and doctors' offices. However, there appears to have been far less segregation of these two functions in the last century than there is today, so that the foregoing data can be considered as being reasonably valid for our purposes. Source of listings: Smith, *op. cit.*, pp. 105–121.

[45] Tabulated from *loc. cit.*

[46] Tabulations made from *Boston City Directory,* 1944. All names which were appended by the term "phys" or "surgeon" or both which were located on Beacon, Marlborough, Commonwealth, Newbury, and Boylston streets, between Arlington street and Charlesgate East, and all cross streets between these, as well as Bay State road to Granby street were tabulated.

[47] The American Medical Association, in its last report, lists 2,934 physicians as practicing in Boston as of 1942. Data furnished by Massachusetts State Medical Board.

Charlesgate East. This distribution is significant. It reveals that streets such as Newbury and Boylston which have greatly deteriorated in prestige value do not attract doctors, in spite of the abundance of buildings which are available for them at reasonable rentals. Apparently the very streets that are the most residential in character and which still retain some of the old-time aristocratic sumptuousness of nineteenth-century Back Bay are the ones that attract physicians and surgeons. By actual count there are, in the district embraced by the foregoing tabulation, 1,840 buildings. Of these, 176 are occupied by one or more doctors. In other words, 9.57 per cent of the structures in the Back Bay have been occupied by medical practitioners. This proportion varies for different streets; on Newbury street only 1.39 per cent of the buildings are occupied by doctors, while on Bay State road 28.11 per cent, or nearly one in every three buildings, are thus occupied.[48]

This relative concentration of medical practice in a distinct spatial locale is in no way unique to Boston. In New York around Central Park, for instance, there is a similar concentration, and parallels can be found in many other American cities. Even more noteworthy is the fact that in all these cities the area of concentration is in or near the most fashionable in-town residential quarter of the city. This can hardly be a mere coincidence. There would seem to be a very real meaningful significance to this concentration of so many doctors in or near the fashionable residential quarter of large cities. A few reflections on trends in medical practice and on the status of the medical profession may give us some insight into this relationship. To begin with, such a concentration is in large measure a result of the growth of medical and surgical specialization during the past few decades. In earlier days, when the general practitioner was the only type of doctor, a dispersed distribution of physicians was probably most suited to serving a community's medical needs. But the appearance of specialists, with their mutual "referring" of patients and the limited ratio of patients to the total population, seems to dictate central location (though not necessarily at the area of maximal accessibility). This too would account for the widespread phenomenon of clinics and medical centers at which a number of different specialists are available and between whom the referring of

[48] Tabulations from *Boston City Directory*, 1944.

patients is made easy by virtue of the spatial nearness. However, to understand why the area of medical concentration so often corresponds with the area of highest residential prestige it is necessary to invoke other considerations. The medical profession, above all, is not a "business." Both by its own self-estimation and by the evaluation of the community as a whole the medical profession ranks high in occupational prestige. Such a status demands appropriate symbolic representation. A doctor is expected not only to have adequate equipment and a clean, professional-looking office, but he is expected to be located in a suitable vicinity. Such expectations are in no way inherent to the healing function of the medical practitioner but are purely of cultural definition. Their ecological significance, however, is in no way lessened by this fact. In terms of these expectations physicians and surgeons, particularly those who are specialists, are constrained to establish their offices, not in the business center, not in the half vacant transitional zone, and not in the low rent tenement or rooming house districts, but rather in the fashionable in-town residential neighborhood with its high prestige value. Once such an area becomes meaningfully identified with the medical profession there arises an additional attractive force which further motivates doctors to establish their offices in the district. Indeed it becomes economically rational for a doctor to so locate. In this situation we can see how a spatial pattern, originally volitional in its beginnings, gets to be an objective condition to which later locational processes rationally comply. This phenomenon, consisting essentially of a value pattern acquiring the status of an externality from the standpoint of individual social systems, has already been encountered in our analysis of Beacon Hill. In the case of the Back Bay its locational effects are very tangible. Thus a doctor who is able to charge three dollars for an office call in his suburban office can, for the very same services, charge a ten dollar fee for an office call at a Back Bay office. Hence the doctor who wishes to specialize or who desires to establish a wider reputation than is possible through maintaining a local or suburban office will frequently seek an office in the Back Bay. Thus one doctor, a recognized skin specialist from Europe, had for many years maintained an office in Brookline. However, with a view to making himself more accessible to his patients and to references from other doctors he moved to an office on Commonwealth avenue. This move was undertaken at an initial financial sacrifice, though in the end it was amply repaid through a bigger practice. In that sense it was a rational choice of location. But this very rationality operated in a cultural context partaking, on the one hand, of the Back Bay's prestige and, on the other hand, of the high status of the medical profession. The rationality is thus predicated entirely upon factors of a meaningful, valuative character. It is these factors which account for the gradual extension of doctors into the Back Bay so that on a few streets there has been almost a complete displacement of single families by doctors' offices. This process represents a meaningfully selective succession of land uses. The selectivity arises out of the congruence between values attaching to upper class residence and values attaching to the medical profession.

There is another type of land use whose invasion of the Back Bay reveals the same meaningfully selective process of succession. This is the extension of retail business into Newbury and Boylston streets. Once again we find that the encroachment of business upon the Back Bay had its beginning rather soon after the district's original development. A Boston directory for 1886 comments upon the incursion of business at that time as follows:

Boylston street is rapidly becoming a business street; hotels, schools, and stores having already threatened the residences well toward Berkeley street. If but a few months time has been sufficient to wholly change the character of this street from Park square to Church street, what may not be expected to take place during the next few years? Business is fast working Back Bay-ward, rather than South End-ward. . . .[49]

Most of these businesses were specialty shops which catered to the upper class families living in the immediate vicinity. Shopping at that time was done by means of horse and carriage, so that women found it convenient to attend to their purchases by a short run down one of the Back Bay streets to the Boylston street shops. During subsequent decades the Back Bay shopping district underwent a steady expansion. By 1905 most of the Boylston street dwellings, at least as far as Clarendon street, had

[49] Smith, *op. cit.*, p. 108.

been altered so as to accommodate stores on their first floors.[50] Newbury street still remained largely residential. By 1924 the whole length of Boylston street had been occupied by businesses and some fifteen or twenty residences on Newbury street had been altered into shops and picture galleries.[51] Today even Newbury street has been largely appropriated by business except for a nondescript segment of some three blocks occupying the middle of its length. This whole portion of the Back Bay has become Boston's distinctly smart shopping district. Its stores cater expressly to purchasers of more expensive tastes and the goods retailed by its stores consist largely of status symbols — gowns, furs, antiques, oriental rugs, hats, etc. The appeal is almost wholly to women of the upper income levels. Not infrequently items will be found which are identical to those on sale at the Tremont or Washington street stores but which have been considerably marked up in price.

The meaningful congruence between stores of this type and the fashionable reputation of the Back Bay is quite evident. By virtue of this congruence specialty shops find it advantageous to locate in the district. Indeed for such businesses the prestige value which attaches to the Back Bay actually renders the area a more productive agent than it would be in terms of transportation accessibility alone. But not every type of social system is able to capitalize upon this greater productivity of space. A second hand shop, a tavern, a garage, a grocery store, or even such a highly economizing land use as a moving picture theater, would gain very little by locating in such a district, even if it could afford the rent. Its prestige value would not accord with the meaningful connotations which attach to the Back Bay. In all likelihood such a social system would be barred by real estate operators who, knowing the ill effects that such a business would have for adjoining land values, would prefer to convey a lot to some less profitable land use so as to maintain property values in the surrounding area. For these values owe their magnitude almost entirely to the reputation of the Back Bay — a factor that is purely of cultural derivation and which has little or no basis in accessibility to shoppers. Consequently the kinds of social sys-

[50] See *Wilson* v. *Massachusetts Institute of Technology*, 188 Mass. 565.
[51] *Allen* v. *Massachusetts Bonding and Insurance Co.*, 248 Mass. 378.

tems which locate in the Back Bay are those which are meaningfully congruent with the fashionable reputation of the district. Specialty shops do have enough prestige in the present urban scheme of values to reconcile with the Back Bay's reputation. Hence they are the social systems which appropriate the commercially available portions of the Back Bay. Such a process of succession in land use cannot be understood obviously except in terms of the cultural component. One might argue that specialty shops occupy the Back Bay rather than other types of businesses because they are the only ones which can pay the high rents of the district. But this argument misses the crucial point that these rents are as high as they are mainly because land uses of an appropriate prestige character remain in the district. If cheaper businesses were to occupy the Back Bay there would undoubtedly be a sharp drop in rentals, such as happened in the South End. In a very real sense it can be said that rents in the Back Bay are as high as they are largely because there happen to be retail businesses having enough prestige so that they are able to capitalize upon (i.e., turn to productive use) the reputation of the district. If these social systems did not possess such prestige they could not convert the fashionable reputation of the Back Bay to profitable ends and hence there would not be the demand for commercial sites by which rents have attained their present scale.

In spite of the meaningful appropriateness of apartment houses, doctors, and specialty shops with the aristocratic reputation of the Back Bay there has been a certain amount of conflict resulting from the steady encroachment of the former upon single-family residences. Most of this conflict has centered around the violation of deed restrictions. For this reason it throws into rather clear relief the interaction between spatially referred values and interests. To be sure there has never been anything like the degree of affect toward the Back Bay that there is toward Beacon Hill. But the prestige of the Back Bay has engendered in the minds of some residents sufficient affect toward the area so that a moderate resistive force has been presented toward the invasions of other social systems. Unlike the Beacon Hill situation, however, interests have in this case prevailed over values. Thus we are afforded some additional insight into the interaction between these two types of ends.

As early as 1893, for instance, the Commonwealth granted the release of a Boylston street lot from restrictions against mercantile use of the property. A number of other releases of this kind were subsequently made in cases where no damage to residential properties seemed to be involved.[52] In 1904 the Massachusetts Institute of Technology, then located on Newbury street between Berkeley and Clarendon streets, was authorized to enlarge its buildings in violation of the original terms of the deed. Immediately two families residing near by on Newbury street brought suit, claiming that such an enlargement of buildings would depreciate the value of their lots for residential purposes. The Supreme Court ruled in their favor, thus upholding the continued applicability of the deed restrictions.[53] But violations of deed restrictions did occur in other parts of the Back Bay. In 1915 a garage was erected on Newbury street in violation of the deed restrictions applying to that segment of the street.[54] In 1917 two strictly commercial buildings were constructed at 526–528 and 530–532 Commonwealth avenue, in express violation of deed restrictions against mercantile uses on that street.[55] It is of course a point of law that if a person erects or alters a building in violation of deed restrictions that are applicable to all the lots in a neighborhood, and if other property owners in the area fail to register protest until the former party has already made considerable expenditure, there can be no enforcement of the deed restrictions.[56] In most of the foregoing violations it is evident that this is precisely what happened. As apartment houses, doctors' offices, and specialty shops invaded the Back Bay the market value of properties went up. Hence, in the absence of any strong affective attachment to the area, most property owners simply waived their rights to enforce the deed restrictions and passively allowed near-by properties to be converted to nonresidential uses, knowing full well that the value of their own lots would be enhanced in future sales.

[52] Massachusetts House Document No. 277, 1924, op. cit.
[53] Wilson v. Massachusetts Institute of Technology, 188 Mass. 565.
[54] Vorenberg v. Bunnell, 257 Mass. 399.
[55] Loc. cit.
[56] Stewart v. Finkelstone, 206 Mass. 28.

Now and then there were exceptions. Thus in 1926 efforts were made to erect an apartment house on the water side of Beacon street in violation of deed restrictions governing yard space. A number of local residents who owned near-by lots brought suit to forbid construction of the building. The Supreme Court upheld their position.[57] Again, in 1928 a petition was brought before the Board of Zoning Adjustment to alter the height limits of Arlington street, between Beacon and Boylston streets, so as to permit the construction of several 155-foot apartment buildings. The plan was to construct a row of high class apartment hotels along this portion of Arlington street.[58] However the petition met with strenuous objections from many of the local residents. In the words of one Back Bay resident:

Generally speaking, except for Boylston and Newbury streets, the Back Bay, since it was filled in by the Commonwealth, has retained the residential character for which it was originally laid out. . . . Under those circumstances, unless it is proposed to do away with the whole residential character of the Back Bay it seems unfair that those who wish to live in a normal residential district should not be allowed to do so when the only reason for changing the residential character is to add some value to the properties of a few of their neighbors.[59]

Proponents of the alteration in height limits argued that the Back Bay had "ceased to be a family residential section" and had "outlived its present usefulness." [60] At hearings before the Board of Zoning Adjustment 58 persons opposed, and 13 persons favored, the alteration in height limits.[61] A committee of three was appointed to investigate the problem and in the end the height limits remained unaltered. Even on Newbury street there has been some resistance to business encroachment. Thus, as late as 1929, property owners on that street protested a bill which had been submitted to the legislature by certain business and real estate interests that would have released the deed restrictions governing

[57] *Bancroft* v. *Building Commissioner of the City of Boston*, 257 Mass. 82.
[58] *Boston Transcript*, December 22, 1928.
[59] Robert Homans, quoted in the *Boston Herald*, January 5, 1929.
[60] *Boston Herald*, January 5, 1929.
[61] *Boston Herald*, January 12, 1929.

building setbacks from the street and thereby enhance its usefulness as a business thoroughfare. They argued that such a release
from deed restrictions would ruin their land for residential purposes.[62] Because of this opposition the deed restrictions are still
in force on most of Newbury street; only that segment of the
street which lies between Arlington and Clarendon streets has
thus far been widened. One of the principal objectives of the
Back Bay Association today remains that of gaining a release
from the Newbury street deed restrictions so that the remainder
of the street may be similarly widened.[63]

On the whole rational adaptation has prevailed over volitional
adaptation in the Back Bay, sometimes in direct contradiction to
the latter. Thus the Ritz-Carlton, a 155-foot hotel on Arlington
street, was constructed within the zoning height limits area of 80
feet — this despite the opposition of the Beacon Hill Association
and many Back Bay residents. Construction of the building required a special variation in the zoning law for the particular lot
in question. In its authorization of this variation the Board of
Appeal of the Building Department reasoned as follows:

It appeared at the hearing that the proposed structure in question is
a hotel of first class construction. . . . Due to its location the lot is
an extremely valuable one and it is located within half a block of the
155 foot district. The neighborhood and the whole of Newbury street
for a considerable distance is rapidly changing for business purposes.[64]

Opponents of the undertaking brought the matter before the Supreme Court. In its decision the Court ruled that the Board of
Appeal had been quite within its rights in varying the zoning law,
pointing out that:

. . . the reasons stated on the record in the case at bar, while not
overpoweringly convincing, cannot be pronounced erroneous as matter
of law. With their soundness in point of fact we have nothing to do.[65]

[62] Massachusetts Senate Document No. 3, 1929, op. cit.
[63] James A. Smith, executive secretary of the Back Bay Association.
[64] Quoted in Norcross v. Board of Appeal of the Building Department of
the City of Boston, 255 Mass. 177.
[65] Quoted in Norcross v. Board of Appeal of the Building Department of the
City of Boston, 255 Mass. 177.

In this and other cases interests have prevailed over values in the locational processes of the Back Bay. But this triumph of interests over values has been of a selective character. Not every rational land use has been able to invade the one-time aristocratic residential quarter. And the very rationality of those social systems which have invaded the district has been predicated upon certain values which, by their exteriority to the social systems in question, are really in the nature of an external condition. These values must be rationally complied with by the succeeding land uses in the same way that such objective factors as accessibility and rent must be dealt with. Their existence thus exerts a selective influence upon the social systems which seek location in the Back Bay. This selectivity is in terms of the meaningful congruence between the fashionable reputation of the Back Bay and the relative prestige of succeeding land uses. Apartment houses, respectable rooming houses, physicians' and surgeons' offices, and high class specialty shops all have sufficient prestige value to harmonize with the reputation of the Back Bay. Hence they are the social systems that have been gradually preëmpting the area.

CHAPTER VIII

THE ROLE OF OCCUPATIONAL AND KINSHIP PATTERNS IN LOCALIZED ANOMIE: THE SOUTH END

THUS FAR we have seen that rational adaptation, though it be a very real locational process, derives its whole character from a particular kind of value system. In the case of the commercial center of Boston the very existence of retail stores is a result of historically unique cultural patterns. Likewise the peculiar importance of accessibility for the functioning of retail stores is of cultural definition. Thus even in the retail district of a large city, where one would expect to find the closest approach to the premises of methodologically rationalistic ecology, we find that both the rational orientation of social systems and the impeditiveness of physical space has been structured by a context of social values. So too the invasion of more rational land uses into an area having prestige connotations is subject to a selective influence. This process has been observed in the Back Bay area of Boston. In such a selective process the values which the area symbolizes have a certain "objective exteriority" to which succeeding land uses must rationally comply.

Our analysis, however, has shed very little light upon the social or group implications of an overall value system for the persons who occupy a given locality. To be sure, our treatment of Beacon Hill and the North End showed how the value systems unique to those communities did influence social relationships within them. But these were strictly localized value systems which had no broader base than the particular communities in question. At present our concern is with values having a much greater inclusiveness than this. We wish now to ascertain the localized "associational" effects of a value system which in some degree is borne by all the communities within a given society. Already we have found in contractualism the distinctive feature of associational patterns in western society. Its role in the spatial distribution of certain types of social systems, namely retail business establishments, has been demonstrated. But the question which now confronts us is this: what bearing if any does a contractualistic value system have for the nature of social interaction in a specific community?

We have chosen to deal with this problem by analyzing the South End district of Boston and indicating how certain features of American occupational and kinship structure have conditioned associational patterns there. The South End above all is a rooming house area or, as it is more commonly called in Boston, a lodging house area. Its population consists mainly of dependent aged persons and transient middle aged "service workers." A high proportion of these persons are entirely removed from kinship ties. In the case of the older people they are typically widowed; in the case of the younger adults they are unmarried, separated, or divorced. Those who have employment are generally working in insecure service jobs characterized by a high rate of turnover among personnel. As will be seen in our subsequent analysis, both of these features (detachment from kinship ties and employment in transient service occupations) are corollaries of an historically unique value system, essentially contractualistic in nature, which has brought into being appropriate kinship and occupational patterns. By virtue of these patterns there exists in every large city a homeless, footloose, and impoverished population which typically gravitates to a special portion of the city where single rooms may be had at low rentals. There, owing to the close juxtaposition of so many "social isolates" within a limited area, there develop certain *sub rosa* interaction patterns which violate the moral sensibilities of the larger society. Nonetheless, objectively viewed, these localized amoral actions are the logical consequence of the kinship and occupational patterns implied by a contractualistic value system. They are the necessary functional corollaries of present day social organization.

Physical Setting of the Rooming House Area. In a sense such amorality may be likened to the refraction of a light beam through a prism and the splitting up of that light beam into derivative light beams. By this analogy an overall value system, impinging upon a particular physical setting made up of houses having a certain design, and streets having a certain layout, and upon a population made up of a certain age, sex, and marital composition is going to "refract" into derivative values. The *sub rosa* inter-action patterns of the South End are just such "refractions." They exist implicitly in the larger overall value system but remain latent until they are "catalyzed," so to speak, by a particular physical and demographic setting. Thus the localized anomie of the South End is the by-product of a particular kind of value system impinging upon a particular physical layout and upon a particular population make-up. We must know this objective setting, therefore, if we would understand the anomie which is so typical of rooming house areas like the South End.

At the outset it is necessary, for purposes of statistical enumer-ation, to delineate precisely what we shall mean by the term "South End." In common usage the name is applied to a large and heterogeneous area lying south of the Boston and Albany Railroad tracks, on both sides of Washington street, and extend-ing down to Northampton street. Within these bounds are to be found rooming houses, tenement houses, factories, and nation-alities of the most diverse kind. Obviously statistical tabulations made for so heterogeneous an area would have very little signifi-cance. Since we are interested only in the land use type which is most distinctive to the South End and from which the district gets its peculiar character, namely the rooming house, it is neces-sary for us to delineate the South End much more precisely. The technique which we have resorted to is somewhat open to criti-cism. Improperly applied it could easily lead to conclusions about the South End which had already been indicated in the very defi-nition of the area. We shall have to be wary of making tautolo-gous generalizations. Briefly the procedure was this: On the reasonable assumption that a rooming house area will have a negligible child population, all the census tracts in and around the South End were ranked according to the percentage borne by their respective populations under 20 years of age to their respec-tive total populations.[1] Those census tracts having 25 per cent or more of their populations in age groups 20 and over were eliminated. In this way the tenement quarter lying to the east of Washington street and which has nothing in common with the

[1] Data from *Population and Housing — Statistics for Census Tracts, Boston, Massachusetts,* Sixteenth Census of the United States, 1940, Table 2.

rooming house district lying to the west of Washington street
either in physical layout or in population, was excluded from our
delineation of the South End "proper." There then remained the
following census tracts: G3, J1, J2, J3, J4, J5, K5, I3, L1, L2,
L3, L4, L5, and L6. Of these G3 is in no sense of the word a
residential area. It is almost wholly occupied by garages, warehouses, taverns, and retail businesses. For this reason it was
eliminated from our delineation of the South End. Finally there
remained the problem of income status. The South End rooming
house area, unlike that of the Back Bay, is occupied by a population of lower working class and marginal upper working class
persons. To include high rent census tracts like K5 and J3 in the
same area with such low rent census tracts as L1, L4, and L5
would be to conceal that which is most distinctive about associational patterns in the South End rooming house area. For this
reason it was decided to eliminate all census tracts having a
median monthly contract rent of more than $25.00.[2] One excep-
tion was made to this rule: census tract L2, having a median rent
of $25.94, was left in the South End on the basis of personal
observations. Some of the better South End rooming houses are
located in this neighborhood but socially and culturally the area
is indistinguishable from the rest of the South End. In no sense
of the word can it be classified with the Back Bay, which lies
just across the railroad tracks. Out of this process of elimination
there remains a residual area composed of census tracts J2, I3,
L1, L2, L3, L4, L5, and L6. (See map.) Even this delineation
is not wholly satisfactory. Within it there exists a sizable Syrian
community which has nothing in common with the surrounding
rooming house population. However there seems to be no way of
excluding these Syrians from the area of delineation without at
the same time excluding much of the rooming house area itself.
Furthermore, census tracts L5 and L6, the only ones lying east
of Washington street by our delineation of the South End, differ
in one respect from the remainder of the district. The presence
within them of the City Hospital and of a Catholic school has
introduced somewhat different population characteristics into the
vicinity than those which are found elsewhere in the South End.
In these two areas women slightly outnumber men, whereas every-

[2] Rental data obtained from *Population and Housing*, Table 5.

where else in the South End the reverse is the case. The presence
of a good many nurses and nuns is responsible for this difference.
These two tracts also contain somewhat larger proportions of
children than the other tracts, though not sufficiently so as to
remove them from the rooming house category. Finally a good

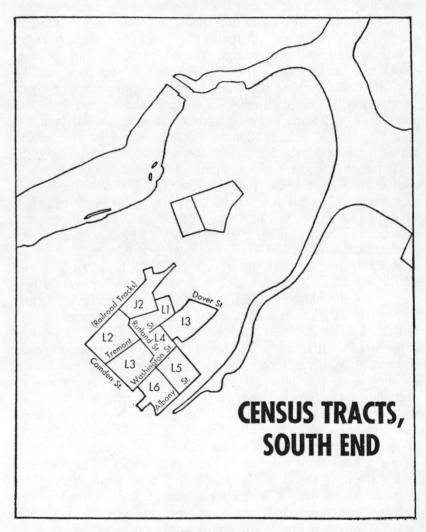

FIGURE 18

many internes live in the area because of its proximity to the City Hospital. However the basically rooming house character of these census tracts and the dubiousness of excluding them on so arbitrary a ground as their slightly different population make-up has induced us to leave them within our delineation of the South End. Exclusion of them might lay us open to the charge of "picking" our areas so as to prove a case. Moreover, both tracts share with the rest of the South End the mobile, family-less character that is so typical of the rooming house phenomenon. In general whatever error may have been introduced by our inclusion of them is on the conservative side, so that there certainly can be no danger of making faulty generalizations about the South End in terms of them.

There is one additional index, wholly independent of that which we have used, which tends to support our own delineation. In a special tabulation made for the Boston Health Department from unpublished 1930 census tract data there is included among other things the number of persons in each census tract who were living in boarding houses and lodging houses. The ratio which this population bears to the total population of the respective census tracts should therefore be a fairly good index to the rooming house character of a given area. In terms of this index every one of the census tracts appearing in our delineation except two show maximum ratios of boarding house and lodging house population to total population.[3] The exceptions are census tracts L5 and L6, the ones whose inclusion was somewhat dubious by our previous index. For reasons already mentioned however we have chosen the conservative course of retaining the delineation described above.

Let us turn then to an analysis of the objective physical setting of the South End district. Our purpose will be to take note of those objective factors which in some degree condition both the demographic make-up and, indirectly through that demographic make-up, the associational characteristics of the district. After this analysis we shall go on to the next step. Having seen that the demographic make-up of the South End is the result of a

[3] Data from *"Census Tract Data, 1930 Census,"* unpublished material from Fifteenth Census of the United States, 1930, compiled by Boston Health Department, Table 11.

particular occupational and kinship system impinging upon a particular physical setting, we shall now observe how that demographic make-up itself becomes an objective factor. In this capacity it too serves as a catalyst by which the occupational and kinship system is "precipitated" into associational patterns that would be inconceivable had there been a different physical setting and a different demographic composition. We may, then, begin by noting the outstanding physical features of the South End, starting with housing.

On the whole the dwellings within this great rooming house district are in sound structural condition. From 1855 to 1870, as the reader will recall from Chapter II, these dwellings were occupied by upper class families. In keeping with the standards of that time the houses were solidly built, being arranged side by side in the form of a continuous wall of brick and masonry. Today one half of these dwellings are more than sixty years old, and 91 per cent of them are more than forty years old.[4] In spite of this they remain in fairly good condition. According to census criteria 6.31 per cent of the dwelling units within the South End, as we have delineated it, are in need of major repairs.[5] This compares quite favorably with housing conditions in the North End, South Boston, and Charlestown. One evidence of the basic structural soundness of houses in the South End is the fact that an attempt was actually made during the late 1920's to rejuvenate part of the area for fashionable occupancy. In 1927 a Dr. Wilson moved with his family to a home on Union Park. The next year a friend and colleague of his, Dr. George Smith, likewise moved with his family to Union Park. Later a Mrs. Sears and a few other friends followed suit. Some of these families went to con-

---

[4] The Finance Commission of the City of Boston, *A Study of Certain of the Effects of Decentralization on Boston and Some Neighboring Cities and Towns* (Boston: 1941), p. 12. These figures apply to the broader South End, which includes the newer but more dilapidated tenement buildings lying to the east of Washington street. The age of the buildings within our delineation is on the whole greater but their structural condition is much better.

[5] Computed from census tract data in *Population and Housing — Statistics for Census Tracts, Boston, Massachusetts,* Sixteenth Census of the United States, Table 6. In the broader South End, 26.8 per cent of dwellings are in need of major repairs. (Boston City Planning Board, *Building a Better Boston,* Boston, 1941, p. 30.)

siderable expense in refurbishing and repairing their homes. A real estate writer at the time commented on the possibilities of this incipient rejuvenation as follows:

Boston possesses . . . a district which is really far lovelier than Beacon Hill and it cries aloud for rejuvenation. This is the South End section which has been allowed to deteriorate shamefully in the past half-century. Its natural advantages are far superior to the Hill, but because it has not been publicized and crooned over who in Boston outside of the lodging-house and tenement population that lives there has ever given it a thought? To be sure a very few people with commendable courage restored some of the fine houses in the most beautiful part of the district, Union Park, but the movement, if such it may be termed, never grasped the lethargic imagination of the general public.[6]

Unfortunately the financial crash of 1929, which in a sense terminated Beacon Hill's own revival, also frustrated this small scale attempt to re-establish the South End. Most of the upper class families have now left Union Park, although the *Social Register* for 1943 listed three such families as still residing there. Whether or not the revival would ever have extended to other portions of the district is questionable, but the fact does remain that structurally a good deal of the South End is apparently in sound enough condition to have attracted people of social standing and means. In the absence, however, of adequate maintenance and repair the buildings have undergone considerable deterioration. One evidence of this is the decline in total assessed valuation of the South End as a whole, including both the rooming house and the tenement house districts. The accompanying data portray this decline clearly:

$$1925 — \$44,232,600$$
$$1940 — \ \ 29,277,100$$

This represents a drop of 33.8 per cent during a fifteen year period; the city as a whole experienced a drop of 19.2 per cent during the same period.[7]

[6] Thomas Devine, in the *Boston Transcript*, September 28, 1932.
[7] *Building a Better Boston*, p. 29.

Even more serious than this, in terms of the South End's residential desirability, is the arrangement of the dwellings. The direct contiguity of every building with adjoining buildings prevents the side ventilation and light which is so important by present day housing standards. Along with this overcrowding of buildings there is an overcrowding of population. As may be seen from Table 8, page 173, the South End is nowhere near so congested as the North End. But it ranks along with the West End, East Boston, and Charlestown as being one of Boston's more congested residential districts. Part of this congestion results from landladies' efforts to maximize their slender incomes. In the typical rooming house every room except the kitchen and the landlady's room or apartment will be let out to tenants. On the first floor are front and rear parlors, each generally occupied by a single individual. These rooms always command the highest rents. On the upper floors are square rooms and side rooms, the latter commonly being unheated and meagerly furnished, but each let out to an individual tenant. The only bathroom in the house is usually on the second floor and it must be shared by all the tenants in the building.[8] Thus a typical rooming house will be occupied by from ten to fifteen tenants, each in his own room, and utterly isolated from his fellow residents. The imperious necessity of making her house yield as much income as possible causes the landlady to let out every available room to tenants. This practice of converting every room into a living quarter, with no provision being made for common parlors or visiting rooms, has been held by some observers to contribute in no small measure to the social problems that are so characteristic of rooming house districts.

Four other objective features of the South End bear notice as conditioning associational patterns in the district. These are: the existence of several heavy traffic arterials running through the area; the extension of the elevated railway directly through the heart of the district, along Washington street; the presence of a great many cafés, taverns, and cheap amusement facilities; and the proximity of coal yards, factories, and other industrial establishments. Together these objective factors exert a serious blight

---

[8] Albert Benedict Wolfe, *The Lodging House Problem in the City of Boston* (Cambridge: 1913), chap. 5.

upon the whole vicinity. The eight major thoroughfares which traverse the South End are avenues for a continuous flow of heavy truck and auto traffic. The elevated railway casts a perpetual shadow along the whole length of Washington street and is responsible for much of the noise and din which blights that artérial. The cafés, taverns, and amusement places — whose location in the area is of course a result of the kind of people who live there — are responsible for further blight attendant upon brawling, drunkenness, and tawdry appearance. And the industrial establishments account for much of the smoke and dirt which pervades the district. Finally, the South End, in spite of and perhaps because of its position athwart some of Boston's major thoroughfares, is isolated from social contact with the rest of the city. Thus directly adjoining its western border is the Back Bay. But along that border runs the New York, New Haven, and Hartford Railroad, which is as insuperable a barrier to interaction between the South End and the Back Bay as would be a river. Along the whole length of this border there are only three bridges for auto traffic; pedestrian traffic is possible only by means of elevated iron foot bridges which extend across the railroad tracks at several points. Except along Massachusetts avenue there is no direct means of transportation between the South End and the Back Bay, although both districts lie side by side. So too the South End lacks any direct connection with South Boston, because of the water barrier formed by South Cove, which runs between the two districts. Only northern Roxbury, lying just to the south across Northampton street, is in regular communication with the South End. Yet that community merges itself into the South End, both in physical layout and in population characteristics, so that one can hardly speak of this contact as involving the transmission of social values from one community to the other.[9] Every day a constant procession of automobiles, trucks, trolley cars, and buses streams through the South End, but none of this represents social contact between residents of that area and residents of the outlying communities. All communications in the South End are pointed toward the city center and that is the only place at which

[9] See Howard Parad, "Two Roxbury Tenement Groups and the Surrounding District," unpublished honors' thesis in Area of Social Science, Harvard University (no date).

South Enders interact by direct contact with members of other communities in the Boston metropolitan area.

Objective factors such as these are fully recognized as undesirable by residents of the South End. An inquiry into the grievances of rooming house keepers on Union Park, for instance, showed that most of these people wanted fewer saloons and cafés, more open spaces, more one-way streets, and less heavy truck traffic.[10] In view of these people's rational apprehension of the South End's physical setting it is reasonable to suppose that this physical setting does have a selective influence upon the type of people who will live in such an area. In this indirect way, as well as immediately, some rather important physical influences are brought to bear upon associational patterns in the South End. The nature of these influences will become clearer in the course of the subsequent analysis. Preliminary to that we shall have to outline some of the main population characteristics which have developed with respect to the South End's physical setting.

Socio-Economic Characteristics of the Rooming House Area. The total number of persons living within the South End by our delineation of the district is 31,418. Of these, 56.30 per cent are native white, 26.57 per cent are foreign born white, and 17.13 per cent are nonwhite.[11] Of the foreign born persons almost one half are Canadians or Irish and are therefore quite similar to the native white population in social and cultural characteristics. Syrians, English, and Greeks are, in that order, most prominent among the remaining foreign born persons.[12] Except for the Canadians and the Irish these foreign born persons do not constitute part of the South End rooming house population. Rather they live in tenements scattered throughout the side streets of the district, generally in cohesive sub-communities of their own. The Syrians center around Union Park and Shawmut avenue; the Italians and Greeks are most numerous in census tracts I2 and I3. The Negro population, heavily concentrated along the New York, New Haven, and Hartford Railroad, appears most numerous in

[10] Cited in *Building a Better Boston,* pp. 38–39.

[11] Calculated from data in *Population and Housing — Statistics for Census Tracts, Boston, Massachusetts,* Sixteenth Census of the United States, 1940, Table 1.

[12] Calculated from data in *Population and Housing,* Table 3.

census tracts J2, L2, and L3. The Negroes are gradually expanding northward and eastward, having recently located to the east of Washington street in violation of that traditional boundary line. Most of these minority peoples have remained rather solidary with their respective value systems; they have their own churches, lodges, and other organizations, and they generally live in family units. In no sense of the word do they typify the South End rooming house population. For that reason they are not of

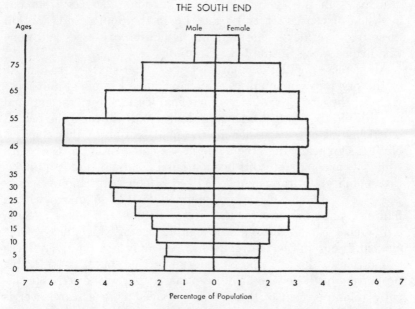

FIGURE 19. POPULATION COMPOSITION, SOUTH END

primary concern to us in the present connection; they have been mentioned only for the sake of an empirically complete characterization of the South End's population.

The real rooming house population in the South End is predominantly of American (or Canadian and Irish) stock, mainly middle aged or elderly, and more male than female. These age and sex characteristics are revealed by figure 19, which portrays the population composition of the census tracts embraced in our delineation of the South End.[13] Two observations may be made

[13] Calculated from data in *Population and Housing,* Table 2.

on the basis of this graph. First of all, the male and female populations are about equal in the childhood and younger adult age groups as well as in the extremely advanced age groups. But in the age groups 35–54, representing the middle years of adulthood, males outnumber females by nearly two to one. Secondly, the modal age group of the male population is the rather advanced one of 45–54 years. For females too the proportion of persons in the upper age groups is atypically great. The relative prominence of females in the age group 20–29 no doubt derives from our inclusion of census tracts L5 and L6 in the South End. Within these tracts resides a considerable population of nurses and nuns who live near the Boston City Hospital.

All of these population characteristics differ sharply from those of the previous communities which we have examined and from those of the city as a whole. Their implications for associational activities in the South End are profound and will form the principal theme of our discussion in the final section of this chapter. No less significant than the age and sex composition of the South End is its marital status, its occupational make-up, and its population mobility. Of the population aged fifteen years and over only 38.23 per cent is recorded as married; [14] this compares with a figure of 50.46 per cent for the city of Boston as a whole.[15] Such a difference is a sizable one, the significance of which will become evident in our subsequent analysis. Not only is a relatively large proportion of the adult population unmarried, but a considerable proportion of those who have been married are widowed. Specifically 10.96 per cent of the population aged 15 years and over is widowed.[16] It should be evident from these indices that the South End rooming house population is largely removed from kinship attachments, comprising instead a highly individualized and atomized community. The occupational structure too is very different from the ones which we have found in our other study

---

[14] Data are for 1930, there being no data by census tracts on marital status. *Census Tract Data, 1930 Census,* by Boston Health Department, Table 7.

[15] Computed from data in *Abstract of the Fifteenth Census of the United States,* "Population," 1930, Table 120.

[16] Calculated from census tract data in *Census Tract Data, 1930 Census,* by Boston Health Department, Table 7.

areas. Table 28 presents the percentage distribution of employed persons according to type of occupation.

TABLE 28

PERCENTAGE DISTRIBUTION OF EMPLOYED PERSONS IN THE SOUTH END, BY OCCUPATIONS, 1940

Occupations	Total	Male	Female
Total employed............................	100.00	61.85	38.15
Professionals.............................	9.11	3.29	5.82
Semi-professionals........................	1.61	1.01	0.60
Proprietors, managers, officials.............	3.31	2.81	0.50
Clerical, sales workers.....................	12.01	7.05	4.96
Craftsmen, foremen, etc....................	10.48	10.09	0.39
Operatives................................	14.97	9.15	5.82
Domestic service workers...................	7.23	1.40	5.83
Service workers (excluding domestic)........	34.90	21.11	13.79
Laborers..................................	5.32	5.23	0.09
Unreported...............................	1.06	0.71	0.35

Calculated from data in Sixteenth Census of the United States, 1940.

The preponderance of service workers in this occupational structure is striking. Most of these workers are employed by laundries, restaurants, hotels, and the like, in very menial capacities: as dishwashers, waiters, chefs, laundry workers, etc. Characteristically they are poorly paid, highly transient, uneducated, and more or less "emancipated" from accepted institutions in the community. Among the other occupations clerical workers, salesmen, clerks, factory operatives, foremen, and craftsmen are most important. These groups are characterized by the same mobility, instability, and moral emancipation as are the service workers. There is one further aspect of occupational structure in the South End which bears notice. That is unemployment, and its corollary of relief. Both during the pre-war depression and during the war period the South End has far outranked every other district in Boston as to the proportion of families receiving public assistance. In 1932–33, during the depths of the depression, 46.3 per cent of the families in the South End were on relief.[17] The North End was next, with 34.2 per cent of its families receiving public

[17] Boston Council of Social Agencies, *Social Statistics by Census Tracts in Boston* (Boston: 1935), II, 14–18. This figure applies to the broader South End, which includes the tenement area as well as the rooming house area.

assistance, East Boston, with 25.5 per cent, and so on down to
the Back Bay which had only 4.6 per cent on relief.[18] Dependency during the war period is revealed by the data on public
assistance for March, 1944, shown in Table 29.[19]

TABLE 29

PUBLIC ASSISTANCE IN BOSTON AND ITS HEALTH AND WELFARE DISTRICTS
DURING MARCH, 1944

District	Dependent Aid; Cases per 1,000 Population	Old Age Assistance; Cases per 1,000 Persons over 66 Years
Boston	4.45	228
Back Bay	2.70	188
Brighton	1.42	189
Charlestown	3.77	318
North Dorchester	2.40	212
South Dorchester	1.42	163
East Boston	4.45	188
Hyde Park	1.83	178
Jamaica Plain	0.75	170
North End	8.47	202
Roslindale	0.86	118
Roxbury	6.30	300
South Boston	3.96	238
South End	20.70	403
West End	7.72	213
West Roxbury	0.51	145

Source: Greater Boston Community Council, *The People of Boston and its Fifteen
Health and Welfare Areas*, 1944, Table 10.

Thus a very large percentage of residents in the South End are
or have been on relief. The proportion whose income is just
enough to keep them above the dependency line is even greater.

The third socio-economic characteristic of the South End which
helps condition associational patterns is population mobility.
Quantitative evidence of the mobility of the South End is afforded
by tabulations made from the *Police Lists*. As the reader will
recall, the *Police Lists* indicate opposite the name of every resident both his present address and his address of one year previously. From such lists it is rather simple to classify persons
according to change of residence and then calculate relative mo-

[18] *Loc. cit.*

[19] Greater Boston Community Council, *The People of Boston and its Fifteen Health and Welfare Areas* (Boston: 1944), Table 10.

bility rates. In Table 30 we have presented such data for both the South End and the North End, for the pre-war year of 1938.[20]

TABLE 30

NUMBER AND PERCENTAGE OF PERSONS IN THE SOUTH END AND THE NORTH END OF BOSTON GROUPED ACCORDING TO CHANGES IN ADDRESS BETWEEN JANUARY 1, 1938 AND JANUARY 1, 1939

Residence on 1-1-39		Same place on 1-1-38 as on 1-1-39	In district 1-1-38 at a different address from 1-1-39	Outside of district, but inside Boston, 1-1-38	Outside of Boston, 1-1-38
South End	Number....	1140	415	163	146
	Per cent....	61.16	22.26	8.75	7.83
North End	Number....	2101	162	38	23
	Per cent....	90.41	6.97	1.63	0.99

Quite obviously the two main slum districts of Boston have very different mobility rates. More than one-third of the South End's population on January 1, 1939 had changed addresses during the preceding year and nearly one-fifth of it had come to the district from elsewhere during that period. From these data it would appear that the outstanding feature of population mobility in the South End is change of address within the district. Impressionistic knowledge of the area supports this inference. The typical rooming house dweller is forever on the hunt for a better room with lower rent. This lends to the area a highly fluid character which obstructs any development of community consensus.[21]

If now we inquire into the motives which prompt so many rooming house dwellers to live in the South End we may come to realize how physical setting exerts its demographically selective influence. The "ideal typical" resident of the South End has been found to be male, single, late middle aged, uneducated, transient, and poor. His housing requirements are pretty nearly dictated by these factors. Since he is living alone he will generally desire a

[20] Calculated from *Police Lists*. (Full title: City of Boston, *List of Residents 20 Years of Age and Over as of January 1, 1939;* same for 1938.)

[21] Harvey W. Zorbaugh, "The Dweller in Furnished Rooms: an Urban Type," in Ernest W. Burgess (ed.), *The Urban Community* (Chicago: 1926), p. 100. Zorbaugh found in the Lower North Side of Chicago a complete population turnover every four months.

single room, rather than a whole apartment or flat. Since he is
transient he will demand a room that is already furnished and
equipped with bedding, towels, and other household necessities.
Being poor he will desire a room of moderately low rent. Now,
housing facilities that are adapted to these requirements cannot
be found in every part of the city. The tenements of the North
End, with their lack of central heat and their arrangement of
rooms into flats, are wholly unsuited to housing transient single
persons. The respectable rooming houses of the Back Bay command rents that are quite beyond the reach of the underpaid
service worker. In the suburbs the houses are either three-decker
flats meant for multiple family occupancy, or they are single family dwellings whose locations and structural conditions are such
as to command rents prohibitively high for the service worker.
In the South End, on the other hand, rents are necessarily low
since the physical environs, particularly the factories, the traffic,
the elevated railway, and other such factors, repel persons who
are able to pay for quiet and clean living accommodations. Moreover, the construction of the houses — originally designed for
single family occupancy, with rooms for maids and servants — is
such that the buildings in their present form are better suited to
rooming house purposes than to tenement purposes.[22] The number of rooms in each house is sufficiently great so that conversion
of a building to rooming house purposes can be a paying proposition. Thus, by virtue of its physical setting and layout the South
End is admirably adapted to the housing requirements of single,
poor, and transient persons. In this way the objective physical
layout of the district selectively attracts a population having
appropriate demographic and occupational characteristics.

That considerations such as these are indeed the ones which
prompt single and transient persons to live in the South End may
be gathered from remarks that they make regarding their place
of residence. One elderly man, asked if he liked his present living
accommodations on Tremont street, replied:

I'm fairly comfortable, but I have to be alone and do things by myself
because of my handicap. [Partial blindness.] I'm moving over to

---

[22] It is possible that conversion to tenement buildings would have yielded
considerably greater revenues to the proprietors of South End buildings.

Columbus avenue and live with some friends of mine. The rent's just as good there. Of course, the Negroes are all around but there's not so much thieving and holding up, you know. Around here something's always being stolen at night.

A middle aged worker, asked why he lived in the South End, replied:

H——, why don't I live in Back Bay! The rent's better here. . . . I've lived here off and on for twenty years — every time I come to Boston. I'm handy to downtown so I can walk to work.

Another informant who lived in a rooming house on Shawmut avenue, in the midst of the Syrian district, replied to a query as to why he lived there:

I live here because it's kind of quiet.[23] Some nights it's quiet and sometimes it isn't. (Do you get better rent here?) No. (Have you any friends here?) Some people have friends but I'm all alone.

From these statements it is clear that considerations of rent, environs, and convenience are very much in the minds of South End rooming house dwellers. The choice of residence which these people make is thoroughly rational, for it represents the deliberate selection of a "least costful" location which is fully recognized by the person to be such. This correspondence between the objective least costfulness of an action sequence, and the subjectively anticipated least costfulness on the part of the person (or other social system) who has chosen that action sequence is the distinctive feature of rational action.

Kinship and Occupational Preconditions to the Rooming House Phenomenon. At this point a question forces itself into our analysis. Can it be said that the rooming house phenomenon, as we have depicted it in the South End, "naturally" follows from the objective factors of physical setting and population composition? Can we regard it as inevitable, given the rationality of people seeking cheap, furnished, single rooms? If so, we would have discovered a case in which spatial adaptation did indeed fit the deductions of the methodologically rationalistic theories. In other

---

[23] "Quiet" refers to lack of rowdyism, drunken hilarity, and trouble.

words, the rationality of the social systems (rooming house dwellers) and the impeditivcness of spatiality (the physical setting of the rooming house district) would in such a case be objective givens; the territorial patterns growing out of them would be passive epiphenomena in which space, immune from any other influences, became allocated among various uses with a maximum of rationality.

But can such a position really be held? Certain considerations seem to point to a negative answer. To begin with, why are there people who must live alone, detached from kinship ties, ever on the move, and forever driven by the necessity of finding cheap rooms in which to live? It must be evident that no answer to this problem can be found in the objective physical setting of the South End nor in the population composition and socio-economic characteristics of that area. These factors exercise their causal power only mediately through a broader, larger value system. Apparently we are obliged once again to invoke factors of a cultural nature if we would understand the causation of land use patterns in urban communities. The South End, in spite of its undesirability as a place in which to live and in spite of its social atomization and disorganization is just as much the product of an overall value system as the retail district of downtown Boston is or, for that matter, as are the organized communities of Beacon Hill and the North End. The clearest indication of this fact may be found in the socio-economic characteristics which have been outlined above. There we found that the great majority of rooming house dwellers in the South End were unmarried or widowed, and that they were unemployed or were engaged in underpaid transient jobs. Now these are not in any sense "self-created" social phenomena. They are corollaries of a particular patterning of kinship and occupational relationships which would be inconceivable outside of a contractualistic society. In the absence of this particular patterning of kinship and occupational relationships there would never be a "rooming house phenomenon." There would not be the transient, unattached, and impoverished persons who seek cheap furnished single rooms to rent by the week or month. And without such a population type the objective physical setting of areas like the South End would play a very different role in urban land use structure. It behooves us then to take note of those features of American kinship and occupational structure which are most relevant to the rooming house phenomenon. Once we have understood the cultural context out of which the rooming house dweller has emerged as a social type we shall be in a position to analyze the associational patterns which follow from the existence of such a social type. Then, recalling our earlier data on the physical setting of the South End and its selective attraction of a population with appropriate socio-economic characteristics, we shall be able to show why these associational patterns are localized. In this manner we shall have demonstrated the cultural contingency of localized anomie such as prevails in the South End rooming house district.

Let us begin with kinship structure. Perhaps the outstanding feature of family organization as it has developed in American society is what Parsons has called "the structural isolation of the individual conjugal family." [24] To a striking extent the American family is a strictly "domestic" unit, in which consanguine and sibling links have become extremely weak. This means that, in the ideal-typical case, the person who never marries is not a functioning member of any family at all. It means too that when married persons are widowed they find themselves removed from kinship ties. To be sure, exceptions to this are common. But that in no way detracts from the force of the argument. For what really matters is the fact that the person who fails to marry, the person who remains with his or her parents through much of his adult life, and the person who is widowed and goes to live with his matured children — all of these persons become foci of strain in the kinship system. Not only are they as individuals beset with personality conflicts but they precipitate such conflicts in those with whom they live. Such "irregularities," however frequent they may be in fact, simply do not accord with social expectations. One is not *supposed* to preserve consanguine solidarities with his parents or with his children beyond a certain point. In such a system unmarried persons and elderly widows and widowers are morally expected to take care of themselves if they can possibly do so. They are supposed to maintain separate residence and economic independence from their parents or their children. This

[24] Talcott Parsons, "The Kinship System of the Contemporary United States," *American Anthropologist,* 45: 22–38 (January–March, 1943), p. 28.

is, on the level of family organization, the logical consequence of a contractualistic value system. For, in its exclusive stress upon the conjugal bond, the American family approaches the status of a "special interest" group, in which marital relations become wholly separated from other spheres of life interest. Marriage is but one area of social interaction among many others, and to a very large degree a person is free to "rationally" decide whom he will marry or if he is going to marry at all.

Now in point of fact there are many people who never do marry, and a large proportion of those who do marry are eventually widowed. As a result one will find in every urban community a rather sizable population which is wholly detached from family participation. In rural areas, where the extended family has more nearly maintained itself, this isolation of single persons from kinship ties is nowhere near so frequent as it is in large cities. The conjugal pattern, with all its atomizing consequences, finds its fullest expression in the great urban agglomerations of which Boston is one example. Now, given a large population of unmarried and widowed persons in a city such as Boston there emerge some rather unique housing requirements. The lone person, whether he is middle aged and employed or is elderly and retired, will often if not generally have a minimum of furniture and other heavy belongings. Moreover, unless he does considerable entertaining of friends, he has little occasion for a whole house or even for an apartment. A single room will take care of his needs. Furthermore he will often desire freedom of movement so that he can change his place of residence with a minimum of bother. These are as characteristic of women as they are of men. The rooming house, providing single. furnished rooms, central heat, short term rent, and a minimum of property commitments is the response to these unique housing needs.

But the rooming house phenomenon cannot be fully explained in terms of kinship structure alone. The transiency and impoverishment which characterize so many rooming house dwellers are attributable to other features of American society. They have their origin in the functional requirements of an industrial economy with its unique occupational structure. Above all an industrial economy presupposes an adequate supply of unskilled and mobile workers. Certain jobs, such as those of restaurant bus boys and dishwashers, laundry scrubbers and ironers, traveling salesmen and clerks, factory operatives and janitors, require very little skill. There is not the prolonged apprenticeship which characterizes a handicraft economy in which production is in the hands of craftsmen. Hence such jobs can be filled by almost anybody. The consequence of this is that the bargaining power of persons engaged in such employment is low, their tenure is insecure, and their place can easily be filled by another. Persons engaged in such work are therefore "underpaid" in terms of the living levels valued by the larger society, and they are frequently "out of a job." Moreover, the kinds of persons who must take such employment are those who lack the training and aptitude for any other sort of work. Their socialization has commonly been deficient in regard to such traits as ambition, regularity, "steadiness," and the like, all of which are esteemed in the scale of values of the larger society. Lacking in such traits the unskilled person is very likely to be mobile. This mobility is only heightened by his low income and uncertain employment, by which he is always driven in quest of better and surer employment.

There is another corollary to the occupational structure that has developed *pari passu* with the contemporary industrial economy. This is the phenomenon of "retirement." A good many of the operations necessary to the functioning of an industrial economy require a certain degree of agility, sensory acuity, and physical stamina — characteristics which elderly people generally do not have. The man who could successfully hold down a job as chef, factory operative, or janitor during his middle age and late middle age finds himself increasingly unable to perform the necessary tasks as he reaches old age. His ability to hold one job or to get a new one deteriorates rapidly. At some point in this process he becomes, in fact if not in intention, "retired." The ramifications of such retirement extend much further than merely the sudden cessation of income. As Parsons has indicated, retirement from one's job entails a sudden removal of the individual from the very scheme of status ascription.[25] This results from the preëminent position which occupation has assumed in present day society in the determination of personal status. It is little wonder,

[25] Talcott Parsons, "Age and Sex in the Social Structure of the United States," *American Sociological Review*, 7: 604–616 (October, 1942), p. 616.

then, that with retirement and disengagement from the most important status-determining element of American social structure, namely the job, there follow a whole range of associational consequences for the elderly person. In Parsons' words:

> In view of the very great significance of occupational status and its psychological correlates, retirement leaves the older man in a peculiarly functionless situation cut off from participation in the most important interests and activities of the society. There is a further important aspect of this situation. Not only status in the community, but actual place of residence is to a very high degree a function of the specific job held. Retirement not only cuts the ties to the job itself but also greatly loosens those to the community of residence.[26]

The retired elderly person, particularly the one whose prior occupation has not enabled him to save for his old age, finds himself confronted with poverty and loneliness. What adjustment he will make depends upon his marital status, his financial means, and the means of his matured children. In a very large number of cases he will be single or widowed, unable or unwilling to find accommodations with whatever children he may have, and faced with the necessity of living on a very slender income (insurance, relief, or contributions from children). The elderly woman, though she does not "retire" in the same sense as does the man, nonetheless is confronted with very nearly the same problems as the elderly single man when she reaches old age without a husband and without siblings or children able or willing to board her. Given a sizable population of persons such as these — transient and poorly paid service workers and retired, elderly, and impoverished persons — there must be provided housing accommodations of a suitable kind. Transiency, low income, lack of personal possessions, and the fact of living alone, all dictate single furnished rooms with low rent as being the appropriate type of dwelling unit.

This, then, is the kinship and occupational structure in terms of which the rooming house as a distinct type of land use has emerged. In all likelihood there would be no such phenomenon in a society whose family relationships were structured along con-

[26] *Loc. cit.*

sanguine lines and in which status, rather than being determined primarily by occupation, was determined say by one's possessions in land. In such a society the unmarried person (if indeed such a type would be socially tolerated) might maintain residence either with his parents or with his siblings of a certain lineage. And, what is of even greater importance, such an arrangement would be wholly in accord with his own and his kinsmen's legitimate expectations. Of course many other variants besides this would be possible, but it is hardly likely that any of them would, under the specified conditions, bear any resemblance to the detached, atomized, and quasi-stigmatized way of life which characterizes the rooming house dweller.

So too, in a society whose productive processes were maintained on a handicraft basis, involving a high degree of skill and prolonged apprenticeship, there would hardly exist the unskilled, transient, and freely mobile population such as one finds in the rooming house area of any large American city. Finally, "retirement" in the sense of a complete cessation of participation in occupational life and a complete removal from the very criteria of status ascription would be inconceivable in an economy where lineage rather than occupation was the basis of status ascription. Looking at the matter positively it would seem as though the rooming house is a functionally necessary land use phenomenon, given a kinship system organized almost exclusively along conjugal lines and given an occupational system which involves for many persons transiency, insecurity, and eventual retirement with attendant removal from the elements of status ascription.[27] So long as these patterns prevail — and they are probably inextricable from the whole contractualistic organization of personal relationships which pervades western society — there will always be a sizable population of single, transient, elderly, and low-income persons whose housing requirements can only be met by the availability of inexpensive and furnished single rooms.

The Localization of Anomie. The causal sequence in the establishment of a rooming house district is thus clear. In terms of a unique patterning of kinship and occupational relations there exists in every large city a sizable population of isolated, transient, and financially straitened persons in middle age and old age.

[27] Cf. Wolfe, *op. cit.*, pp. 167–168.

This population, because of its socio-economic characteristics, is impelled to seek housing accommodations of a very definite kind in which single rooms, available at low rentals and already furnished and centrally heated, are the outstanding features. Now housing accommodations that meet these specifications are not available in every part of a city. In Boston, as well as in many other cities, they are to be found principally in one-time single family residential quarters which have long since been by-passed in the course of the city's growth. They are typically found near the city center, amidst objectionable physical environs, and under conditions of some deterioration.

As a result of this process one finds in the South End of Boston a population distinguished by its social isolation, its transiency, and its poverty. The associational implications of such a socio-economic composition are unmistakable. Briefly they involve a high degree of social anomie. The community structure that has evolved in the South End approaches very nearly the extreme pole of nominalism. What Zimmerman has said regarding the nominalist community applies quite literally to the South End:

> The idea of "nominal community" or nominalist element in the community implies that the group is integrated largely by geographic proximity. The members have very little in common as regards tradition, language, origin, national background, or common experience.[28]

The reasons for this state of affairs in the South End are not hard to find. Life in a rooming house is utterly devoid of companionship and intimacy.[29] One's fellow tenants are forever on the move, remaining in one place for a few weeks or months and then finding a room with better heat or lower rent and moving away. The constant succession of new roomers makes social distance and mutual suspicion almost a necessity if one would not run the risk of theft or personal abuse. The heterogeneity of ages, the absence of family identification by which to "legitimize" one's self, the diversity of ethnic, occupational, and religious affiliations, and the lack of any "stake" in the local area — all of these fac-

---

[28] Carle C. Zimmerman, "The Evolution of the American Community," *American Journal of Sociology*, 46: 809–817 (May, 1941), p. 809.

[29] Wolfe, *op. cit.*, p. 109.

tors prevent any solidarization of personal relationships. Even the landlords and landladies themselves are highly mobile. Many of them own their homes on a mortgage and are often unable to meet their obligations. Real estate speculators have sometimes deliberately "arranged" foreclosures after a landlady has paid off a good deal of her mortgage, by steering roomers away from her house or by removing phony roomers that had been placed there when she made her first payment.[30] Under such conditions even the landladies constitute an unstable and mobile element in the South End's population.

The kinds of associations which are attracted to such an area are even more disintegrative of solidarity. Cheap cafeterias, usually serving liquor, locate along the main avenues of population flow. Gambling joints, taverns, variety stores, and other such establishments develop to serve the recreational tastes of the population. In such places one can play the slot machines, buy "numbers," meet women of dubious character, and otherwise engage in activities that are morally censurable by the scale of values of the larger society. In the absence of durable personal relationships there are few sanctions short of legal coercion that may be brought to bear upon the amoral person. His anonymity and isolation give him an immunity from the moral controls which operate in "real" communities, such as gossip, ridicule, ostracism, and the like. In the absence of any rewards for proper behavior there is an actual weakening of moral inhibitions and an atrophy of conceptions of right and wrong. Such norms, however well rooted they may have been in individual consciousnesses, tend to deteriorate when the individual is removed from the social context of reward, punishment, and reinforcement in which they were originally defined. It is not surprising then that "the prob lem of furnished rooms has long been connected with the city problems of vice and immorality." [31]

Let us consider in a little more detail some of the manifestations of this localized anomie. On the whole the South End is one of Boston's major areas of vice and crime. Police squad cars and patrol wagons are ubiquitous features of the South End's land-

[30] *Ibid.*, pp. 67–71.
[31] Edith Abbott, *The Tenements of Chicago, 1908–1935* (Chicago: 1936), p. 324.

scape. The majority of Boston's "career criminals" live in either the South End or the West End. Petty pilfering, theft from rooms, street brawling, jackrolling, narcotic peddling, and prostitution are typical of the illegal activities which characterize the area. These offenses are for the most part by mature men. Juvenile delinquency, while rather high, is not so great as in the West End or even in the North End. Table 31 reveals the position of the South End relative to other districts in the rate of juvenile delinquency. It should, however, be borne in mind that delinquency in the South End is undoubtedly much greater than these

TABLE 31

APPEARANCES OF BOSTON JUVENILES UNDER 17 YEARS IN MASSACHUSETTS
COURTS PER 1,000 POPULATION 7–16 YEARS OF AGE, BY DISTRICTS

District	1936–1940 (pre-war)	1941–1943 (war period)
Boston	14.2	14.7
Back Bay	11.8	22.2
Brighton	7.0	8.8
Charlestown	18.6	23.9
North Dorchester	10.3	9.8
South Dorchester	6.9	5.2
East Boston	23.5	19.3
Hyde Park	7.0	6.1
Jamaica Plain	8.5	13.1
North End	26.5	19.7
Roslindale	5.6	7.8
Roxbury	18.2	23.3
South Boston	16.8	13.1
South End	24.3	28.5
West End	27.8	35.7
West Roxbury	3.1	3.1

Source: Greater Boston Community Council, *The People of Boston and its Fifteen Health and Welfare Areas* (1944), Table 8.

figures would suggest. The data refer only to the place of residence of the juvenile offender. Now the unique thing about much of the amoral activity which pervades the South End is that it is engaged in by people who live in other parts of Boston. By virtue of its atomization and anonymity the South End provides a refuge for persons who wish to engage in activities that are legally or morally prohibited in their own communities. This is particularly true of juvenile offenders. Youths who are "looking for a thrill" readily gravitate to the South End where they can escape detection and perhaps pass as adults. There too they can get liquor (denied them by law in their own neighborhoods), they can take up rooms with companions of the opposite sex, they can rob and easily escape, etc. Hence the incidence of juvenile offenses in the South End is in all likelihood very high. Headlines in the *Mid-Town Journal,* a community newspaper published in the South End and circulating in that district as well as in adjoining portions of Roxbury and the Back Bay, indicate something of the character of juvenile offenses in the district.

"HOLD YOUTH, 16, IN $5000 BAIL FOLLOWING ASSAULT ON GIRL, ROBBERY, AND BURGLARY" [32]

"RUNAWAY SISTERS, 13–15, TELL INVESTIGATORS OF WILD BOOZE ORGIES AND FUN WITH MEN" [33]

"HOLD YOUTH, 19, ON LARCENY RAP" [34]

The fact remains, though, that most offenders in the South End are adults. The criminal acts which these adult offenders commit are generally of a "base" sort, whether judged in terms of the values of the larger society or in terms of those of the professional criminal world. Thieving, brawling, and prostitution are statistically the most common offenses. Some quantitative evidence is available as to the frequency of morals offenses in the South End relative to that in other districts of Boston, from unpublished records of the Boston Police Department.[35] These data concern the number of arrests made in various police divisions within the city of Boston, classified according to type of offense, for the year ending November 30, 1943. Their frequency in the various police divisions of Boston is apparent from Table 32. Insofar as these data are significant it is clear that the South End exceeds any other district in the incidence of morals offenses. Of the 1,088 arrests made in Boston during the year in question, on grounds of transgressing the morals laws, fully 301, or 27.67 per

[32] *Mid-Town Journal,* August 27, 1943.

[33] *Mid-Town Journal,* September 10, 1943.

[34] *Mid-Town Journal,* December 10, 1943.

[35] Data furnished from files of Boston Police Department, Division of Statistics, through courtesy of Messrs. Lieber, Murphy, and DeValerni.

TABLE 32

ARRESTS FOR MORALS OFFENSES IN THE CITY OF BOSTON FOR YEAR
ENDING NOVEMBER 30, 1943, BY POLICE DIVISIONS

Police Division	Adultery	Fornication	Illegitimacy	Lewd and Lascivious Cohabitation	Open and Gross Lewdness
1 (North End)	3	1	1	3	4
2 (Downtown)					4
3 (West End)	28	32	2	28	38
4 (*South End*)	49	141	10	79	22
5 (no such division)					
6 (South Boston)	7	6	7	14	2
7 (East Boston)			2	4	3
8 (police boat)					
9 (North Roxbury)	50	33	7	31	8
10 (Roxbury Crossing)	60	59	23	29	35
11 (Dorchester)	17	4	6		10
12 (no such division)					
13 (Jamaica Plain)	2		1		1
14 (Brighton)		2	2	1	4
15 (Charlestown)	1		6	3	6
16 (Back Bay)	39	40	1	52	9
17 (West Roxbury)				1	2
18 (Hyde Park)			5	4	3
19 (Mattapan)			1	2	7
Bureau of Criminal Investigation	4	9	6	7	5
Totals	260	327	80	258	163

Source: Records of Boston Police Department.

cent took place in the South End. This is higher than the rate for
any other single police division in the city. But of even greater
significance is the particular type of morals offense which is predominant in the South End. From the table it can be seen that
fully 141 of the 327 arrests for fornication — i.e., 43.12 per cent
— were in the South End. This is evidently the type of morals
offense which is most distinctive to the rooming house district.
The reason for this is not hard to find. Ordinary prostitution with
unmarried women would be the sexual adjustment which transient, unmarried men in middle age and late middle age would
tend to make. Adultery, illegitimacy, and other morals offenses
have a very different significance. It is noteworthy, for instance,
that the number of arrests for adultery were highest in Roxbury
Crossing. This district has a very large Negro population among
whom marital fidelity tends to be rather lax.

Of course these data must not be taken at their face value. Statistics on arrests may deviate very considerably from actual offenses. There is reason to suppose that the number of arrests on morals charges in the South End falls very much short of the actual number of offenses in the district, for the reason that the isolation and anonymity of most persons allows a great deal of amoral activity to go on undetected. Such undiscovered amoral activity is undoubtedly much more common in the South End than in other districts where population stability and homogeneity make undiscovered morals offenses relatively few in number.

How much of the amoral activity revealed in Table 32 is attributable to "residents" of the South End and how much is attributable to outsiders who go to the district "looking for trouble" is impossible to judge. It is difficult, for one thing, to know who is a resident and who is not, since so large a proportion of the South End population is transient. There is little doubt, however, that the socio-economic characteristics of the South End population have a great deal to do with its social and cultural anomie. Consider for instance the sex ratio and marital status of the South End. With almost two-thirds of its population unmarried and with men between 35 and 54 years of age outnumbering women in that age group by nearly two to one, the problems of sexual adjustment are bound to be difficult. Inevitably a certain proportion of unmarried persons, lacking the socializing influences that would make for moral inhibition, will transgress prevailing norms regarding sexual behavior. Prostitution is one manifestation of the adjustments which such persons will make.[36] Throughout the South End, particularly on the main thoroughfares, there are houses which rent rooms to unmarried couples. There are many others which are plain brothels. One such case is recorded by the *Mid-Town Journal:*

Two runaway girls, one but 13, the other 15, who had been reported missing from their homes in Roxbury for the past two weeks were discovered by police of the Warren ave. division in a Dover st. rooming house where they had been living since their departure, entertaining

[36] Walter C. Reckless, "The Distribution of Commercialized Vice in the City: a Sociological Analysis," in Ernest W. Burgess (ed.), *The Urban Community* (Chicago: 1926), pp. 196–197.

soldiers and sailors and other guests and allegedly turning their earnings over to the landlord who was taken into custody and held on serious charges after the two children told police the story of their two week orgy in the alleged brothel.[37]

Another adjustment that is made, though with much less frequency, is common law marriage. There is reason to believe that many of the persons recorded as "married" in census returns are not so in fact.[38] Such common law marriages are often of long duration, as in the following case described by the *Mid-Town Journal*:

A romance which began six years ago in which the participants loved each other well but not wisely ended in Warren ave. police station cells after complaints and investigation by police and social organizations into the marital status of a couple, the parents of four children, living in harmony, but in alleged violation of the morals laws, on which charges they were booked when taken into custody by police.[39]

Associational patterns such as these would be inconceivable in a community characterized by solidarity and moral consensus. It is significant that in the North End, where the objective physical setting of the community is far worse than in the South End, violations of morals laws are very few in number. There the identification of Italians with an integrated value system, and the solidarity which such persons have toward local Italian associations, utterly precludes the moral license which characterizes the South End. Slum conditions as such are not responsible for amoral activity. Rather it is the socio-economic character of a community — its age and sex composition, its marital status, income level, and population stability — that most tangibly correlates with cultural anomie and its amoral consequences. And this socio-economic make-up is conditional upon an historically unique structuring of kinship and occupational relations without which there would not even exist a rooming house area with its anonymity, transiency, and poverty.

[37] *Mid-Town Journal,* October 1, 1943.
[38] Zorbaugh found that in the Lower East Side of Chicago fully 60 per cent of persons living as couples were not legally married. *Op. cit.,* p. 100.
[39] *Mid-Town Journal,* November 26, 1943.

It is worth repeating at this point that much of the amoral activity which characterizes the South End is attributable to outsiders. Most of the elderly people in the district, and undoubtedly many of the younger residents as well, have staunchly maintained their personality integration around values which are esteemed by the larger society. For them life in a poverty-stricken and vice-ridden rooming house district has been dictated by financial and marital circumstances, and they remain wholly aloof from the amoral activities which surround them. What matters most, however, is the fact that the very transiency of these people, their very heterogeneity, and their very lack of "legitimized" status in terms of family participation, creates a situation in which moral sanctions are utterly ineffective. There is not the stability of personal relationships nor the consensus upon values which are so essential to social control. In their absence persons whose socialization has been deficient, so far as inculcation of moral inhibitions is concerned, are attracted to an area in which anonymity and transiency give an immunity to the moral and legal offender. Thus the distinctive socio-economic character of a rooming house district provides a suitable "medium" for the emergence of amoral activities.

Certain theoretical implications of this point are rather interesting. The thought occurs that perhaps the functional requirements of a stable community, considered as a social system, may establish definite limits to the amount of spatial mobility which can be "tolerated." Possibly a degree of mobility in excess of such limits is inherently disruptive to certain associational processes that are functionally necessary to a community. Beyond these limits the very maintenance of the community's identity as a going social system may be threatened. It does seem evident that a "real" community — one in which the behavior of individuals accords with accepted moral values — is only possible where there is some degree of spatial fixity between members.[40] The ramifications of this hypothesis would lead us rather far afield from our immediate problem and it is enough now to have merely taken note of it.

For the present it is more important to realize that the localization of social anomie such as typifies the South End rooming

[40] Acknowledgment is due Mr. Luke M. Smith for much of this insight.

house district is a locational phenomenon which cannot be understood in terms of the methodologically rationalistic premises. To be sure, the rooming house dweller is very rational in his selection of a place in which to live. So, too, the relation of space to his achievement of ends is largely that of an impediment. But these two factors gain their locational significance only by virtue of a particular kinship and occupational structure which has created the rooming house dweller as a social type. The things about which the rooming house dweller is rational and the particular way in which space impedes his attainment of ends are predicated upon the peculiar nature of his requirements as a particular kind of "social system." And to understand that we have to know the kinship and occupational patterns in terms of which the rooming house dweller has his being.

CHAPTER IX

SOME IMPLICATIONS AND APPLICATIONS OF A
CULTURAL ECOLOGY

OUR SURVEY of land use in central Boston has followed a certain logic. First we considered the variability of spatial patterns taken on by land uses both past and present within the larger metropolitan area. Our purpose was to find out how real were the uniform patterns that have been set down by the idealized descriptive schemes. Then we proceeded to an analysis of certain communities and ancient historical sites within Boston. Here we were interested in learning whether space is always put to its most economic use according to the empirically rationalistic formula. Finally we turned to the commercial core of the Boston metropolitan area and to two communities that have been peculiarly affected by its expansion. Here we wished to discover whether locational processes could properly be abstracted away from a cultural context as the methodologically rationalistic theories had claimed.

In every case our findings were negative. Land use patterns within the metropolitan area have been much too variable to warrant our forcing them into simple concentric or sector schemes, at least for purposes of rigorous scientific analysis. Similarly the frequency with which spatial areas, sometimes well suited to occupancy by highly economic uses, are maintained in dis-economic uses, seriously challenges the empirically rationalistic theories. For one thing, those theories fail to account for the persistence and recuperation of dis-economic land uses. Moreover they fail to explain why such uses may have a real utility for the community. In the case of Beacon Hill, the historic sites, and the North End we have seen that space may become the symbol for certain values which, embodied in the end-repertoires of social systems, give rise to locational processes that defy a strictly economic analysis. Finally the culturally contingent character of locational processes as shown by certain commercial and residential land uses, sheds doubt upon the "purity" of the methodologically rationalistic theories. Investigation of areas like the retail center of Boston, the Back Bay, and the South End has demonstrated that rational land use is itself contingent upon a particular value system. The resulting locational processes do not at all follow "naturally" from the character of social systems as disparate beings nor from space as a physical phenomenon. Apparently the very nature of social systems as locational agents and of spatial distance as an impediment derives from historically unique values which may not be the same in different societies.

Closer examination of these findings shows that they all point to a single factor as the one which is missing in the older theories. That is the cultural component in spatial adaptation. Despite superficial differences between the idealized descriptive schemes, the empirically rationalistic theories, and the methodologically rationalistic theories, there is a common denominator to all of them, viz., their exclusion of the cultural component. All of them invest physical space with a "non-cultural givenness" and all of them consider social systems as passive, compliant and disparate adapters. Now if the conclusions that we have drawn from our empirical survey are at all correct it would seem that this theoretical construct is invalid or else sterile. Spatiality, we have found, is not only an impediment but may be a symbol as well. This symbolic quality is referable only to a system of social values through which space may become invested with certain meaningful properties.' More than this, the very impeditiveness of space itself does not reside in it as a physical phenomenon but rather in the costfulness which it imposes upon social systems that have to deal with it. In other words, impeditiveness is a function not only of physical space but also of the make-up of the social systems which must deal with it. This constitution of social systems is itself the product of a particular value system which defines the very being and conditions of survival for those social systems. Thus both the character of space and the make-up of social systems are of cultural origin. From this it would seem to follow that the cultural component is central to locational processes. Only in terms of this component can we fully understand why land is put to the uses to which it is. In terms of it, land can be put to uneconomic and even dis-economic uses — all because certain values have become attached to a locality and have in that way found symbolic representation. In terms of it, too, land gains its impeditive character, by which particular social systems cannot function unless they find suitable locations. Obviously a variable so important as this one must be systematically incorporated in ecological theory.

This is the point to which our study has led us. It has not been designed to lead us any further, for that would be a separate study by itself. But we are obliged, if we are to make of our findings something constructive, to suggest certain lines of development by which the cultural component can be integrated into a systematic ecological theory. We are also obliged to indicate, at least briefly, some of the practical implications of our findings, with special reference to the Boston Hub. Several ideas, all in some degree supported by our data, present themselves.

Probably the most important of them is the idea that ecological theory must take as its point of departure the community as a real social system, having certain functional requirements for its maintenance of identity. Even a nominalistic collectivity like the South End is a community, for it represents a stable *Gestalt* of associational processes articulated by physical space. So too the larger collectivity comprised by Boston is a community and as such possesses a sociological reality. The functional requirements of a community may be viewed as localized counterparts to the more inclusive value system of a society. In the prevailing contractualistic regime of western society such spatially-relevant functions as transportation, retailing, manufacturing, and residence are paramount. Under a value system which lay primary stress upon symbolic relationships between man and the transcendental — for instance certain "theocentric" cultures — worship, ceremony, priestly housing, and burial of the dead might be the main land use requirements. Many other variations are possible. But in all of them it is important to consider the community as a going social system whose functioning requires, among other things, such an allocation of space to various ends as comports with its maintenance of identity. The "terms" for its maintenance of identity will of course be laid down by the more inclusive value system of the society and will be different according to whether the city's *raison d'être* is primarily commercial, or religious, or military. Under each of these, however, there is a problem of allocating space. In such allocation there must always be a *proportionalization of ends*. This arises out of the fact that every community has a multiplicity of component ends, and not merely one or a few ends. Hence it becomes necessary to achieve a certain "balance of sacrifices" in order that every component end of the community will in some degree be attained.

There is of course nothing particularly new in this idea of proportionality in the allocation of space to various functional requirements of a city. Indeed it lies at the very basis of all city planning, as we shall presently see. One need only recall Aristotle's list of urban requirements (food, arts, arms, revenue, religion, and courts), each with its proper spatial arrangement, to realize that proportional allocation of space to city functions has long been recognized by ecologists and "pre-ecologists." [1]

Let us then imagine a city that is made up of certain ends defined for it by the value system of the society in which that city exists. We can postulate that there will be an hypothetical point at which the amount and "kind" [2] of space devoted to a particular end or function balances off with the spatial requirements of each other end or function comprising the city. At this point the total deprivation of all the ends comprising the system is at a minimum. It is important to recognize that this "end-deprivation" is not synonymous with "cost" in the economic sense of the word, since it refers not only to dearth of scarce goods but also to thwarting of intangible and non-empirical ends which are just as real functional requirements of a city. All of these ends and functional requirements must be attained, yet no one of them can be pursued to an unlimited degree lest others be unduly deprived. That point along the "deprivation continuum" of a particular end, at which point the degree of deprivation comports with a minimal deprivation of all other ends comprising the community, may be called point *x*. Now, by definition, any deviation away from *x* will entail increased deprivation to one or more of the other ends comprising the community as a system. Thus an allocation of too much space to park and recreational facilities

---

[1] See: Aristotle, *Politics* (tr. by William Ellis), Everyman's Library (New York: 1919), Book VII, chaps. 9–12.

[2] In terms of accessibility and meaningful fittedness to the end in question.

will obstruct certain other requirements of the city as a functioning social system, such as commerce or manufacturing. Likewise the allocation of too little space to park and recreational facilities will obstruct the "best" functioning of the community as a system. Reasoning deductively, then, it may be suggested that departure from point *x* in either direction as to degree of deprivation of a particular end is accompanied by a *progressive* increase in deprivation to the system as a whole — more specifically, to one or more of the other ends comprising the system. The relationship may be diagrammed as follows:

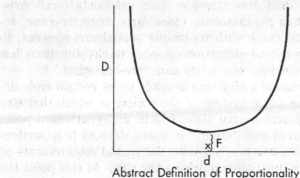

Abstract Definition of Proportionality

FIGURE 20

In the figure, *d* indicates deprivation of a particular spatially contingent end; *D* indicates deprivation of all the other ends comprising the system. At *x* along the *d* continuum the overall functioning of the system is being least obstructed, or, to put the same thing positively, the overall functioning is being most fully attained. Just enough space in terms of area, and just the right distribution of space in terms of suitability (accessibility or meaningful congruence) to the respective ends, has been allocated to the several ends comprising the system as to comport with the "best" — i.e., least thwarted — functioning of the system. Departure from *x* entails increasing deprivation to the system as a whole, and the greater the departure the greater the *proportional* increase in deprivation; in other words, the relationship is an exponential one. Symbolically it may be defined as follows:

$$D = k(d - x)^{2m} + F$$

K and m are constants for whatever particular social system is being depicted.[3]

This, then, is a highly deductive definition of proportionality in the allocation of space to the various spatially contingent ends that comprise a community as a social system. It is logically predicated upon our conception of the community as a reality *sui generis*, composed of a number of spatially contingent ends (as well as other ends that are wholly autonomous of spatiality) all of which must be in some degree attained if the community is to function and maintain its identity as a system. Along with this theoretical construct there are a number of important logical corollaries. In the first place it is necessary to recall our previous deductions made in regard to the variable contingency of different ends upon space. Which ends are most contingent upon space is a matter of cultural definition. In mediaeval cities defense was one of the principal municipal functions and such subsystems and activities as pertained to military operations were highly contingent upon what was for them an optimal location. They therefore became spatially preëmptive activities. In a contractualistic value system, on the other hand, highly specialized exchange functions represent the principal *raison d'être* of a city. Hence retailing becomes one of the more spatially contingent activities. As such it assumes a certain preëmptive role in contractualistic land use patterns. In both cases the unequal contingency upon space as between various urban functions means a differentiation between spatially preëmptive and spatially residual functions. Hence in any proportionalizing of land uses a city will, insofar as it approaches our deductive construct, tend to assign "priority" to the spatially preëmptive functions. Failure to do so will represent a deviation from point x in our diagram and will manifest itself in the form of strains and conflicts among rival land uses.

A second important theoretical corollary to our deductive definition of proportionality is what Zipf has aptly termed the "in-

---

[3] Symbolic representation such as this does not by itself add anything to our knowledge of the phenomenon, but is merely another way of defining it. Sometimes, however, it affords possibilities of new insights and more inclusive integrations not otherwise conceivable. Particular acknowledgment for aid in this formulation is due Mr. Richard F. Arens, Teaching Fellow in Mathematics at Harvard University, and Mr. William J. Firey.

tegrality of territory." Without committing ourselves to his specific theory we can agree with his generalization that a social system — whether a nation, a region, or a city — does function "best" when it has sufficient territory at its disposal so that all of its spatially contingent functions find spatial articulation.[4] Boston is an interesting case of a community which lacks "integrality of territory." Its corporate limits are so laid out that many of its proper functions as a community have been appropriated by suburban communities. Viewed analytically this represents a situation in which the "deprivation" of certain functional requirements consequent upon the pursuit of other functional requirements is not distributed evenly over the real community comprised by Greater Boston. Instead certain deprivations impinge wholly upon corporate Boston whereas the complementary ends are spatially articulated outside the city's corporate limits. Expressed crudely, one might say that people who live in the suburbs have all the advantages of participation in Greater Boston, but none of the disadvantages. Boston would have integrality of territory only if suburbanites shared some of the welfare and relief costs, highway and transit costs, and other such functional requirements which are inextricable corollaries of the greater community in which those suburbanites themselves participate.[5] The implications of this for metropolitan planning are profound and must receive some consideration before we conclude our analysis.

The final corollary to our deductive construct is the problem, dealt with in Chapter IV, of utility to a community *versus* utility to the component members of a community. It was Pareto's insight to have shown that these need not coincide at all, except at a certain point which he called Q. Now, it is possible that our theory of proportionality permits a more exact definition of the relationship between utility of the whole and utility of the part. Briefly it may be suggested that below the minimal point x on the d continuum of our diagram, every accretion in utility to a subsystem correlates with an accretion in the utility to a system. Beyond x, however, further accretions in utility to a subsystem entail

[4] Cf. George Kingsley Zipf, *National Unity and Disunity* (Bloomington: 1941), pp. 33, 201ff.

[5] "Second Prize Program," *The Boston Contest of 1944* (Boston: 1945), p. 30.

a progressive disutility or deprivation to the system as a whole. The reasoning behind this hypothesis is simple. Each end or functional requirement of a community, whether retailing, worship, manufacturing, or residence, becomes the very reason for being of a lesser system. Thus, retailing can properly be viewed as a requirement for a community's maintenance of identity. In that sense it is an end for the community *per se*. But on another level that end becomes the very reason for being of a subsystem. The community "need" for retailing becomes the functionally specific end of a host of stores and markets. Now clearly the more space which a city allocates to retailing and the better such space is located relative to accessibility, the more stores it can have and the more fully it can attain its functional requirements in the way of retailing. Thus increasing utility of the subsystems (stores) coincides with increasing utility of the system (the community). But a point will eventually be reached (point *x* on our diagram) at which further allocation of space to business will unduly deprive the city of space which is necessary for other functional requirements, such as recreation or the expression of sentiments. Beyond this point further increases in the utility of subsystems (stores) consequent upon further allocation of space to business purposes will entail a decrease in the utility of the community as a whole.

The theory of proportionality thus suggests itself as a possible avenue for ecological systematization. Unlike the deterministic schemes formulated by Burgess, Hoyt, McKenzie, Park, Weber, and others, the theory of proportionality makes of the cultural component its *point d'appui*. This it does through taking the community as its central variable and noting which of its constituent ends (whether interests, values, or functions) are spatially contingent. That of course is dependent entirely upon the larger value system or culture within which that city has its being, as well as upon the lesser values which are unique to that particular city. Knowing the relative contingency upon space of the various ends comprising the community it is then possible to specify which are preëmptive and which are residual land uses. Likewise it is possible, at least analytically, to detect the strains and disfunctions which accrue to a city through departing from a strict proportionality in its allocation of space to various land uses. The idea of territorial integrality, too, points up certain foci of strain resulting from a faulty legal delineation of territory relative to the functions which a community must perform and for which it needs space.

When these deductions are put to a pragmatic test there emerge some rather significant implications for land use planning. In this respect our empirical analysis of land use in the Boston Hub gains a new and practical meaning. We have seen that the community, in our case Boston, can be taken as a reality *sui generis*. Boston, in other words, does possess a communal reality. As such it has functional requirements of its own which are not the same as the functional requirements of retailers, suburbanites, roomers, or shippers taken individually. These community requirements should be embodied in any realistic metropolitan plan.

Specifically, one such requirement has been found to be symbolic representation. Boston, more than most other cities, has a great many historic sites which serve as "reminders" of its civic identity. The presence of old colonial dwellings, venerable cemeteries, ancient public buildings, hallowed churches, and distinctive neighborhoods exerts a definite civic-building influence upon the residents of a community. Out of such an influence emerges the kind of sentiments upon which real citizen participation depends — loyalty, a feeling of belongingness, and a purposefulness that goes beyond individual ambitions. Boston needs these sentiments. Through them it can win the interest and support of its people in civic improvements. Without them it can only appeal to the varied special interests of pressure groups to accomplish its objectives. Sentiment is one of the surest community-building forces that any city can have. And since sentiments are so readily sustained by objective symbols, like historic sites, it behooves Boston to preserve and restore those which it has. No city or metropolitan plan would be complete which overlooked this. To be sure, the allocation of space to symbolic uses does diminish the amount of space that can be put to productive uses. But productivity, we have seen, is not the only functional requirement of a community. Symbolic representation is just as real a requirement, for reasons indicated in our fourth chapter. A comprehensive city plan will be one that strikes a balance between these two requirements, according to the theory of proportionality in land use.

One should not forget, moreover, that some tangible economic benefits can accrue to Boston through the preservation and restoration of its historic sites. To begin with, these sites are national shrines. They attract tourists and travelers from all over the country. In this way they are a source of income which might be many times increased if suitable improvements were made on them and on their immediate environs.[6] But, more than this, the proper landscaping and architectural treatment of some of these places might be a means of reëstablishing the Hub as a desirable residential area. We have already seen that for several decades the Hub has been losing its population to the suburbs. This has been particularly true of the population that has means and is therefore best able to pay for essential municipal functions. Somehow an attraction must be provided that will restore the Hub as a desirable place in which to live. In the words of one prize-winning plan drawn up for Greater Boston: "It is evident that the urban center must be made more attractive to the population to draw desirable citizens back to the city center."[7]

This plan goes on to suggest a strategy of "infiltration" as the one most likely to effect a rehabilitation of residential areas.[8] A clue as to just how such infiltration might be accomplished is afforded by the Beacon Hill case. There a handful of persons, quietly developing one old house after another but maintaining a certain architectural consonance for the whole neighborhood, brought about the rejuvenation of an area that had been fast deteriorating. In all likelihood similar methods might be used with advantage in the rejuvenation of other portions of central Boston. Thus the North End, with its Paul Revere House, Old North Church, Copp's Hill Burying-ground, and other such historic symbols, might be rehabilitated as a desirable apartment house district for young couples or single people working downtown. Abortive revivals such as took place in the South End could well be anticipated and helped to a more successful consumma-

---

[6] See *The Boston Contest of 1944*, especially "First Prize Program," p. 20, and "Third Prize Program," p. 87.

[7] *Ibid.*, "First Prize Program," p. 18.

[8] *Ibid.*, "First Prize Program," p. 19.

tion. Through such infiltration whole neighborhoods might be reclaimed and made attractive to people of moderate means. In this way the steady loss to central Boston of its revenue-yielding land uses would be arrested and reversed. Thus the symbolic qualities of space may become actual economic assets to the city. They should be capitalized upon by measures which will preserve their symbolic character.

Foremost among such measures would be assessment and tax adjustments, zoning alterations, and the authorization and promotion of urban redevelopment corporations.[9] These are drastic measures and could not possibly be taken up individually. They would only succeed as parts of an overall, long-range planning program which would in some degree shift the incidence of taxation away from real property and onto income; would put assessment procedure on an equitable and scientific basis; and would convert zoning from a negative, "keep out" kind of instrument to a positive, constructive program.

Once again the case of Beacon Hill illustrates the importance of these measures in preserving symbolic areas. Had it not been for the rezoning of the Hill to lower height limits and to exclusively residential use (through the strenuous efforts of the residents themselves) it is unlikely that the revival begun in 1905 could have endured to the present time. Thus protective zoning was an indispensable element in the preservation of this symbolic area. Similarly, the actual redemption of the Hill was brought about by a group of persons operating, privately and without rights of police power to be sure, in much the same manner as would an authorized urban redevelopment corporation. Official promotion of such agencies could accomplish an even more extensive reclamation of old sites and neighborhoods. Finally, the importance of assessment and tax adjustments for the preservation of symbolic areas can be seen in what is happening to Beacon Hill today. Once again the Hill has begun to show incipient signs of retrogression. Well-to-do families are more and more being deterred from living on the Hill because of the exorbitant assessments on property, far in excess of true market values. If this policy were long continued Beacon Hill might yet become a cheap rooming house district like the South End. Were that to happen,

[9] Cf. *loc. cit.;* also, "Third Prize Program," p. 101.

Boston would have lost, along with the Back Bay, one of its few income-yielding residential districts. But an intelligent planning program can save Beacon Hill for Boston. People of means do like to live there, owing to the Hill's historical associations. Preserved as an upper class residential district Beacon Hill can yet remain an enduring source of revenue for the city treasury if it is not over-assessed and over-taxed. But this presupposes a complete overhauling of present assessment and taxation practices in the city of Boston. Such a step is essential to the redemption of all central Boston. Without it the city can look forward to a continued loss of its population and a continued decline in its taxable values. In this measure, and the others that have been proposed, is of course implied the idea that symbolic representation is a real function of space and that, properly balanced off with other spatially-contingent functions of the community, it can enhance the utility of the larger whole. The theory of proportionality does lend a certain plausibility to this assumption and our earlier empirical analyses give a factual support to it.

There are some further practical implications that follow from the idea of proportionality in land use. Consider the problem: how large an area must be encompassed in a city plan? So far as accessibility to the Hub is concerned, Cambridge is more a part of Boston than is Mattapan. Yet Cambridge is an independent city, with its own zoning ordinance and its own city plan, over which Boston has no authority whatsoever. Can any plan succeed which applies only to separate municipalities, irrespective of their real functional interdependence? Our previous analysis points to a negative answer. Boston as a functioning community far overruns its legal boundaries. Hence any plan which fails to encompass the territory that is functionally integrated to the Hub will very likely fall short of its objectives. The idea of territorial integrality, which follows logically from the theory of proportionality, must be incorporated in an overall metropolitan plan.

The very fact that there already exist several metropolitan authorities, all designed to cope with one or another of the problems which confront Greater Boston, testifies to a "functional requirement" which cannot be met within the existing governmental structure, which arbitrarily splits up the real metropolitan unit. There is the Boston Metropolitan District (concerned mainly with transit), the Metropolitan District Commission (administering metropolitan sewerage, water, and parks, with its own police force), the Metropolitan District Water Supply Commission, the Metropolitan District Sewer Construction Commission, and the Metropolitan Boston Smoke Abatement District. There is little coördination between any of these agencies and their territories are all different from one another. Moreover their authority is limited to only a few of the problems which call for concerted metropolitan planning. A plan for Boston must be a plan for Greater Boston, or it will not work. It is significant that all three of the main prize-winning programs submitted to the *Boston Contest of 1944* propose a single Metropolitan Authority, District, or Region with power of one degree or another over police, health and sanitation, recreational facilities, transportation, welfare, and planning. The plans differ as to the precise powers, jurisdiction, and make-up that should be given such an Authority, but they are unanimous in recognizing the need of developing an administrative and planning unity for the area embraced in the real functioning Boston. Such an Authority should be empowered to revaluate all property under its jurisdiction so as to remedy the gross discrepancies in assessments as between Boston and the surrounding towns. The tax rate should also be equalized over the whole metropolitan area. Only thus can a proportion be achieved between the territorial layout of services received and the territorial layout of taxes incurred. Naturally the very assumption by the Metropolitan Authority of certain powers now dispersed among various municipalities will serve to rectify the present territorial unbalance between services needed and ability to pay. Municipal Boston is so delineated that its functional requirements far exceed its ability to pay for those requirements. Only a political unit that corresponds to the territorial integrality of Greater Boston can avert bankruptcy to the metropolitan core, with all the dire consequences for the entire area that would attend such a debacle.

If we turn to another corollary of our theory of proportionality we find further practical implications for metropolitan planning. There can be no gainsaying that slums represent a disutility to the community as a whole, whether measured in terms of health and welfare costs, the difference between taxes yielded and services required, or any other index. Yet individual tenement buildings are often a lucrative source of profit to their owners. Clearly slums represent a departure from proportionality in land use, in that the maximum utility of the community, as a system, is being sacrificed to the maximum utility of tenement owners, as subsystems. It follows then that slum clearance will not generally be achieved by appealing to the interests of individual tenement proprietors. It can only be achieved through the use of police power, either directly by the state or city, or through such authorized agencies as urban redevelopment corporations. Even when a dilapidated building is no longer yielding any profit to its owner there is very little incentive for him to remove it. The actual costs of demolition and replacement may exceed the amount of funds that he can raise. As a result the building stands, barely meeting its minimum operating costs and blighting the whole neighborhood in which it is located.[10] The proposal has recently been advanced that buildings be insured for their life expectancy, with the amount of the policy being paid the owners when costs of maintenance exceed potential income.[11] Through such property life insurance as well as through urban redevelopment corporations and the enforcement of higher building standards, it should be possible to rehabilitate the slum districts of the Hub.

Of course every program of slum clearance must reckon with the future housing of displaced persons and families. To force low-income families out of one slum, so that they must locate elsewhere and create a new center of blight, merely creates two problems where there was one before. Our analysis of the South End, for instance, showed that the provision of cheap, single furnished rooms for transient, detached and impoverished individuals was a functional necessity for every large city. Any proposal for the demolition of existing structures in the South End would have to reckon with the serious social problems that might ensue — the dispersal of vice to other parts of the city, the conversion of single-family dwellings to cheap rooming houses, etc. Boston, like every other large city, must plan with full knowledge that it will have a low-income, transient population which must be

[10] Herbert B. Dorau and Albert G. Hinman, *Urban Land Economics* (New York: 1928), p. 193.

[11] *The Boston Contest of 1944,* "Second Prize Program," p. 38.

housed. An intelligent plan will be one that accepts this fact and endeavors to maintain housing standards as high as possible and ameliorate the problems of vice that inevitably accompany such a population. A number of specific steps suggest themselves as meriting consideration in an overall metropolitan plan. So small a detail as parlor rooms might be a case in point. An ordinance requiring a common parlor room in every rooming house could go far toward mitigating social isolation in a district like the South End.[12] Moreover it would allow persons to bring callers to their residence without incurring the dangers and implications that follow from bringing guests of the opposite sex into one's own room. Finally, it would enable people to talk with one another without having to go to the tavern for a place to visit. Such an ordinance would of course impose an added cost upon landlords and landladies. However, if tax adjustments were made in line with our previous suggestions, so that *ad valorem* property taxation was no longer the principal source of municipal revenue, this added expense would be more than offset by the lower tax rate. The development of additional parks, the enactment and enforcement of higher housing standards (working realistically in terms of the physical structures already present), and possibly the construction of federally subsidized low rent "hotels" for transient men—these and similar steps might be followed in the redemption of such an area as the South End. The rehabilitation of tenement areas like East Boston, Charlestown, or the West End would involve very similar measures except that housing must here be planned for family units rather than for isolated individuals. Foremost among these measures should be subsidized low rent housing which would conform to approved standards of ground coverage and population density, additional parks and playgrounds, and perhaps the development of distinct neighborhood centers with their own collocations of stores and services.[13] Needless to say, any such program of rehabilitation will damage the interests of some groups within the community. But it will

[12] For this suggestion, made some thirty years ago, see Franklin Kline Fretz, *The Furnished Room Problem in Philadelphia* (Philadelphia: *circa* 1912), pp. 47–49.

[13] Recommended in the "First Prize Program," *The Boston Contest of 1944*, p. 19.

contribute immeasurably to the utility of the community as a whole and in that way restore a certain proportionality in the use of land.

Finally we may look to our last corollary of proportionality for a further insight into metropolitan planning. According to this corollary, which we arrived at through our analysis of the retail district of Boston, different kinds of social systems are unequally contingent upon spatial distance. In a contractualistic society such as our own, commercial activities and particularly retail stores depend upon a high degree of accessibility for their functioning. They thus become preëmptive land uses. Residences, on the other hand, varying with their rental value, become residual land uses. Other social activities can be ranged along the same continuum of preëmptiveness and residuality. Any city or metropolitan plan must recognize this unequal contingency upon space as between various urban functions. In laying out prospective zoning areas a city plan must assign priority to the preëmptive land uses if it is not to lay the basis for future strains and conflicts. But there is a proportion to be achieved even here. It is possible to assign too much space to the preëmptive land uses. It is also possible to misjudge what areas are best suited to the preëmptive land uses. A little of both seems to have taken place in Boston's zoning program. At the time the 1924 zoning ordinance was being prepared the assumption prevailed that commercial expansion would continue indefinitely and that most of this expansion would be to the southwest. Accordingly a great deal of the South End was zoned for general and local business, far beyond the space requirements of Boston commerce. Moreover business expansion actually took more of a westward than a southward course, heading into the Back Bay rather than the South End.[14] As a result 114.17 acres are now zoned for general business with only 26.89 acres being thus used. The consequences for residential land use in the South End are obvious. Property owners, anticipating future sales to business or office establishments, inflate values beyond their real worth. Moreover, any incentive to repair and modernize dwellings is destroyed, since the property owner has no assurance that a store will not locate

[14] Boston City Planning Board, *Building a Better Boston* (Boston: 1941), pp. 30–31.

near by and damage his home for residential purposes.[15] Thus departure from proportionality in land zoning has worsened the blight which afflicts the South End. Boston of course is no worse in this respect than many other American cities, all of whom prepared zoning programs at a time when little was known about the actual space requirements of different kinds of land uses.[16]

The fact does remain, though, that priority must be assigned retail businesses if a proportion in urban land use is to be achieved. In this respect Boston's retail district has become so laid out as to seriously depart from such a proportion. Owing to the position of the Common, wedging directly into the heart of the downtown area, Boston's shopping district has assumed an elongated pattern. This pattern seriously reduces the accessibility of stores to prospective shoppers, owing to the walking distance that it imposes upon people. Much could be done to mitigate this inconvenience through proper planning. One architect has suggested that a civic center be located at the corner of the Common which wedges into the Tremont-Boylston street intersection.[17] Such a center would create a focus of high population flow which could tie together the two segments of the city's shopping district. Other measures to facilitate accessibility of retail stores might be undertaken. The construction of parking areas at convenient points in the Hub is almost essential to the preservation of downtown business. The elimination of narrow alleys in the Hub and the widening of main thoroughfares would contribute to the same end.[18] Through such measures the spatial requirements of retail business could be more adequately met than they have been, and some of the serious strains that beset the heart of the metropolitan area would thus be mitigated.

These are some of the practical implications of the theory to

[15] Loc. cit.

[16] See Harland Bartholomew, Urban Land Uses (Cambridge: 1932), pp. v–vi, 71–73, 77; Harold M. Mayer, "Patterns and Recent Trends of Chicago's Outlying Business Centers," Journal of Land and Public Utility Economics, 18: 4–16 (February, 1942), p. 15; George Le Roy Schmutz, "Economic Effects of Zoning," Annals of the American Academy of Political and Social Science, 155 (Part II): 172–177 (May, 1931), pp. 174–176.

[17] See "First Prize Program," The Boston Contest of 1944, p. 15.

[18] Loc. cit.; also "Second Prize Program," pp. 63–67; "Third Prize Program," p. 104, ibid.

which our survey has led us. They may not all be sound or feasible, and they may not all have been properly deduced from our theoretical construct, although every effort has been exerted to make them so. In any event they are suggestive avenues for urban redevelopment, not only of Boston, but of other cities as well. And they do represent the kind of pragmatic test to which any ecological theory must be adequate.

BIBLIOGRAPHY

BIBLIOGRAPHY

A. Books and Pamphlets Pertaining to Ecology

Alihan, Milla Aïssa, *Social Ecology* (New York: Columbia University Press, 1938).

Aristotle, *Politics* (New York: Everyman's Library, 1919).

Arkin, Herbert, and Raymond R. Colton, *An Outline of Statistical Methods,* fourth edition (New York: Barnes and Noble, Inc., 1939).

Babcock, Frederick M., *The Valuation of Real Estate* (New York: McGraw-Hill Book Co., Inc., 1932).

Bartholomew, Harland, *Urban Land Uses* (Cambridge: Harvard University Press, 1932).

Bernard, L. L., editor, *The Fields and Methods of Sociology* (New York: Ray Long and Richard R. Smith, Inc., 1934).

Black, John D., and Albert G. Black, *Production Organization* (New York: Henry Holt and Co., 1929).

Brunhes, Jean, *Human Geography* (New York: Rand McNally and Co., 1920).

Burgess, Ernest W., editor, *The Urban Community* (Chicago: University of Chicago Press, 1926).

Cooley, Charles Horton, *Human Nature and the Social Order* (New York: Charles Scribner's Sons, 1922).

Dawson, Carl A., and Warner E. Gettys, *An Introduction to Sociology* (New York: The Ronald Press Co., 1929).

Dean, William H., Jr., *The Theory of the Geographic Location of Economic Activities* (Ann Arbor: Edwards Bros., Inc., 1938).

Dorau, Herbert B., and Albert G. Hinman, *Urban Land Economics* (New York: The Macmillan Co., 1928).

Durkheim, Emile, *The Elementary Forms of the Religious Life,* translated by Joseph Ward Swain (London: G. Allen and Unwin Ltd., 1915).

Ely, Richard T., and George S. Wehrwein, *Land Economics* (New York: The Macmillan Co., 1940).

Ford, James, *Slums and Housing* (Cambridge: Harvard University Press, 1936).

Fretz, Franklin Kline, *The Furnished Room Problem in Philadelphia* (Philadelphia: University of Pennsylvania Press, 1912).

Gries, John M., and James Ford, *Home Finance and Taxation,* vol. II in the President's Conference on Home Building and Home Ownership (Washington: Published by the Conference, 1932).

Hoyt, Homer, *The Structure and Growth of Residential Neighborhoods in American Cities* (Washington: Federal Housing Administration, 1939).

Hurd, Richard M., *Principles of City Land Values* (New York: The Record and Guide, 1903).

Knight, Frank H., *The Ethics of Competition and Other Essays* (New York: Harper and Bros., 1935).

Lavedan, Pierre, *Qu'est-ce que l'Urbanisme?* (Paris: H. Lauren, 1926).

Linton, Ralph, *The Study of Man* (New York: D. Appleton-Century Co., 1936).

Malinowski, Bronislaw, *Coral Gardens and their Magic* (New York: American Book Co., 1935).

Maunier, René, *L'Origine et la Fonction Économique des Villes* (Paris: V. Giard and E. Brière, 1910).

McKenzie, R. D., *The Metropolitan Community* (New York: McGraw-Hill Book Co., 1933).

National Resources Committee, *Population Statistics, 2. State Data* (Washington: United States Government Printing Office, 1937).

Palander, Tord, *Beiträge zur Standortstheorie* (Uppsala: Almqvist and Wiksells boktryckeri, 1935).

Pareto, Vilfredo, *Mind and Society* (New York: Harcourt, Brace and Co., 1935).

Park, Robert E., and Ernest W. Burgess and R. D. McKenzie, *The City* (Chicago: University of Chicago Press, 1925).

Park, Robert E., editor, *An Outline of the Principles of Sociology* (New York: Barnes and Noble, Inc., 1939).

Parsons, Talcott, *The Structure of Social Action* (New York: McGraw-Hill Book Co., 1937).

Plato, *The Dialogues of Plato,* translated by B. Jowett (New York: Charles Scribner and Co., 1871).

Ratcliffe, Richard U., *The Problem of Retail Site Selection,* Michigan Business Studies, vol. 9, no. 1 (Ann Arbor: School of Business Administration, Bureau of Business Research, University of Michigan, 1939).

Schütz, Alfred, *Der Sinnhafte Aufbau der Sozialen Welt* (Wien: J. Springer, 1932).

Sert, José Luis, *Can Our Cities Survive?* (Cambridge: Harvard University Press, 1942).

Simmel, Georg, *Soziologie,* third edition (München, Duncker and Humblot, 1923).

Sombart, Werner, *Der Moderne Kapitalismus,* first edition (Leipzig: Duncker and Humblot, 1902).

Sorokin, Pitirim A., *Contemporary Sociological Theories* (New York: Harper and Bros., 1928).

——, *Social and Cultural Dynamics* (New York: American Book Co., 1937 and 1941).

——, *Social Mobility* (New York, Harper and Bros., 1927).

——, *Sociocultural Causality Space Time* (Durham, North Carolina: Duke University Press, 1943).

——, Charles J. Galpin, and Carle C. Zimmerman, *A Systematic Source Book in Rural Sociology* (Minneapolis: University of Minnesota Press, 1930).

Steiner, Jesse F., *Readings in Human Ecology,* mimeographed (Seattle: University of Washington, 1936).

Thornthwaite, C. Warren, *Internal Migration in the United States* (Philadelphia: University of Pennsylvania Press, 1934).

Weber, Alfred, *Theory of the Location of Industries,* translated by Carl Joachim Friedrich (Chicago: University of Chicago Press, 1929).

Weimer, Arthur M., and Homer Hoyt, *Principles of Urban Real Estate* (New York: The Ronald Press Co., 1939).

Zimmerman, Carle C., *The Changing Community* (New York: Harper and Bros., 1938).

——, *Consumption and Standards of Living* (New York: D. Van Nostrand Co., Inc., 1936).

Zipf, George Kingsley, *National Unity and Disunity* (Bloomington, Indiana: The Principia Press, Inc., 1941).

B. Articles Pertaining to Ecology

Angell, Robert C., "Discussion," *American Sociological Review,* 1: 189–192 (April, 1936).

Chapple, Eliot D., "Measuring Human Relations: an Introduction to the Study of the Interaction of Individuals," *Genetic Psychology Monographs,* 22: 3–147 (1940).

Davie, Maurice R., "The Pattern of Urban Growth," in George Peter Murdock, editor, *Studies in the Science of Society* (New Haven: Yale University Press, 1937).

Engländer, Oskar, "Kritisches und Positives zu einer allgemeinen reinen Lehre vom Standort," *Zeitschrift für Volkswirtschaft und Sozialpolitik,* 5 (n.s.): 435–505 (1926).

——, "Standort," in *Handwörterbuch der Staatswissenschaften,* fourth edition (Jena: Verlag von Gustav Fischer, 1926).

Gettys, Warner E., "Human Ecology and Social Theory," *Social Forces,* 18: 469–476 (May, 1940).

Gibbard, Harold A., "The Status Factor in Residential Successions," *American Journal of Sociology*, 46: 835–842 (May, 1941).

Haig, Robert Murray, "Towards an Understanding of the Metropolis — the Assignment of Activities to Areas in Urban Regions," *Quarterly Journal of Economics*, 40: 402–434 (May, 1926).

Maunier, René, "La Distribution Géographique des Industries," *Revue Internationale de Sociologie*, 7 (July, 1908).

Mayer, Harold M., "Patterns and Recent Trends of Chicago's Outlying Business Centers," *Journal of Land and Public Utility Economics*, 18: 4–16 (February, 1942).

McKenzie, R. D., "Human Ecology," *Encyclopedia of the Social Sciences* (New York: Macmillan and Co., 1933).

Park, Robert E., "Human Ecology," *American Journal of Sociology*, 42: 1–15 (July, 1936).

———, "Succession, an Ecological Concept," *American Sociological Review*, 1: 171–179 (April, 1936).

Parsons, Talcott, "Age and Sex in the Social Structure of the United States," *American Sociological Review*, 7: 604–616 (October, 1942).

———, "The Kinship System of the Contemporary United States," *American Anthropologist*, 45: 22–38 (January–March, 1943).

———, "The Motivation of Economic Activities," *The Canadian Journal of Economic and Political Science*, 6: 187–202 (May, 1940).

———, "The Professions and Social Structure," *Social Forces*, 17: 457–467 (May, 1939).

Pfeifer, Gottfried, "Über raumwirtschaftliche Begriffe und Vorstellungen und ihre bisherige Anwendung in der Geographie und Wirtschaftswissenschaft," *Geographische Zeitschrift*, 34: 321–340, 411–425 (1928).

Predöhl, Andreas, "Das Standortsproblem in der Wirtschaftstheorie," *Weltwirtschaftliches Archiv*, 21: 294–321 (April, 1925).

———, "The Theory of Location in its Relation to General Economics," *Journal of Political Economy*, 36: 371–390 (June, 1928).

Quinn, James A., "The Burgess Zonal Hypothesis and its Critics," *American Sociological Review*, 5: 210–218 (April, 1940).

———, "Human Ecology and Interactional Ecology," *American Sociological Review*, 5: 713–722 (October, 1940).

———, "The Hypothesis of Median Location," *American Sociological Review*, 8: 148–156 (April, 1943).

Schmid, Calvin F., "Land Values as an Ecological Index," *Research Studies of the State College of Washington*, 9: 16–36 (March, 1941).

Simmel, Georg, "The Persistence of Social Groups," *American Journal of Sociology,* 3: 662–698 (March, 1898); 3: 829–836 (May, 1898); 4: 35–50 (July, 1898).

——, "Über räumliche Projektionen socialer Formen," *Zeitschrift für Sozialwissenschaft,* 6: 287–302 (1903).

Sombart, Werner, "Einige Anmerkungen zur Lehre vom Standort der Industrien," *Archiv für Sozialwissenschaft und Sozialpolitik,* 33: 748–758 (May, 1910).

Usher, Abbott Payson, "Comment se Placent les Usines. L'example des Etats-Unis," *Annales d'Histoire Économique et Sociale,* 1: 524–550 (October, 1929).

Weber, Alfred, "Industrielle Standortslehre," in *Grundriss der Sozialökonomik,* vol. 6 (Tübingen: J. C. B. Mohr, 1914).

Zimmerman, Carle C., "The Evolution of the American Community," *American Journal of Sociology,* 46: 809–817 (May, 1941).

C. Books and Pamphlets Pertaining to Boston

Abbott, Edith, *The Tenements of Chicago, 1908–1935* (Chicago: University of Chicago Press, 1936).

The Beacon Hill District: Similar to the Washington Square Greenwich Village Section; no author, publisher, or publication date indicated; pamphlet available in Landscape Architecture Library, Harvard University.

Beebe, Lucius, *Boston and the Boston Legend* (New York: D. Appleton-Century Co., Inc., 1935).

Boston City Planning Board, *Building a Better Boston* (Boston: City Planning Board, 1941).

——, *Report on the Income and Cost of Six Districts in the City of Boston,* E. R. A. Project X2235–F2–104 (Boston: City Planning Board, 1934).

Boston Contest of 1944, The (Boston: Boston University Press, 1945).

Boston Council of Social Agencies, *Social Statistics by Census Tracts in Boston,* two volumes (Boston: published by the Council, 1935).

Boston's Growth (Boston: State Street Trust Co., 1910).

Bridgman, Thomas, *Memorials of the Dead in Boston* (Boston: B. B. Mussey and Co., 1853).

Brown, Abbie Farwell, *The Lights of Beacon Hill* (Boston: Houghton Mifflin Co., 1922).

Bushee, Frederick A., *Ethnic Factors in the Population of Boston,* Publications of the American Economic Association (New York: Macmillan and Co., 1903).

Chamberlain, Allen, *Beacon Hill, its Ancient Pastures and Early Mansions* (Boston: Houghton Mifflin and Co., 1925).

Chamberlin, Joseph Edgar, *The Boston Transcript, a History of its First Hundred Years* (Boston: Houghton Mifflin Co., 1930).

Child, Irvin L., *Italian or American?* (New Haven: Yale University Press, 1943).

Committee for the Preservation of Park Street Church, *The Preservation of Park Street Church, Boston* (Boston: published by the Committee, 1903).

Copeland, Robert Morris, *Essay and Plan for the Improvement of the City of Boston* (Boston: Lee and Shepard, 1872).

Curtis, John Gould, *History of the Town of Brookline, Mass.* (Boston: Houghton Mifflin Co., 1933).

Dorion, E. C. E., *The Redemption of the South End* (New York: The Abington Press, 1915).

DuWors, Richard E., "The Dominant Educational Area of Boston," manuscript (Boston: 1937).

Early, Eleanor, *And This is Boston!*, second edition (Boston: Houghton Mifflin Co., 1938).

Ellis, George E., *Bacon's Dictionary of Boston* (Boston: Houghton Mifflin Co., 1886).

Ennice, Ruth, "Back Bay" (Boston: unpublished master's thesis at Boston University, 1941).

Finance Commission of the City of Boston, *A Study of Certain of the Effects of Decentralization on Boston and Some Neighboring Cities and Towns,* reprint of City Document No. 56 (1941), Boston.

Greater Boston Community Council, Research Bureau, Community Studies, *The People of Boston and its Fifteen Health and Welfare Areas,* mimeographed bulletin (Boston: published by the Council, 1944).

Greene, Charlotte, *While on the Hill; a Stroll Down Chestnut Street* (Boston: The Four Seas Co., 1930).

Haven, Franklin, Alexander H. Rice, and Peleg W. Chandler, trustees, *A Statement in Regard to the Huntington Avenue Lands, in the City of Boston* (Boston: Trustees of the Huntington Avenue Lands, 1879).

Herlihy, Elisabeth M., editor, *Fifty Years of Boston* (Boston: published by the Tercentenary Committee, 1932).

Herndon, Richard, *Boston of To-Day* (Boston: Post Publishing Co., 1892).

History of the House of Hovey (Boston: C. F. Hovey Co., *circa* 1920).

Howe, M. A. De Wolfe, *Boston Common, Scenes from Four Centuries* (Cambridge: Riverside Press, 1910).

Huse, Charles Phillips, *The Financial History of Boston* (Cambridge: Harvard University Press, 1916).

The Inaugural Addresses of the Mayors of Boston (Boston: published by the City Registrar, 1896).

Kimball, Richard Bowland, *Christmas Eve on Beacon Hill* (Boston: Atlantic Monthly Press, Inc., 1918).

King, Moses, *The Back Bay District and the Vendome* (Boston: Hotel Vendome, 1881).

Lawrence, Robert Means, *Old Park Street and its Vicinity* (Boston: Houghton Mifflin Co., 1922).

Mangione, Jerre, *Mount Allegro* (Boston: Houghton Mifflin Co., 1943).

Mathews, Lois Kimball, *The Expansion of New England* (Boston: Houghton Mifflin Co., 1909).

McKeever, J. Ross, "The Beacon Hill District" (Cambridge: unpublished master's thesis at Massachusetts Institute of Technology, Architecture Library, 1935).

Otis, Harrison Gray, *An Address to the Members of the City Council on the Removal of the Municipal Government to the Old State House* (Boston: J. H. Eastburn, 1830).

Parad, Howard, "A Study in Social Science and Social Work Based Upon an Analysis of Two Roxbury Tenement Groups and the Surrounding District," unpublished honors' thesis, Harvard University, Area of Social Science, no date.

Proceedings of a Public Meeting Held at Faneuil Hall, June 7, 1876 (Boston: Rand, Avery and Co., 1876).

Report of a Committee of Citizens, *The Public Rights in Boston Common* (Boston: Rockwell and Churchill, 1877).

Report on a Survey of Business and Industrial Buildings in the City of Boston, 1935, E. R. A. Project No. X2235, F2, U46 (Boston: Boston City Planning Board, 1935).

Rosen, Ben, *The Trend of Jewish Population in Boston,* Monographs of Federated Jewish Charities of Boston, vol. 1, no. 1 (Boston: Federated Jewish Charities, 1921).

Rositter, William S., editor, *Days and Ways in Old Boston* (Boston: R. H. Stearns and Co., 1915).

Ross, M. D., *Estimate of the Financial Effect of the Proposed Reservation of Back-Bay Lands* (Boston: John Wilson and Son, 1861).

Samson, Josephine, *Celebrities of Louisburg Square* (Greenfield, Mass.: The Record Press, 1924).

Sartorio, Enrico C., *Social and Religious Life of Italians in America* (Boston: Christopher Publishing House, 1918).

The Seventy-Fifth Anniversary of the Consecration of Saint Paul's

Church, Boston, Sunday, May Twenty-six, 1895 (Boston: published by the parish, 1895).

Shackleton, Robert, *The Book of Boston* (Philadelphia: The Penn Publishing Co., 1916).

Shultz, John R., *Beacon Hill and the Carol Singers* (Boston: The Wood, Clarke Press, 1923).

Smith, Dexter, *Cyclopedia of Boston and Vicinity* (Boston: Cashin and Smith, 1886).

Snelling, George H., *Memorial, with Remarks and Letters, in Favor of a Modification of the Back Bay Plan,* reprint from Senate Document No. 186, 1859 (Boston: 1860).

Sullivan, T. R., *Boston New and Old* (Boston: Houghton Mifflin Co., 1912).

Tucker, Thomas W., *Bannisters Lane, 1708–1899* (Boston: Shepard Norwell and Co., 1899).

Urban Land Institute, *A Survey in Respect to the Decentralization of the Boston Central Business District* (Boston: published by the Institute, 1940).

Venticinque Anni di Missione fra gl'Immigrati Italiani di Boston, Mass., 1888–1913 (Milano: Tipografia Santa Lega Eucaristica, 1913).

Warner, W. Lloyd, and Paul S. Lunt, *The Social Life of a Modern Community* (New Haven: Yale University Press, 1941).

Wheildon, William W., *Sentry, or Beacon Hill; the Beacon and the Monument of 1635 and 1790* (Concord, Mass.: published by the author, 1877).

Whyte, William Foote, *Street Corner Society* (Chicago: University of Chicago Press, 1943).

Winsor, Justin, *The Memorial History of Boston* (Boston: J. R. Osgood and Co., 1880–1881).

Wirth, Louis, *The Ghetto* (Chicago: University of Chicago Press, 1928).

Wolfe, Albert Benedict, *The Lodging House Problem in Boston* (Cambridge: Harvard University Press, 1913).

Woods, Robert A., *Americans in Process* (Boston: Houghton Mifflin Co., 1903).

———, *The City Wilderness* (Boston: Houghton Mifflin Co., 1898).

D. ARTICLES PERTAINING TO BOSTON

Beacon Hill Association, Zoning Defence Committee, "The Menace to Beacon Hill," leaflet (Boston: 1927).

Brown, Abram English, "Beacon Hill," *The New England Magazine,* 28 (n.s.): 631–650 (August, 1903).

Brown, Frank Chouteau, "Boston's Growing Pains," *Our Boston,* 1 (November, 1926).

———, "Boston: More Growing Pains," *Our Boston,* 3 (February, 1927).

Bruce, James L., "The Rogers Building and Huntington Hall," *Proceedings of the Bostonian Society* (1941), 29–36.

Bushee, Frederick A., "Italian Immigrants in Boston," *The Arena,* 17: 722–734 (April, 1897).

Chamberlain, Allen, "Beacon Hill Christmas Candles," *Old-Time New England,* 26: 69–73 (October, 1935).

———, "The Beacon Hill of the Forefathers," *Old Days on Beacon Hill, 1824–1924* (Boston: Women's Municipal League, 1924).

"Freedom and the Old South Meeting House," *Old South Leaflets,* no. 202 (Boston: Old South Meeting House, 1910).

Furness, Clifton Joseph, "Walt Whitman Looks at Boston," *The New England Quarterly,* 1: 353–370 (July, 1928).

Gillespie, Harriet Sisson, "Reclaiming Colonial Landmarks," *The House Beautiful,* 58: 239–241 *et seq.* (September, 1925).

Gilmore, H. W., "The Old New Orleans and the New: a Case for Ecology," *American Sociological Review,* 9: 385–394 (August, 1944).

Jones, Joshua H., Jr., "Happenings on Boston Common," *Our Boston,* 2: 9–15 (January, 1927).

Kennedy, Albert J., "The South End," *Our Boston,* 2: 13–19 (December, 1926).

Kiley, John C., "Changes in Realty Values in the Nineteenth and Twentieth Centuries," *Bulletin of the Business Historical Society,* 15 (June, 1941).

"The Parker-Inches-Emery House, 40 Beacon Street, Boston," *Bulletin of the Society for the Preservation of New England Antiquities,* 4: 2–11 (August, 1913).

Porter, Alexander S., "Changes of Values in Real Estate in Boston the Past One Hundred Years," *Collections of the Bostonian Society,* 1: 57–74 (1888).

"The Regeneration of Beacon Hill: How Boston Goes About Civic Improvement," *The Craftsman,* 16: 92–95 (April, 1909).

Warren, William Marshall, "Beacon Hill and Boston University," *Bostonia, the Boston University Alumni Magazine,* 4: 3–21 (November, 1930).

Whyte, William Foote, "Race Conflicts in the North End of Boston," *The New England Quarterly,* 12: 623–642 (December, 1939).

E. Newspapers

The Back Bay Leader, October 19, 1939.
The Back Bay Ledger and Beacon Hill Times, 1939–1944.
The Boston Globe, 1900–1923.
The Boston Herald, 1900–1931.
The Boston Post, 1900–1930.
The Boston Transcript, 1900–1933.
The Christian Science Monitor, 1922.
The Italian News, 1943–1945.
The Mid-Town Journal, 1943.

F. Directories, Censuses, Registers, Etc.

Assessed Values of Real Estate in Boston (Boston: Real Estate Publishing Co., 1901; Boston Real Estate Exchange, 1920–1941).
Atlas of the City of Boston: Boston Proper and Back Bay (Philadelphia: G. W. Bromley and Co., 1902, 1922, 1938).
Board of Public Trustees, Boston Elevated Railway Co., Report, sheets 18 and 19 (Boston: January, 1944).
Catalogue of 38 Lots of Land on the Back Bay, Belonging to the Commonwealth of Massachusetts, fronting upon Commonwealth Avenue and Marlborough Street, to be Sold by Public Auction on Thursday, April 9, 1863 (Boston: N. A. Thompson and Co., 1863).
City of Boston, Assessing Department, Public Copy of the Valuation Lists (tax lists), 1944.
City of Boston, *City Document — No. 56,* 1863, Report of Committee on the Preservation of the Hancock House (Boston: 1863).
Boston City Directory, 1846, 1938–1945.
Census of the United States (Washington: United States Government Printing Office)

> Eleventh — 1890
> Twelfth — 1900
> Thirteenth — 1910
> Fourteenth — 1920
> Fifteenth — 1930
> Sixteenth — 1940

"Census Tract Data, 1930 Census," Unpublished material from Fifteenth Census of the United States, 1930, tabulated for the Boston Health Department.
Directory of the Larger Manufacturers, Boston Industrial Area, pamphlet (Boston: Boston Chamber of Commerce, Bureau of Commercial and Industrial Affairs, 1940).

First Annual Report of the Boston Transit Commission (Boston: published by the Commission, 1895).

List of Residents 20 Years of Age and Over as of January 1, 1932 (Police Lists), Boston: City of Boston, 1932.
Same for 1937, 1942, 1943.

Massachusetts Reports — Cases Argued and Determined in the Supreme Judicial Court of Massachusetts (Supreme Court Decisions), Boston: Little Brown and Co.

Massachusetts House Documents, No. 277, 1924.

Massachusetts Senate Documents, No. 2, 1927; No. 3, 1929.

"Our First Men": A Calendar of Wealth, Fashion, and Gentility (Boston: published by all the booksellers, 1846).

Records of the Boston Police Department, Division of Statistics.

Records of the Building Department, City of Boston.

Registry of Deaths, in Department of Vital Statistics, State House, Boston.

Social Register, Boston (New York: Social Register Ass., 1894, 1905, 1914, 1929, 1943).

APPENDIX

Number of Families Listed in the *Social Register* for
1943 as Living in Towns of the Metropolitan Area

Arlington	3	Newton	247
Belmont	21	Quincy	0
Boston	962	Revere	1
Brookline	372	Saugus	0
Cambridge	257	Somerville	0
Chelsea	0	Stoneham	0
Dedham	99	Wakefield	0
Dover	52	Waltham	6
Everett	0	Watertown	2
Lexington	4	Wellesley	53
Lynn	1	Weston	60
Malden	0	Westwood	30
Medford	2	Winchester	3
Milton	202	Winthrop	0
Nahant	7	Woburn	0
Needham	45		

Total 2429

INDEX